WITHDRAWN
UTSA Libraries

POETIC AFFAIRS

Verbal Art STUDIES IN POETICS

Lazar Fleishman and Haun Saussy, Editors

POETIC AFFAIRS

Celan, Grünbein, Brodsky

MICHAEL ESKIN

Stanford University Press · Stanford, California 2008

Stanford University Press
Stanford, California

Printed in the United States of America on acid-free, archival-quality paper

Library of Congress Cataloging-in-Publication Data

Eskin, Michael.
    Poetic affairs : Celan, Grünbein, Brodsky / Michael Eskin.
        p.   cm.—(Verbal art : studies in poetics)
    Includes bibliographical references and index.
    ISBN 978-0-8047-5831-4 (cloth : alk. paper)
    1. Celan, Paul—Criticism and interpretation.   2. Grünbein, Durs—Criticism and
interpretation.   3. Brodsky, Joseph, 1940–1996—Criticism and interpretation.
4. Poetics.   5. Subjectivity in literature.   I. Title.

PT2605.E4Z5977 2008
831'.914—dc22

                                                                    2007026524

The publication of this book was supported by a grant from the Harriman Institute,
Columbia University.

For Kathrin, with love

and for
Derek Attridge and Durs Grünbein,
with admiration and gratitude

Contents

Acknowledgments

This book could not have been written and completed without the involvement, support, and generosity of the following persons and institutions, to all of whom I am extremely grateful: Kathrin Stengel, Derek Attridge, Boris Gasparov, Dmitrij Bobyšev, Tomas Venclova, Karen Leeder, Ed Cohen, Ulrich Baer, Amir Eshel, Martin Puchner, Sidney Sussex College, University of Cambridge, Columbia University, New College, University of Oxford, and the Beinecke Rare Book and Manuscript Library at Yale University. I would also like to thank Lazar Fleishman, Haun Saussy, Norris Pope, Emily-Jane Cohen, Tim Roberts, Alice Rowan, Rob Ehle, David Jackson, and Stanford University Press for giving this book a home and releasing it into the world in its present shape. Finally, I would like to express my deepest gratitude to this book's main interlocutors for their invaluable gifts of poetry and philosophy.

Paul Celan's poems are used with permission from *Atemwende*, © 1967 by Suhrkamp Verlag, Frankfurt am Main; William Shakespeare, *Einundzwanzig Sonette: Deutsch von Paul Celan*, © 1967 by Suhrkamp Verlag, Frankfurt am Main; and *Gesammelte Werke*, © 1983 by Suhrkamp Verlag, Frankfurt am Main. Durs Grünbein's poems are used with permission from *Schädelbasislektion*, © 1991 by Suhrkamp Verlag, Frankfurt am Main; and *Eklärte Nacht*, © 2002 by Suhrkamp

Verlag, Frankfurt am Main. Joseph Brodsky's "Twenty Sonnets to Mary Stuart" is used by permission: "Dvadcat' Sonetov k Marii Styuart" by Joseph Brodsky, copyright © 1983 by Joseph Brodsky. The translation into English is authorized for this use only and not for reprint. An authorized translation by the author of "Dvadcat' Sonetov k Marii Styuart" was first published in *To Urania* (1988) and reprinted in *Collected Poems in English* (2000). Earlier versions of parts of Chapters Two and Three have previously appeared in *New German Critique,* volume 91, and *arcadia,* volume 39, number 2, respectively.

Prefatory Note

Notwithstanding the unity of this book's overall argument, which unfolds progressively from section to section, Chapters Two through Four can meaningfully be read as discrete interpretations of, respectively, Celan's, Grünbein's, and Brodsky's lives and works. Some of the research that has gone into the writing of this book, although not directly relevant to its main argument, is of sufficient critical significance to be made available in an appendix for the interested reader's perusal. Throughout this book, all unidentified translations are my own. For the purposes of ensuring maximum clarity of exposition, I have provided strictly literal translations of Celan's, Grünbein's, Brodsky's, and others' poems, which are accompanied by the originals only if required by the argument. With the exception of established English spellings of Russian proper names—such as Brodsky, Pushkin, Mandelstam, and Akhmatova—all transliterations from the Russian follow System 3 in J. Thomas Shaw's *The Transliteration of Modern Russian for English-Language Publications* (New York: Modern Language Association, 1979). To allow for a smooth reading experience, note numbers are placed, for the most part, at the end of any given sentence or period; quotations in the main text are referenced in the notes in sequential order if more than one quotation appears in any given sentence or period.

One might . . . be justified in saying that . . . beings . . . are designed with a view to our attention. . . . But we give them being, we acknowledge them as being, only from the moment when they become for us, in no matter what degree, centers or focal points, when they evoke in us a reaction of love and respect, or a contrary reaction . . . as soon as beings are looked at in this perspective, they can no longer be introduced as simple unities or totalities. . . . I need a word to describe these conglomerations which are not totalities, and I shall . . . call them "constellations."

—Gabriel Marcel, *The Mystery of Being*

Introduction

On Poetry, Life, Method, and Sundry Affairs

> *After all, what goes into writing a book—be it a novel,*
> *a philosophical treatise, a collection of poems, a biography, or*
> *a thriller—is, ultimately, a man's only life: good or bad but*
> *always finite.*
>
> *In any given book, the foreword is the first and the last*
> *thing; it serves either as an explanation or as a justification*
> *and a defense against criticism . . . [1]*

For several years now, I have been engaged—as a reader, critic, and teacher—with the lives and works of three outstanding poets: Holocaust survivor and arguably the "greatest French poet of the German language" Paul Celan (1920–1970); Dresden native and one of the most significant living German poets Durs Grünbein (1962–); and Leningrad native, U.S. poet laureate, and Nobel Prize winner Joseph Brodsky (1940–1996).[2] Above and beyond each poet's literary-historical significance, biographical factors, and personal taste, and beyond the inevitable *je ne sais quoi* behind any reader's or critic's penchant for a particular poet, writer, artist, group of artists, or period, my initial interest in this particular group of authors was triggered by the fact that all three consider themselves heirs to the legacy of Osip Mandelstam (1891–1938), the Russian-Jewish poet and cofounder of the Acmeist movement in Russian poetry who, owing to his tragic fate at the hands of the Stalinist regime as a more or less direct corollary of his supreme artistry, has come to epitomize the precariousness, necessity, integrity, and moral force of poetry in the face of sociopolitical adversity. What especially intrigued me about this literary constellation was not so much its genealogical dimension *per se*—after all, as Seamus Heaney reminds us, there is hardly anything extraordinary about poets turning to the "great masters of the past" to follow their "artistic inclinations" and "imaginative needs"—but rather its significance within a literary-historical trajectory that culminates in Grünbein's extensive reception of and response to both Celan's and Brodsky's readings of Mandelstam.[3] (Of the three poets, I should note, only one, Grünbein, has seriously engaged with the other two; at best, Brodsky and Celan took marginal note of each other.)

The more time I spent in the company of Mandelstam and his self-proclaimed poetic descendants, however, and the longer I studied the ways in which they received and interpreted Mandelstam's legendary poetic "letter in a bottle" addressed to a "more or less distant, unknown interlocutor," whose "embrace" and "love" the poet longed for (thus Mandelstam's erotic depiction of poetry as transhistorical dialogue), the clearer it became to me that much more is at stake in examining Celan's, Grünbein's, and Brodsky's recourse to "Russia's greatest [modern] poet" than understanding one strong poet's impact on and survival in the works of a handful of self-appointed poetic successors.[4] I gradually realized that the significance of the ways in which the three poets can be said to have appropriated and creatively put to use in their own lives and works Mandelstam's *polyphonic organicism* and *ethical realism*—that is, his conception of poetry as a living organism born of and participating in the ever-unfolding polylogue of the voices "of all ages" *and* as an ethical-existential force bespeaking the poet's love and concern for the world and "human society"—by far exceeds the purview of literary genealogy and history, crucially bearing on the much more fundamental question of the very workings of poetry (and literature in general) as an articulation of *life*, and hence as an ethical practice.[5]

Thus, what had begun as a comparative study in literary genealogy and history soon gave way to a more conceptually oriented inquiry into the *poetological* significance of Celan's, Grünbein's, and Brodsky's respective poetic practices, which programmatically blur the line between life and art.[6] Furthermore, in the course of my concomitant engagement with the three poets in light of their genealogical affinities, I couldn't help at least strongly intuiting, if not clearly discerning at first, that from a poetological viewpoint as well they were best studied in conjunction; that is, although each of them individually may certainly have something to teach us about the workings of poetry, it is their cumulative, combined artistic effort that holds the most interesting theoretical lessons on the internal and external life of poetry as a form of utterance constitutively bound up with life.

As I was trying to come up with an adequate response to what I experienced as the three poets' demand to be read side by side—in other words, as I was trying to determine how their poetic projects could be made to fit together conceptually—the following overarching argument gradually developed that allows each poet's theoretical significance to come to the fore with particular clarity while emphasizing the embeddedness of their poetic projects within a framework of mutual imbrication and complementarity: by looking at how Celan, Grünbein, and Brodsky go about their craft individually, we can learn a great deal about the anatomy and physiology of the poetic text, as well as about how it symbiotically relates to the extrapoetic—to its material, biographical, and sociohistorical conditions. Moreover, by approaching their poetics as mutually complementary (in a sense yet to be elaborated), we are afforded an unprecedented *comprehensive* view of how poetry works. I should stress that although my overarching argument may have developed empirically on the basis of and certainly draws on the three poets' genealogical and historical (if limited) ties, it does not conceptually presuppose or depend on those ties. Adopting a *catalytic* interpretive method that valorizes aesthetic reception over production, I juxtapose Celan, Grünbein, and Brodsky in light of their yet-to-be-disclosed mutual *poetological* complementarity.[7]

Given its inductive, twofold thrust—that is, its concern with the lives and works of a particular set of authors *and*, through them, with general questions of poetics—my argument necessitates the concurrent pursuit of three interlocking goals: to offer inventive readings of Celan's, Grünbein's, and Brodsky's lives and works; to probe, through these readings, in an innovative mode the relationship between literature and life and, specifically, the ways in which this relationship gets staged and articulated in poetry; and finally, to point, on the basis of the three poets' translations of life into poetry (and vice versa), to creative new ways of conceiving of the workings of poetry as an ethical practice.

If it is not to remain merely formal, this threefold goal that stakes out the parameters of my interpretive endeavor necessitates in turn a number of steps aimed at infusing my argument with concrete historical, thematic, and conceptual content. Thus such abstract and general notions as *life, lives and works,* and *the workings of poetry,* which are central to my argument, must be specified and concretized in order to be tackled meaningfully in the first place. After all, if we want to talk about life and literature, we can do so only on the basis of concrete manifestations of both, as well as in specific thematic and conceptual respects. In my approach to Celan, Grünbein, and Brodsky I consequently focus on a handful of concrete, contextually significant real-life *events,* as well as on a limited number of texts and poetic encounters *in light of these events.* More specifically, I attend to how Celan, Grünbein, and Brodsky poetically respond to and metabolize these events so that their particular modes of translating life into poetry cannot fail to acquire unprecedented poetological and ethical force. In order to be able to argue the latter persuasively, I in turn map the thus disclosed interface between literature and life onto a stratigraphically specified conceptual grid developed in response to Celan's, Grünbein's, and Brodsky's poetics and devised signally and comprehensively to capture and do justice, at a theoretical level, to what may well be considered the fundamental, mutually imbricated building blocks of the life of poetry: the constitution of poetic signification, the subsequent emergence of poetic subjectivity on the basis of poetic signification, and finally, the assumption of poetic and (by extension) ethical agency on the part of the thus-created poetic subject.[8] In particular, this conceptual grid, which allows me to bring into sharp relief what I consider to be especially innovative about the three poets' poetics, is informed by Celan's emphasis on the poetic process as the condition of subjectivity and agency, by Grünbein's focus on and emphatic staging of subjectivity as a poetic invention, and finally by Brodsky's postulate that "aesthetics is the mother of ethics."[9]

Before turning to the events in question and apprising the reader of the specifics of my take on Celan, Grünbein, and Brodsky against the foil of these events, a few explanatory remarks regarding my overall treatment of the life-literature nexus are in order. Heeding my three poets' emphasis on the irreducible entwinement of poetry and life (without in any way implying that "art can be explained by life"), and relying on the notion of literature in general as a form of utterance (and hence as essentially saturated with the contexts of its articulation), I am concerned with life only to the extent that it has become a determinant *literary fact*.[10] What do I mean by this?

Following the Russian formalists, who distinguished between the literary order, or *series,* and other, extraliterary *historical series* (such as biography, history, politics, and so on), while acknowledging the indelible, if complex, link between literature and "extraliterary orders," I mean by *literary fact* anything at all insofar as it has become an element of the literary series, or literature, *tout court*.[11] "Although it is getting ever more difficult to define literature," Jurij Tynjanov notes, "anyone . . . will be able to point out a literary fact. He will be able to say that this or that does not belong to literature but, rather, to the poet's everyday or personal life, while this or that, conversely, is an emphatically literary fact."[12] Tynjanov's fellow formalist Boris Tomaševskij offers a helpful explanation of the difference between a literary and an extraliterary fact: It is not an author's biography *per se*— his or her "curriculum vitae or the investigator's account of his life"—that makes for a literary fact, but rather the author's "legendary" or "literary" biography, his "biographical legend," that is, his *life and times* insofar as they have become a "living and necessary commentary to his works . . . a legendary concomitant to his poetry."[13] Thus, a few illuminating instances of life-turned-literary-fact are Gustave Flaubert's trial in February 1857 for publishing the presumably immoral *Madame Bovary*, the scandal surrounding the publication of Nabokov's *Lolita* in 1955, and the 1928 publication and subsequent reception of D. H. Lawrence's *Lady Chatterly's Lover* (1928), including the 1960 obscenity trial of Penguin Books for printing an unabridged version of the work—all of which would count, in Tomaševskij's view, as literary facts. After all, all of these real-life events have been absorbed into the lives of the books that occasioned them; or to put it differently, neither *Madame Bovary* nor *Lady Chatterly's Lover* nor *Lolita* would be what they are without the scandals surrounding their publication, and the consternation and indignation they triggered (and continue to trigger) among readers.[14] The inclusion of "On a Book Entitled *Lolita*"—the essay on the novel's genesis and aesthetic rationale that Nabokov wrote in response to charges of pornography shortly after the novel's publication—in all subsequent editions of the novel is a particularly good example of the enmeshment of the extraliterary with the literary.

With these considerations in mind, I now turn to a preliminary discussion of the cluster of real-life events that have provided this book's historical-biographical skeleton, as well as of the three poets' responses to and poetic transpositions of these events. The events in question are the so-called Goll affair, in the course of which Celan was wrongfully accused of plagiarizing the work of poet Yvan Goll and which overshadowed his life from the early 1950s until his suicide in 1970; the banishment of Stoic philosopher and statesman Lucius Annaeus Seneca to the Mediterranean island of Corsica in 41 B.C.E. on the charge of adultery with Emperor Claudius' niece, Julia Livilla—an event that has become central to Grünbein's self-fashioning as a contemporary poet; and finally, what I would like to call comprehensively the "Brodsky affair," which set the tone for virtually all of Brodsky's oeuvre and which comprises the poet's trial and conviction on the trumped-up charge of social parasitism in 1964 and subsequent expulsion from the Soviet Union in 1972, as well as his momentous liaison with and betrayal by Marianna Basmanova. I should note right away that the ostensible interpretive imbalance created by my decision to home in on three events that are not biographically homologous—two of the events did actually happen to two of the poet's involved and one did not (Seneca's exile obviously did not happen to Grünbein)—has no essential bearing on my overall concern with the interface between literature and life: The fact that what I would like to dub the "Livilla affair" did not directly happen to Grünbein neither diminishes its status as a real-life, historical event nor means that it cannot, like any event, become and be treated as significant in any number of contexts other than the context of its initial occurrence. In other words, the fact that, unlike the Goll and Brodsky affairs, which did transpire in Celan's and Brodsky's lives, the Livilla affair did not transpire in Grünbein's life is contingent from a literary-factual viewpoint. What is important is that, as I show, Grünbein *treats it* as central to his life and poetics.[15]

What do the three poets do, poetically, in response to these events, the significance of which in and for their lives and works can, as I illustrate, hardly be overestimated? How do they respond to and translate these affairs so that their responses can be said to cast the question of poetry as an ethical practice in a novel light?

Clearly it would be facile to assume that any serious, existentially motivated response to any given situation or event could ever be reduced or boiled down to a single, essential aspect or feature; any attempt at such a reduction would presuppose willfully disregarding the inherent complexity and multifacetedness (semantic, pragmatic, intentional) of human action. This means that the three poets' respective dealings with the above-mentioned affairs cannot possibly be reduced to a single feature. This being said, however, it is not only possible but plausible—if not to say ineluctable, given the inevitably perspectival nature of human cognition—to consider any given phenomenon, including responses to situations or events, in light of what to the observer appears to be its contextually most remarkable or dominant trait, its overall thrust, so to speak.[16] Consequently, it is in light of what emerges as the contextually dominant, most remarkable feature shared by all three poets' responses to the events in question that I wish to interpret them. Whatever else the three poets may be said to have done poetically in response to the Goll, Livilla, and Brodsky affairs, respectively, all three have translated these events, as I document in great detail, into *affairs of poetry*—into *poetic affairs* (in an amatory, erotic sense, above all); all three, in other words, can be said to respond most memorably to these events by displacing their "affair-quality" (that is, their sociopolitically extraordinary, transgressive, and scandalous character) onto the level of poetry and reenacting it in emphatically erotic terms. In so doing they not only succeed in putting, as I explain, existentially and ethically significant and unexpected spins on the three affairs, but they also adumbrate and stage (in tacit homage to Mandelstam's erotic poetics) an unprecedented conception of *poetry as love affair*—that is, a conception of poetry as not primarily linguistic (hinging on the interplay of the six basic functions of language, with the poetic function dominating the others) but as what I would like to call *affairistic*—as predicated on the ethical-existential and erotic categories of love, fidelity, and betrayal.[17]

This is of course not to suggest that the verbal aspect of poetry is downplayed by the three poets, but rather that it is recognized and staged as embedded and already unfolding within an affairistic framework. In and through their *affairistic* appropriations, displacements, and rewritings of the three events, Celan, Grünbein, and Brodsky succeed, I argue, in sounding, in an innovative key, the workings of poetry, approached through the threefold question of the constitution of poetic signification (Celan), the subsequent emergence of poetic subjectivity (Grünbein), and finally the assumption of poetic and (by extension) ethical agency on the part of the thus-created poetic subject (Brodsky).

While grounding my critical reflections and observations in detailed, contextually motivated interpretations of Celan's, Grünbein's, and Brodsky's overall poetic projects, I disclose and document their specifically affairistic thrust on the basis of their respective dialogues with three choice interlocutors: Celan's with Shakespeare, Grünbein's with Seneca, and Brodsky's with Lord Byron. I focus first on Celan's translations of Shakespeare's sonnets, which develop and instantiate, I argue, an erotic conception of poetic translation and hence of poetic signification *tout court* (insofar as translation is the basic mode of signification), thereby enabling Celan to countervail and parry (if not, in the long run, to withstand) poetically the Goll affair's pernicious impact in the shelter of the loving embrace of Shakespeare's poems—in the "truth" of what I reveal as the two poets' love affair.[18] I then proceed to a detailed discussion of Grünbein's idiosyncratic engagement with the question of poetic subjectivity, giving special attention to what I disclose as his poetologically momentous liaison with Seneca—most vividly staged in his "Seneca Studies." I conclude with a sustained exploration of the ethical dimension of Brodsky's poetics; in particular, I zero in on Brodsky's dialogue with Lord Byron as it most extensively and memorably unfolds in the collection *New Stanzas to Augusta*, which I construe as Brodsky's attempt to countervail political disempowerment and personal betrayal by poetically and, as I argue, ethically recouping agency in the arms of his beloved "English Muse."

By assigning my discussion of the questions of poetic signification, poetic subjectivity, and poetic and ethical agency to three different chapters devoted to distinct poetic conversations (Chapters Two through Four), I am not in any way suggesting, and thereby retracting my initial emphasis on their mutual imbrication, that these constitutive aspects of the literary could ever be encountered in isolation in the real lives of concrete poetic texts. Every poem, every literary text, constitutively performs all three aspects (to a greater or lesser degree of visibility) that can be separated and situated along a linear, discursive axis for heuristic purposes only. In other words, because in the actual life of poetry all three aspects are by definition intertwined, my sequential treatment of each of them must be recognized as a hermeneutic necessity resulting from the linear nature of discursive reasoning rather than being an attempt at a just portrayal of poetic reality. Concomitantly, the particular order of my engagement with Celan, Grünbein, and Brodsky must be viewed as a function of the stratigraphic logic underlying what I have advanced as the mutual imbrication of the questions of poetic signification, subjectivity, and agency—to wit, signification as the condition of subjectivity, which in turn becomes agency. Each poet, respectively, I suggest, stages exemplarily one of the three constitutive aspects of the poetic here discussed; and although all three aspects are by definition operative in the works of all three poets, the works of each are not equally suited as model instantiations of all three aspects.

Thus, although Celan certainly attends to, as I show, the questions of poetic subjectivity (what he refers to as "the naming and addressing I") and agency (most explicitly in his notion of poetry as "counter-word"), his main contextual contribution to our thinking about and understanding of the workings of poetry consists, I suggest, *not* primarily in the "answers" he provides to these questions (approached in the well-worn dialogic terms supplied by Herder, Buber, and Mandelstam, among others), but in what I reveal as their reliance on, and hence subordination to, the more fundamental question of poetic signification as the condition of subjectivity and agency.[19] The singularly innovative thrust of Celan's engagement with the question of poetic signification in turn consists, I argue, in his affairistic practice of poetic translation, which sublates both the Romantic commonplace, according to which "all poetry is translation," and the semiotic commonplace, according to which "the meaning of any . . . sign is its translation into some further, alternative sign."[20] In Grünbein's texts, conversely, it is the question of the emergence of poetic subjectivity that moves to the forefront of poetic attention and to which the sibling questions of poetic meaning and agency can be said to be subordinated. The novelty of Grünbein's take on the question of subjectivity consists, I argue, in casting it in affairistic (as opposed to, for instance, epistemological or cognitive) terms: The subject reveals itself as the fruit of the poet's love affair with a literary interlocutor. Finally, Brodsky puts explicit emphasis on the question of the interface between poetry and ethics, thereby relegating the questions of poetic signification and subjectivity to second and third place (in no particular order), without in any way obliterating them. Echoing Celan's and Grünbein's affairistic presentations of the constitution of poetic signification and subjectivity, respectively, Brodsky in turn casts the poetic subject's accession to agency in affairistic terms. To enable the reader to follow my argument closely in its full historical, thematic, and conceptual scope, in the first chapter I provide

comprehensive accounts of the three affairs that constitute my argument's historical focus, followed by detailed explanations of its key terms and concepts. On a
final preliminary note, I should point out that although Celan's, Grünbein's, and
Brodsky's lives and works, including a number of the issues addressed here, have,
as I document, received a fair amount of critical attention, neither their specifically affairistic dimension nor their poetological complementarity—that is, the
cumulative, combined import of their poetics—have hitherto been probed. It is
in attending to the latter two aspects of the three poets' poetic projects, I argue,
that their unprecedented significance and innovative force can be most saliently
thrown into relief.

CHAPTER I

Creative Fidelities

. . . how the event becomes the occasion from which the poetic line emerges.

I like to be particular in dates. . . .

The purpose of poets, then, is "to tell truths," but in ways necessarily complicated. . . .

Fidelities . . . she recognizes it as the word on which all hinges.[1]

Affairs to Remember

"UNE VRAIE AFFAIRE DREYFUS"

In early November 1949—more than a year after arriving in Paris, where he would reside until his suicide in April 1970—Celan made the acquaintance of Surrealist poet Yvan Goll (1891–1950).[2] Hoping to find sympathy, so the story goes, from a "Jewish fellow sufferer . . . for his German 'poems after Auschwitz,'" Celan presented the senior poet, who was dying of leukemia, with his first collection of poems, *Der Sand aus den Urnen* (The sand from the urns), published in Vienna in September 1948 after Celan's immigration to France.[3] Both poets were deeply impressed with each other. Celan considered Goll a "true poet" and a "Mensch"—the "first one," he wrote to a friend in Vienna, "I have encountered in Paris." Goll in turn admired Celan's "clair génie" and endorsed his "mission de poète."[4]

Between November 1949 and Goll's death on March 14, 1950, Celan paid the dying poet several visits at the American Hospital in Neuilly.[5] It was probably during one of these visits that Goll asked the young émigré to translate his French poems into German. Celan obliged. After Goll's death his widow, Claire Goll, encouraged Celan to continue translating her late husband's poems. By the end of 1951 Celan had translated three of Goll's collections: *Élégie d'Ihpétonga suivi de Masques de Cendre* (Elegy of Iphétonga followed by the masques of ashes), *Les Géorgiques Parisiennes* (Parisian georgics), and *Chansons Malaises* (Malaysian songs). Celan's translations, however, were never to see the light of day. After sending the batch to Goll's publisher, Celan was surprised to find it rejected on account of its alleged unfaithfulness to the original.[6] This rejection led to a falling out between Celan and Claire Goll, who had just published her late husband's posthumous collection, *Traumkraut* (Dream weeds, 1951).

What was to enter the annals of literary history as the so-called Goll affair began soon after the publication in December 1952 of Celan's second collection of poems, *Mohn und Gedächtnis* (Poppy and memory), which includes the poems previously published in *Der Sand aus den Urnen*. In August 1953, after having been alerted to textual similarities between *Mohn und Gedächtnis* and *Traumkraut*, Claire Goll wrote an unofficial defamatory letter to various German publishers, broadcast stations, and newspapers accusing Celan of plagiarizing her late husband's work.[7] The plagiarism "campaign" gained momentum throughout the 1950s as a result of Goll's letter, earning Celan notoriety as a "master plagiarizer, who repeats in his own poems in a mediocre way what Yvan Goll had brought to perfection;" the campaign reached its apex in 1960–1962, following the publication, at the end of April 1960 of another letter by Claire Goll titled "Little-Known Facts About Paul Celan," and did not abate until the late 1960s.[8] Significantly, the publication of Goll's second letter occurred precisely when Celan was rising to prominence in Germany after being awarded, in May 1960, the Georg Büchner Prize, Germany's most prestigious literary recognition.

The charges publicly renewed by Claire Goll in her second letter were immediately revealed as untenable. Thus, in an open letter in defense of Celan published shortly after Claire Goll's "Little-Known Facts," Marie Luise Kaschnitz, Ingeborg Bachmann, and Klaus Demus (Celan's friend and fellow poet, who had accompanied him on at least one of his visits to the hospitalized Goll) pointed out that the alleged parallels between Celan's *Mohn und Gedächtnis* and Yvan Goll's *Traumkraut* adduced by the latter's widow in support of her plagiarism charges were "the result of . . . the juxtaposition of sloppily cited passages from Goll's poems dating from 1949 to 1950 with equally sloppily cited passages from Celan's poems already contained in the volume, *Der Sand aus den Urnen*, published in Vienna in 1948."[9] "As Goll's widow, who owned it, very well knew," the authors continue, "the volume had been withdrawn from circulation shortly after its appearance due to an inordinate amount of misprints and had remained virtually unknown outside Austria; its uncomfortable date could be suppressed all the more easily given that the majority of its poems—written between 1940 and 1948 in the Bukovina, Romania, and Vienna—had not been widely known prior to their inclusion in *Mohn und Gedächtnis*."[10] Notwithstanding the untenability of Goll's trumped-up charges, however, her second letter spawned a series of articles in the German media addressing Celan's poetry in the light of Goll's allegations, and bestowing, by virtue of their sheer existence, the semblance of a certain degree of validity on the matter.[11]

For Celan the Goll affair was part of what he perceived as a revival of National Socialism in Germany at the time: "What is new about this Nazi renaissance," Celan noted in 1962, "is that they know how to do it better than Hitler."[12] It put into question his existence and self-understanding as a Jewish poet "after Auschwitz" and his identity as a survivor: "it is a veritable Dreyfus affair"—"une vraie affaire Dreyfus"—Celan observed in the same year, "sui generis, of course. . . . It is a true mirror of Germany, the 'new' forms assumed by Nazism. . . . "[13] Celan's racialist reading of the Goll affair was motivated by Claire Goll's reference to his and his family's fate at the hands of the Nazis as a "sad legend" in conjunction with the flaring up of anti-Semitic activity throughout Germany after the December 1959 Bundestag's decision not to sign into law an already ratified antiracism bill.[14]

The Goll affair proved to be *the* traumatic literary-existential event in Celan's life after settling in France. As he put it, rather euphemistically, in a letter to Alfred Andersch (July 27, 1956), "this matter, absurd though it may be, is now indelibly part of my life, and what is part of my life I take very personally, it touches me."[15] Furthermore, because it originated in a poet's request to be translated, the affair threatened the very core of Celan's poetics of dialogue and encounter, the basic enactment of which can be witnessed precisely in and through translation as the originary manifestation of poetic encountering.[16] In view of Celan's belief that the poet "remains given" to his poetry and that "poetry is life," his poetic output dating from this period in particular can be expected to bear palpable traces of the affair.[17] In fact, it is above all to his poetry and translations (as an integral part of his oeuvre) that we have to look for a serious response on Celan's part to Claire Goll's charges. Celan, who was not willing to take a stance publicly and rebut Goll's allegations, would have *naturally* (I say *naturally* having in mind Celan's notion of poetry as *the* "counter-word" *par excellence* in the name of human life) relied on the power of his poetry to contravene the "pure infamy," as he remarked to Andersch, of the attacks to which he was exposed.[18] How exactly Celan went about mounting what one critic has called his "lyrical offensive" against Goll and her supporters is documented on the basis of his poetologically unprecedented translations of Shakespeare's sonnets.[19]

"FOR WHICH ANNAEUS SENECA WAS ALSO EXILED"

In 41 C.E., during the first year of Emperor Claudius' reign, philosopher and statesman Lucius Annaeus Seneca (1–65 C.E.) was accused and convicted of adultery with the emperor's niece, Julia Livilla, and subsequently banished to the Mediterranean island of Corsica.[20] Seneca's banishment was the result of a court intrigue initiated by Claudius' first wife, Valeria Messalina, who was renowned for her insatiable sexual appetites and lust for power. Messalina "became enraged at her niece Julia [Livilla]," Dio Cassius writes, "because she neither paid her honor nor flattered her; and she was also jealous because the girl was extremely beautiful and was often alone with Claudius. Accordingly, [Messalina] secured Julia's banishment by trumping up various charges against her, including that of adultery (for which Annaeus Seneca was also exiled) and not long afterward compassed her death."[21] Not until the intervention of Claudius' second wife, Agrippina, eight years later, would Seneca be recalled to the imperial court in Rome.[22] According to one contemporary, Publius Sullius, the philosopher's exile was a "well-deserved" punishment for the "pollution of the couch of imperial princesses." Seneca himself, however, insisted on his innocence in the matter.[23]

The Livilla affair put Seneca's Stoic beliefs, which he had hitherto been practicing under the favorable conditions of the busy life of an attorney and public official in the imperial capital, to the test.[24] In Corsica, the philosopher would indeed have to prove himself to be a *sapiens*, a wise man and prototypical Stoic subject: steadfast, apathetic, and impervious to the "slings and arrows of outrageous fortune." Little did Seneca know that "two-thousand years later" his "peaceful rest" would be "disturbed" by a descendant of those "louts who caused / trouble for you along the borders of your empire"—a German. Durs Grünbein's election of Seneca as one of his choice poetic and existential interlocutors is indelibly linked to Grünbein's self-fashioning and self-positioning as a contemporary poet.[25] The ways in which Grünbein engages with Seneca for the purposes of crafting a unique poetic subject are the focus of my *affairistic* reflections on the poet and the philosopher.

THE BRODSKY AFFAIR

On November 29, 1963, an article entitled "A Quasi-Literary Drone" appeared in the Leningrad daily *Večernij Leningrad*.[26] In this article, a budding, virtually unknown poet whose publication record to date comprised no more than a handful of literary translations and original poems was accused, among other things, of "decadence, modernism, . . . pessimism, pornography, . . . intended treason [and] a parasitic way of life."[27] Two weeks later, on December 13 1963, one of the article's authors presented his case against Joseph Brodsky to the Soviet Writers' Union, which in turn filed a complaint with the state authorities, accusing the poet of social parasitism.[28] As a result, Brodsky was arrested, indicted, tried (February 18 and March 13, 1964), convicted of social parasitism, and sentenced to "five years of forced labor in a remote location" in the Soviet Union.[29] "L'affaire Brodski"—a "veritable . . . Dreyfus affair," according to poet Samuil Maršak—immediately made the headlines around the globe and was significant in several ways.[30] First, it was the result of false allegations and lies. "In it," Brodsky remarked at his trial in reference to "A Quasi-Literary Drone," "only my name and surname are correct; even my age is wrong; even the poems mentioned are not mine; according to this article, I am friends with people whom I hardly know or do not know at all."[31] Second, even under the harsh statutes of the Soviet Criminal Code, the poet should have been acquitted of the trumped-up charge of social parasitism. Between 1956, when he quit school at the age of fifteen, and 1963, Brodsky had been, as he was able to substantiate at his trial, consistently employed in various occupations.[32] Third, it set a precedent, in the post-Stalinist era, for the state's dealings with artists deemed anti-Soviet and was a preview of literary trials to come.[33] Finally, and most important in the present context, it gave new currency to "a remarkable theme that runs," as Brodsky observes, "all through Russian literature, 'the poet and the tsar.'"[34] This means that from the get-go Brodsky coded his run-in with the state as a "literary fact," as one of the links in the long chain of fallings-out between poets and the powers-that-be marking Russian literary history. (Think, for instance, of the harsh treatment of Pushkin and Dostoevsky by Aleksandr I and Nikolaj I, respectively; of Gumilev's execution by the Bolsheviks; and of Mandelstam's death at the hands of Stalin.) Brodsky's declaration, in response to Judge Savel'eva's questioning of his credentials as a poet, that his calling as a poet was a matter of divine dispensation ("it's . . . from god") underscores the "legendary" (in Tomaševskij's sense) quality of his "dramatic and comical" ordeal.[35] Furthermore, like Pushkin, Lomonosov, Deržavin, and others, Brodsky resorted to the Horatian topos of the longevity of art as opposed to the brevity of life in an attempt to refract, shape, and make sense aesthetically of a particular situation that he would describe many years later as "the bleakest time in my life;" "I wrote poems," he averred at his trial; "this is my line of work; I am convinced . . . that what I have written will be of service to humankind and not only to my contemporaries but also to future generations."[36]

In March 1964, Brodsky set out for the village of Norenskoe in the Russian north in order to serve his five-year sentence; however, as a result of the intervention on his behalf by a number of prominent public figures, his sentence was soon commuted and he was permitted to return to Leningrad in September 1965—only to be expelled from the Soviet Union for good in June 1972.[37]

"Dramatic" though it may have been, it was not the *official*, judiciary side of the Brodsky case that avowedly preoccupied its protagonist the most. "At that time"—that is, at the time of his arrest, trial, and sentencing, Brodsky would remark yeas later—"I was, for the first and only time in my life, involved in a serious triangle. A *ménage à troi*—a sufficiently common thing, two guys and a girl—and that's why I was mostly preoccupied by this. What goes on in your head troubles you much more than what happens to your body"; " . . . that was the time," Brodsky reminisces on another occasion, "which coincided . . . with my greatest personal trouble, with [my betrayal] by a girl, etcetera, etcetera . . . and a kind of triangle overlapped severely with the squares of the solitary confinements. . . . I was more fired up by that personal situation than by what was happening to my body."[38]

What happened? In early summer of 1962, Brodsky met and fell in love with Leningrad artist Marianna Basmanova. "It was roughly at that time," Brodsky's friend, fellow poet, and rival Dmitrij Bobyšev reminisces, that "Brodsky began showing up with Marina Basmanova. . . . "[39] So strong were Brodsky's feelings for Basmanova that, legend has it, he did not heed his friends' advice to steer clear of Leningrad until the *Večernij Leningrad* scandal had blown over: "It so happened that when 'A Quasi-Literary Drone' was published Brodsky was in . . . Moscow, and his friends were trying to convince him not to return to Leningrad. But he was in love. Love took the upper hand over reason; he returned and was immediately arrested."[40]

It is at this point that the plot of Brodsky's "greatest personal trouble" begins to thicken. While Brodsky was incarcerated and subjected to "forensic psychiatric assessment," from late December 1963 through early January 1964, Basmanova and Bobyšev struck up an affair.[41] "Before the New Years Eve party," friends of Bobyšev's and Brodsky's remember, "Bobyšev [announced] that he was bringing a girl. The girl turned out to be Marina Basmanova. Bobyšev explained that Joseph had asked him to take care of her while he was away."[42] Bobyšev himself describes the events thus:

> the year 1963—a year of turmoil—was drawing to a close. . . . Marina wanted to cel-
> ebrate the new year with me. . . . I told her where I would be on new year's eve and
> left for our winter dača. . . . When she arrived [at the new year's eve party] the event
> suddenly became meaningful: as if time itself had been renewed, ticking differently,
> with a fresh, almost feral energy. . . . We grabbed two candles each and walked out
> into the dark, leaving the illuminated windows behind. . . . I kissed her and smelled
> the snowy fragrance of her hair. . . .

At this point Bobyšev presumably asked Basmanova, "What about Joseph? We used to be friends. . . . Doesn't he consider you his bride . . ?" "I don't consider myself his bride," Basmanova responded (according to Bobyšev); "whatever he may think, it's his business. . . . " "We returned to the Dača, dancing," Bobyšev continues; "Marina's candle set one of the festoons on fire and the flames spread to the curtains. . . . After the fire had been put out we went upstairs and fell asleep 'under the covers'."[43] Whatever the truth about the personal details of the situation may be (unfortunately we don't have Basmanova's side of the story), it did apparently entail a face-off between the two rivals during the brief interval between Brodsky's release in early January 1964 and his re-arrest on February 13 of the same year. "In order to outspeed rumors," Bobyšev reminisces, 'I decided to confront [Brodsky] in person":

> I found him in a gloomy mood—apparently rumors had already reached
> Brodsky. . . . I cut straight to the chase: " . . . There have been some changes in my
> life that . . . concern you, too. . . . I am joining my life with Marina." "What does this
> mean?" "It means that we are—an item." "Did you sleep with her?" "I will not answer
> such questions. I am joining my life with her. My life—do you understand?" "But did
> you sleep with her?" "What difference does it make? We are together now. So, please,
> leave her alone." "Beat it!" "Yes, I'll leave in a moment. I just want to say that, per-
> sonal matters notwithstanding, there's literature, in which we are on the same side."

Of course this was not to be the end of the story. Apparently guilt-ridden, Basmanova visited Brodsky at the psychiatric hospital after his re-arrest on February 13. She needed time to think. Brodsky was sentenced. Basmanova broke up with Bobyšev, who scoured Leningrad looking for her, until he found out that she had followed his rival into exile. Bobyšev left for Norenskoe: "So—this is it—Norenskoe," Bobyšev exclaimed upon arriving in the village in the spring of 1964,

> huts in an open field. . . . But—look—there's Marina. . . . She is all set to
> leave. . . . Joseph . . . is standing by. . . . "Marina," I shout, " . . . I've come to get
> you." . . . Joseph yells: "No! . . . Marina . . . you're not going anywhere." . . . The

three of us enter the hut across the street . . . a desk, cluttered with books and manu-scripts, two cots—a box containing cigarettes . . . hanging on the wall over one of the cots: an axe. "What do you want?" Joseph asks. " . . . I've come to get her." "She's not going anywhere." "Oh yes, she is, with me." We both look at the axe. "I am not leaving without her. . . . " "She's staying here." Another look at the axe. "No, she's leaving." "No, she isn't." At this point Marina interferes, saying to Joseph: "I told you I'm leaving." "No, you can't! . . . " "No matter. I have to. . . . " We went outside and walked in the direction of the nearby forest . . . Brodsky one step behind. . . . We could see the end of the field and a narrow path leading into the wood. Enough, I thought, I must stand up for Marina. . . . [44]

To cut a long story short, Basmanova and Bobyšev returned to Leningrad—albeit not as an "item." Brodsky was freed a year and a half later, returned to Leningrad, reconnected with Basmanova, who conceived a child by him, separated from him again, went back to Bobyšev nine months pregnant, and did not stay with him either.[45] "Forget Tolstoy," Bobyšev muses, "even Dostoevsky couldn't have come up with anything even remotely close to [this] parody of what might have been bliss."

What appears to be the critic's subscription to the "voyeuristic genre of biogra-phy," his sensationalist desire to muck about in other people's "personal affairs"—which are not, according to Brodsky, an "object of public property"—is in fact a most legitimate, nay, necessary step in my attempt to do full justice to certain as-pects of Brodsky's (and *mutatis mutandis*, Celan's and Grünbein's) oeuvre—aspects that are predicated on the poet's explicit transformation of biography and histori-cal fact into "biographical legend" and "literary fact," and that consequently en-join the reader to familiarize himself, if minimally, with the historical, both public and private, contexts of Brodsky's poetry.[46] Again, this is not to say that "art can be explained by life," nor is it to pay undue attention to "biographical material," which Brodsky views, somewhat facetiously and with a strong dose of *mauvaise foi*, as "irrelevant . . . to the analysis of a work of art in general."[47] It is, however, to emphasize that life—and especially the poet's "greatest personal trouble"—cannot but inform, if in complex ways, Brodsky's overall poetic output and, emphatically, what he considered the "chief accomplishment of [his] life," namely, *New Stanzas to Augusta: Poems to M. B., 1962–1982*, which is addressed in its entirety to Mari-anna Basmanova and which is the focus of my subsequent reflections on Brodsky's work: "this is a collection of poems written over a span of twenty years with more or less a single addressee, and to a certain extent this is the chief accomplishment of my life. . . . I was looking through all these poems and suddenly saw that they formed a kind of plot in an astonishing way. . . . "[48] In a nutshell, Brodsky's poetic project can be described as, among other things, a sustained attempt at navigating the impossible straits of two ostensibly mutually exclusive claims: the claim that "what goes into writing a book . . . is, ultimately, a man's only life" and the concomitant claim that a "poet's real biography is in his vowels and sibilants, in his meters, rhymes, and metaphors."[49]

It is in his sustained dialogue with Lord Byron in particular, I argue, that the full affairistic force of Brodsky's poetic response to the Brodsky affair comes to the fore most palpably and poignantly.[50] With the help of Byron, Brodsky succeeds in poetically turning himself from patient into agent, from victim into victor.

Definitions

Before proceeding to the nitty-gritty of my affairistic exploration of Celan's, Grünbein's, and Brodsky's poetic practices, I would like to explain the key terms and concepts that enable and inform my particular approach to the modalities of poetry's interface with and articulation of life: *event, affair, truth, fidelity, love,* and *interlocution.*

EVENT

By *event* I mean, in the most general terms, a private or public occurrence, matter, happening, or encounter; a coming into being of something that somehow or other exceeds and transgresses the ordinary, interrupts the historical flow of the everyday, pierces through accepted matrices of making sense and going about things, and creates an indelible point of historical, political, and semantic reference henceforth to be reckoned with. My use of *event* and its adjectival cognates is informed, in particular, by its uses by Wilhelm Windelband, Alain Badiou, Reinhart Koselleck, and Derek Attridge, as well as by Celan's conception of poetry as the event of an "encounter . . . reminiscent of all our dates" and by Grünbein's emphasis on the "evental [*ereignishaft*] character of poetic speech."[51]

The Neokantian philosopher Windelband distinguishes between *being* and *event,* whereby the latter, in contrast to the former, emphatically "concerns the human being" and takes place "for him." This means that an event is *not* to be understood in purely ontological or structural terms (along the lines of von Ranke and Heidegger), that is, as more or less independent of the perceiving, interpreting subject *for whom* it is and, as such, constitutes itself as an event in the first place. Alain Badiou specifies the event as an irreducible singularity, the "beyond-the-law" or supplement to any given situation—in the form of a momentous encounter, invention, creation, or action—which cannot "be named from within the situation"; the event makes it possible "that a . . . truth relative to the situation deploy itself." Reinhart Koselleck suggests thinking of *event,* which he defines as "the sum of [related] occurrences," in terms of extension, if ever so small, over time. Derek Attridge, finally, develops an evental concept of literature whereby literature—the event of the literary—is understood as the inventive displacement, if ever so slightly, of the cultural matrix within which it happens.[52]

AFFAIR

By *affair* I mean specifically a kind of event involving more than one person, pivoting on the interplay of fidelity and betrayal, and typically of an ethically, sociopolitically, and erotically extraordinary character—potentially but not necessarily secretive, transgressive, illicit, and scandalous. In my affairistic readings of Celan's, Grünbein's, and Brodsky's poetic responses to and translations of life, I focus above all on the amatory and the erotic. I am concerned in particular with the three poets' modes of poetically appropriating and rewriting the Goll, Livilla, and Brodsky affairs, respectively, in light of their poetic agendas.

TRUTH

An event has its own truth. It generates the parameters of its unfolding. It is the *truth* of an event that makes the event an event. The truth of an event is not derivative, not merely an instance or avatar of a truth already known and acknowledged. Rather, it ought to be understood as "the coming-to-be of that which is not yet," manifesting itself in and being attested to by the fact that henceforth the actions and beliefs of those taking part in the event will have, in one way or another, been determined or informed by it, will appeal to and unfold in accordance with the event.[53] In the broadest sense, *truth* may be defined, to use William James's words, as "agreement . . . with reality"; the rub is, as James concedes, "what may precisely be meant by the term *agreement,* and what by the term *reality.*"[54]

Clearly, the concept of truth at work here is not ontological, logical, correspondential (adequational), or verificationist; it is rather a lived, experiential kind of truth—impossible to determine "objectively," yet not any less "real" for that matter.[55] It is the kind of truth intuited by Celan when, alluding to his poetic encounter with Mandelstam as the experience of "the Irrefutable and the True," and in the process inverting St. Augustine's "one does not enter truth except by way of love,"[56] he writes:

A Booming:
truth itself

among the humans
has stepped,
into the midst of the
flurry of metaphors.[57]

It is the kind of truth or knowledge about "reality"—the reality created and determined by the event—that is best conceived of in terms of conviction, moral stance, or attitude. It is the attitude Brodsky presumably has in mind when he defines *love* as "an attitude toward reality" and the poem as an "act of love . . . for . . . reality," which facilitates "truth resulting in lyricism or, better still, lyricism becoming truth." It is the kind of truth that is, as Iris Murdoch writes, a "true vision . . . which reveals to us all things as they really are" and that Hemingway intimates when he sets out to "write one true sentence . . . the truest sentence that you know."[58] Agreement with reality, then, signifies a certain kind of bond between agent and situation, a certain kind of almost ineluctable demand on a person or a group of persons as the result of an event.

FIDELITY

I wish to specify the bond or agreement between agent and event as *fidelity*. The truth of an event obtains and transpires, as Badiou suggests (following Gabriel Marcel), in the "process of . . . fidelity to [the] event," in the "fidelity to the possibility opened by the event." As Marcel explains, fidelity is "a certain relation which is felt to be inalterable, and therefore an assurance which cannot be fleeting."[59] To be faithful to an event means, Badiou notes (again following Marcel), being compelled "to *invent* a new way of being and acting in [and according to] the situation." The event's truth "bids me," Marcel observes, "invent a certain *modus vivendi* which I would otherwise be precluded from envisaging."[60] In other words, fidelity is essentially inventive or, to use Marcel's term, creative: true fidelity is perforce "creative fidelity."[61] Yet a "being who is faithful is also one who can betray" and be betrayed.[62] Fidelity cannot be thought of without its opposite—betrayal, which is as much a "possibility opened by the event," as much a *modus vivendi et agendi* in view of "the Irrefutable and the True" as fidelity. For both presuppose our concrete experience and awareness of the truth of the event in question. The interface between fidelity and betrayal plays a crucial role in my affairistic approach to relations between texts as well as relations between contexts and texts.

LOVE

> *I know the word exists, and the heart doubtlessly has a name*
> *for it, but its interpretation remains an uncharted bay every*
> *man must fathom for himself.*
>
> *Truth is spoken, if it ever comes to be spoken, in love.*[63]

Brodsky conceives of poetry as of an "act of love," Grünbein underscores that "the service of Love" is one of the poet's "most noble pursuits," and Celan suggests, as I explain later, that the poetic word is essentially an expression of profound affection for and loyalty to the beloved singular other.[64] To do justice to the three poets' engagement of *love* as a specifically poetic category, I suggest interpreting it—without in any way disregarding its commonly accepted array of meanings as an emotional, psychological, and social force—in emphatically hermeneutic terms, in line with a long tradition ranging from Plato through St. Paul and St. Augustine to Paul Tillich, Gabriel Marcel, Iris Murdoch, and Alain Badiou (to name only a handful of authors staking out the historical trajectory of the Western philosophical discourse on love).[65] I should note that I do not discuss the specific differences between the varieties of love, traditionally captured in such terms as *eros, philia, agape,* and *epithymia;* rather, I employ the term in a broad, amatory-erotic sense.[66]

In its various forms, love has been credited with a special kind of hermeneutical, cognitive force: "Eros," Diotima explains to Socrates, is "at once desirous and full of wisdom [*phroneseos*]." According to St. Paul, love (*agape* or *caritas*) holds out the promise of a future state of privileged knowledge. "He who knows [the] truth," Augustine proclaims, "knows it . . . love [*caritas*] knows it." According to Tillich, in and through love "reality manifests itself." For Marcel, "love is the . . . starting point for the *understanding* of . . . body and soul." For Murdoch, love is "knowledge of the individual" predicated—and here she joins forces with Brodsky—on the lover's "attention . . . towards the great surprising variety of the world." Finally, Badiou defines love as "the production . . . of a truth."[67]

Love, in other words, ought to be viewed as a particular—novel, inventive, unprecedented—mode of engaging with and interpreting the world and reality (in the most general terms), as a force that creates meaning(s) and establishes new semantic structures and connections as a result of the lover's concern with "this or that detail of the universe" in light of his fidelity to the truth of an event.[68] Or to put it differently, fidelity to the truth of an event articulates itself emphatically in and through love.

INTERLOCUTION

Insofar as love is thought of, if not exclusively, as a hermeneutical force, as a mode of understanding and knowing, it must perforce be recognized as intentional—an "attitude toward reality," as Brodsky puts it—and hence as relational.[69] I wish to specify the particular hermeneutical bond established in and through love, understood as the medium of fidelity to the truth of an event, in terms of *interlocution,* which fuses the relational (*inter*) and the hermeneutic (*locution*). *Interlocution* should not be read as synonymous with *dialogue, conversation,* or *colloquy.* By *interlocution* I mean a hermeneutical relationship between agents or entities, such as texts. I mean the kind of relationship Walter Benjamin has in mind when he stipulates that poetic "translation . . . must *lovingly* adopt within its own language [the original's] mode of meaning." I mean the kind of relationship Brodsky considers characteristic of the interface between poetry and life, which he defines, as already mentioned, as "an act of love, not so much of an author for his subject as of language for a piece of reality."[70] Interlocution has less to do with real dialogue, written or oral, than with a certain way of taking into account and engaging with (the texts of) others. Thus, from the perspective of interlocution, there is no contradiction or paradox in the fact that although Grünbein views poetry as essentially monologic, his actual poetic practice evinces a high degree of interlocution. Concomitantly, the fact that Celan views poetry as essentially dialogic would not in itself automatically guarantee the interlocutionary character of his poetry.

Interlocution also highlights the fact that the loving relationship intended here transpires and is articulated in and through language as the hermeneutical medium *par excellence.* Fidelity to the truth of an event can consequently be specified as articulating itself with particular force through love unfolding as interlocution. Insofar as interlocution is essentially verbal and insofar as it hinges on the question of fidelity and betrayal with regard to the truth of a particular event, it cannot but signally bear on the question of fidelity and betrayal as it plays out in the practices of reading, interpretation, and translation, especially the practices of reading, interpreting, and translating works of literature.

~

In tracing Celan's, Grünbein's, and Brodsky's translations of life into poetry (and vice versa), then, I am specifically concerned with the ways in which they can be said to exercise their fidelities to the truths of the three events at the heart of this book, as well as the ways in which their fidelities get articulated in their interlocutions with such literary predecessors as Shakespeare, Seneca, and Byron, among others. I should stress yet again that I do not presume to have privileged access to Celan's, Grünbein's, and Brodsky's respective *experiences* of their own and others' lives, and that this book is not an exercise in sociological, psychological, or biographical criticism. What I am after are the ways in which the three poets can be said to have become *inventive* and *creatively faithful* to the truths of the Goll, Livilla, and Brodsky affairs, respectively; the ways in which they can be said to have stood by their various truths, allowing them to unfold in and through their poetry.

Insofar as the truth of an event is directly accessible—to the extent that it is accessible at all—only to the person actually living and experiencing the event, we necessarily depend on personal testimony for an *account* of a person's fidelity to this truth. In other words, if, as Celan puts it (with a nod to Sartre), "Nobody / testifies to the / Witness" of an event, only an *account* of the witness's fidelity to the truth of the event can guarantee the latter's necessarily delayed and mediated witnessability. Or to put it differently, the truth of an event can be attested to only *metaleptically*—as the (chrono)logically anterior referent of an inevitably belated hermeneutics of *indication*.[71]

If being faithful to an event means being emphatically creative vis-à-vis the demands the event makes on those upon whom it impinges, looking at constitutively creative accounts of evental fidelity is the hermeneutically obvious path to take in the present context. For my engagement with Celan, Grünbein, and Brodsky, this means that any observations or claims I will have made about their respective modes of inventiveness and creativity with regard to the aforementioned affairs must perforce begin from and end with their poetic practices—the most vivid manifestations and articulations of their creative powers. All three poets engage these affairs, which are, as I illustrate, threaded into the very warp and woof of their poetics, as catalysts and horizons for sustained poetic-existential reflection. What *are* the evental truths elaborated and staged by Celan, Grünbein, and Brodsky? To what ends can they be said to harness these affairs poetically so as not to betray what will have emerged as their respective truths? It is to a detailed elaboration and discussion of Celan's, Grünbein's, and Brodsky's individual poetic stagings of their respective fidelities to the truths of the events in question to which I now turn.

CHAPTER 2

From Encounter to Tryst

Celan and Shakespeare

O let me true in love but truly write. . . .

Everything happens in the world because of encounters.[1]

Paul Celan has become the epitome of "poetry after Auschwitz."[2] His oeuvre has been engaged, for the most part, in light of his experience of the Holocaust—as a survivor's exemplary poetic testimony to one of modern history's darkest chapters. As one critic succinctly puts it, "the dominant image of Celan [is] a mixture of darkness, death, dejection, and grief."[3] Although this *tragic* view of Celan as "poet, survivor, [and] Jew" (thus the subtitle of John Felstiner's acclaimed book on the poet) is more than justified in view of the bare facts of Celan's biography *and* in view of his poetry's sustained concern with the Holocaust, it is by no means the only plausible and productive interpretive stance toward the poet and his legacy. As a number of critics have pointed out, Celan's poetry ought not to be pigeonholed as or reduced to the status of "poetry of witness," that is, poetry the main function of which consists of mourning, commemoration, and bearing witness to suffering—in this case, the "suffering of Auschwitz and that which it stands for."[4] Celan's poetry can also and indeed ought to be read as a "lyrical offensive, a counter project" in the face of such suffering, *his* mode (idealistic and politically ineffective in any sense of immediacy though it may be) of countervailing, if belatedly, through poetry the very possibility of catastrophe.[5] What crucially, if by no means exclusively, enables and sustains Celan's lyrical offensive against the abiding trauma of National Socialism, against what he experienced, especially in connection with the Goll affair, as the continued, if disguised, irruption of an atrocious past into the present, is, I suggest, his reliance on the salvific power of love. The force of love—especially erotic love—ought to be viewed as Celan's most stalwart *ally* in his lifelong attempt to cope poetically with and respond adequately to "what happened."[6]

Consequently, if we want to grasp the full force of Celan's creative fidelity to the truth of the event that he avowedly experienced as the most palpable manifestation of what he perceived as the continued presence of National Socialism in Germany—the Goll affair—we ought to attend to his poetic deployment of the topoi of love and eroticism, especially in those texts that most poignantly metabolize the affair, such as his translations of Shakespeare's sonnets, as I illustrate in this chapter. In the course of what I disclose as his interlocution with Shakespeare, Celan not only poetically succeeds in parrying Goll's charges, but he also develops and stages what emerges as an idiosyncratic, affairistic conception of poetic translation, and hence poetic signification *tout court*.

I begin my interpretation of Celan's oeuvre in the key of love by attending to the conceptual and intertextual dimensions of his poetics as articulated in his scant prose (mainly in two speeches: one delivered on January 26, 1958, upon being awarded the Literary Prize of the Free City of Bremen; the other, entitled "Der Meridian," delivered on October 22, 1960, upon receiving the Georg Büchner Prize), with a view to disclosing its amatory underpinnings.[7] I then move on to a detailed analysis of Celan's engagement with Shakespeare—the most palpable and exemplary staging of his poetics of love.

"Beloved Lucile"

"Long live the king!" These words, uttered by Lucile Desmoulins, whose husband, Camille, a prominent revolutionary, has just been executed on the orders of the revolutionary tribunal at the end of Georg Büchner's drama *Danton's Death* (1835), serve Celan as an exemplary *avant la lettre* instantiation of his conception of poetry as counter-word, as "a singular human being's speech having become Gestalt"[8]:

> Someone who . . . hears the one who is speaking, "sees him speak," who has apprehended language and Gestalt and . . . at the same time breath, that is, direction [*Richtung*] and fate [*Schicksal*] . . . this someone is Lucile. . . .

And here, where everything comes to an end . . . as Camille . . . dies . . . here comes Lucile . . . for whom language is something personal and perceptible . . . with her sudden "Long live the King!"

After all those words uttered on the stage (it's the scaffold)—what a word!

It is the counter-word [*Gegenwort*] . . . an act of freedom [*Akt der Freiheit*]. . . .

Certainly . . . this sounds at first like a pledge of allegiance to the "ancien régime."

But here—you'll allow someone who grew up with the writings of Peter Kropotkin and Gustav Landauer to stress this—here there's no paying homage to monarchy or to a preservable Yesterday.

Homage is being paid to the majesty of the absurd, testifying to the presence of the human [*Gegenwart des Menschlichen*].

And that . . . is, I believe . . . poetry.[9]

Lucile's word of response to and protest against the Jacobin reign of terror is an "act of freedom" that seals, as she very well knows, her own fate (professing loyalty to Louis XVI in Paris in 1794 is equal to signing one's own death warrant). Celan interprets this response against the foil of the reign of terror of the "thousand darknesses of death-bringing speech" which he had experienced firsthand during the Third Reich and to which he had lost his parents, among others.[10] Celan suggests that poetry as counter-word—and Lucile as an allegory of poetry as counter-word—is capable of withstanding, in one way or another, the onslaught and strictures of state power and history in the name of the singularly human.[11]

As Celan himself points out, his take on Lucile's "Long live the King!" is indebted in particular to revolutionary socialist and anarchist Peter Kropotkin (1842–1921) and, more importantly, to radical socialist Gustav Landauer (1870–1919), both of whom had published extensively on the French Revolution.[12] Celan's reading of Lucile's exclamation and thus his overall notion of poetry as counter-word is informed in particular by Landauer's conception of freedom and its relation to poetry, the main function of which he defines as "objection" (*Einspruch*) and "contradiction" (*Widerrede*).[13]

Although Landauer had already laid out his views on the significance of individual existence vis-à-vis the historical and political in his 1907 treatise *Die Revolution*, it was in the course of his lectures on Shakespeare, delivered shortly before his death and posthumously published by Martin Buber (one of Celan's central poetic-existential interlocutors), that an emphatically ethical-existential concept of a "freedom . . . in the human" (*Freiheit . . . im Menschlichen*), a "freedom from formulae, theoretical and moral conventions," was developed. This concept aims not at historical or political conditions but rather at the very "aliveness and inner core" of our singular "human existence," and it captures a person's existential "direction" (*Richtung*) and "fate" (*Schicksal*).[14] Although the question of "freedom . . . in the human" is negotiated, according to Landauer, more or less explicitly in all of Shakespeare's works, it is staged with particular force, he suggests, in *Romeo and Juliet*: "the divine necessity of the human, which we call freedom, comes to life [most palpably] at the very moment when the power of love manifests itself between them."[15] Thus, if we read Celan's take on Lucile's "Es lebe der König!" in light of his engagement with Landauer, and particularly in light of the latter's elaboration of his notion of freedom through the prism of Shakespeare's dramatic meditation on the tragic vagaries of love, Lucile's counter-word—as an "act of freedom" in the name of "the singular human being" and rife with "direction" and "fate"—can *a fortiori* be read as a declaration and an act of love.

Reading Celan's notion of poetry as counter-word via Landauer in the key of love is all the more plausible given that it is enjoined by Büchner himself. Is not Lucile's final "Long live the king!" first and foremost, a disguised expression of pain, despair, longing, and profound love on the part of a wife in view of her beloved husband's violent death?[16] (Immediately prior to uttering these words she is heard screaming and exclaiming "My Camille! Where shall I look for you?") Is it not a disguised expression—in a certain sense absurd indeed in comparison with the ostensibly greater historical and political significance of the project of the revolution, which cannot do without the occasional victim, as it were—of one person's desperate desire for the preservation and continuation of the other's very being?[17] Can it not be read, if by no means exclusively, as a ruse on Lucile's part—a ruse that, in sealing her fate at the hands of the Jacobins, will allow her to be reunited in death with her beloved husband, whose heart-wrenching letters ("My dearest Lucile! My most beloved Lucile!") written to her from the Luxembourg prison in the days before his execution testify to their profound and passionate mutual attachment?[18]

Taking cognizance of and acknowledging the amatory dimension of Celan's conception of poetry as counter-word has important consequences for an adequate and contextually productive understanding of his concomitant conceptualization of poetry as an en*counter* with a (poetic) interlocutor or *counter*part, a conceptualization that he developed under the spell of his own momentous encounter in May 1957 with Osip Mandelstam's works—and through them, as he would claim, with the poet himself:

> The poem is lonely. It is lonely and underway. The one who writes it remains given to it.

But doesn't the poem, consequently, stand, here already, in the encounter [*Begegnung*]—in the secret [*Geheimnis*] of the encounter?

The poem wants to reach an Other, it needs this Other, it needs an interlocutor or counterpart [*Gegenüber*]. It seeks it out, speaks toward it. . . .

The poem becomes . . . dialogue [*Gespräch*].

In the space of this dialogue, the addressed constitutes itself gathers [*versammelt es sich*] itself around the addressing and naming I.[19]

In view of the obvious lexematic, morphological, and semantic kinship between *Gegen*wort, *Begegn*ung, and *Gegen*über—*counter*-word, en*counter*, and *counter*-part—Celan is more than justified in establishing a conceptual and existential link between poetry as *counter*-word and poetry as a "word of en*counter*."[20] The counter-word of poetry happens only in and through en*counter*ing the other. If, however, the poetic counter-word is perforce a word of love—insofar as it conceptually derives from and is modeled on Lucile's "Long live the King!"—Celan's poetics of encounter and dialogue will have always been already (also) a poetics of love.[21] At its most poetic, the counter-word of poetry cannot but be a word of love, Celan suggests; concurrently, love *articulates* itself exemplarily in the poetic counter-word.

Surprising and unexpected though it may seem to cast Celan's poetics as a poetics of love—especially on the basis of his engagement with Büchner (of all authors), which has been interpreted for the most part in the light of the *darker*, *tragic* side of the biography and poetics of Celan as a poet "after Auschwitz"[22]—it is plausible indeed, if we bear in mind the following "corroborating factors":

(1) Celan's attention to the critical function of the human hand in and for the progress of the "lonely" poem toward its interlocutor—only the "true hands" of a "singular and mortal being," Celan observes, "write true poems. . . . I see no essential difference between a handshake and a poem"[23]—is certainly informed by Büchner's linking, in the play *Leonce and Lena,* of the desire to be loved with the desire to touch and be touched by the other: "O God, I could love," Lena remarks, "we walk through life lonely . . . groping for a *hand* that would hold us until the undertaker separates our *hands*. . . ."[24] If we grant that Lena's and Büchner's voices resonate in Celan's equation of poetry with a handshake, and if we concurrently grant that Celan's poetic handshake testifies to and is an integral part of the event of poetic encountering, then we are more than justified in reading the latter in the key of love.

(2) To the extent that Celan's poetic notion of *encounter* is profoundly indebted to Martin Buber, it is always already imbued with the latter's notion of the

"dialogic eros," which binds the "I and you" in the "secret" / "secrecy" (*Geheimnis*) of their "mutuality."[25]

(3) Finally, insofar as Celan develops his poetics in explicit dialogue with Mandelstam—significantly, his emphasis on Lucile's being a witness to the "presence of the human" harks back to his characterization of Mandelstam's poetry as evidencing the "existence of the singular human being"—the Russian's erotic conception of poetic dialogue, which presumably culminates in the fulfillment and gratification of the poet's desire for the "interlocutor's embrace" and for "loving with his love," must perforce be heard resonating in Celan's notions of poetic encountering and "shaking hands."[26]

In view of the above, and mindful of Celan's emphasis on the secret, clandestine (*Geheimnis*), and intimate character of the poetic encounter, I suggest thinking of that encounter in terms of being a *tryst*—a notion that implies secrecy and is by definition eroticized. In other words, I suggest interpreting Celan's poetics of dialogue as a poetics of erotic communion—as interlocution. The poem itself becomes the site and medium of assignation, the "space," as Celan notes, in which the lovers gather (that is, constitute themselves)—both the "one who writes" the poem, "the addressing and naming I," and his "interlocutor," his "you," to whom the "I" owes its coming "into itself."[27]

Although Celan's engagement with the themes of love and eroticism in his poetry can certainly be traced back to his earliest extant texts written in Czernowitz, he first adumbrated what I have disclosed as his poetics of the loving counter-word and brought it into focus in a conceptually and theoretically somewhat-comprehensive manner in "Der Meridian"—that is, virtually in direct response to Claire Goll's second defamatory letter, which had been published shortly before Celan received news in mid-May 1960 of having been awarded the Büchner Prize.[28] Insofar as the poetic counter-word is, according to Celan, the exemplary mode of protest against injustice and abuse in the name of the "singular human being," it is, I should reiterate, to his poetry above all that we have to look for an adequate response on Celan's part to an affair that he experienced as an assault on his very being as a Jewish poet "after Auschwitz." Celan's poetic output dating from the late 1950s and early 1960s in particular—the period during which the Goll affair peaked—can be expected to bear the most palpable traces of the poet's involuntary entanglement in and attempts to free himself from the web of lies and deceit spun by Goll and her supporters. (The fact that whatever "public statements" we have by Celan on the Goll affair are to be found in his poetry makes sense only—unless, that is, we impute to Celan a complete lack of desire for self-preservation—from within the logic of his poetics. Celan would indeed *not* have done *all* he could have done to defend himself against Goll's charges had he not relied on the power—oblique though it may be—of his poetic word to denounce their untruth and set the record straight, as it were.) More specifically, given that Celan considered translating others' poetry "no less important than writing his own verse" (in the wake of his encounter with Mandelstam he abandoned the distinction between poetic translation and *original* creation) and given that from a semiotic viewpoint poetic translation is the most basic form of poetic signification, Celan's most expeditious and *effective* counter-word in response to an affair that, *qua* translation affair, threatened the very core of his poetics of dialogue and encountering (insofar as its basic enactment is witnessable precisely in and through translation) must perforce be sited in his poetic translations, especially those dating from the period in question.[29] Not surprisingly, throughout the most heated phase of the Goll affair, in the first half of the 1960s, Celan's activity and public presence as a translator outweighed his visibility as an "original" poet.[30]

Among the many poets whom Celan chose to engage with closely and translate throughout the 1950s and 1960s, especially during the most heated phase of the Goll affair—such as Mandelstam, Emily Dickinson, Jules Supervieille, Vladimir Majakovskij, René Char, Sergej Esenin, and Henri Michaux—and who in one way or another and to a greater or lesser extent fed into the elaboration of his poetics, one poet stands out: on Celan's own testimony, Shakespeare—the author whom, as John Felstiner notes, he "most esteemed"—played a particularly important role in his dealings with the Goll affair.[31] "Shakespeare had always been a source of consolation," Celan is reported as saying shortly before his death, "especially in times of persecution, during the Goll affair, or during the periods of psychiatric treatment."[32] And it is the specific kind of consolation evidenced and documented in Celan's translations of Shakespeare's sonnets that, I argue, attests to their unprecedented affairistic significance: Celan's dialogue with Shakespeare spanned virtually his entire career and unfolded with particular intensity in his versions of Shakespeare's sonnets dating from the late 1950s to the mid-1960s and published in book form as *Einundzwanzig Sonette* (Twenty-one sonnets) in 1967. It is in this dialogue that the full force of Celan's poetics of love is released to produce one of the most memorable events in the history, theory, and practice of poetic translation.[33] In Celan's translations of Shakespeare's sonnets, the semiotic—or rather, *sem-erotic*—underpinnings of his poetics of love are exemplarily revealed and instantiated.

"To Truths Translated"

I hate inconstancy. . . .

By dint of translating . . . , he became . . . his most faithful reader.[34]

"WHILST I ALONE DID CALL UPON THY AYDE . . . "

Why Shakespeare? Why would Celan have singled out Shakespeare as his prime "source of consolation" and support during the Goll affair (and beyond)?[35] A number of factors can be adduced as motivating Celan's choice:

1. Given Celan's racialist reading of the affair as a manifestation of the abiding presence of National Socialism in Germany and hence as an attack on his very being as a *Jewish* poet, it is not at all surprising that, in a situation requiring the strongest possible and most effective counter-word on his part, he should have sought succor from the poet he considered the greatest of all poets, who would thus have logically presented himself as the strongest possible and most advantageous ally, as it were: Shakespeare.[36] Hauntingly, the first two lines of Shakespeare's seventy-ninth sonnet—"Whilst I alone did call upon thy ayde, / My verse alone had all thy gentle grace," which Celan translates as "Als ich um Hilfe zu dir kam, allein, / da warst du meinem Vers allein gewogen"—proleptically vindicate Celan's decision to turn to Shakespeare for help and consolation, to engage him as his advocate and ally.[37]

2. As a tale about a poet's entanglement in a web of desire, deceit, infidelity, and poetic rivalry, and last but not least about poetry's power to capture truthfully, shape, and outlast the vagaries of life, Shakespeare's sonnet sequence presented itself to Celan as a welcome prism through which to refract, comment on, and articulate faithfully, in *his* own poetic terms, the truth of the real-life web of lies, deceit, and accusations in which he was embroiled at the time.[38]

3. Last but not least, I should point out that in securing Shakespeare as an ally for his lyrical counteroffensive against his German detractors in the name of "truth"—the truth of his innocence, in particular—Celan succeeded in undermining the very premise of the affair's perceived racialist dimension. Let me explain: In the late 1950s, when Celan set out in the midst of the storm of the Goll affair to render Shakespeare's sonnets in German, he embarked on an enterprise of extreme personal *and* cultural significance. Unlike any of the other poets whom Celan chose to engage with closely and, frequently, to translate, especially during the various phases of the Goll affair, Shakespeare was not only the poet he most revered, but also the poet who occupied a very special place in the German cul-

tural imagination since he was first mentioned in German print toward the end of the seventeenth century.[39] No other (foreign-language) poet has been the subject of such abiding fascination, reverence, and emulation among Germans; no other (foreign-language) poet has played as prominent a role in the formation of Germany's cultural and national identity as Shakespeare. The young Goethe and the authors of the *Sturm und Drang* viewed his works as the very embodiment of "nature"; the romantics considered him a genius more German than English; the Young Germans invoked the author of *Hamlet* to denounce political complacency and oppression ("Deutschland ist Hamlet!"); the National Socialists endeavored to cast him as a German classic on a par with Goethe and Schiller; Karl Jaspers and Carl Schmitt engaged his dramatic treatments of moral questions as foils for dealing with Germany's Nazi past; and most recently, Durs Grünbein has called him (with a nod to Goethe) a "natural constant . . . of the kind of the number π."[40] Probably, the most eloquent testimony to the scope and depth of Germany's ongoing affair with Shakespeare consists in the fact that he has emerged as one of the playwrights whose work is most frequently performed on German stages, and that, as Franz Josef Czernin observes, the sonnet sequence has not been translated, completely or in part, into any other language as frequently as into German. Translating Shakespeare's sonnets has become, Grünbein observes, a veritable "ritual" for German poets.[41]

In view of Shakespeare's place at the dead center of Germany's long-standing preoccupation with its own national and cultural identity, Celan's decision to translate Shakespeare's sonnets into German could not help but appear as an intrusion on the part of an "outsider" into what had ostensibly consolidated, over the course of two centuries, into an emphatically German affair. (It is worth remembering at this point that Hans Egon Holthusen, a former Nazi and member of the Waffen SS and after the war an influential critic and member of the Berlin Academy of the Arts, branded Celan a "stranger and outsider to poetic speech."[42]) After all, the fact that a Romanian-born, Jewish, and naturalized French poet who had gained prominence in Germany primarily as the author of texts (such as "Death Fugue") denouncing the suffering of Jews at the hands of Germans would have had the audacity to create *his* "international" version of Shakespeare *in German* could not help but mark a break in the established tradition of Germany's arrogation and colonization of Shakespeare as a "German" author.[43] Thus, in winning Shakespeare over to his Jewish side, so to speak, Celan can be said to have ironically suggested, "If the most 'German' of German authors, Shakespeare, thinks that I am innocent, why are you attacking me?" With Shakespeare—and this means with that which is presumably "great and . . . beautiful" about German culture—on his side, Celan could not fail to unmask Goll's German supporters as the tacit promoters of a notion of Germanness predicated on the ostracism of precisely such Germans as Celan (and Shakespeare).[44]

~

In my approach to Celan's engagement with Shakespeare, I focus on three inter-related aspects that most saliently testify to Celan's creative fidelity to the truth of the event of the Goll affair: (1) the ways in which Celan's most pressing poetic-existential concerns at the time are poetically metabolized; (2) the ways in which the nexus of poetry and love—one of the sonnet sequence's central themes *and* the foundation of Celan's poetics of the counter-word—is staged; and (3), the poetological surplus value of Celan's *interlocution* with Shakespeare—of what I disclose as the adumbration and poetic enactment of an affairistic, erotic notion of translation and hence of poetic signification *tout court.*

Before embarking on a detailed discussion of Celan's versions of Shakespeare's sonnets, however, I should note that I will attend to linguistic, rhetorical, and prosodic specificities only insofar as they pertain to my overall argument, being well aware of the fact that Celan takes great liberties—if one applies parameters of linguistic, prosodic, and lexematic fidelity—in his poetic translations and that Shakespeare's sonnets have been translated into German in completely different, more faithful ways.[45] I should also point out that two semiotic assumptions inform my approach: (1) although any translation signifies, first and foremost, the original, it necessarily develops its own referential and semantic "universe"; and (2) it is in and through the tension among the referential, semantic, and rhetorical constitutions of original and translation that new meanings emerge. In the case of Shakespeare's sonnets and their translations by Celan, this tension is produced, for instance, by Celan's inscription of Shakespeare's aesthetic-erotic themes within the context of his own life. Thus, to give one preliminary example: Shakespeare's apostrophes throughout the sonnets—to the "young man" (Sonnets 1–126) and the "dark lady" (Sonnets 127–154)—undergo a redirection in Celan's translations, which in addressing themselves to Shakespeare and his addressees (from a purely semiotic viewpoint) can be read as emphatically, yet not exclusively, directed at the world-at-large around Celan, summarily at his contemporaries and detractors, as well as at himself—through the detour of second-person apostrophe.[46] Finally, I should mention that my slightly acontextual treatment of Shakespeare's texts, as well as my "biographizing" treatment of Celan's translations, is justified only in view of my overall focus on the literary-factual significance of the Goll affair and in view of Celan's programmatic ("the one who writes [the poem] remains given to it") and well-documented poetic inscription of life.[47]

Significant to the present context, the first sonnet Celan chose to translate (begun in September 1959 and completed in January 1960) in the thick of the Goll affair was Sonnet 90, in which Shakespeare meditates—adopting a quiet tone of resignation and mourning—on his impending separation from the young man.[48] With its recognition of "the spight of fortune" it is particularly apt to capture "the blows . . . that are [Celan's] lot" at the time:[49]

Then hate me when thou wilt, if ever, now,	Mußt du mich hassen, haß mich unge-säumt,
Now while the world is bent my deeds to crosse,	Gesell der Welt dich zu, die mir den Weg vertritt,
Join with the spight of fortune, make me bow,	groll mit dem Schicksal, beug ihn, der sich bäumt,
And doe not drop in for an after losse.	und sei nicht du das Letzte, das entglitt.

(lines 1–4)

(Must you hate me, hate me without delay,
join the world, which obstructs my way,
join in with the wrath of fate, bend the one who balks/protests/resists
and be not the last that [will have] slipped away.)

Celan's emphatic *must,* which tips the first line's rhetorical balance to the side of the imperative, thus outweighing its conditional gist (in the sense of "If you must hate me . . . "), can be read as foregrounding—especially in conjunction with the contiguous repetition "hassen, haß"—the sheer facticity and inevitability of "the spight of fortune," as it presumably articulates itself in a media campaign obstructing and aggravating Celan's "way" as a translator-poet. The plausibility of reading Celan's version of these lines as an implicit denunciation of the Goll affair is shored up by his decision to complement Shakespeare's plea—"Join with spight of fortune, make me bow"—with a clear expression of resistance (completely absent in the original) to worldly obstructions by stating (and thereby prosodically echoing Shakespeare's final "bow" in line 3) that he is one "der sich bäumt" (who resists).

The autobiographical motivation and import of this poetically expressed resistance—paratextually corroborated by a note of Celan's from June 1961, located (fittingly) in a folder containing his correspondence with Claire Goll: "J'assume—Je résiste—Je refuse" (I assume responsibility—I resist—I refuse)[50]—comes to the fore most palpably when compared to other translations of this line, especially those with which Celan was familiar and which he endeavored "to steer clear of," such as those by Gottlob Regis, Otto Gildermeister, Eduard Saenger, Stefan George, Terese Robinson, and Rolf-Dietrich Keil, none of whom takes the liberty, as does Celan, of turning Shakespeare's resignation into resistance. Regis translates line 3 as "Hilf dem Verdruß des Glücks mir weh zu tun" (Help the chagrin of fortune to hurt me), Gildermeister as "Verbündet mit dem Schicksal führ' den Streich" (Allied with fate carry the blow), Saenger as "Folg meinem Glück, so trifft mich Streich auf Streich" (Follow my fortune, so blow after blow attains me), George as "Erdrück mich—hilf dem schicksal das mich hetzt" (Crush me—help fate that is chasing me), Robinson (following Gildermeister) as "Verbünde dich dem Schicksal, führ' den Streich" (Ally yourself with fate, carry the blow), and Keil as "Beug jetzt mich, wo Fortunas Groll mich hetzt" (Bend me now that Fortune's wrath is chasing me).[51] Concomitantly, the rhetorical force of Celan's prosodically nugatory *Mußt*, followed by the repetition of *hassen, haß* in line 1, is particularly palpable against the backdrop of such more faithful renderings as those by Regis ("So hasse mich denn, wann du willst"), Gildermeister ("Drum hass mich, wann du willst"), George ("Nun hass mich wenn du willst"), Robinson ("Doch hasse mich, willst du mich hassen"), and Keil ("So haß mich, wenn du willst").[52]

Sonnet 70 serves Celan as a mouthpiece to denounce further the "spight of fortune":

That though art blam'd shall not be thy defect,
For slanders mark was ever yet the fair;
The ornament of beauty is suspect,
A crow that flies in heavens sweetest ayre.
So thou be good, slander doth but approve
Thy worth the greater, being woo'd of time,
For Canker vice the sweetest buds doth love,
And thou present'st a pure unstayined prime.
Thou hast past by the ambush of young daies,
Either not assayled, or victor being charg'd;
Yet this thy praise cannot be soe thy praise,
To tye up envy evermore inlarged.
If some suspect of ill maskt not thy show,

Nicht an dir liegts, daß sie dich schmähn und schmähen:
kaum zeigt sich Reines, schon wirds schlechtgemacht.
Wo Himmel blaun, da fliegen bald die Krähen.
Der Schönheit Zierde: Argwohn und Verdacht.

Verlästert du, geliebt auch von den Tagen:
ist Güte dein, dies alles mehrt sie bloß.
Die Knospe duftet und der Wurm muß nagen;
du bist ein Erstling und bist makellos.

Die vielen Hinterhalte schon in jungen Jahren:
du gingst hindurch, zuweilen siegtest du.
Dies ist dein Ruhm, der so wie keiner klare,
-

Then thou alone kingdomes of hearts
   shouldst owe.

den Mund der Neider schließt auch er nicht
   zu.

Du, müßtest du nicht so: beargwöhnt, sein,
im Reich der Herzen herrschtest du allein.

(It's not your fault that they slander you and slander:
no sooner does the pure appear than it is denigrated.
Where skies are blue, soon crows are flying.
Beauty's ornament: mistrust and suspicion.

Slandered you, may the days love you:
is goodness yours, all this makes it greater still.
The bud scents and the work must gnaw;
you are a first and are immaculate.

The many ambushes already in early years:
you went through, sometimes you won.
This is your fame, as clear as no other,
the mouth of the envious even it does not shut up.

You, would you not have to thus: suspected/mistrusted, be,
in the empire of hearts you would reign alone.)

Addressing himself, as it were, through Shakespeare's apostrophe to the young man, Celan appears to be condemning, while exculpating himself ("It's not your fault"), the slanderous campaign to which he is exposed. The repetition of *schmähn und schmähen* (slander . . . and slander) (line 1), the transposition of the original's *suspect* (line 3) into the hendiadys *Argwohn und Verdacht* (mistrust and suspicion) (line 4), the emphatic placement of the neologism *Verlästert* (slandered) at the very beginning of line 5, as well as the emphatic—mark the colon—*so: beargwöhnt* (thus: suspected/mistrusted) (line 13) can be read as foregrounding the intensity of the translator's antidefamatory intent.[53] The latter's articulation is equally facilitated by lines 9 to 10 of Sonnet 119: "O benefit of ill! Now I find true / That better is by evil still made better," which Celan translates as "Gewinn des Übels! Bessres wird, ich merk / durch Übel besser noch, als es je war" (Gain of evil! What is better becomes, I notice / through evil even better than it ever was).

Shakespeare's "Thou hast past by the ambush of young daies" (Sonnet 70, line 9), which Celan renders as *du gingst hindurch* (you went through) (line 12), furnishes Celan with a bridge to the biographical-historical core of his own poetics insofar as it is based on his firsthand experience of the Holocaust. Celan's *gingst hindurch* uncannily echoes his depiction of the fate of language in the Third Reich in his Bremen Prize speech:

> Language had to . . . go through its own answerlessnesses, go through terrible silencing, go through the thousand darknesses of death-bringing speech. It went through and did not deliver words for what happened; but it went through this event. Went through and was permitted to reemerge into the light of day again. . . .

> [Die Sprache] mußte . . . hindurchgehen durch ihre eigenen Antwortlosigkeiten, hindurchgehen durch furchtbares Verstummen, hindurchgehen durch die tausend Finsternisse todbringender Rede. Sie ging hindurch und gab keine Worte her für das, was geschah; aber sie ging durch dieses Geschehen. Ging hindurch und durfte wieder zutage treten. . . . [54]

The poetic, historical, and biographical import of Celan's *gingst hindurch* in his version of Sonnet 70 is intensified by his nugatory—from the viewpoint of lexematic and semantic fidelity to the original—use of *Verfinstrungen* (darkenings) in his translation of Sonnet 5 (completed on February 12, 1961):

For never resting time leads Summer on To hideous winter and confounds him there,	Ist Sommer? Sommer *war*. Schon führt die Zeit den Wintern und Verfinstrungen entgegen.

(lines 5–6)

(Is summer? Summer *was*. Already time leads
toward winters and darkenings.)

The use of *Verfinstrungen* here, despite the absence of an equivalent in the original, alerts us to Celan's impetus, which comes to the fore with particular clarity against the foil of the passage cited from his Bremen Prize speech, in which the morphologically related term *Finsternisse* (darknesses) is employed with reference to the "night"—to use Elie Wiesel's term—of the Holocaust.[55] By linking his depiction of the fate of language in the Third Reich to his response to Shakespeare, Celan saturates the latter with the theme of his experience and survival of the Holocaust, thus denouncing, via Shakespeare, what he interpreted as a revival of National Socialism in Germany, of which he considered the Goll affair an offshoot. Celan's use of *Verfinstrungen* in Sonnet 5 most poignantly testifies to the intimate connection between life and literature established in his poetic translations, which are imbued with the translator's more or less immediate life context and existential concerns.[56]

Sonnet 60 lends literal support to the biographical significance of Celan's use of *Verfinstrungen*. Its *eclipses* (line 7)—literally, *Finsterniss*—along with time's destructive power (line 8) provide Celan with a viable prism through which to allude to and refract what he himself went through in the early 1940s at the hands of the Nazis, thus squarely placing the Goll affair in the context of his ongoing concern with the Holocaust and its aftermath:

Nativity, once in the maine of light,	Geburt, ins volle Licht gerückt, sie kraucht
Crawles to maturity, wherewith being crown'd,	zur Reife hin; und so, gekrönt, umglänzt noch eben,
Crooked eclipses gainst his glory fight,	wird sie in schiefe Finsternis getaucht,
And Time that gave doth now his gift confound.	und sie, die Zeit, zerstört, was sie, die Zeit, gegeben.

(lines 5–8)

(Birth, drawn into full view, it slouches
toward maturity; thus, crowned, radiant a moment ago,
it is bathed in crooked darkness,
and it, time, destroys, what it, time, has given.)

Translating these lines enables Celan to fuse history and personal trauma with the dismay at what must have felt to him like an attack on the very core of his being as a (Jewish) poet and survivor. In the context of the Goll affair, such other Shakespearean lines as "Then thou whose shaddow shaddows doth make bright" (*Du, dessen Schatten Schatten hell durchwebt*) (Sonnet 43, line 5), which thematizes the addressee's radiant presence in the speaker's sleep, and "That some-times anger thrusts into his hide" (*den ich es fühlen laß in meinem Zorn* (Sonnet 50, line 10), which expresses the speaker's weariness and anger at being carried away from his lover on the "beast that bears me" (line 5), also acquire pressing significance in Celan's hands. Shakespeare's nightly "shaddows" can be read as being translated by Celan into the context of the plagiarism charge—which literally overshadowed his life and work at the time—*and* into its political reinterpretation by him. In Celan's version, it is Shakespeare's own shadow, Shakespeare's poetic presence, that the translation suggests brightens the "Crooked eclipses" (*schiefe Finsternis*) of the Goll affair. Concomitantly, Celan's personalized version of line 9 of Sonnet 50—in the original, "anger" is the active subject of the clause, whereas in Celan's translation the speaker emerges as the agent, emphasizing his *Zorn* through the demonstrative *meinem*—can be read as an index of Celan's anger at the Goll affair.[57] Clearly, as the sonnet sequence's major themes (such as love, jealousy, anger, and artistic pride) are played out in the sonneteer's relations to his two main addressees—the "young man" and the "dark lady"—they are muted in Celan's versions in favor of his own pragmatic-poetic agenda.[58]

Couched within this poetic-biographical nexus, Celan's translation of Shakespeare's Sonnet 105 uniquely thematizes and stages, by self-consciously exploring and probing the dimension of love in poetry, what it might mean to translate poetry, what is at stake in a "marriage of true mindes" (*treue Geister sich vermählen*) (Sonnet 116, line 1). This translation vividly testifies to the emphatically poetological dimension of Celan's engagement with Shakespeare, who responded, as I mentioned earlier, to Celan's isolated request for help, "Als ich um Hilfe zu dir kam, allein, / da warst du meinem Vers allein gewogen" (Whilst I alone did call upon thy ayde, / My verse alone had all thy gentle grace) (Sonnet 79, line 1). Sonnet 105, along with sonnets 57, 71, and 116, is one of the few sonnets included in *Einundzwanzig Sonette* that explicitly mentions *love,* one of the sonnet sequence's central themes. The significance in the present context of Celan's selection of these sonnets lies less in their explicit thematics than in the fact that they deal with love in connection with poetry—with the very activity of transforming the sonneteer's erotic-emotional intent into writing. Shakespeare's treatment of love undergoes a translational redirection by Celan, and it is precisely the poetological surplus value brought to bear in and through Celan's reinscription of the theme of love as an integral component of the translator's work that is of particular interest here. To gauge fully the significance of Celan's version of Sonnet 105, I will first attend to some of the contextually relevant semantic transactions in Sonnets 57, 71, and 116.

Sonnet 57 deals with the speaker's enslavement to his love interest, with his readiness to act at the young man's bidding—"Being your slave, what should I doe but tend / Upon . . . your desire? I have no . . . time . . . to spend / Nor services to doe, till you require" (lines 1–4)—and ends with an observation on love—"So true a foole is love that in your Will, / (Though you doe anything) he thinks no ill" (lines 13–14). In Celan's translation these ruminations are given a poetological twist: "Da ich dein Sklave bin, was kann ich tun, als deinen / Wünschen entgegenharrn . . . / Die Zeit . . . ist mir wie irgendeine. / Und Dienste? Keinerlei, eh du's mir aufgetragen" (As I am your slave, what can I do but your / wishes to await . . . / Time . . . is all the same to me. / And services? None, unless you have engaged them); "Solch treuer Narr ist Liebe: nimmer sieht / sie Arg in deinem Tun—was auch geschieht" (Such a faithful fool is love: never sees / it ill in your doing—whatever happens). The translator, Celan suggests, is the primary author's *slave,* awaiting instructions regarding the task to be carried out—in this case, the very act of translating; furthermore, the translator's *enslavement* to the original (and to its author) is a function of his love for it—more specifically, of his love's foolishness, insofar as it is faithful. In other words, the translator's work is motivated by his faithful devotion to and love for the original; whatever happens, the translator-lover will stand by his interlocutor, will not allow his love's work to be contaminated by the thought that the interlocutor's actions could be motivated by bad intentions or insidiousness—by *Arg*. Celan's translation of *ill* as *Arg* is highly significant in this context; it subtly links this version to his earlier-discussed version of Sonnet 70, which contains the hendiadys *Argwohn und Verdacht* (mistrust and suspicion) and which can be read as an articulation of the translator's antidefamatory stance vis-à-vis the plagiarism campaign.[59]

Continuing the theme of love and poetry, Sonnet 71 allows Celan to explore further the translator's loving work:

No longer mourne for me when I am dead
Than you shall hear the surly sullen bell
Give warning to the world that I am fled
From this vile world with vildest worms
    to dwell:
Nay, if you read this line, remember not,
The hand that writ it, for I love you so,
That I in your sweet thoughts would be
    forgot,
If thinking on me then should make you
    woe.
Oh if (I say) you look upon this verse
When I (perhaps) compounded am with
    clay,
Do not so much as my poore name re-
    herse;
But let your love even with my life decay;
Lest the wise world should look into your
    mone,
And mocke you with me after I am gon.

Du sollst, bin ich hinweg, so lang nur
    klagen,
als du die Glocke hörst, die düstere, vom
    Turm;
so lange, als sie braucht, der Welt zu sagen:
Der bei dir wohnte, ging und wohnt beim
    Wurm.

Dies schreibe ich, doch du, hast du's ge-
    lesen,
vergiß, wers schrieb. Denn sieh, ich liebe
    dich:
ich wollt, ich wäre nie in deinem Sinn
    gewesen,
wenn, da du mein gedenkst, dich Gram
    beschlich'.

Du laß, ruht einst dein Blick auf diesen
    Worten,
derweil ich Staub bin, Staub bin und nicht
    mehr,
die Liebe werden, was auch ich geworden,
und meinen Namen, sag ihn nicht mehr
    her:

Die Welt, klugäugig, sucht schon deine
    Tränen,
mich, da ich fort bin, mit dir zu verhöh-
    nen.

(You ought, when I am gone, mourn only for as long
as you hear the bell, the gloomy, from the belfry;
for as long as it needs to tell the world:
He who lived with you is gone and lives with the worm.

This I am writing, but you, when you've read it,
forget who wrote it. For see, I love you:
I wish I had never been on your mind,
should, when you think of me, grief sneak up on you.

You let, when some day your gaze rests upon these words,
while I am dust, dust and nothing more,
love become, what I, too, have become,
and my name, don't pronounce it any longer:

The world, smart-eyed, is already looking for your tears,
to malign/taunt me with you, once I am gone.)

Delving into the midst of Celan's translation of this sonnet, we cannot fail to observe that Celan turns Shakespeare's depersonalized reference to poetic creation as an accomplished process—expressed in the quite matter-of-fact mention of "this line" (line 5) accompanied by the synecdochic "The hand that writ it" (line 6)—into a personal statement on the translator's creativity *in actu*: "Dies schreibe ich" (This I am writing). The introductory deictic *Dies* together with the active construction *schreibe ich* highlight the translator's responsibility for his text—notwithstanding its status as a translation. However, an unexpected tension between the translation's stress on personal authorship and the alleged insignificance of the author's identity is created by the subsequent emphatic shift (through the repetition of *du*) of the poem's pragmatic center from author to reader through the adversative "doch du, hast du's gelesen" (but you, when you've read it) (line 5), followed by the injunction to forget (*vergiß*, line 6) the lines' author. The logic underlying this tension is immediately addressed in the conjunctive "for I love you so"—"Denn sie, ich liebe dich" (line 6). *Because* the poetic transaction thematized in the sonnet is predicated on love, the author's and, more importantly, translator's identity can be obliterated. Celan's imperative *sieh* underscores the implied logical motivation of the injunction to forget. Notwithstanding the author's responsibility for his text, within the dimension of interlocution the question of identity—and hence of subjectivity— recedes into the background in favor of the loving relationship itself. While acknowledging the translator's authorship of the version in question, the reader is enjoined to focus not on the poem's subject but on love's very work—on the poetic process itself unfolding before him rather than on its author and his name. Celan thus makes good on Walter Benjamin's oblique stipulation that the process of a poetic translation's "loving" adoption, "to the very last detail," of the original's "mode of meaning" brings about the translator's demise or obliteration (*Aufgabe*).[60]

Celan's rewriting of lines 9 to 12 subtly corroborates the import of the preceding lines. Instead of following Shakespeare's mournful and rather hopeless "let your love even with my life decay" (line 12), Celan enjoins his interlocutor to allow love to *become*—not *decay*—what *he*, Celan, will have become. Although Celan ostensibly preserves the overall meaning of Shakespeare's mournful plea by soliciting his addressee to let love become dust, his choice of *werden* (become) (line 11), repeated twice, in this context, with its emphasis on potentiality and openness toward the future (even in death), redirects the original's semantics along the lines of a certain kind of hope and continuity. After all, does not Celan's translation unfold—if we attend to the reading process itself—as "Du laß . . . / die Liebe werden" (You let . . . / love become), before flowing into the subclause "was auch ich geworden" (what I too have become)? In other words, the speaker's injunction is, first and foremost and prior to any qualification of property in the logical sense, to let "love become." Yet Celan's *geworden* is far from unambiguous. While ostensibly demanding to be read as an abbreviated form of the accomplished future tense ("werde geworden sein" / "will have become"), it literally signifies the speaker's developmental state at the moment of enunciation, that is, what he *has*, rather than *will have*, become. What has the speaker become? In Celan's semantic redirection of Shakespeare's lines and in the thus-established intratextual context, the translator has become a lover, emphatically voicing his love ("Denn *sieh*, ich liebe dich"). He enjoins his addressee to accomplish nothing less than to let love itself become loving, that is, to allow love ever to *become* love. Again, the uniqueness of Celan's translation comes to the fore with particular clarity if it is juxtaposed with some of his predecessors' versions of these lines:

O kommt dir, ruf' ich, dieser Vers ins Haus	Ich sage, wenn du schaust auf dies Gedicht,
Lange vielleicht nach meines Leibs Ver-modern,	Indes ich selbst vielleicht im Staub zer-stiebe,
Sprich meinen Namen selbst nicht aus,	Dann hauch' selbst meinen armen Namen nicht;
Laß mit dem Leben Liebe gleich ver-lodern:	Mit meinem Leben welk' auch meine Li-ebe,
(Ah, should, I say, this verse come to your house,	(I say, when you look at this poem,
Long, maybe, after my body's decay,	While I may be dispersing as dust,
Do not pronounce my name itself,	Then don't even whisper my poor name;
Let with life love equally burn up . . .)	With my life may your love, too, fade . . .)
(Regis)	(Gildermeister)

O—sag ich—siehst du dann auf dies
    gedicht
Wenn ich vielleicht verschüttet bin mit
    Staub:
Dann nenn auch meinen armen Namen
    nicht—
Dein lieben schwinde mit des lebens raub

Ach, blickst du, sag' ich, dann auf dies
    Gedicht,
Wenn ich vielleicht schon eins mit Schutt
    und Graus,
Dann nenne meinen armen Namen nicht,
Mit meinem Leben sei dein Lieben aus

(Ah—say I—should you then look at this
    poem
When I am perhaps covered with dust:
Then also don't speak my poor name—
Your loving may vanish with the rape of
    life)
(George)

(Ah, should, say I, then look at this poem,
When I am perhaps one with rubble and
    horror,
Then do not speak my poor name,
With my life may your loving be over)
(Robinson)

What does it mean to allow love ever to become love? It means—as suggested by the sonnet in its entirety and, *a fortiori*, by the translation—not to continue mourning after a prescribed period (first quartet), to realize that I—the real and implied reader—am loved by the author/speaker (second quartet), to enter the dimension of love, in which proper names, identities, and subjectivities—in short, the workings of language, with its attendant ambiguities and fallacies—yield to something greater (third quartet) that exceeds and leaves behind the malicious attitude of the "wise," "smart-eyed" world waiting to deride the interlocutors. (The sonnet's final couplet, of course, makes it especially amenable to being inscribed within Celan's overall poetic engagement with the Goll affair.) In other words, the reader—of Shakespeare's reading and writing translator in particular—is asked to become a lover in and through the loving activity of reading and responding to the lover's address.[61]

Celan's translation adumbrates and enacts a conception of writing and reading poetry (with poetic translation fusing the two) predicated on, informed by, and subtended by love. Its interlocutionary appeal is all the more audible if we bear in mind that Celan's version of Sonnet 71 continues, expands, and elaborates on—emphatically, by virtue of the initial *Du sollst*—the interlocutionary theme sounded, yet not further explored, in his version of Mandelstam's poem "Rakovina" (Shell):

No ty poliubiš, ty oceniš
Nenužnoj rakoviny lož.

Doch sie, die leer und unnütz ist, du sollst
sie lieben, deine Muschel dort.

(But you will love, you will value
The useless shell's lie(s).)

(But it, which is empty and useless, you
    ought
to love it, your shell there.)[62]

As I have argued elsewhere, in the context of Celan's encounter with Mandelstam, loving the "shell there" signifies, first and foremost, loving the poet of the original himself in lovingly translating his poem. The very act of poetically responding and, consequently, of translating—insofar as responding implies grasping meaning, and meaning is predicated on translation—is cast as a gesture of love, while love is cast in hermeneutic terms.[63] Celan's prosodically nugatory, yet poetologically central, "du sollst / sie lieben, deine Muschel dort" (you ought / to love your shell there) clearly reappears in the equally prosodically nugatory *Du sollst* in line 1 of his version of Sonnet 71.[64]

Finally, Sonnet 116 yet again drives home the point that the translator's response to the original is informed by love, while picking up the theme of resistance addressed in Sonnet 90:

Let me not to the marriage of true mindes	Ich laß wo treue Geister sich vermählen,
Admit impediments: love is not love	kein Hemmnis gelten. Liebe wär nicht sie,
Which alters when it alteration findes,	wollt sie, wo Wandlung ist, die Wandlung
Or bends with the remover to remove.	wählen;
	noch beugt sie vor dem Beugenden die
	Knie.

(lines 1–4)

(I let, where faithful/true spirits marry,
no impediment obtain. Love wouldn't be itself,
if it, where change is, change chose;
neither does it bend before the bending its knees.)

Continuing to personalize Shakespeare's text, Celan transforms the hortatory "Let me" into the emphatic *Ich laß* (I let); in transposing Shakespeare's nominal "the marriage of true minds" into the active, verbal *treue Geister sich vermählen,* Celan stresses the nuptials' processual character, thereby replicating the very activity of translating itself, as it were. On this reading, then, Shakespeare's "impediments," by which "love" will not allow itself to be vanquished or bent, acquire particularly pressing significance in light of the plagiarism charges. The world that is "*bent* to crosse" Celan's "deeds" and that he resists in Sonnet 90 ("beug ihn, der sich bäumt") reappears in the "impediments" of Sonnet 116 and in the speaker's articulation of love's steadfastness and un*bend*ingness in the face of such impediments. That Celan can indeed be heard rearticulating and hence underscoring his already expressed resistance is evidenced most acutely in his idiosyncratic and lexically semantically unfaithful translation of the fourth line of Sonnet 116. The repetition of the root *beug* (bend) in *beugt* and *Beugenden* achieves two contextually relevant goals. First, it articulates and underscores resistance on the semantic and rhetorical levels, especially in conjunction with the adversative *noch* (neither). Second, in imitating (along with the preceding repetition of *Wandlung*) Shakespeare's ety-mological figures in lines 3 to 4 ("alters . . . alteration," "remover . . . remove"), it brings about the culmination of the *material enactment* of the quartet's theme of constancy and continuity in the face of worldly obstructions.

In the course of my discussion thus far, it has become sufficiently clear that Celan's interlocution with Shakespeare is steeped in the "blood, sweat, and tears" of the real-life battle of the Goll affair. In being ostensibly *unfaithful* to Shake-speare—from a squarely linguistic, semantic, and rhetorical viewpoint—Celan succeeds in structurally (re)staging and (re)enacting the themes of fidelity and betrayal as they unfold in Shakespeare's sonnets *and* in giving voice to what he evidently experienced, in the context of the Goll affair, as a betrayal of his very integrity as a poet and survivor. Concomitantly, in advancing love's power to countervail the "spight of fortune," Celan underscores the centrality of love for his poetics, whose full erotic-affairistic force reveals itself in his translation of Shakespeare's Sonnet 105—to which I now turn.

"ALL MY ARGUMENT"

While the previous sonnets merely mention love, accept it as a given, as it were, Sonnet 105 presents a sustained reflection and meditation on the very character of this love:

Let not my love be cal'd Idolatrie,	Ihr sollt, den ich da lieb, nicht Abgott
Nor my belovèd as an Idoll show,	heißen,
Since all alike my songs and praises be	nicht Götzendienst, was ich da treib und
To one, of one, still such, and ever so.	trieb.
Kinde is my love to day, tomorrow kinde,	All dieses Singen hier, all dieses Preisen:
Still constant in a wondrous excellence,	von ihm, an ihn und immer ihm zulieb.
Therefore my verse to constancie	
confin'de,	Gut ist mein Freund, ists heute und ists
One thing expressing, leaves out differ-	morgen,
ence.	und keiner ist beständiger als er.
Faire, kinde, and true, is all my argument,	In der Beständigkeit, da bleibt mein Vers
Faire, kinde and true, varrying to other	geborgen,
words;	spricht von dem Einen, schweift mir nicht
And in this change is my invention spent,	umher.
Three themes in one, which wondrous	
scope affords.	"Schön, gut und treu", das singe ich und
Faire, kinde, and true, have often liv'd	singe.
alone,	"Schön, gut und treu"—stets anders und
	stets das.
	Ich find, erfind—um sie in eins zu bringen,

Which three, till now, never kept seate in
one.

sie einzubringen ohne Unterlaß.

"Schön, gut und treu" so oft getrennt, ge-
schieden.
In Einem will ich drei zusammenschmie-
den.

(You ought/shall, whom I there lov', not idol name,
Not idolatry, what I am doing and was doing/did there.
All this singing here, all this praising:
of him, to him and always for the love of him.

Good is my friend, is't today and is't tomorrow,
and no one is more constant than he.
In constancy, there my verse remains sheltered,
Speaks of the One, doesn't stray about.

"Fair, good and true," this I am singing and singing.
"Fair, good and true"—constantly different and constantly this.
I am finding, inventing—in order to bring them into one,
to bring them in without intermittence.

"Fair, good and true" so often separated, divorced.
In one I want to forge three.)

Among Shakespeare's 154 sonnets, Sonnet 105 alone is explicitly devoted to a reflection on the ways in which we think and talk about love, on how we conceive
of it, as well as on what it actually means or *is* for the speaker ("Kind *is* my love,"
line 5).[65] It thus focalizes Shakespeare's discourse on love throughout the sonnet
sequence and serves as a metatext and internal commentary on one of the sonnets' central themes. Owing to its fusion of a reflection on love with the theme of
poetic creation, it also emerges as a fundamentally metapoetic text—not merely
with regard to poetry or love in general but, more importantly, with regard to
poetry insofar as it is predicated on love, insofar, that is, as it is an *act of love*.
Consequently, Celan's translation can be read as a poignant poetic articulation of
his notion of poetic dialogue as interlocution (subtended by and fundamentally
unfolding in and through translation), and as an intervention on the poet-transla-
tor's behalf in view of oppressing real-life concerns.

How does Celan respond to Shakespeare in his version of Sonnet 105? Harking
back to his translation of the imperative at the beginning of Sonnet 71 ("No longer mourne . . . ") as *Du sollst* (You ought), Celan turns Shakespeare's introductory "Let not" into the plural imperative *Ihr sollt . . . nicht* (You ought . . . not).

He then transforms the original's reference to "love" as a concept or emotion (indicated by the subsequent "Idolatrie," which would not make any sense in reference to a person) into the personalized, active subclause *den ich da lieb* (whom there I lov'). By dint of the relative pronoun *den* (whom), together with the deictic marker *da* (there)—which could, however, also be read as a particle of emphasis, employed mostly in colloquial speech, as in "what are you doing there"—Celan clearly signifies that his speaker's love is directed toward a person, who is suggested as present (even if only in and by way of his text, to which he "remains given"). The shift in meaning between original and translation is obvious: whereas Shakespeare is concerned to note that his "love" is not to be perceived as and "cal'd Idolatrie," Celan's first priority is to stress that his lover—"over there"—is not an *Abgott* (idol). And although Celan makes good on the translator's task to follow the original closely by referring to Shakespeare's "Idolatrie" in line 2, his initial emphasis on interpersonal, active loving is not thereby diminished. On the contrary, through the subclause *was ich da treib und trieb* (what I am and was doing there) (line 2), which prosodically catches up with Shakespeare's "love" in line 1, Celan underscores that he is actively and emphatically engaged in loving. For the verb *treiben* (literally, to engage in, to practice, to do, to float), the repetition of which in the present and past tenses marks Celan's insistence on the speaker's uninterrupted, active participation in "loving," signifies activity both *qua* verb and by virtue of replicating its grammatical character as a verb on the semantic level. Celan further stresses the interpersonal as it unfolds in and through love in the threefold repetition in line 4 of the third-person-singular pronoun—*von* ihm, *an* ihn *und immer* ihm (of him, to him and always for the love of him)—as opposed to Shakespeare's twofold "To one, of one," as well as in the placement at the very end of the same line of the lexeme *zulieb,* which contains the root *lieb* (lov'). Once again, Celan's particular spin on Shakespeare's text can be brought into sharp relief against the foil of other, more faithful versions of these lines:

Nicht Götzendienst nennt meine Liebe! Nimmer
Betrachtet als mein Götzenbild den Freund:
Denn all mein Singen, all mein Loben, immer
Von einem, nur auf einen ist's gemeint.

(Not idolatry call my love! Never
Consider my idol the friend:
For all my singing, all my praising, always
Of one, only for one it is meant.)
(Regis)

Nennt meine Liebe nicht Abgötterei,
Und mein Geliebter soll kein Abgott scheinen,
Weil all mein Lied und Lob stets einerlei,
Sich immer gleicht, von Einem, an den Einen.

(Call my love not idolatry,
And my lover shall not appear to be an idol,
Because all my song and praise ever equal
Is with itself, of One, to the One.)
(Gildermeister)

Nennt meine liebe nicht abgötterei
Drin den geliebten ihr als götzen seht—
Sagt nicht—mein sang und lob sei einerlei:
Einem—an einen—immernoch und stet.

(Call my love not idolatry
Therein the lover you as an idol see—
Say not—my song and praise is ever the
    same:
For one—to one—still and constant(ly).
(George)

Nennt meine Liebe nicht Abgötterei,
Sagt nicht, daß ich ein Götzenbild errich-
    tet,
Weil meiner Lobgesänge Einerlei
Nur einen preist, an Einen nur gerichtet.

(Call my love not idolatry,
Say not that I have erected an idol,
Because my praising songs' sameness
Only one praises, to one addressed.)
(Robinson)

Celan further personalizes his response: Shakespeare's "love" in line 5, which in this context signifies, as explained earlier, the emotional-conceptual dimension of *love*—notwithstanding the grammatical plausibility of reading it in reference to the young man—is unambiguously rerouted by Celan to refer to his *Freund*— the "beloved" first encountered in the first stanza.[66] Celan's shift in reference engenders an immediate second referential-semantic displacement: the constancy and "wondrous excellence" (line 6) of Shakespeare's "love" is redirected to refer to the beloved himself. Because this would not make any sense in Shakespeare's text, it bears out my earlier claim that Shakespeare's "love" in line 5 pertains to the emotional-conceptual rather than to the personal. By the time readers have reached Sonnet 105 in the sonnet sequence, they are already well aware of the young man's inconstancy and infidelity (in the erotic-sexual sense) with regard to the speaker. This may explain, on the semantic level, Celan's decision to dispense with the original's "wondrous excellence" in his translation. Although Shakespeare is indeed justified in being surprised at the abiding constancy ("*Still* constant") of his own love for the young man in view of the latter's infidelities, Celan's high moral assessment of his *Freund* in line 6 (*und keiner ist beständiger als er* [and no one is more constant than he]) is logically predicated on the friend's continuous goodness, as expressed in the previous line, and thus engenders neither wonder nor surprise. Shrewdly, however, Celan alludes to the young man's inconstancy and thereby retroactively captures the legitimacy of Shakespeare's articulation of his love's "wondrous excellence" when, in line 8, he writes "dem Einen" (the One) in the same breath as "schweift mir nicht umher" (does not stray about).[67] In translating Shakespeare's "thing" (line 8) as *dem Einen* (with a capital E), Celan continues personalizing the original, making it refer explicitly to the *Freund* rather than to a theme or subject.[68] The subsequent liberal translation of "leaves out difference" as *schweift mir nicht umher* (doesn't stray about), which specifies the constancy of *mein Vers* (my verse) in line 7, reads like a subtle, indirect condemnation of the young man's behavior as implied in Shakespeare's "Still constant in a wondrous excellence" and in the suggested opposition between the young man's inconstancy and the "constancy" (line 7) to which Shakespeare's "verse" is "confin'de."

Celan further develops the ethical significance of his version in employing *treu* (as opposed to *wahr*) to render Shakespeare's "true" from the triad "Faire, kinde, and true" (line 9). Although *treu* is one of the literal German equivalents of "true" (the other being *wahr,* literally *true* in the logical sense), it reduces the latter's semantics to one aspect only, namely, the moral aspect of fidelity, at the cost of obliterating its (epistemo)logical dimension (still present in the original), that is, its reference to truth in the logical-philosophical sense. To be sure, the fact that Celan's use of *treu* may be phonologically and morphologically motivated, neatly echoing Shakespeare's "true," does not diminish its ethical import, which is corroborated by Shakespeare's continuous attention to *kindness* and *constancy* throughout the poem. Celan emphatically relates his ethical take on Shakespeare's sonnet to the activity of writing and translating poetry, as suggested by the repetition of *singing* in "das singe ich und singe" (this I am singing and singing) (line 9), as well as by the etymological figure in "Ich find, erfind" (I am finding, inventing) (line 11). Celan's insistence in the third stanza on active involvement, on the process of his response in the very act of its performance, dovetails with his initial stress on the immediacy of writing in the first stanza.

Although one of the main features of Shakespeare's inventiveness in this sonnet is the articulation of what Helen Vendler has called an "erotic religion" through the juxtaposition of "Christian [doctrine] and aesthetic Platonism," Celan's (additional) inventiveness can be located in the transposition of Shakespeare's "aesthetic eroticism" along the lines of a squarely biblical paradigm.[69] This has immense consequences for the interpretation of the text and fully corroborates the version's already-mentioned idiosyncratic ethical impetus. In contrast to the original's initial request or plea, the first line of Celan's translation—*Ihr sollt, den ich da lieb, nicht Abgott heißen* (You ought/shall, whom I there lov', not idol name)—reads as a commandment, performing the biblical formula *Ihr sollt* followed by an infinitival verb form, as in *Ihr sollt euch nicht zu den Götzen wenden* (You shall not turn to idols) (Lev. 19:4; trans. Luther) or *Ihr sollt euch keine Götzen machen* (You shall not make idols) (Lev. 26:1; trans. Luther). The fact that Celan rewrites Shakespeare's plea in the form of a commandment—a rewriting already operative in his version of Sonnet 71 with its initial *Du sollst*—infuses his response with an ethical force by far exceeding Shakespeare's attention to *love, kindness,* and *constancy.* Valorizing the ethical force of Celan's *sollt* is all the more plausible, philosophically speaking, in view of the fact that at least since Kant the *ought* has functioned as the paradigmatic expression of the ethical.[73] Given the translation's pragmatic orientation both toward the original and, more importantly, toward its own readership, Celan's *Ihr* emphatically addresses his readers, who are commanded to view neither Celan's translational endeavor as a whole as idolatry—or as adultery—nor the subject of his love "there" as an idol. Celan's *sollt* creates a very particular frame of reception that is totally absent from Shakespeare's original by laying down as "moral law," as it were, what in the original reads like a mere plea subtended by reasoning and rhetoric—by "argument" (line 9).[71]

In light of this initial commandment, the sonnet's insistence on the *legitimacy* and *truth* of the beloved's adoration by the poet, on the beloved's trinitarian oneness, is not merely a matter of *argument* but rather a matter of the reader's *trust* or *willingness* to engage with the poet's love and with the poetry it generates in terms of faith and fidelity. The fact that Celan replaces Shakespeare's "argument" with *das singe ich und singe*, which stresses the performance of poetic creation, is of crucial importance. Celan does not reason with the reader but stipulates, as a matter of trust or faith on the reader's part, that his text testifies to utmost moral integrity, being motivated by the most sincere and faithful of intentions. That Celan dispenses with "argu[ing]" his case is further evidenced—in addition to his elision of Shakespeare's "argument" in line 9—by the fact that he also dispenses with Shakespeare's logical conjunctions "Since" (line 3) and "Therefore" (line 7), restricting himself to the simple articulation of *All dieses Singen hier . . . In der Beständigkeit* (All this singing . . . In constancy) (lines 3 and 7). Celan suggests that there is nothing to argue here, that if we do not trust in the integrity of his love as a poet and translator, no argument or pleading will convince us of its truth.

Given that Sonnet 105 has been read, as Vendler points out, as a defense of poetry against real or potential detractors, it is particularly amenable to being reinscribed within the heated context of the Goll affair.[72] In line with his unwillingness to engage in a public refutation of the plagiarism charges, Celan contents himself, in his translation of Sonnet 105, with mere acknowledgment and declaration. True to his view that poetry "attempts to be true," that it has to do with "truth"—that is, truth not predicated on logic, adequation, or verifiability, but an ethical truth that "emerges from the reality in which the poem has been created"—Celan lets his translation articulate its own truth *and* his fidelity to it, neither of which is in need of logical-rhetorical back-up.[73]

Retaining the moral implications of Shakespeare's defense against the charge of "idolatry" while not being concerned with its strictly theological or religious intent, Celan emphasizes the structural tension between *idolatry* and *orthodoxy* insofar as it signifies, beyond questions pertaining to Christian doctrine, the difference between what could be called *falseness* or *infidelity* and *truthfulness* or *fidelity*. It is in this sense that we are enjoined to read Celan's commandment not to view his work of love as *idolatry* or his lover as an *idol*. His translation and by extension his poetry in general, we are commanded to recognize, are created in the spirit of fidelity, integrity, truth, and love. Celan intimates what this love involves in excess of its status as an emotional-psychological state that can only be experienced, not argued. His specific view of the translator's love for his pretext comes to the fore most vividly in the subclause *was ich da treib und trieb* (what I am doing and was doing there) (line 2).

I should note at this point that Celan's translation is characterized by one feature that I have not hitherto fully addressed and that must be registered: its *bathetic* character. In contrast to Shakespeare's text, which throughout is kept in an elevated style, Celan's translation creates a contrast between high and low style. The parenthetical *den ich da lieb*—with its colloquial *da* (there) followed by the shortened verb form (*lieb* ["lov"] instead of *liebe* ["love"])—which breaks up the ponderous main clause, *Ihr sollt . . . nicht Abgott heißen* (You ought/shall . . . not idol name);[74] the impatient and almost colloquial rhetoric of *All dieses Singen hier, all dieses Preisen* (All this singing here, all this praising); the contractions in *ists heute und ists morgen*; and finally, the parlando of *schweift mir nicht umher* (does not stray about) all contrast with the gravity and seriousness of the sonnet's "argument," or theme.[75] Celan's bathetic rhetoric signally captures the tension running through the entire sonnet sequence, between the serious treatment of such "elevated" topoi as fidelity, truth, and "true love," on the one hand, and the coarser, more "lascivious comments" (Sonnet 95, line 6) on such "low" topoi as sexual infidelity, promiscuity, jealousy, and lust, on the other. As the following lines from Sonnet 115 suggest, Celan in fact aims at highlighting precisely the erotic-libidinal, stylistically "lower" dimension of Shakespeare's text:

Those lines that I before have writ doe lie,	Wie log ich, als ich schrieb, ich würde dich
Even those that said I could not love you deerer:	zu keiner Zeit noch heißer lieben können.
Yet then my judgment knew no reason why	Ich sah nicht, wie das volle Feuer sich
My most full flame should afterwards burne cleerer.	Noch steigern sollte, brünstiger entbren-nen.

(lines 1–4)

(How I lied when I wrote I would
at no time be capable of loving you hotter / more ardently.
I saw not how the full/blazing fire would
grow even stronger, flare up more with more passion / more randily.)

In contrast to the original's subdued eroticism—expressed in the familiar metaphor of the burning flame—Celan's version is emphatically sexualized. Where Shakespeare speaks of loving the young man "deerer," Celan writes (following Terese Robinson) *heißer* (with more passion / more ardenly); where Shakespeare creates the image of a "full flame" burning "cleerer," Celan writes *brünstiger* (more randily).[76]

In light of these differences, Celan's unexpected use in Sonnet 105 of the verb *treiben* in reference to translating and writing poetry acquires pressing significance. It turns Shakespeare's nominal rhetoric in the sonnet's first two lines not only into emphatic activity but, more importantly, into an activity that has, in German, definite sexual overtones. Although *treiben* in itself means "to engage in," "to practice," "to do," in light of the sonnets' overall erotic-sexual dimension, in light of this particular sonnet's treatment of the speaker's *constancy* as opposed to the beloved's *inconstancy*, the German reader cannot fail to overhear yet another sense of *treiben* materially absent from Celan's translation yet semantically invoked within its overall erotic-sexual context. The colloquial *es treiben* (to do it), especially in the context of love and eroticism, means "to do it (with someone)," to engage in sexual intercourse with someone.[77] What Celan tacitly advances, then, is nothing less than a sexual-erotic notion of poetic translation and, by extension, the constitution of poetic meaning in general. He enjoins us to view his translation in its very performance as a sexual act, as intercourse with Shakespeare, who emerges as the one "whom [Celan] there love[s]." The plausibility of reading Celan's translation of Sonnet 105 as the adumbration and enactment of an erotic-sexual conception of poetic dialogue—with poetic encountering seen as intimate physical contact between bodies (of texts)—is corroborated by his depiction of his imagined encounter with Mandelstam in the poem "Es ist alles anders" (Everything is different), which dates from the same period as his Shakespeare translations and in which the importance of the proper name and, by extension, of language and verbal (mis)communication gives way—as in Celan's translation of Sonnet 71—to physical communion: "der Name Ossip kommt auf dich zu . . . / du löst ihm den Arm ab von der Schulter, den rechten, den linken, / du heftest die deinen an ihre Stelle, mit Händen, mit Fingern . . . / —was abriß, wächst wieder zusammen" (The name Osip is coming toward you . . . // you detach his arm from his shoulder, the right one, the left one, / you attach yours in their place, with hands, fingers . . . / —what tore apart grows together again).[78] Unlike Shakespeare's young man (or dark lady), Celan's friend and lover—Shakespeare, that is—is indeed, as he himself reiterates, "constant" and "kinde," allowing Celan, who is beset by attacks on his very being as a poet, to be sheltered in the secrecy of their tryst—in the erotic communion of their poetic love affair.[79]

How are we to understand concretely Shakespeare's *constancy* and *kindness* as they are perceived by Celan? In the context of Celan's life at the time *and*, concomitantly, in the context of his engagement with other poets, Shakespeare's constancy and kindness can be understood as the simple fact that he offered Celan, in and through the poetry to which he will have remained given, a space of security and truth, constantly and generously, as it were, providing Celan with lines that allowed him to express his anguish and anxieties in the language of poetry. By virtue of his poetry, Shakespeare offered him a loving, physically intimate shelter from the vicissitudes of life. The sonnets thus participate in the poetic-existential meridian that Celan considered a guarantee for the possibility of a poetic kind of existence. Celan's above-quoted poetic-existential "confession," mediated through the words of Shakespeare's Sonnet 79, can be read as a poignant commentary on my approach to Celan's interlocution with Shakespeare and on the significance of Shakespeare's place in Celan's (poetic) universe: "Als ich um Hilfe zu dir kam, allein, / da warst du meinem Vers allein gewogen" (Whilst I alone did call upon thy ayde, / My verse alone had all thy gentle grace).

An awareness of Celan's erotic "conception" of poetic dialogue, adumbrated and subtly staged in his versions of Shakespeare's sonnets, is important for a productive reassessment of Celan's oeuvre—which has, as mentioned at the beginning of this chapter, predominantly been broached in light of the question of a politically tainted (poetic) language (German) and its relation to (personal) history and (personal) trauma—in the healing keys of love and eroticism. Engaged through the prism of his Shakespeare translations in particular, Celan emphatically emerges as a poet who accords a central place to love and eroticism in his writings. Attending to Celan's poetic treatment of love and eroticism, reading him as a poet of love, productively complements and enriches his reception as a "survivor-poet" by shifting the critical focus from the indisputably "tragic" and "dark" to the "brighter" and more "uplifting" moments in his life and oeuvre. The ironic upshot of this reading is that the trauma of the Goll affair for Celan was accompanied by a very different affair—his poetic love affair with Shakespeare. While Shakespeare may have been the dupe of a society that did not recognize the young man's promiscuity and infidelity for what it was, namely, "faults" (Sonnet 96, line 4) and "errors" (line 7), taking it instead for a truth that it was not, thereby allowing it to be "To truths translated" (line 8), Celan succeeds in translating the untruth of the Goll affair into his fidelity to the truth of his interlocution—his poetic love affair—with Shakespeare and, by extension, into the truth of his life and poetry.

Celan's poetics of interlocution comes full circle in his already-quoted version of Shakespeare's Sonnet 115:

Those lines that I before have writ doe lie,
Even those that said I could not love you
  deerer:
Yet then my judgment knew no reason
  why
My most full flame should afterwards
  burne cleerer.
But reckoning time, whose milliond ac-
  cidents
Creepe in twixt vows, and change decrees
  of Kings,
Tan sacred beautie, blunt the sharp'st
  intents,
Divert strong mindes to th' course of al-
  tring things:
Alas! Why fearing Time's tiranie,
Might I not then say, 'Now I love you
  best,
When I was certaine ore in-certainty,
Crowning the present, doubting of the
  rest:
Love is a Babe, then might I not say so,
To give full growth to that which still doth
  grow.

Wie log ich, als ich schrieb, ich würde dich
zu keiner Zeit noch heißer lieben können.
Ich sah nicht, wie das volle Feuer sich
noch steigern sollte, brünstiger entbrennen.

Doch frißt die Zeit in Eid und Schwur
  sich ein,
ihr Zufall löst, was Königsworte waren,
stumpft Plan und Ziel, und stumpft der
  Schönheit   [Schein,
lenkt starken Sinn zum Wandelbaren.

"Nie liebt ich dich wie jetzt": darf ich
  nicht, da
ich mich vor ihr, der Zeit, fürcht, solches
  sagen?
Daß nichts Bestand hat, ach, ich weiß es ja.
Ich krön das Heute! Zweifl' an weitern
  Tagen!

Die Liebe ist ein Kind, das wächst. Ich ließ
sie reif sein, ganz,—ich durfte dies!

(How I lied when I wrote I would
at no time be capable of loving you hotter / more ardently.
I saw not how the full/blazing fire would
grow even stronger, flare up more with more passion / more randily.

Yet time eats itself into oath and pledge,
its contingency dissolves what royal words used to be,
blunts plan and goal, and blunts beauty's sheen,
diverts strong determination toward the alterable.

"Never did I love you as (I do) now": may I not, as
I am of it, time, afraid, say such things?
That nothing lasts, ah, I know it well.
I crown (the) today! Am doubtful about future days!

Love is a child that grows, I let
it be mature, wholly—I was allowed (to do) this!)

Dated October 31, 1963, Celan's version documents the culmination of his long-lasting poetic affair with Shakespeare, whom he avowedly never loved with as much ardor and passion as "now": *now* that "the world is bent [his] deeds to crosse"; *now* that he is "blam'd" and "slandered"; *now* that his exposure to the "spight of fortune" is, presumably, at its most painful, and most difficult to endure—so painful, in fact, that he showed the first signs of psychosis toward the end of 1962 (in part, arguably, as a result of the Goll affair) and would henceforth require intermittent psychiatric treatment until the end of his life.[80]

More important, however, this version establishes an intimate connection between his poetic love affair with Shakespeare and what I have advanced as his overall poetics of love. In *crowning* the *Heute* (today)—thus his translation (following Regis and George) of Shakespeare's "present" in line 12—Celan establishes an explicit link between the "now" of Shakespeare's abiding, sheltering presence in his life (already conjured as the "shaddow" that "shaddows doth make bright" in Sonnet 43) and the *Hier und Jetzt* (here and now) of the true poem, which has only "this one, singular, punctual presence (*Gegenwart*)" and which is, in the "Meridian," crowned—*qua* antidote to the uncertainty of the flux of time—with the *Akut des Heutigen* (acute accent of the today) as opposed to the *Gravis des Historischen* (grave accent of the historical) and the *Zirkumflex . . . des Ewigen* (circumflex . . . of the eternal).[81] The truth of poetic interlocution, Celan suggests, expresses itself in the "here and now" of its very loving performance and singular "actualization."[82] Like Lucile's "Long live the King!" Celan's translational response to Shakespeare is a word of protest directed at the world at large—stating the truth of his innocence in the Goll affair, as it were—and a word of creative fidelity to the truth if his love for Shakespeare; a response that concretely and extensively stages what has been intimated throughout Celan's oeuvre, yet never fully enacted—until, that is, his extended tryst with Shakespeare under the sign of infamy. Celan's Shakespeare translations are not merely the culmination of one particular poetic love affair; they are also the most poignant and extensive performance and instantiation of Celan's overall poetics of love.

In translating the Goll affair into his love affair with Shakespeare, Celan succeeds in poetically reflecting on and problematizing, as it were, the interface between fidelity and betrayal on the social-ethical *and* poetic levels: To the extent that translation—given the irreducible incongruity between any two languages—cannot help betraying the original in one way or another in its very attempt at being faithful to it, Celan's many linguistic, semantic, and prosodic infidelities with regard to Shakespeare's text can be read as signifying what he experienced as a profound betrayal on the part of the "smart-eyed world."[83] Conversely, Celan's uniquely creative way of articulating *his* erotic, interlocutionary fidelity to Shakespeare—albeit as a diachronically extended and qualitatively transformed poetic presence and interlocutor—and through him to the truth and truthfulness of his poetic practice and hence to his very existence as a poet can be read as signifying the ultimate "victory" of the event of poetry *qua* tryst over any attempt at its denigration or destruction. And although Celan may know that "nothing lasts" and be "doubtful about future days," deep down he holds out the hope that the "child" that is "Love" will continue to "grow."[84] Inverting and personalizing St. Paul's triad of "faith, hope, and charity" (1 Cor. 13:13) while poetically enacting his subsequent claim that "the greatest of these *is* charity," Celan writes, in a poem dated August 21, 1961, "Ich liebe, ich hoffe, ich glaube"—"I love, I hope, I believe."[85] No words could poetically articulate more fully and more succinctly the love and fidelity to the truth of poetry that finds its most comprehensive and most detailed instantiation and enactment in Celan's interlocution with Shakespeare, whose own triad "Fair, kinde, and true" resounds in and can in turn be said retroactively to be informed by Celan's Pauline profession of faith.

In contrast to the common *metaphorical* application of the moral-sexual concepts of fidelity and infidelity to the act of translation—most conspicuously embodied in the traditional notion of the *belles infidèles*—Celan's understanding and practice of *translation as love affair* must be viewed, from within the logic of his poetic ontology, in its literal specificity.[86] Insofar as the poet "remains given" to the poem, which "embodies [the poet's] gestalt in its directedness, [and] hastens forward," which "strives to reach through time . . . not beyond time," and which is the poet's mode of "sending [him]self ahead [into the future]," Celan's affair with Shakespeare is, in the most literal sense, only possible and real *as* poetic interlocution.[87] Concomitantly, the notion of poetic signification *as* affair staged in Celan's interlocution with Shakespeare ought not to be taken metaphorically, for if, as I have stated elsewhere, poetry performs, according to Celan, its author's "motion through the 'space of time'" even after his death—like the light of certain stars that reaches the earth long after their factual extinction—carrying its respective source's gestalt with it, then Shakespeare's text and, by extension, poetry in general, is not to be conceived of as essentially distinct from its author but, rather, as a unique, diachronically extended state of its author's aggregation, as it were.[88] Celan's love affair with Shakespeare is real—as real as it gets, in fact, given that at the time of its unfolding, one of the lovers had been dead for more than three centuries.

CHAPTER 3

Metaphors of Subjectivity

Grünbein and the Philosophers

I am—well, what?

In the desperation of this exile he recognized his own destiny and . . . staid with him during the first days of exile and then for weeks and months on end . . . by way of a curious, childish kind of toying with tradition.

Among all of the available masks, the I may be the best.[1]

In the previous chapter I offered a reading of Celan's poetics in the key of love with special attention to what I have cast as his affairistic conception of poetic translation—and hence of poetic signification *tout court*. In Celan's translations of Shakespeare's sonnets, I have argued, the affairistic underpinnings of the poetic constitution of meaning are articulated in an exemplary manner. I now proceed to the question of the *agent* or *subject* of poetic signification: Who assumes responsibility for it? Who is this subject? Who is the "I" that constitutes itself, according to Celan, in and through poetic interlocution?

As announced in the Introduction, I approach these questions by way of Durs Grünbein's poetics. Not only does Grünbein tackle and poetically instantiate these questions in a particularly forceful and vivid manner, but also his poetics reveals itself, from within the interpretive frame of my inquiry, as an especially productive and illuminating complement to and continuation of Celan's poetics of love. If

Celan's poetics can be said to address exemplarily the problem of the (poetic) constitution of meaning as interlocution predicated on creative fidelity, Grünbein's
poetics, I aim to substantiate, can be said to engage exemplarily with the question
of the makeup of the subject of poetry as a function of poetic signification.

A few clarifying remarks on my use of *subject* and *subjectivity* are in order. In
the present context, following common linguistic and philosophical usage, the
two terms signify, on the one hand, the *I* and the mode of experiencing oneself
as and being (perceived as) "I"; *and on the other hand,* following Alain Badiou,
a singular, "site-specific configuration" (that is, person) faithfully abiding by the
truth of a particular event.[2] More specifically, I wish the *subject of poetry* or *poetic
subject* to be understood as an invented figure that in complex ways is not only
continuous with but also a signal manifestation of the historical-epistemological
subject. As Émile Benveniste pertinently notes, "'subjectivity' is the speaker's capacity to posit [that is, invent] himself as a 'subject.' . . . Language is only possible
because every speaker posits himself as a *subject.* . . . "[3] Karl Heinz Bohrer's notion
of *aesthetic subjectivity,* which signifies the category of the subject insofar as "it
semantically finds, invents itself" in the literary work, is an apposite precedent to
my notion of poetic subjectivity.[4]

Thus, although I inquire specifically into the emergence of the *poetic* subject,
I should stress that poetic subjectivity must be recognized—in line with Celan's,
Grünbein's, and Brodsky's insistence on the inseverability of literature and life,
text and context—as constitutively open to the influx of the extra-textual and
contextual, and vice versa, from which it came and on which it will in turn have
had an impact. In other words, the subject of poetry cannot, in one way or another and to a greater or lesser degree, fail to be grounded in, point to, overlap with, and articulate the historically and existentially situated poet himself. In
Grünbein's terms, the poet's poetic personae, whomever they may be, are invariably linked to (the concerns of) a "little man in Germany," who is of course none
other than the poet himself. Consequently, in being a poetic agent, the subject of
poetry, cannot help, as I elaborate in my final chapter, already and always being
an ethical agent as well.[5]

In my exploration of Grünbein's poetic engagement with the question of subjectivity, I attend first to his sustained dialogue with René Descartes. I then explicate the poetic significance of his conception of subjectivity as a function of
metaphor. Finally, I trace the concrete emergence of the poetic subject on the
basis of one exemplary text: the poem "Julia Livilla," in which the creation of
subjectivity is subtly yet unambiguously cast as the result of the poet's affair with
his interlocutor.

Invenio, Ergo Sum

The question of the springs of poetic subjectivity has been at the heart of Grün-bein's poetics since he first broke into print in the late 1980s. From the "unsus-tainable I" of *Grauzone morgens* (Grey zone in the morning, 1988) through the "animal I," the "I [as] mere syllable remnant," and the "I [as] conditioned reflex" of *Schädelbasislektion* (Skull crash course, 1991) and *Falten und Fallen* (Folds and traps, 1994) to the "I made of paper" of *Vom Schnee, oder Descartes in Deutschland* (On snow, or Descartes in Germany; 2003), Grünbein has offered a variety of po-etic responses to the basic question: "Who is I?"[6] "Who is really capable of saying *I* without suppressing a smile?" Grünbein asks in one of his most pointed (and funny) meditations on the question of subjectivity. "If you could," he goes on,

> you would prefer to keep your mouth shut. This near-sibilant [referring to the Ger-man "Ich"] might quickly turn out to be a burp, and wouldn't everything be betrayed then? Embarrassingly inevitable though it may seem, the *I* is the unmistakable bodily scent of speech, bad breath congealed into a pronoun. Its primary feature is the fact that nobody can suppress it. . . . As soon as you speak in your own name, everything you say exudes a pungent smell, which can quickly turn into a stench. No grammatical trick will help you to cover it up like deodorant, even though not everybody is endowed with a sense of smell as keen as a dog's to be able to sniff out the foot print. . . . Even if you keep your fangs . . . hidden behind your blandishing lips, the *I* marks the moment when the palate is exposed. Saying I foils all of shame's ruses. . . . [7]

That Grünbein's poetic "inquiry" into the constitution and significance of subjec-tivity ought to be viewed as more than just one among the discourses and themes that have emerged as the hallmarks of his oeuvre to date—for example, the dis-courses of physiology, anatomy, the presumed postmodern urban experience of continual dislocation, and the experience (and memory of) *Realsozialismus*—is evidenced in the fact that the legacy of René Descartes, the inaugurator of the reign of modern subjectivity, occupies a central place in Grünbein's poetic uni-verse.[8] In addition to such Cartesian bits sprinkled across Grünbein's texts as "The *I think* was merely a hematoma," or "psychic tricks or syllogisms like this Cogito ergo . . . ," the singular import of Descartes' life and work for Grünbein is at-tested to by the poet's choice of the mask of a "Cartesian Dog" as one of his most memorable poetic personae, and most saliently by the fact that he created an en-tire novel in verse, *Vom Schnee oder Descartes in Deutschland*, devoted to the poetic exploration of Descartes' life and work.[9] Grünbein's epistemological conception of poetry as a "comprehensive cognitive act" that proceeds according to its own "poetic logic," which parallels and complements philosophical "logic," equally bespeaks the poet's debt and proximity to the philosopher.[10]

What I would like to ask in view of the variety of 'answers" to the fundamental question of subjectivity provided by Grünbein is whether something like a unifying, comprehensive vision or notion of subjectivity can be uncovered in his poetics—a notion that can be said to enable, subsume, subtend, and sustain the functionality and viability of the panoply of poetic *I's* populating his texts. In other words, does Grünbein's heterogeneous staging of subjectivity imply that a master concept or master trope of subjectivity governs his multiple poetic subjects or personae? The philosophically obvious starting point for elaborating a response to this question is Grünbein's engagement with Descartes.

In his early programmatic essay "Galilei Measures Dante's Hell and Gets Hung Up on the Measurements," which is among other things a response and tribute to as well as an emulation of Mandelstam's groundbreaking essay "Conversation About Dante," Grünbein approvingly cites the Russian's designation of the Italian as "the Descartes of metaphor":[11] "I compare, therefore I exist, Dante could have said. He was the Descartes of metaphor; for it is only through metaphor that our consciousness gains access to the material world; for there is no being beyond comparing, as being itself is a simile."[12]

According to Mandelstam—who implicitly relies on the conceptions of metaphor and simile (going back to Aristotle) as more or less identical tropes—being the "Descartes of metaphor" means existing by dint of comparing, which is to say, by dint of creating metaphors, and this in turn means by dint of creating poetry *tout court*, insofar as poetry is taken to be predicated on the "capacity for metaphor," which, according to Aristotle, "alone cannot be acquired from another, and is a sign of natural gifts."[13] (As I explain later, Grünbein shares Aristotle's and Mandelstam's views of poetry as the art of metaphor *par excellence*.) In other words, Mandelstam's "I compare, therefore I exist" can be read as more or less equivalent to saying "I write poetry, therefore I exist." Given that "Conversation About Dante," Mandelstam's aesthetic *summa*, is as much about Dante as it is about Mandelstam himself, and given that calling Dante "the Descartes of metaphor" is in itself a complex act of metaphor (and metonymy), Mandelstam ought be taken as suggesting that he too is a "Descartes of metaphor"—that he too lives by dint of poetry, that for him as well the motto "I write poetry, therefore I exist" holds true.[14] In approvingly citing this poetic-philosophical nexus in his own Dante essay, Grünbein in turn aligns himself with Mandelstam's (and Dante's) view and practice of poetry as a mode of existence.

However, as *Vom Schnee*, Grünbein's most extensive and in-depth engagement with Descartes, suggests, Grünbein does more than simply endorse and follow Mandelstam's functionalization of Descartes as a philosophical anchor for more general poetic-existential concerns. Giving the screw of Mandelstam's metaphor another turn, Grünbein reconceives of Descartes, whom Mandelstam leaves intact as an historical-biographical entity, as the very *creation of metaphor*. In Grünbein's hands, "the Descartes of metaphor" becomes "the Descartes *born* of metaphor"— that is, a Descartes born of poetry, a metaphorical, poetic Descartes. What does it mean to be "the Descartes of metaphor" in this second sense?

It means, first and foremost, that Grünbein reinscribes both Descartes the man and, more important in the present context, the ontological and epistemological formula "Cogito, ergo sum," with which the philosopher has come to be identified metonymically, as poetic creations. Rather than following Mandelstam in implicitly subscribing to the common practice of reading the name *Descartes* as the marker of a particular historical-philosophical configuration, as the signifier of the stipulated historical moment of the inception of modern philosophy fundamentally conceived of as bound up with the question of subjectivity (Descartes as the "father of modern philosophy" *qua* philosophy of the subject), Grünbein suggests the metaphorical—that is, poetic—constitution of this very moment and its begetter.[15] Contrary to the philosophical propensity to read *Descartes* metaleptically through the prism of what, for better or worse, has solidified into the historical-philosophical category of *Cartesianism*—that is, as Habermas points out, into a putative philosophy of "abstract subjectivity" traceable to a specific historical moment (for instance, the night of November 10 to 11, 1619, when Descartes had three dreams in the course of which, as he recorded in his journal, the "foundations of a miraculous science" were revealed to him)—Grünbein points to the poetic or figurative/figural dimension of *Descartes* as the embodiment of the "cogito."[16] To what extent is such an approach to Descartes' life and work plausible and justified?

Far from bespeaking a denial of history along the lines of an extremist and simplistic reading of Hayden White's metahistorical critique, Grünbein's poeticization of *Descartes* reveals itself as an inventive, creatively faithful response to Descartes' own engagement with and deployment of the poetic mode in the course of elaborating his philosophical method.[17] After all, does not Descartes begin the *Discourse on Method* (1637), his first published work, which would secure his fame as the "father of modern philosophy," with the programmatic caveat that rather than intending to "teach a method that everyone must follow in order to use his reason well," he instead wishes his account "of the manner in which [he] has endeavored to use his reason" to be read "as nothing more than a story [*histoire*] or, if you prefer, a fiction [*fable*] in which one may find some examples worthy of imitation as well as numerous others which one will have reason not to follow"?[18] This means, among other things, that what has been accepted as Descartes' historically and philosophically most influential pronouncement—the indubitable and "necessary truth" of the axiom "*I think, therefore I am . . .* the first principle of philosophy"—ought to be read above all as part of the overall "fiction" of the *Discourse on Method* and not primarily, as has commonly been done as a matter of course, as an apophantic, contextually independent philosophical declaration aiming at universal validity.[19] In other words, if we take seriously Descartes' insistence—facetious and rhetorically motivated though it may be—on the "fabulistic" character of his account, the putative birth of modern subjectivity in his realization that my existence and my thinking that I exist are functionally interdependent reveals itself as part of a narrative or story, that is, as an emphatically literary event. In addition to Descartes' programmatic caveat itself, such a reading is borne out by the fact that the *Discourse on Method*'s philosophical disquisition on the methodological necessity of universal doubt for the acquisition of true knowledge about oneself and the world is couched within the autobiographical frame narrative—presented "like a painting"—of its author's life and intellectual trajectory up to 1637.[20]

That Grünbein homes in, in particular, on the fabulistic (that is, poetic) dimension of Descartes' philosophical project is clearly evidenced, among other things, by such facts as that he entitles Chapter Thirty-Six in *Vom Schnee* "Homo in Fabula" and, most important, that the novel as a whole (and hence Grünbein's overall dialogue with Descartes) is preceded by and thus placed under the sign of one of the most concretely narrative, and hence fabulistic, passages from the *Discourse on Method*, in which the philosopher presents the birth of his method as linked to the *story* of his sojourn in southern Germany in the winter of 1619-1620:

> I was in Germany then on the occasion of the wars that are not finished there yet and that has summoned me there; and as I was returning to my army post from the coronation of the emperor [Ferdinand II, July 1619], I was held up by the onset of winter in quarters where, with no conversation to disturb me and, fortunately, no other care or passion to trouble me, I would stay all day long cooped up in a heated room and converse with my own thoughts. . . .[21]

To be the "Descartes of metaphor," then, in Grünbein's second sense is to be a subject born not of the strictures of a methodically applied universal skepticism—presented though it may be, for rhetorical purposes, in the guise of a fable—but of poetry; it is to be the product of poetic creativity and inventiveness in line with

Descartes' own emphasis on the fabulistic structure of the *Discourse on Method*:
"Invenio, ergo sum,"—I invent, therefore I exist—could be the maxim of Grünbein's poetic subject. To sum up what I have elaborated in terms of an answer
to my initial question about whether a master concept or trope of subjectivity
governs Grünbein's motley crew of poetic subjects and personae—whatever else
the "subject" may be, it is *a fortiori*, Grünbein suggests, a *poetic invention*. Consequently, if we want to understand and witness the subject's coming-into-being,
we ought perforce to look to the emergence and constitution of the *subject of
poetry*.[22]

Certainly Grünbein is not the first to reread Descartes in light of and as a function of the onto-epistemological significance of the poetic. His take on the question of the subject is avowedly filtered through the scathing critique of modern
philosophers' penchant for stipulating subjectivity as an ontological given brought
to bear by Friedrich Nietzsche, whom Grünbein considers "one of the most influential thinkers of all time."[23] "There are still those harmless self-observers,"
Nietzsche writes, jabbing at the followers of Descartes, Kant, Hegel, and Schopenhauer, "who think that 'immediate certainties,' such as 'I think,' or . . . 'I will,'
exist—as if cognition could ever access its object in its purity and nakedness, as a
'thing in itself.' I will repeat a hundred times that 'immediate certainty,' 'absolute
cognition,' and 'thing in itself' imply a contradiction in terms. It is high time that
we finally freed ourselves from the seduction of words!"[24] For it is "language that
seduces us," Nietzsche goes on, into thinking that "all action is conditioned by an
agent, a 'subject.' . . . But there is no such substratum; there is no 'being' behind
the doing, acting, becoming; the 'doer' is merely a *poetic invention/fiction* added to
the doing [*'der Thäter' ist zum Thun bloss hinzugedichtet*]—doing is all there is."[25]
Like Nietzsche, Grünbein points to the poetic constitution of subjectivity. Unlike
Nietzsche, however, who lumps together Descartes' epistemology with other theories considered to be predicated on the tacit disavowal of their poetic conditions,
Grünbein is attuned to the fact that Descartes is—in stark contrast to Nietzsche's
attempt to cast him as one of "those harmless self-observers"—very much aware of
the crucial contribution of the work of the imagination to the development and
viability of his method.[26]

Avowedly, Descartes' most fundamentally inventive and innovative insight,
and the indubitable foundation of his "miraculous science," namely that the prop-
osition "*I think, I exist [Ego sum, Ego existo]*, is necessarily true whenever I utter
or think it [*a me profertur, vel mente concipitur*],"[27] is enabled and facilitated by
the algorhythmic application of a particular method of thinking consisting of the
interplay of four basic methodological "maxims" or precepts of reasoning:

1. "To accept nothing as true that I do not evidently know to be true [and] that I have occasion to doubt. . . . "

2. "To divide each problem . . . into as many parts as possible and necessary for its solution. . . . "

3. "To conduct my reasoning in an orderly and organized fashion, beginning from the most simple and most easily knowable data. . . . "

4. "To tally and review completely and comprehensively so as to be able to ascertain that nothing has been omitted."[28]

In view of the significance of Descartes' theory of the subject for Grünbein's poetics we in turn have to ask, what enables and facilitates Grünbein's "postulate" of the poetic constitution of subjectivity? Or to put it differently, what dynamic or mechanism allows Grünbein to trace poetically and testify to the emergence of subjectivity? For clearly, working in the poetic mode, Grünbein can hardly be expected simply to *apply* Descartes' fourfold analytical method, which is geared specifically to finding the "truth in the sciences," onto the practice of poetry, which unfolds according to its own discursive strictures, according to its own "laws." To "every logic," Grünbein notes, "there corresponds a poetic logic; to every epistemological axiom there corresponds a poetic axiom."[29] What is the specific logic of Grünbein's poetics? The answer is *metaphor*; the logic of metaphor is Grünbein's method, so to speak. The poetic subject comes into being, Grünbein suggests, by dint of metaphor. How exactly this happens is the focus of the next section.

Subject in Time

I began with the desire to speak with the dead.

Make my soul pass the equinoctial line
Between the present and past worlds, and hover
Upon their airy confine. . . .

The times divested themselves of their names, bled into and
permeated each other.

The great majority of the human race . . . live in plural times
and spaces, interpenetrant and durcheinander.[30]

Like Aristotle and Mandelstam, among others, Grünbein links the practice of poetry in general and the constitution of the subject of poetry in particular to the force of metaphor. In "Erklärte Nacht" (Night explained), one of his most poetologically eloquent poems, he has the following to say about poetry and metaphor and their existential and historical import:

The poetic line is a diver, it pulls you into the deep, searches for treasures
At the bottom of the sea, out there in the brain. It conspires with the stars.
Metaphors are these flat stones that you hurl into the open sea
From the shore. They skip across the water's surface,
Three, four, five, six times if you are lucky, before breaking, heavy as lead,
Plumblike through the mirror. They are tears that go through the ages.
Philosophy in meters, music of the joyful leaps from word to thing.
Gifts some say, others: cunningly crafted.
What remains are poems. Songs as mortality sings them.
A tourist guide, the best, for the exodus from humanity's night.[31]

Metaphors—here used metonymically as more or less synonymous with *verse* and *poems*—break through the surface of the sea of time, tear time's fabric. They are not subject to or bound by chronology. In and through these tears they establish and keep open channels of communication with the depths of time; they locate and recover treasures from the ocean floor of history and guarantee their survival and preservation into the future. Due to the power of metaphor, Grünbein suggests, with an approving nod to Hölderlin, "What remains are poems."[32] What metaphors make possible, then, first and foremost, is travel through time and history by surfing the "memory wave" into which the poet "transform[s] [him]self."[33] They are the prime vehicles, the surf boards, the shuttle cocks of memory. On more than one occasion Grünbein notes that the experience of a "fundamental anachronism," which has attuned him to the "contemporaneity of the noncontemporaneous," informs and motivates his writing.[34] By disabling the "dictates of time," poetry—in and through its fundamentally metaphorical makeup and operations—is especially capable of doing justice to the sense that it is not necessarily true "that we exist today only, strictly chronologically."[35] Ensconced in the multifarious "vehicle" of his poetry ("A tourist guide, the best") and mindful of Mandelstam's conception of poetry as animated "by the breathing of all ages," Grünbein conceives of and depicts himself (and the poet in general) as "underway along the spiral path / of the dead voices of the ages . . . condemned to hurtle / Through history."[36] By dint of metaphor, Grünbein is capable of apprehending and immersing himself in what he calls (via Mandelstam) "the noise of time"; by dint of metaphor he is capable of exploring both real and imagined times and spaces; owing to metaphor, he can allege to have "journeyed with Odysseus, centuries ago, across the Mediterranean."[37]

Grünbein's most significant move in the present context consists of reconceptualizing metaphor, which has traditionally functioned primarily as a *semantic* trope, in terms of *temporality*—as a figure of *time* and *history* rather than *logic*. In other words, rather than thinking of metaphor in purely semantic terms, that is, primarily in terms of the presumably synchronic *transfer, translation, transport, carrying over,* and *passage* (these being the literal meanings of the Greek *metaphora*) of semantic-referential data, Grünbein takes *metaphor* literally. He valorizes and attends to the essentially temporal dimension of the term's cluster of interlacing meanings, to its essentially diachronic signification (the meanings just listed necessarily imply the passage of time).[38] In contrast, however, to Mandelstam (and Celan), whose poetry is emphatically oriented toward the future (without, for that matter, disavowing the significance of the past), toward the not-yet-born "reader in posterity," Grünbein prefers traveling *back in time,* sojourning in the bygone worlds of and visiting with the "precious dead" (thus the title of one of Grünbein's collections of poetry—*Den Teuren Toten*). "The bridge to antiquity, to all past cultures and epochs is," Grünbein confesses, "more important to me than being in sync with the manifestations of the present;" the Greek and Roman classics in particular, he avers, "are not simply classics to me, but they have something to say to me directly. . . . Juvenal's Rome in 100 C.E. is very similar to today's New York [and], to a certain extent, Berlin;" their poetic legacy "has become a means of interpretation of his own existence."[39]

The poem "Metaphor," a rewriting of Lucian's dialogue between Charon and Hermes on the occasion of the ferryman's brief visit among the living, palpably stages the centrality of metaphor for Grünbein as the bridge or conduit along which the dead and the living are enabled, as W. G. Sebald remarks, to "move back and forth as they like" across time and space "according to the rules of a higher form of stereometry":[40]

Metaphor

"Pop they must all," jokes Lucian
In Charon's voice. The latter
Is in stitches, a visitor on earth.

He means the bubbles, all the human lives,
Like foam bubbling up beneath the waterfall.
A picture for the gods, their perky becoming
And disappearing within the briefest of time spans.

Some are small and pop right a way, some
Last longer, he says scornfully. They merge
With others, forming airy herds.

Chimeras of air all of them, the many lives,
Some great, others negligibly unimportant.
Bloated they are, eternally weighted
By gravity, all these nothings.

For instance the tombs of the heroes of Troy—
"They are really not big at all," scoffs the ferryman
On our shore. With arms and horses
Buried, only a green hill remained.

Niniveh, Babylon, Ilion, Mycene: show me the cities,
He is telling Hermes. All gone,
Embarrassing the remains, the divine companion replies.

The trip was worth his while. What a life
They lead, the poor ones, marked by unhappiness.
"Nobody thinks of Charon," he sums up disconcertedly.[41]

Although Grünbein's intensive engagement with the past—with classical antiquity in particular—in an attempt to make sense of and shape his own situation would appear to be neither novel nor extraordinary in the context of modern Western culture's unremitting appropriation and reinscription of the classical legacy, it should not in fact be viewed, as I elaborate later, as merely one among the plethora of contemporary instantiations of the belief that knowledge "about ancient times helps us understand our own."[42] In other words, Grünbein's metaphorical explorations of history's depths and its manifold conversations with the "voices of the ages" should not, I suggest, be read as bespeaking the poet's facile subscription to the presumed truth of Machiavelli's influential dictum that "all the things in this world in every era have their counterpart in ancient times" and that consequently "anyone wishing to see what is to be must consider what has been." Nor should they be read as simply self-serving acts of cultural exploitation and functional appropriation in line with the work of those, as the critic Hermann Korte argues, "who, like Heiner Müller [and other contemporaries], are attracted to antiquity because it provides them with a treasure trove of images, figures, topics [and] cues [for] making literary diagnoses about the present on the one hand and for creating self-portraits and engaging in poetic self-reflexion on the other."[43]

As I explicate later, in Grünbein's texts past and present are mutually engaged and interlaced in such a way as to produce and open up a qualitatively novel dimension of significance in which neither past nor present are left where they presumably are and in which poetic subjectivity emerges as the very focus and conduit of their enmeshment. Postponing an in-depth discussion of the idiosyncrasies of Grünbein's metaphorical "bridge to antiquity" until the next section, at this point it is enough to note that Grünbein's fidelity to the past (and the present) is of a different kind, that for Grünbein, traveling back in time and history by dint of metaphor is a function of what has been, in his view, the "poets' typical professional illness" since, at the very least, the age of Juvenal and Martial:

insomnia. "Insomnia seems to have been," Grünbein observes, "the most widely spread illness in [first- and second-century] Rome. Thus, for the poet Martial [as for the satirist Juvenal], peaceful sleep at night was part of the very definition of the poet's happiness;" subsequently, insomnia became "a watchword capturing virtually all of the symptoms of the disease called 'modernity'."[44] Insofar as traveling through and sounding the depths of time and history are the symptoms and manifestations of an illness, which bespeaks (or generates?) the poet's desire to have intercourse with the dead (rather than going to sleep), it is in a sense ineluctable. This means that speaking in metaphors—which, according to Grünbein, is equivalent to engaging metaphorically with the past *tout court*—is something the poet cannot help "contracting" or "coming down with." Metaphor reveals itself *a fortiori* as an anthropological category, as the prime component of the poet's very mode of being (as a poet).[45] Restlessly lying awake at night, the din of the city receding into the background and yielding to the "noise of time" itself, the "sick" poet tunes into the "tangle of voices of many ages," rides the "memory wave" and gives himself over to his desire to have intercourse with the "precious dead."[46] Like Mandelstam before him (in the untitled 1915 poem that begins "Sleeplessness. Homer. Taut sails. / I have read half way through the catalogue of ships . . . "), Grünbein immerses himself in the "dark sea" of culture and history, which "roars / And thudding heavily laps [his] pillow."[47] (The very beginning of *Vom Schnee*, where the text's speaker calls on Descartes to wake up—"Monsieur, wake up"—and thus to regain the state of sleeplessness, most palpably speaks to and underscores the nocturnally intimate character of Grünbein's mode of intercourse with the dead.)

Yet again we find Nietzsche lurking behind Grünbeins poetic-physiological functionalization of *insomnia*. In his disquisition on the "advantages and disadvantages of history for life," the significance of which for himself Grünbein acknowledges, for instance, in the autobiographical poem "Vita Brevis" ("For history was a disadvantage for me"), Nietzsche observes that "there is a degree of insomnia, of rumination, [indicative] of an historical sense that is harmful to everything that lives and that, ultimately, destroys it, be it a human being, a people, or a culture."[48] A "human being who would be historical through and through," Nietzsche continues, "would resemble a person who would be forced to abstain from sleeping. . . . ;" insomnia is symptomatic, according to Nietzsche, of a hypertrophied, noxious "historical sense" that disables and incapacitates human creativity and action; famously, Nietzsche wants to cure what he considers the "historical illness" of his age—the age of historicism—through a balanced diet consisting of the "ahistorical and suprahistorical," whereby the former signifies the "capacity to forget" while the latter suggests a "viewpoint" beyond history oriented toward that "which gives being the character of eternity and sameness."[49]

Unlike Juvenal, Martial, and Nietzsche, however, Grünbein does not aim at overcoming insomnia, because without it he would not be able to immerse himself in the sea of time; unlike Nietzsche in particular, Grünbein, who does not believe that humans can be anything but "historical through and through," is neither interested in forgetting the past nor in assuming a suprahistorical viewpoint. Far from it: what Nietzsche treats as an illness to be cured with the help of the antidotes offered up in his untimely meditations, Grünbein is keen on perfecting and fine-tuning (notwithstanding his agreement with Nietzsche as to calling it an "illness"). Grünbein converts the "historical illness" into a positive condition, and thus into a constitutive element of the poet's existence. Tacitly inverting his predecessors' variously motivated condemnations of insomnia—whether in the name of peace and happiness (Juvenal and Martial) or in the name of life and the freedom to act and shape culture and history (Nietzsche)—Grünbein not only accepts the "illness" of insomnia as a positive phenomenon, as a mode of being that allows the poet to fulfill his desire for intercourse with the past under the protective cover of the night; but more than that, he also elevates it to the status of "the poet's—the time traveler's with perfect pitch—refuge on earth."[50] It all depends, Grünbein implies, on one's capacity and strength to translate what may well be experienced and perceived as the curse of an aggravating chronic condition into the blessing of a positive state. This transformation is predicated on the valetudinarian's capacity and creative energy—Nietzsche calls it "plastic power"—to "incorporate and transform the past and the foreign" rather than be overwhelmed by it.[51] The insomniac himself is revealed as the metaleptic creation of the cultural translation and transformation that transpire in the course of his metaphorical travels and multiple conversations with the dead; the insomniac himself "produces the [space-]time from within which and into which he projects himself."[52]

Among the persons whom Grünbein—the self-appointed postmodern successor of Odysseus, Aeneas, and Dante—encounters on *his* insomniac's journey through the dominion of the dead, philosopher and statesman Lucius Annaeus Seneca stands out with particular clarity. As the following avowal on Grünbein's part poignantly attests, Seneca has been one of his most long-standing, intimate, and cherished interlocutors: "I have been conversing with the philosopher Seneca for many years now. His essay 'On the Brevity of Life,' for instance, is one of a handful of books that I like to carry with me on transatlantic flights and similar occasions."[53] Fully testifying to the poet's extraordinary "plastic power," Grünbein's dialogue with the philosopher and statesman exemplarily instantiates the theoretical-methodological cluster of issues—that is, questions about subjectivity, *metaphor,* and so on—presented in connection with the rhetorical conundrum "the Descartes of metaphor," and reveals his poetics to be profoundly attuned to my overarching affairistic inquiry.

In my discussion of what I disclose as Grünbein's interlocution with Seneca, I focus on one particular text from the cycle "Seneca Studies," namely, the poetologically programmatic poem "Julia Livilla."[54] I first trace Grünbein's strategies in creating a polyphonic poetic subject made up of his own and the philosopher's voices. I then disclose the affairistic dimension of his relationship with Seneca on the basis of this vocal entanglement I should note that my decision to home in on one specific text rather than on a range of contextually apposite examples is methodologically and, to a lesser degree, pragmatically motivated: methodologically insofar as the viability of my argument, which is emphatically topical and problem oriented, does not depend on exemplification by quantity (this means that one exemplary staging that supports my literary-biographical, affairistic take on the emergence of the subject of poetry shall suffice as "proof" of its viability); and pragmatically given this book's limited framework.

"My Dear and Only Faithful Friend"

> *Every culture has its own version of antiquity; so does every century; so should, I believe, every individual.*
>
> *Wherever the two would be seen together in those days, they would elicit the kind of malicious and, at times, invidious talk with which a society . . . built on marriages of convenience . . . prosecuted every alleged or actual affair. . . .* [55]

Featuring one of Grünbein's most memorable insomniacs, "Julia Livilla" vividly stages, as I document in great detail, the affairistic, interlocutionary emergence of poetic subjectivity as a function of metaphor:

Julia Livilla

(1) Mein lieber, einzig treuer Freund, es ist soweit. Ich bin,
Wie Du vor Jahren schon befürchtet hast, verbannt.
Mein neuer Wohnsitz heißt nun Korsika. Das graue Kinn
Rom zugewandt, steh ich am schroffen Felsenrand.
(5) Verzeih den Stolz, doch ein Exil auf kargen Inseln
Ist, wie Du weißt, das Schicksal aller Querulanten—

Des Philosophen Ziel. Denn wenn ein Blutgerinnsel
Dir deine Sterblichkeit beweist, hast du verstanden:
Fortuna läßt nur, was du selbst gewollt, geschehn.
Kein Grund zur Klage, schaut man von der üblen Seite
Aufs Leben, als es sorglos war, kaum abzusehn.
So spielt im Atrium, beschützt, das unbewußte Kind.
Auch wenn das einzig Feuchte (nimm das Meer beiseite)
Hier weit und breit, das Peinlichste, die Tränen sind—
(15) Du hattest recht mit deiner Warnung. Eine Frau,
So schön, so ungewöhnlich, muß Verderben bringen.
Doch wenn die Grazie deinen Weg kreuzt, himmelblau
Dich Klugheit streift mit manikürten Schwingen,
Bist du bereit zu manchem Risiko. Denn so ist Liebe—
(20) Sie übersteigt, was immer du an Argumenten hast.
Nicht daß ich einsam wär, allein mit meinen Diatriben.
Mir scheint nur, Freund, wir hätten zuviel Zeit verpaßt,
Indem wir das Intime mieden. Weiß ich, was du weißt?
Und weißt du, was ich wirklich denke, wenn der Husten
(25) Spätnachts zurückkehrt und mein Schmerz mich beißt?
Nennst du das Ehebruch: wir beide taten, was wir mußten.

Julia Livilla

(1) My dear and only faithful friend, at last, I am—
Years ago, you already feared that this would happen—banished.
My new place of residence is Corsica. My gray chin
Facing Rome, I am standing on the steep cliff.
(5) Pardon my pride, but exile on barren islands
Is, as you know, the fate of all trouble makers—
The philosopher's end. For when a blood clot
Proves your mortality to you, you've understood:
Fortune allows only what you yourself wanted to happen.
(10) No need to complain, if you look from the bad side
At life, when it was without cares, barely foreseeable.
The oblivious child plays like this, protected, in the atrium.
Even if (not counting the sea) my tears are far and wide
the only moist and most embarrassing thing here—
(15) You were right in warning me. A woman,
So beautiful, so unusual, must bode disaster.
And yet—when grace crosses your path, sky-blue
Prudence brushes up against you with manicured wings,
You are willing to take risks. For such is love—
(20) It surpasses whatever arguments you may produce.
It's not that I am lonely, alone with my diatribes.

It just seems to me, my friend, that we wasted too much time
Avoiding intimacy. Do I know what you know?
And do you know what I really think, when my cough
(25) Returns in the middle of the night and the pain bites me?
Call it adultery: We both did what we must do.[56]

The poem as a whole revolves around a significant erotic-political event and "its aftermath"—an event on account of which the poem's speaker, a philosopher (line 7), has presumably been exiled to the "barren island" of Corsica (lines 2–5), from where he is addressing his absent "only faithful friend" (line 1).[57] The quick yet detailed strokes with which the speaker's situation is limned (lines 4–5, 13–14) indicate the friend's absence (if he were present there would be no need on the speaker's part to apprise his addressee of the fact that he now resides in Corsica and is standing at the edge of a steep cliff, looking toward Rome; lines 3–4). The event in question is the speaker's encounter, falling in love, and subsequent—presumably adulterous—affair (lines 19, 23, 26) with an unusual, beautiful, and intelligent woman (lines 15–17) whose name is, Grünbein suggests, none other than the poem's title, "Julia Livilla." The speaker's implied longing for Rome (line 4) indicates that the city is both his previous place of residence and the locale in which the affair unfolded and came to an end. A philosopher's banishment from Rome to Corsica as a result of events concerning a woman named Julia Livilla unmistakably points to Lucius Annaeus Seneca as the poem's subject. As briefly outlined in Chapter One, in the year 41 C.E. Seneca was relegated to the Mediterranean island off the Italian coast after being charged with and convicted of adultery with Julia Livilla, Emperor Claudius' niece. The philosopher was not allowed to return to Rome until the intervention of Claudius' second wife, Agrippina, in 49 C.E.

What does Grünbein do with this material? To begin with, he has his speaker address a close friend, his "only faithful friend," in the manner of Seneca's extant missives to Lucilius and others. The unspecified friend has obviously been privy to the goings-on at the imperial court for quite some time and must thus have been, like Seneca, a high-standing official in the Roman bureaucracy. The historical identity of the putative Seneca's addressee is not critical to the poem's agenda—all the more so given that Seneca himself tended to make use of his addressees as mere pretexts for exposing his ideas.[58] What is important, though, is the very liveliness and immediacy of the gesture of address—the impersonation of Seneca addressing a close friend.

The attempt to render Seneca's fictitious words immediate and realistic relies primarily on having the putative Seneca adopt the words and tone of the historical Seneca. Thus, Grünbein's "steep cliff" and "barren islands" (lines 4–5) directly echo the philosopher's own depictions of Corsica.[59] Concomitantly, his matter-of-fact treatment of exile and of its significance for the one having to endure it (lines 5–7) harks back to Seneca's own discussions of the topic. "Exile," he writes to his mother from Corsica, is merely "a change of place." It is part and parcel of the human condition that "through unknown regions restless man has made his way." "Different people," he continues, "have been impelled by different reasons to leave their homes. But at least this is clear: none has stayed in the place where he was born."[60]

In presenting exile both as an existential-historical fact *and* as the "philosopher's end" (line 7) in general, Grünbein imbues the speech of his poetic persona with the overall Stoic discourse on exile and cosmopolitanism and, like Seneca himself, embeds it in real history. Exile and philosophy have been linked at least since the banishment of Anaxagoras from Athens on charges of impiety.[61] Since then, many a philosopher has been forced to leave his home for political reasons: Diogenes, for instance, had to leave Sinope, Aristotle had to leave Athens, and Cicero had to leave Rome; and as Seneca himself points out to his mother, in 161 B.C.E. the Roman senate ordered all Greek "philosophers . . . to leave this very city [that is, Rome] as being corruptors of the youth."[62] While not all exiles relocated to remote, barren, or craggy islands as Seneca did, Aristotle, for one, did indeed spend the remainder of his life in the city of Chalkis on the island of Euboea off the Boetian coast. Grünbein's "exile . . . on islands [if not necessarily "barren" ones] / Is . . . the fate of all trouble makers / The philosopher's end" (lines 5–7) is thus indeed (to some extent at least) borne out—*pace* its hyperbolic thrust—by historical fact.

But there is another sense in which exile could be construed as the philosopher's "end." Upon being reproached for his banishment, Diogenes is said to have replied, "Nay, it was through that, you miserable fellow, that I became a philosopher."[63] Diogenes' reinterpretation of exile as a necessary stage in the making of a philosopher leads to the logical conclusion that, insofar as becoming a philosopher means living in exile, philosophers as essential exiles are at home anywhere and nowhere. In other words, the philosopher is the prototypical cosmopolitan—cosmopolitanism being the positive version of exile. Thus, when asked "where he came form," the same Diogenes would reply, thereby laying the foundations of cosmopolitanism (which the Cynics and the Stoics shared, among other things), "I am a citizen of the world [*kosmopolites*]."[64] Following Diogenes via Crates and Zeno, Stoics of all colors believed that the true home of the "wise man"—the *sophon* or *sapiens*—is "the entire universe."[65] Not surprisingly, Seneca devotes ample space to the discussion of his own exile in light of the Stoic doctrine of cosmopolitanism. "Our school refuses," he writes with specific reference to Chrysippus, to allow the wise man [*sapientem*] to attach himself to any sort of state [*rem publicam*]. . . . I ask you to what state should the wise man attach himself? To that of the Athenians, in which Socrates was sentenced to death, from which Aristotle fled to avoid being sentenced? . . . Surely you will say that no wise man will wish to attach himself to this state. . . . And so the [wise man] can never suffer exile [*nec exulare umquam potest*], since [he] is free . . . and at home in every world and every age [*omni mundo omnique aevo par*] . . . view[ing] the world as the universal home of mankind [*mundum ut unam omnium domum spectat*].[66]

The Stoic theme is further elaborated in the speaker's quite unsentimental ("No need to complain," line 10) acceptance of his mortality (line 8), as well as in the avowal that "fortune allows only what you yourself wanted to happen" (line 9). The poem's *amor fati* is a virtually direct echo, for instance, of the following lines from Seneca's sixty-first letter to Lucilius: "Let us therefore so set our minds that we may desire whatever is demanded of us by circumstances, and above all that we may reflect upon our end without sadness."[67] Similar formulations, with particular reference to the state of exile, can be found, for instance, in "De providentia": "We should offer ourselves to Fortune in order that, struggling with her, we may be hardened by her. . . . Good men labour, spend, and are spent, and withal willingly. Fortune does not drag them—they follow her and match her pace. . . . Good men . . . are sent into exile [*exilium*]; why not, since sometimes they voluntarily leave their native land?"[68] The pride (line 5) with which Grünbein's Stoic actively meets fortune's challenges (and for which he facetiously apologizes) is yet another echo, for instance, of Seneca's following admonition addressed to his friend Serenus: "The wise man does not need to walk timidly and cautiously; for so great is his confidence in himself that he does not hesitate to go against fortune, and will never retreat before her."[69]

Grünbein's closing reference to nightly coughing and pain poignantly anchors the poem in the philosopher's very corporeality. Seneca, who suffered from a debilitating respiratory condition since early childhood and frequently refers to experiencing "physical pain" (*corporis dolores*) would certainly not have benefited from Corsica's reputedly harsh falls and winters.[70] In his fifty-fourth letter to Lucilius, which provides the subtext to lines 23 to 25 of "Julia Livilla," Seneca talks about his ailment in detail:

My ill-health had allowed me a long furlough when suddenly it resumed its attack. . . . I have been consigned . . . to one special ailment . . . it is well-enough described as "shortness of breath" [*suspirium*]. Its attack is of brief duration . . . it usually ends within an hour. Who indeed could breathe his last [*exspirat*] for long? I have passed through all the ills and dangers of the flesh, but nothing seems to me more troublesome than this. And naturally so; for everything else may be called illness, but this is a sort of continued "last gasp" [*animum egerere*]. Hence physicians call it "practising how to die" [*meditationem mortis*]. . . . Do you think I am writing this letter in a merry spirit, just because I have escaped? It would be absurd to take delight in such supposed restoration to health. . . . Yet in the midst of my difficult breathing [*suffocatione*] I never ceased to rest secure in cheerful and brave thoughts.[71]

But there's more to Seneca's coughing and pain in Grünbein's poem than meets the eye. In addition to rendering the poem viscerally palpable and immediate by underlaying it with the dramatized speaker's bodily presence, Grünbein's attention to coughing—the only reference in the poem, if oblique, to the human voice, to breathing, speech, and language in general—ought to be read as a poetological pointer and, by extension, as an invitation to attend to semantic layers above and beyond the matrix of historicizing dramatization. After all, according to Grünbein, poetry is not merely a "picture puzzle," but is, more specifically, a "picture puzzle of physiological origin." Poems are charades of the continual transformation of *experience* "from nerve into writing" on the part of the poet, who is mindful of the "veto of [his] intestines."[72] It is in and through the physiologically saturated and historically situated human voice, in and through concrete and singular speech acts, that the word is "brought to life" and "redeemed . . . from its lexical deep sleep."[73]

Having established the historical and psychological veracity of the poem's speaker and framed the poem with words that the real Seneca may plausibly have used, and having thus allowed the reader to ensconce himself in the comfortable belief that "Julia Livilla" is the dramatic staging of a specific event "and its aftermath" in Seneca's life, Grünbein introduces into the poem a voice that radically departs in tone, rhetoric, and content from what we have been led to expect, on the basis of lines 1 through 10, from the putative Seneca. Beginning with line 10 and continuing through the poem's ending via the resurfacing of the "real" Seneca's voice in lines 24 and 25, the contours of an utterly un-Stoic, un-Senecan subject emerge. And it is Grünbein's unexpected twist or variation on the *theme of Seneca* that imbues the poem with a tension easy to miss if we allow ourselves to be taken in by the poem's ostensible dramatic straightforwardness.

Clearly the subject of the poem's second half is not the Stoic Seneca, as we know him from his moral essays and letters. We know him as a man concerned with leading a virtuous life informed by "justice, . . . temperance, . . . prudence and righteousness and the proper apportionment of all duties"; a man who aims to attain a state "beyond the reach of any desire," who considers (physical) pleasure and lust "lowly, servile, weak, and perishable," and who admits libido only to the extent that it is *necessary* for reasons of health and procreation ("libido qua necesse est fluat" [may libido unfold according to necessity]); in short, a man whose entire existential-philosophical project consists in subduing the passions so as to attain the happy state of "settled calm" and "tranquility."[74] The subject of the second half of the poem is, rather, someone who is very much aware of and in tune with the libidinal, erotic powers of female beauty; who has been willing to take risks (line 19) for the sake of erotic fulfillment; who by ironically deploring that tears and salt water are the only wet substances to be ashamed of on the island (lines 13–14) betrays his unabated erotic desire; who avows that something that could be construed as adultery had indeed transpired between himself and said woman; who holds the woman in question (presumably Julia Livilla) in very high esteem, calling her "grace" (line 17), and considers her, without any historical justification, the personification of "Prudence"; who has actively succumbed to the powers of love after too long a delay (lines 22–23) and posits the superiority of love and, by extension, passion over reason and argument (lines 19–20).[75]

Both the philosopheme of lines 19 and 20 and the thrust of the preceding lines jar with Seneca's previously outlined Stoic views. In fact, the Dantean-Pascalian "For such is love—/It surpasses whatever arguments you may produce" flouts everything that Seneca professes throughout his writings about the ultimate superiority of reason over passion.[76] Concomitantly, the poem's final apodictic declaration, "Call it adultery: we both did what we must do," is belied by Seneca's obsequious (quite un-Stoic) attempt—most explicitly expressed in his missive to Polybius—to ingratiate himself with emperor Claudius and declare his innocence in the "Livilla affair." "For he [that is, Claudius] has not cast me down with no thought of ever lifting me up. . . . Be his the care—howsoever he shall wish, such let him account my case. Let either his justice discern that it is good, or his mercy make it good; whether he shall discern that I am innocent, or shall wish me to be so—either, in my eyes, will equally show his kindness."[77] With its quite un-Senecan timbre, the self-assured and almost self-righteous note struck in the poem's final verse dovetails with the acknowledgment—ostensibly apologetic—of pride on the speaker's part earlier in the poem. For in light of the poem's conclusion, the "Pardon my pride" of line 5 can be read ironically, not so much as the Stoic profession of confidence and courage in the face of ill fortune, which may be mistaken for haughtiness and pride, but precisely as the profession of what is literally, almost cynically, stated—namely, pride—in the vein of someone saying "pardon my French" with no intent of stopping to swear. This is a far cry from anything the historical Seneca may be expected to endorse. In fact, it explicitly goes against Seneca's ideal of a virtuous life. Foremost among the vices, Seneca emphasizes, are none other than "haughtiness, a too high opinion of one's self and a puffed-up superiority."[78] Furthermore, Grünbein's reinterpretation of the Livilla affair in terms of necessity—mark the final, emphatic *mußten* (must)—blatantly subverts Seneca's unambiguous condemnation of the practice of adultery, and his belief in what the Stoics conceive of as cosmic reason or natural necessity, especially in matters libidinal. Grünbein applies the philosophical category of necessity to a situation that explicitly exceeds the confines of rationality and reason (lines 19–20) (as well as of temperance and moderation, the latter's corollaries), a situation whose supposed erotic underpinnings are precisely the opposite of necessity and thus bespeak the real Seneca's view of "blind and unthinking love . . . extravagant joy springing from very small and childish causes . . . and degeneracy"—all of which Seneca explicitly classifies as pertaining to vice. Grünbein thus turns Seneca on his head, again indicating that more than one sense position (the Stoic), more than one worldview, and more than one poetic persona are vying for the reader's attention.[79]

Who in the poem's duet could be this other, whose voice breaks through the cracks of Seneca's plight, who appears through the interstices of the Stoic mask? Grünbein drops—playfully and with the exuberance of one writing for the initiated—only one, albeit unmistakable, hint: Seneca's other is none other than the one who knows how it is to look on from the "bad side"—"schaut man von der üblen Seite" (line 10). And this is, of course, none other than the poet himself. "I was asked by an American once," Grünbein notes in a 1991 interview, "after I had told him that I was from Berlin: 'Free side or bad side?' I have known ever since that everything that I have done so far [*was ich bisher getrieben habe*] is *Poetry from the bad side.*"[80]

What does this twist do in, with, and for the poem? To begin with, it clearly reinscribes the poem's geographical axis—Rome-Corsica—and its attendant significations as the speaker's home and exile, respectively, within recent European, German, and more specifically, Grünbein's own history. In having the putative Seneca refer to his place of exile as "the bad side" (line 10), Grünbein blurs the semantic-referential boundaries between Seneca's confinement in Corsica and his own erstwhile confinement ("in the shadow of the . . . wall, territorially confined to a space only a bit larger and . . . no less uncanny than Albania") in East Berlin and the German Democratic Republic (GDR), and hence between the philosopher and himself *tout court*. The poem's subject is thus (at the very least) double; the one addressing his "only faithful friend" is Seneca as much as (the stylized) Grünbein himself.[81] However, Seneca's exile does not function merely as a negative trope for Grünbein's life prior to the *Wende* (the collapse of the Berlin Wall followed by German reuinification). For if exile is "the philosopher's end" (line

7) in the sense that it implies his becoming a true cosmopolitan, being at home "in every age and every world"—meaning at home nowhere in particular—then Seneca's relegation to Corsica can also be read as a metaphor for Grünbein's life *after* 1989—a life marked by, as Grünbein notes with a nod to Dante and Mandelstam in particular, being "constantly under way . . . nowhere at home and never reaching [a] destination"—the life of an exile, in line with the ideal life of the unattached "wise man," in line with the Stoic reinterpretation of exile as cosmopolitanism's other name.[82] The poet's voice equally resounds in the poem's vision of mortality and *vanitas* through the prism of physiology: "when a blood clot / Proves your mortality [*Sterblichkeit*] to you" (lines 7–8), for instance, directly resonates in tone and thrust with such lines from Grünbein's poetry as the following:

> What you are stands at the edge
> Of anatomical plates.
>   Blathering to the skeleton
> On the Wall about the soul
> Is as untoward
> As in the throat of time
> (Irrespective of cerebellum and brain stem)
> This shitty mortality.[83]

Similarly, the putative Seneca's avowal that in Corsica "my tears are . . . / . . . most embarrassing [*das Peinlichste*]" (line 14) dovetails in content and diction with Grünbein's reference to life in the GDR as "so many years of embarrassment [*Peinlichkeit*] . . . ," and with his previously quoted depiction of the *I* as the "*embarrassingly* inevitable [*peinlich unvermeidbar*] . . . bodily scent of speech [that] foils all of shame's ruses," which is especially noteworthy in the context of my discussion of Grünbein's poetic exploration of subjectivity.[84]

Grünbein's most spectacular intertwinement of his own voice with the voice and concerns of the putative Seneca is staged, albeit subtly, in the poem's final "cough." As I mentioned earlier, the speaker's painful coughing grounds the poem, in its very enunciation, in his corporeality. As I have also mentioned, it is through Seneca's attested respiratory condition, that is, through his very breathing, that Grünbein thematizes the question of poetry and its creation in "Julia Livilla." In other words, that poetry, for Grünbein, is an emphatically somatic, physiological affair is thrown into relief by dint of the putative Seneca's ailment. Rather than merely functioning as an illustrative, material vehicle for the poet's oblique poetological agenda, Seneca is literally inscribed into the very texture of Grünbein's poetics, translated into the poetic figuration of Grünbein's violent conception of language (including, *a fortiori*, poetic language) in terms of "Revenge of the flesh / Through the larynx," which may articulate itself as a "burp."[85] In and through the putative Seneca's coughing, which is presented as uncomfortable and violent (being followed by "pain"), the poem's somatic substratum wreaks its synecdochic "revenge." Seneca's material weight and specificity, signaled in his singularly experienced ailment, are transformed into the allegorical exemplar of Grünbein's poetics, being fully sublated and incorporated into Grünbein's very own voice. The semantic-thematic tensions uncovered in the poem can be ascribed to the tensions between the voices and sense positions of the poem's two respective speakers. The one—Stoic in all of the word's senses and biographical innuendoes—belongs to Seneca; the other—much more in tune with Grünbein's insistence on "sarcasm" as his dominant poetic attitude—arguably belongs to the poet himself.[86]

Insofar as such a reading is indeed plausible, the question arises as to Grünbein's addressee in this poem, as to his "only faithful friend." Who is this friend? What does Grünbein tell us about him (or her)? It is someone who is cautious and circumspect—as suggested in the participle *befürchtet* (feared) (line 2); someone who knows—*wie Du weißt* (as you know) (line 6)—about philosophy and politics (lines 5–7); someone who is sympathetic to the view that the erotic and lustful may be shameful (line 14); someone who had been close to the exiled at Claudius' court and had warned him about the ramifications of taking up with the woman in question (lines 15–16); someone who is wont to use reason and argument, especially in affairs like the one on which "Julia Livilla" hinges—in short, it is someone prudent and very much like the historical Seneca himself![87] What we wind up with, then, is the following complex setup: Grünbein is addressing Seneca while having the putative Seneca's imagined addressee articulate what could plausibly be construed as the philosopher's *de facto* viewpoint, as expressed not only in his writings but, more important, in the poem itself.

The poem's complex discursive network is further complicated if we bear in mind that the putative Seneca is essentially an impersonation, a feat of ventriloquism on Grünbein's part, to begin with. This means that in addressing Seneca, Grünbein *a fortiori* addresses himself-as-hybrid, as the poem's polyphonic subject of enunciation. Grünbein's particular use of the second-person singular pronoun *du* markedly speaks to the issue of addressing self and other. Through line 7, all second-person pronouns are capitalized, as is customary in German when writing a letter. Beginning with line 8, however, all second-person pronouns, including possessive forms—with the exception of pronouns at the beginning of verses (lines 15 and 18), which, in line with the orthographic convention established in the poem, require capitalization—are spelled with a lowercase *d* (lines 8, 9, 17, 19,

20, 23, 24, and 26). The shift to lowercase occurs precisely when the poem's historical-philosophical overture, which establishes the putative Seneca as the poem's ostensible speaker, gives way to the articulation of a central topos of Grünbein's poetics, namely, the entwinement of mortality and physiology—that is, when the putative Seneca's voice is overlaid with Grünbein's. Beginning with the lowercase spelling of the second-person pronoun and its cognate forms—especially against the foil of the hitherto capitalized *Du*—the poem can emphatically be read as a self-address. What the poem can thus be said to signify grammatically—in full agreement with Stoic doctrine—is that addressing a friend is indistinguishable from addressing oneself: in the Stoic view, a friend is an "alter ego."[88] In other words, Grünbein's pronominal charade *grammatically* enacts and replicates the intertwinement of philosopher's and poet's voices, and hence subjectivities, insofar as subjectivity is the result of "the speaker's capacity to posit [that is, invent] himself as a 'subject.'"[89]

In his dealings with the past, Grünbein does not leave the past where it allegedly is, namely, in the past. Rather than having recourse to the past in order to make sense of and shape the present—thereby, of course, necessarily reinterpreting it to some extent—Grünbein engages the present in order to make sense of the past and shape *it* anew! The specific contribution of Grünbein's modes of "structuring history in [his] own personal fashion"[90] to our assessments of and responses to the indelible presence of the past is not merely one of memory, remembering, or commemoration *per se* (although it is that too) but rather of what could be called, to borrow and displace Avishai Margalit's term, *revivification,* whereby the past—especially individuals from the past—is brought to life not so much in essence, which undergoes changes, but, more important, in altered form.[91] Grünbein's poetic coughing, in particular, viscerally beams the Stoic philosopher into our very presence; concurrently, the respiratory trope enables Grünbein—awakened by the noise of his own poetic speech, as it were—to travel back in time metaphorically, in mind and in body. The poem's final image of the sleepless, ailing philosopher and philosophizing poet physically blurs the boundaries between the two speakers' voices and bodies, and can thus be viewed as a palpable embodiment, a poignant figuration, of Grünbein's postulate of the "contemporaneity of the noncontemporaneous." The irreducible somaticity of the poem's coughing insomniac forecloses the plausibility of attempting to distinguish clearly between past and present, to keep the poem's communicating subjects apart in Grünbein's act of rewriting, which fuses both into a figural unity. Past and present reveal themselves as the twofold creation of metaphor: Seneca has mutated into the former GDR citizen and contemporary poet, while Grünbein has taken on the philosopher's gestalt. The subject articulating the poem is indeed "historical through and through" and thus, essentially, a subject of metaphor. We see, hear, and feel Seneca addressing us; yet the Seneca speaking to us, the readers, the ultimate "dear friend" of literature, is certainly not the "commemorated" Seneca of the past but rather a "revivified," newly born hybrid: Durs Seneca a.k.a. Lucius Annaeus Grünbein.[92]

Significantly, Grünbein chooses an affair as the prism through which to address and focalize exemplarily two of the central concerns of his poetics: the question of the subject and the role of the past in and for an aesthetic engagement with the present. This means that whatever happens in "Julia Livilla" on the semantic, thematic, and epistemological levels ought to be read against the backdrop of the poem's central event: Seneca's putative affair with the emperor's niece. (The fact that, as earlier noted, the veracity of the affair will never be established does not in any way diminish or invalidate the significance of Grünbein's treating it *as if* it had actually happened.) Consequently, we need to inquire into the role and import of the philosopher's affair with the emperor's niece and its political consequences for Grünbein's engagement with the question of the constitution of poetic subjectivity. What does the Livilla affair do for Grünbein?

Insofar as Seneca's putative affair with Julia Livilla and, more importantly in the context of my exploration of the constitution of poetic subjectivity, his subsequent relegation to Corsica put to an extreme test his Stoicism, which he had hitherto practiced—without great difficulty, as it were—under the auspices of a successful career, first as an attorney and later as a public official at the imperial court in Rome, it ought to be viewed as the condition for the emergence of a particular kind of subject—the Stoic subject, presumably impassible and unfazed by the "slings and arrows of outrageous fortune"—whom we have come to associate with the name Lucius Annaeus Seneca.[93] In other words, we ought to register the existential-philosophical significance of Seneca's condemnation to exile as *the* event that facilitated the fine-tuning and consolidation of the singular embodiment of an exemplary kind of subjectivity, as it articulates itself emphatically in such signature texts, written in exile, as Seneca's *Ad Helviam matrem de consolatione* (Consolation to his mother Helvia), *De brevitate vitae* (On the brevity of life), and *De constantia sapientis* (On the steadfastness of the wise man).[94] The Livilla affair thus provides Grünbein with a historically saturated and thematically apposite backdrop against which to foreground and throw into sharp relief his own poetic figuration of subjectivity as bound up, among other things, with the condition of exile.

Unlike, however, the historical Seneca, who disclaims any involvement in what Messalina, Claudius, and others cast as his adulterous affair with the emperor's niece, and thus disclaims any fidelity to something that, according to him, never happened, Grünbein's putative Seneca goes out of his way (lines 15–26) to emphasize that an event that could be construed as adultery and in which he was involved did in fact take place—all too late, alas! (line 23)—and that he fully accepts his relegation as the necessary (line 25) existential-sociopolitical manifestation of his fidelity to the truth of his loving encounter (line 19) with the person in question. In other words, Grünbein displaces the significance of the Livilla affair for the constitution of the philosophical-poetic subject from its historically plausible, political dimension onto its poetically motivated, erotic dimension. It is the experience of love and the encounter with beauty that constitute the subject of Grünbein's poem as a subject of fidelity to a particular event and not, as in the case of the historical Seneca, the fact of having to endure the implementation of the Roman penal code.

Why this shift of perspective? It seems to me, in view of Grünbein's thematic emphasis on love and eroticism in "Julia Livilla," that the most productive way of formulating a convincing response to this question is to reread the poem in the light of Grünbein's overall poetic concern and engagement with *love*. Building on the insights gained thus far into the poem's complexities and tensions, I now reread the poem, in a concluding argumentative move, as one of Grünbein's most stunning love poems—not only a poem *about* love but also, emphatically, a poem *of* love; a poem, that is, in which the poet expresses his love for an interlocutor.

Significantly, the "service of love" is, according to Mandelstam and Dante reader Grünbein, one of the poet's "most noble pursuits."[95] So central—if unobtrusively and discretely so—is the question of love to Grünbein's poetic project, in fact, that one critic was emboldened to credit him with having created some of "the most beautiful love poems of our age."[96] How exactly does the poet's "service of love" play out in "Julia Livilla," above and beyond the significance and function of love as a theme within the poem's complex and tension-filled discursive network?

Long before the explicit mention of love in the poem's second half—in reference to the speaker's abiding affection for a "woman / So beautiful, so unusual"—the forces of both love and fidelity have been brought to bear in the speaker's ostensibly formulaic apostrophe: "Mein *lieber, einzig treuer* Freund . . . " Let us consider the words *lieber* and *einzig treuer*. Although *lieber* certainly appears to be and could hence simply be read as a standard German form of friendly address in the sense of "dear," we must not overlook the fact that it already contains the word *liebe* and, consequently, ought be read as part of the speaker's *declaration of love*—if subtle—*for and to his friend*.[97] Thus we are enjoined to read the poem as a whole, from its very beginning, in the key of and under the sign of love between speaker and addressee. The import of love for the speaker is further underscored by the poet's decision to have its initial mention be immediately followed by the friend's emphatic qualification in terms of fidelity: "Mein lieber, *einzig treuer* Freund." In referring to the friend as "My . . . *only faithful* friend," the putative Seneca underscores his addressee's *singular fidelity* to him and acknowledges the inextricable enmeshment of love and fidelity—*Liebe* and *Treue*—in general, thereby implicitly qualifying *his* love for the addressee in terms of fidelity too. The theme of love thus reveals itself as unfolding on at least two mutually imbricated levels—the illocutionary-performative and the thematic. The subtle articulation of the speaker's love for and implicit fidelity to his loving and faithful addressee (performance) is juxtaposed with the speaker's elliptical narrative *about* his love for and fidelity to an event involving a third party (theme).

Taking into account the previously outlined dynamic of the poem's complex staging of the polyphonic constitution of subjectivity, and attending to its overall illocutionary setup, we cannot fail to register that the declaration of love tacitly articulated in its first line bespeaks, first and foremost, *the poet's own love for his main interlocutor*, that is, Grünbein's love for Seneca, who is cast—similarly to Celan's Shakespeare—as a faithful friend and interlocutor. If this further twist to the poem's already convoluted semantics is granted, we cannot but read the speaker's regret about *not having become intimate with his love interest sooner* (line 23)—which means that the two actually *did become intimate*, if too late—as Grünbein's avowal that he views his discursive relation to and verbal intercourse with Seneca *in erotic terms*, as *erotic intercourse*—as interlocution. Grünbein's use of the verb *treiben* in reference to his practice of poetry (in the previously quoted 1991 interview: "everything that I have *done* [*getrieben*] so far") acquires—especially in the light of my emphasis on the erotic, interlocutionary import of Celan's use of the same verb to capture his dialogue with Shakespeare—pressing contextual significance![98] Only if we acknowledge this erotic dimension of Grünbein's engagement with the Stoic does the ascription of the Stoic virtue of "prudence" (line 18) to "grace" (line 17) make sense. For the prudent *Grazie*—in addition to being a reinvented, fictional Julia Livilla (within the putative Seneca's narrative about his love)—is *a fortiori* none other than Seneca himself (within Grünbein's declaration of love). In the light of my erotic take on Grünbein's engagement with Seneca, the final "Call it adultery: We both did what we must do" enjoins being read as Grünbein's reply to the philosopher's preceding implied reproof to his modern-day lover for having seduced and involved him in an affair, to the effect that their love was unavoidable.

It would certainly be going too far to speculate on the poem's possible auto-biographical subtext: Was it inspired by a visit to Corsica—a favorite vacation spot for Germans? Is the Livilla affair, along with a visit to Corsica, a convenient mask for a "real" affair? Does the poet suggest that the practice of poetry as metaphor in the earlier-defined sense, predicated as it is on the poet's nocturnal escapades and trysts with interlocutors from the past, necessarily implies the betrayal—*Ehebruch*—of the poet's real-life commitment to such persons as his wife, to whom the entire volume *Erklärte Nacht* is dedicated? Is this what the volume's title ultimately implies by way of displacing Richard Dehmel's role poem "Verklärte Nacht" (Night mystified), in which (appositely!) a woman confesses to a man that she has committed adultery and conceived a child by another, that is, that it is the poet's attempt to *explain* poetically what he is up to when he lies awake at night—that he can't help actively and faithfully persevering within the ever-unfolding truth of his trysts with the "precious dead"?[99] Finally, doesn't Grünbein tell me, the reader that *we*—poet and I—also engage in something that could be construed as adultery, that reading poetry is necessarily an affair imposing its own interlocutionary parameters of truth, fidelity, and betrayal? Can't "Julia Livilla" be read as a metaphor for engaging in and with poetry *tout court*, insofar as every poem can be said to be—to the extent that it is faithfully responded to—a potential instance or occasion of both betrayal and fidelity for the loving reader, his or her potential Julia Livilla?

In whatever way we may want to read the poem's phatic-pragmatic dimension, clearly Grünbein's personalization and eroticization of his conversation with Seneca suggests that the constitution of poetic subjectivity proceeds fundamentally by way of interlocution, involving the interlocutors' fidelity to the truth of the event of their love—even at the cost of what may be viewed as betrayal from within an extrapoetic frame of reference *not* predicated on the event of their love. After all, Grünbein's fidelity to Seneca (and others) is—like Celan's fidelity to Shakespeare—an emphatically *creative fidelity*—a fidelity, that is, that *finds and invents*, to use Celan's words—a fidelity that is justified only from within the truth of *Grünbein's* love and that may be expected to revivify a Seneca who is not at all the real Seneca but merely his metaphorical double. What *is* necessary, indeed, for the emergence of poetic subjectivity, Grünbein suggests, is above all the inevitable displacement and re*creation* of the past in and through the labor of love.

According to Mandelstam, "the word is psyche"—a "living" organism that "does not designate objects" but rather "freely chooses," animated by the "breathing [and speaking] of all ages," for its "abode . . . this or that material significance, thingness, beloved body" around which it "roams freely, like the soul around the abandoned yet not forgotten body."[100] Grünbein takes literally what I have called Mandelstam's "polyphonic organicism": animated by the "breathing of all ages," Grünbein's poetic word brings to life his interlocutor's "beloved body," whose physicality and somaticity are poignantly staged in the speaker's reference to the real Seneca's respiratory condition. Insofar as the poet is the product or effect of such diachronic, interlocutionary animation or "ensoulment," the speaker's figural coughing ought to be read emphatically as a palpable indication of the poetic subject's physiological rootedness in the most basic, involuntary human reflex: breathing.[101] Furthermore, insofar as the link between physiology and poetry pertains as much to the question of the constitution and existence of the human being as to the question of a particular aspect—the poetic—of human praxis, "Julia Livilla" ought to be considered a prime instantiation of what Grünbein calls (with a nod to Mandelstam) "anthropological realism," which is "inseparable from ethics," derives its "principles from physiology," and posits "the human body as the irreducible telos" and "the highest court of appeal" in all matters of signification.[102] Grünbein's ethical-anthropological realist derives his principles neither from doctrine (presumably in analogy with the historical Seneca) nor from what Mikhail Bakhtin calls *theoretism,* but from the singular (if reinvented) experiencing, suffering, corporeal, and concretely situated human being—for instance, from the sleep-deprived Seneca at the edge of a steep cliff on the island of Corsica.[103] The message of Grünbein's realist ethics is clear: the fidelity of love as interlocution—transpiring poignantly and exemplarily in and through poetry—conquers the "brevity of life"—love is stronger than death.

Again we hear Grünbein subtly resorting to Dante (as always, already mediated through Mandelstam), who provides him not only with the image of the prototypical modern poet-exile but, more important in the present context, with an exemplary precedent of the poetic articulation of the invincible and life-bestowing power of love, even in the face of death: Like Beatrice (among others) in Dante's text, Seneca (among others) is *loved back into the world of the living* in Grünbein's text. Given the avowedly ethical impetus of Dante's conception and treatment of love as the force that pulls him out of the "dark forest" where he finds himself lost midway through his life, Grünbein's election of Seneca—one of the most prominent *ethical philosophers* of all time—as his partner for the purpose of conceiving and creating the love child of poetic subjectivity—would appear to be not at all surprising.[104] But of course the question of the ethical—the question of agency and the conduct of life—the focus of the next chapter, has been firmly ensconced all along in Grünbein's Cartesian boudoir, which features such other regulars as Seneca, Mandelstam, and Dante (among others). For it was none other than Descartes himself who philosophically fused the question of the subject with the question of ethics in casting his philosophical method as an essentially ethical endeavor that would not only help him find his way out of the "middle of a forest" where "many a traveler . . . has lost his way" and attain the clearing of epistemological and ethical truth, but also facilitate the advancement of the general "good of mankind."[105]

CHAPTER 4

What's in a Name?

Brodsky and the English Muse

They made an Exile—not a slave of me.

I'd weep—but mine is not a weeping Muse,
And such light griefs are not a thing to die on. . . .

At all costs try to avoid granting yourself the status of the
victim.[1]

In the two previous chapters I have offered affairistic readings of Celan's and Grünbein's dialogues with Shakespeare and Seneca, respectively. I have focused in particular on the significance of Celan's interlocution with Shakespeare for our understanding of the workings of poetic signification, and on the significance of Grünbein's interlocution with Seneca for our understanding of the constitution of poetic subjectivity. In this final chapter, I pose the question of poetic and, by extension, ethical agency as a corollary of the emergence of the subject of poetry from poetic signification. I do so on the basis of the poetics of Joseph Brodsky, who, like few other modern poets, has been centrally concerned throughout his career with the interface between the poetic and the ethical.[2]

Before embarking on the final leg of my interpretive journey, however, I should clarify what I mean by the somewhat formulaic "poetic and, by extension, ethical agency." *Poetic agency* is the poetic subject's very mode of being. Once the poetic subject has come into being it cannot but be *active*—an agent, engaged in *doing something,* be it minimally *being* a subject.[3] The poetic subject thus by definition bespeaks and is at the same time bespoken by his or her agency, irrespective of its degree of externalization and witnessability. This means that the poetic subject cannot *not* be an *ethical* agent as well, insofar as human agency (the only kind of agency I am concerned with here) constitutively unfolds in and hence essentially implies the realm of the ethical—here understood in line with Aristotle and Brodsky as the axiological, task-ridden world of human sociality both within and without poetry—which it informs and by which it is in turn informed.[4] Poetic subjectivity can consequently be said to precede ethical agency only from a heuristic viewpoint that relies on the tacit deployment of metalepsis vis-à-vis a phenomenon that in practice is not chronologically analyzable: *the poetic subject as ethical agent.* Furthermore, insofar as any text is an utterance that in a more or less immediate manner intervenes in the world at large, any attempt at strictly separating the poetic from the extrapoetic—poetic agency from extrapoetic, ethical agency—will have been foreclosed on (1) *ontological-theoretical grounds,* because poetic agency cannot fail to spill over its putative discursive boundaries to become ethically effective in the real world (admittedly to a greater or lesser degree); (2) *semantic grounds,* because text and context, author and character, real *I* and poetic *I,* are to be situated—according to Celan, Grünbein, and Brodsky (and others)—along the lines of one discursive continuum; and finally (3) *historical grounds,* because examples (including the poets engaged here) that undermine this specious (and indeed impossible) separation abound.[5]

In using the somewhat pleonastic construction "poetic and, by extension, ethical agency" in reference to the poetic subject's very *mode of being,* then, I highlight (1) that the boundaries between the poetic and extrapoetic cannot be upheld in light of the inseverability of text and context, and more important, in light of my three poets' allegiance to *ethical realism,* that is, their particular modes of acknowledging and staging the interface between life and art; (2) that the complex and rich term *ethics* and its cognate forms are to be understood here as exclusively pertaining to and bearing on the concrete, axiological domain of human activity and sociality (both within and without poetry); (3) that the concept of *agency* is used here in strictly ethical terms; and finally (4) that I acknowledge and heed the centrality of ethics in Brodsky's poetics, pointedly articulated in such statements as "every new aesthetic reality makes man's ethical reality more precise. For aesthetics is the mother of ethics. . . . Beauty and its attendant truth are not to be subordinated to any philosophical, political, or even ethical doctrine, since aesthetics is the mother of ethics and not the other way around."[6] If "aesthetics is the mother of ethics," ethical agency is perforce poetic agency's progeny. Indeed, the "art of poetry" can consequently be said to bear witness, as Brodsky notes, "to the vocal and ethical possibilities of man as a species," giving "you an idea of what man ought [*dolžen*] to be, of his vector, of his ethical potential."[7] The following reasoning stands behind Brodsky's ethical conception of poetry: "If what distinguishes us from the other members of the animal kingdom is speech, then literature—and poetry in particular, being the highest form of locution—is, to put it bluntly, the goal of our species;" insofar as poetry is that toward which we inexorably strive, it articulates what humans *ought* to be(come).[8]

Given my three poets' genealogical, poetological, and historical (if limited) ties, and given the fact that Brodsky's most fundamental poetological axiom, the precedence of aesthetics over ethics, dovetails with what I have elaborated as Grünbein's conception and staging of subjectivity as a function of poetic creativity, the Russian's poetics and poetry can be said to complete most productively the threefold theoretical schema governing my overall inquiry: the mutual imbrication of the questions of poetic signification, poetic subjectivity, and poetic and ethical agency. Philosophically speaking, Brodsky's poetics can be said to set in precisely when the subject of poetry has "found himself in Being" and inevitably "becomes a participant" in ethical life, that is, in the world of values, choices, and tasks.[9] Moreover, echoing and complementing Celan's and Grünbein's affairistic instantiations of the constitution of poetic signification and subjectivity, respectively, Brodsky in turn stages, as I elaborate, poetic and ethical agency in affairistic terms.

Methodically adopting the Kantian distinction between that which is empirically and epistemologically "given" to me and that which is "given [to me] as a task"—the latter articulating the exigency of the ethical (of what I "ought" to do)—and seeing as my overall interpretive horizon Brodsky's fundamental ethical-existential stipulation at "all costs . . . to avoid granting yourself the status of the victim,"[10] I approach Brodsky's poetics in light of the following questions: What is given to Brodsky historically and what does he do poetically in response to and with it? In what way can Brodsky be said to articulate his creative fidelity to the event of his love (for Marianna Basmanova, or M. B.) and multiple betrayal—by lover, friend, and country? What kind of ethical subject are we enjoined to construct on the basis of Brodsky's poetry? Who is the ethical agent bodied forth in his texts? In what way can Brodsky be said to bear witness poetically to "the ethical possibilities of man," to live up to "what man ought to be"? To what extent can he be said to have succeeded in realizing poetry's and, by extension, his own and his species' "ethical potential" in staging and facilitating "truth resulting in lyricism, or, better still, lyricism becoming truth"?[11]

In elaborating a comprehensive response to these questions, I begin from the recognition and productive appropriation of what I have diagnosed as a fundamental hermeneutic tension at the heart of Brodsky's poetic project—the tension between the claim that "what goes into writing a book . . . is, ultimately, a man's only life" and the ostensibly contrary claim that poets' "real biographies" are in their "vowels and sibilants, . . . meters, rhymes, and metaphors," that is, in their poetry.[12] Taken together, both claims enjoin the critic to pay scrupulous attention to Brodsky's life without, however, falling into the perilous trap of mistaking it for his poetry's "theme." In other words, whatever may be the modes of life's passage into poetry in Brodsky's case, we are enjoined to approach and interpret their interface emphatically through the "real" biography of "his vowels and sibilants, . . . his meters, rhymes, and metaphors," that is, through his poetry.

With these considerations in mind, I first address Brodsky's particular place and significance within the framework of my inquiry through the prism of his programmatic impersonation of Dante, on the basis of whose ethical-poetic legacy in particular, as I show, he develops his own aesthetic ethics. More specifically, I attend to Brodsky's self-fashioning as a "new Dante" in response to the ethical-poetic challenge to engage adequately with the aggregate forces of what I disclose as the threefold condition of the *void*—the *metaphysical,* the *historical,* and the *poetic*—at the heart of his poetic universe. Insofar as, according to Brodsky, becoming a new Dante means first and foremost, as I will show, accepting and carrying on Dante's ethical legacy, the import for Brodsky of what Dante posits as the ethical force *par excellence*—namely, love—will need to be subjected to particularly close scrutiny in the present context; more specifically, to the extent that in Dante's poetic-existential cosmos love assumes the form of and speaks through Beatrice, Brodsky's self-fashioning as a new Dante will also have to be shown to pivot on the presumably protective presence and intervention of a latter-day Beatrice.

Guided by the logic of my argument, I next proceed to a detailed discussion of the significance of M. B. as the new Dante's "new Beatrice"—ultimately to suggest that Brodsky's impersonation of Dante, which depends on the salvific and loving intervention of *his* new Beatrice, enjoins being read, above all, as a literary-historical and literary-biographical exercise in failure.

In a final interpretive move and with special attention to "Twenty Sonnets to Mary Stuart," the most substantial piece in *New Stanzas to Augusta,* I reread what I have interpreted as the strategic failure of Brodsky's autobiographical master trope—the poet as a new Dante—in light of his concomitant self-stylization as a latter-day Byron (yet another impersonator of Dante). More specifically, I trace

Brodsky's inscription of the contextually relevant events in his life via Byron's biographical legend, with a view to suggesting that in the course of infusing his writing with "a man's only life" through the conduit of Byron, Brodsky succeeds in transforming himself from an ostensible victim—at the personal and political levels—into a victorious agent who can, in the words of Lucius Annaeus Seneca (one of Brodsky's "favorite" thinkers), "receive neither injury nor insult."[13] Like the Stoic who aims at attaining a state of equanimity in the face of the "slings and arrows of outrageous fortune" by subduing the passions, Brodsky's poet too can be said to aim at countering—or better yet, *counter-wording*—the painful impact of fortune's "slings and arrows," albeit by dint of the palliating powers of prosody: "'sorrow controlled by meter' may do . . . as a provisional definition . . . of the entire art of poetry. As a rule, stoicism and obstinacy in poets are results not so much of their personal philosophies and preferences as of their experiences in prosody. . . . "[14]

On a final, methodological note, I should point out that my interpretation of Brodsky's poetic-existential project proceeds archeologically. Rather than cutting straight to the chase and embarking on an explication of what I consider to be Byron's overall ethical-existential significance for Brodsky, I first uncover the hermeneutic strata underpinning and logically subtending the ethics of Brodsky's poetics. In other words, in order to grasp most vividly and productively the cogency of the ethical-existential rationale underlying Brodsky's impersonation of Byron, I retrace Brodsky's poetological steps, as it were, and reconstruct the "poetic logic," to use Grünbein's expression, of his ethics.

Virgil in Paradise

If it were really like Othello *nobody could understand it, however new it might be. And if it were new, it couldn't possibly be like* Othello.

For he loves, in works of art, the ethical stuff and its treatment. . . . [15]

"Unfortunately," Brodsky remarks, "I did not write *The Divine Comedy* and evidently never will. . . . " However, "had I been writing *The Divine Comedy*," he muses, "I would have placed [Virgil] in paradise. . . . "[16] Brodsky's playful resignation in view of the historically and logically impossible, and his concomitant, equally playful, hubristic pointer as to how Dante's masterpiece *should have been written* (and could thus be improved upon), bespeak on the one hand the younger poet's admiration and profound respect for his predecessor, and on the other hand, his desire to emulate (and thus surpass) him. In rewriting Dante's masterpiece *en miniature* in the conditional Brodsky intimates—not all too subtly for that matter—that he may actually have turned out something not merely on a par with Dante's text but something that has incorporated the lessons learned through the "test of time" and in fact placed Virgil in paradise, as it were. Indeed, Brodsky does submit what he considers the "chief accomplishment of [his] life"— the *New Stanzas to Augusta: Poems to M. B., 1962–1982 (Novye Stansy k Avguste)*— as his bid for Dante's seat in the literary Hall of Fame. "I have this secret hope," he confesses, "that the readers will figure this out, that is, that they will in some infinite sense also find themselves on that level."[17] Brodsky's dialogue with and emulation of Dante, which spans virtually his entire career, culminates in his explicit—poetically and, as I explain later, ethically crucial—self-stylization as a new Dante in an elegy written in June 1972 on the eve of his expulsion from the Soviet Union that palpably summons Mandelstam's depiction of Dante as "a copyist, a translator . . . completely bent over in the pose of the scribe, timorously casting a sidelong glance at the illuminated original, which he had borrowed from the prior's library," and writing to the "dictation" of "the breathing of all ages" without "adding a single word of his own":[18]

> I believe in the void [*pustotu*].
> It's like hell, but shittier.
> And the new Dante bends down to the sheet
> And writes a word on the empty [*pustoe*] page.[19]

These few instances that constitute only a tiny fraction of the implicit and explicit references to and invocations of Dante throughout Brodsky's writings clearly attest to the Italian's significance in Brodsky's life and work, and thus can hardly be overestimated.[20] In fact, no other Russian poet after Mandelstam has engaged and vied with Dante as seriously, extensively, and prominently, in terms of worldwide public exposure as Brodsky has. For no other twentieth-century Russian poet would Dante, as mediated through Mandelstam, become as central a poetic-existential reference point and mask as for Brodsky.[21]

Brodsky is very much aware of the fact that his profuse recourse to Dante— the paradigmatic and best-selling modern figure of the poet as exile (and lover)— may well be interpreted as a gesture of rhetorical convenience, potentially undermining any attempt on his part to articulate his own unique poetic-existential vision. After all, "an exiled writer will," Brodsky mockingly notes, "most likely evoke Ovid's Rome, Dante's Florence, and—after a small pause—Joyce's Dublin" when dealing with his own situation.[22] "Since the fourteenth century," Brodsky continues (implicitly ridiculing his own frequent poetic employment of the image of "the woods"), "the woods have given off a very strong sense of *selva oscura* [*dark forest*], and you may recall what that *selva* led the author of *The Divine Comedy* into. In any case, when a twentieth-century poet starts a poem with finding himself at the edge of the woods, there is a reasonable element of danger—or at least a faint suggestion of it": the danger, Brodsky specifies, of having to go through hell and, I should add, of not taking the "road less traveled"—of following the beaten track and slipping into the poetically trivial.[23] Given Brodsky's explicit acknowledgment of the "danger" of engaging Dante as a prism through which to address and focalize his own poetic-existential concerns, his decision to brave this danger and programmatically portray himself as a new Dante in spite of it cannot fail to give pause.

What does it mean to be a new Dante in Brodsky's sense, given that he cannot be assumed to be merely seeking to join the ranks of all those "exiled writer[s]" whom he offhandedly characterizes as invariably prone to take metaphorical recourse to, don the masks of, or identify with (presumably for lack of imagination) the hackneyed cultural props of Ovid, Dante, and "after a small pause," Joyce? What has been *given* to Brodsky such that fashioning himself as a new Dante enables him to respond adequately to this *given*, thereby working toward living up to what according to him "man ought to be," namely poetic and hence ethical through and through? In addressing these questions I begin with a brief discussion of the genealogical dimension of Brodsky's new Dante before proceeding to unpack the logic underlying this autobiographical master trope.

Being a new Dante, as implied by Brodsky's image of the bent-over poet setting down "a word on the empty page," means first and foremost taking on board and, as I presently explain, surpassing Mandelstam's previously cited figuration of Dante (and himself) as a copyist-translator "bent over in the pose of the scribe" and writing to the "dictation" of "the breathing of all ages" without "adding a single word of his own." It means, in other words, appropriating Mandelstam's vision of Dante and making what was presumably state-of-the-art in and for its own time even newer, as it were.[24] Indeed, this is precisely what Brodsky achieves in the very process of recreating Mandelstam's scene by making one crucial alteration to it. Unlike Mandelstam's Dante, who is portrayed as steeped in and thus relying on the plenitude of literary-historical tradition, and who "writes to dictation," merely cribbing and translating from an already available body of texts without "adding a single word of his own," Brodsky's new Dante is given and confronted with the "void," enjoined to assume the task of filling it with words that will presumably have the force of utter novelty, of the "hitherto unutterable."[25] Certainly this cannot possibly mean that Mandelstam should be read as suggesting that Dante is not an *original* poet. Such a reading is foreclosed by Mandelstam's emphasis on Dante's singular inventiveness and poetic ingenuity.[26] Nor can it possibly mean that Brodsky should be read as suggesting that the words of his new Dante are new in absolute terms, that the new Dante is the sole and absolute origin of his text along the lines of a facile understanding of a certain kind of Romanticism. Such a reading is belied by the extreme degree of intertextuality of Brodsky's texts and, more important, by his credo that the poet "is language's means of existence," that he writes to the "dictate of language,"[27] which is constitutively imbued with collective and individual histories and can consequently not fail to bear the traces of the "breathing [and speaking] of all ages." So strong is the pressure of language and tradition on Brodsky, in fact, that he is led to define poetry—if in a facetiously bathetic manner, echoing Mandelstam's observation that "any word is a sheaf with [voices and] meanings sticking out of it in different directions"—as "a dame with a huge pedigree, [whose] every word comes practically barnacled with allusions and associations," and concomitantly to underscore that every poet of course also has "a pedigree, and a much longer one"—an imposing pedigree indeed, considering that it can be traced "all the way back to Adam"![28]

The implausibility of reading the new Dante's claim to novelty in absolute terms is complemented by the logical "iffiness" of positing novelty through repetition. After all, how can the new Dante be new given that the very phrase *new Dante* repeats the old? Concurrently, how can the very idea of a new Dante be reasonably entertained in view of what Brodsky calls the "singular nature of historical occurrence," that is, in view of the fact that "in time nothing happens twice"?[29] Thus, whatever the novelty of Brodsky's new Dante may be said to consist in specifically, it can be only of the kind that Jacques Derrida calls *iterability*, defined as the "alterability of [the] same . . . in the singularity of the event." In other words, the novelty of Brodsky's new Dante can be said to be achieved, as Derek Attridge observes, only "by means *both* of the refashioning of the old *and* of the . . . advent of the new."[30] In what respect can Brodsky's new Dante be said to bring about the "advent of the new" in the "singularity of the event," that is, in his singular historical situatedness?

Insofar as, according to the 1972 elegy cited earlier, the new Dante's putative novelty is presented as functionally dependent on the condition of the "void," we need to inquire into and gain a better understanding of this fundamental given in order to answer this question productively. What do *pustota*—void or emptiness—and its cognate forms signify in the present context, above and beyond their literal meanings? Although Brodsky never defines his use of *pustota,* three central, contextually relevant interrelated aspects of this poetically and existentially crucial given can be extrapolated on the basis of a number of textual instances from across Brodsky's oeuvre in which the term is implicitly or explicitly engaged. Let me dub these aspects, for the sake of rhetorical simplicity, *metaphysical, historical,* and *poetic.*

THE METAPHYSICAL VOID

On numerous occasions Brodsky uses the term *pustota* in reference to the hereafter, which is not only a leitmotif throughout the earlier-cited 1972 elegy and the poems surrounding it in *A Part of Speech* (*Čast' Reči*)—such as "24 December, 1971," "Song of Innocence and—Experience," and "The Year 1972"—but also an aspect of the overall *baroque* thrust of Brodsky's poetics, manifesting itself most palpably in the poet's abiding concern with perishability, loss, and mortality.[31] What comes "after death," Brodsky speculates, is "probably . . . the void."[32] The most effective means of countering the inevitable advent of this void is, as Brodsky had already proclaimed at his trial, the creation of true art—for "art survives life."[33]

THE HISTORICAL VOID

Brodsky's view of and approach to history, as laid out most "systematically" in his 1991 essay "Profile of Clio," which offers a productive entry into tackling this aspect of the condition of the void.[34] Picking up on the image of the new Dante facing the void in the earlier-cited 1972 poem, Brodsky depicts the poet-historian's "predicament" as being "transfixed between two voids: of the past that he ponders and the future for whose sake he ostensibly does this." Suspended between these two voids, the poet-historian strives "to animate the former" and to determine his suspended state's "ethical consequences for the present," because, Brodsky adds, waxing moralistic, "in a society in which the authority of the church is in decline, and the authority of philosophy and the state are negligible or nonexistent, it falls precisely to [the poet-historian] to take care of ethical matters."[35] In view of the later text's specification of the poet-historian's ethical obligation vis-à-vis the double void, and in view of Brodsky's axiom that ethics is born of aesthetics, the novelty of the new Dante, limned programmatically as facing and filling the void, ought to be sited in his assumption of the task of determining the "ethical consequences for the present" of this state of affairs—that is, the poet-historian's suspension "between two voids"—thereby taking care of "ethical matters."[36] The new Dante's novelty reveals itself above all as one of accent. Without in the least jettisoning Dante's long-standing image as one of the patron saints of the un-justly treated, exiled poet and paradigm of what Grünbein calls modern "hell tourism"—crucially enriched by Mandelstam's reinvention of the Florentine—Brodsky zeros in on what he construes as the specifically *ethical import of Dante's poetic legacy* (discussed shortly).[37] In other words, in fashioning himself as a new Dante facing the double void of history, Brodsky can be said to foreground—fully in line, by the way, with Dante's own emphasis on the fundamentally ethical thrust of his poetry—the ethical dimension of his predecessor's poetic legacy and, more generally, the ethical itself in and as a function of the poetic *tout court*.[38]

The concrete historical singularity and cultural-political novelty of Brodsky's interpretive move in turn emerges with special force if the sociopolitical context of its articulation is considered. Given that Brodsky was effectively cut off from the motley crew of aesthetic-intellectual-political developments, movements, and upheavals marking the West in the 1960s and 1970s—living and writing in what may well be conceived of as the historical and cultural "void" of the world behind what he refers to as the "ironic curtain"—his understanding and practice of po-etry as the condition of ethics ought perforce to be read as a direct inversion of the Leninist doctrine of the precedence of ethics over aesthetics (codified in the concept of "socialist realism"), on whose implicit basis he would be accused of social parasitism and eventually expelled from his homeland.[39]

In contrast to Mandelstam, who contented himself with drawing a *metaphori-cal* parallel between Dante's "most dangerous . . . and criminal age" and his own, thus engaging the Florentine emphatically from a poetological perspective as a supreme craftsman and Acmeist *avant la lettre*; true to his view that "one should be very careful about metaphors when dealing with history"; and contrary to Grünbein's reliance on metaphor as *the* historical master trope, Brodsky implies that metaphorical parallels between present and past may simply no longer work, seventy plus years into the twentieth century, when it comes poetically and, by extension, ethically to coping with and withstanding the onslaught and strictures of history (especially in its totalitarian avatars) in their very concreteness.[40] For an acolyte of Urania—"the muse of . . . geography, and also, according to some interpretations, the muse of love"—such as Brodsky, who defines "fate" (*sud'ba*) as the "admixture of geography / to time," metaphorical parallelisms across time and, more importantly, space, while certainly capable of providing the poet with "a more stereoscopic picture of what amounts to [his own] life," are liable to fail when it comes to capturing and poetically articulating a person's unique and unpredictable *sud'ba*—the singularity of what Brodsky refers to throughout his writings as a human being's *vector*.[41]

THE POETIC VOID

In the 1990 essay "Altra Ego," Brodsky maintains that the poet "continually has to get where nobody has ever been before—mentally, psychologically, or lexically"— thus tacitly underlaying with a poetic rationale his erstwhile stint in internal exile in the geographical void of the remote village of Norenskoe. "Once he gets there, he discovers that there's nobody about, save perhaps the word's original meaning or that initial discernible sound. This takes its toll. The longer he is at it—at uttering something hitherto unutterable—the more idiosyncratic his conduct becomes."[42] For the poet, Brodsky suggests, getting "where nobody has ever been before" means saying something that has not hitherto been said, "uttering something hitherto unutterable," that is, being, or rather, producing, the new, pure and simple. The poetically and linguistically new, however, as Brodsky cannot but concede, will have been informed by and will have relied on the old—Brodsky's "perhaps" ought to be read ironically, as implying that "original meanings or that initial . . . sound" will in fact be "about" when the poet "gets there." In other words, the new will have perforce been of an iterable kind. The force or power propelling the poet to "where nobody has ever been before" is the power of language itself. For the poet writes, according to Brodsky, to the "dictate of language," the most fundamental "given" within the framework of his poetic anthropology.[43] Heeding language's dictate is ineluctable: the poet "continually *has to* get where nobody has ever been before" (emphasis added). The fact that language's dictate signally bears on the poet's "conduct" in turn underscores yet again the profoundly ethical thrust of Brodsky's poetics: "life and conduct" have been, after all, the traditional domains and subjects of ethics.[44]

Against the backdrop of what I have elaborated as his threefold conception of the void (metaphysical, historical, and poetic), Brodsky's autobiographical conceit—his impersonation of Dante—can be specified as follows: the new Dante responds to and becomes active (he *does* set down a word on the empty page) in the face of (1) the given of mortality, or the human condition; (2) the given of history or historicity, on whose ontological basis he knows of and experiences his mortality in the first place and on whose concrete existential basis he was tried, sentenced, and exiled—or what could be called the *historical condition*; and finally (3) the given of the necessity of poetic innovation, or what could be called, in view of poetry's status (according to Brodsky) as the "goal of our species," the *poetic condition.* As a human being and poet, Brodsky constitutively finds himself at the mercy of these fundamental conditions or givens that cannot but always already be intuited from within and that must thus be considered in light of the concrete, literary-biographically significant givens or events marking his life at the time and beyond, such as his arrest, trial, internal exile, multiple betrayal (by a friend, a "girl," and his country), and eventual expulsion from the Soviet Union. They enjoin the poet to assume responsibility for his *sud'ba*, to *act* on his own behalf.

What does the poet do? He "sets down a word on the empty page," thereby beginning to fill the poetic and, concomitantly, historical voids. What does he aim to accomplish in so doing? Although his ultimate goal is to countervail (if not, *per impossibile,* overcome) the human condition by working toward his metonymic survival in and through art—a goal that presupposes countervailing the historical condition through the force of poetry—his primary and more immediate goal can be said to consist in sustaining and deflecting the blows and withstanding the pressures of the more or less immediate present. In other words, in order to try his hand at such a grand feat as conquering historicity and, by extension, mortality through art, Brodsky first needs to ensure the continued possibility of agency on the part of the one doing the conquering—that is, his own freedom to act. He needs to make sure that he stays on top of affairs that are more pressing than the question of immortality—affairs that threaten to disempower him, to stymie, curtail, and annihilate his agency, here and now. How does fashioning himself as a new Dante enable him to achieve the goal of safeguarding his ability to act, and thereby to "take care of [the most urgent] ethical matters"? In what sense can Brodsky's choice of Dante as an alter ego be itself read as one of *the* central "ethical consequences" of his complex real-life situation at the time and beyond?

It is at this point that the specifics of Dante's ethics, insofar as they are essentially bound up with and legible through his poetry, come to weigh in on my argument. For the force and persuasiveness of Brodsky's autobiographical master trope depend on the amenability of his existential, ethical, and poetological agenda to being cast in Dantean terms. Only if the ethics of Dante's poetics can be shown to be such that in resorting to them Brodsky is enabled to "take care of [his own] ethical [and hence poetic] matters" with particular efficiency, as it were, and to say "something hitherto unutterable" does it make sense to treat Brodsky's autobiographical conceit as the pivot of his poetics and ethics, as I have implicitly been doing thus far.

The New Beatrice

"Amor," the god of love, dictates the lines of Dante's poetry: "I am the one,"
Dante avers, "who, when Love [Amor] inspires me, takes note, and goes setting
it forth after the fashion which he dictates within me."[45] Love is the center and
fulcrum of Dante's poetics and ethics—the "divine love" that moves "the sun and
other stars"; the salvific, sublimated love that prompts Beatrice to ensure that
Dante finds his way out of the "void" of the proverbial "dark wood," where he
gets lost "midway in the journey of . . . life," and reaches paradise after journey-
ing through hell and purgatory; and last but not least, the erotic and carnal love
experienced and staged by the protagonist of the *Vita Nuova* in particular (and
thrown into sharp relief in Mandelstam's reading of Dante).[46] As one critic aptly
puts it, Dante "raises love to the status of [the] ethical and ethicizing power" *par
excellence.*[47] It is important to keep in mind that, its cosmic and hence abstract
dimension notwithstanding, love assumes the concrete form of Beatrice in Dante's
ethical-poetic universe. Whatever love may be in itself, its concrete experience by
Dante depends on Beatrice—the embodiment of love, the matrix and motor of
his poetry and ethics. Through her, love speaks to him; in her, its truth becomes
palpable.

For Brodsky this means *a fortiori* that in order to be convincing as a new
Dante, he too must be expected to center his ethics and poetics around the question of love and, more important, to produce his own "new Beatrice"—for without a counterpart to Dante's beloved, the new Dante would hardly be convincing
as a Dante to begin with. In other words, in accepting the baton of the ethics of
Dante's aesthetics, Brodsky must perforce acknowledge the ethical centrality of
love, recognizing love as the paramount ethical force. Brodsky makes good on
both expectations, albeit, as I illustrate, with a crucial twist. In order to grasp fully
Brodsky's proximity to Dante on the question of love and its role in the creation
of poetry, we need to dig deeper into Brodsky's postulate that the poet writes to
the "dictate of language."

The dictate of language, Brodsky explains, seeks embodiment and articulates
itself in and through the "voice of the Muse,"[48] whose power over the poet is in
turn bespoken by his passion for a real beloved—the Muse's metonymic, human
stand-in and language's second-order manifestation (the Muse being the first):

> The Muse, née language, plays a decisive part in the sentimental development of
> a poet. She is responsible not only for his emotional makeup but . . . for the very
> choice of his object of passion and the manner of its pursuit. It is she who makes him
> fanatically single-minded, turning his love into an equivalent of her own monologue.

What amounts in sentimental matters to obstinacy and obsession is essentially the dictate of the Muse, whose choice is always of an aesthetic origin and discards alternatives. . . . The intensity of that emotional absolutism is such that at times it overshoots anything that lies near, and often one's very target. As a rule, the nagging, idiosyncratic, self-referential voice of the Muse takes a poet beyond imperfect and perfect unions alike, beyond utter disasters and paroxysms of happiness—at the expense of reality, with or without a . . . reciprocating girl in it.[49]

If the poet's love is the fount and motive force of his creativity *qua* dictate of the Muse/language, and consequently the foundation of his ethics (conceived of as the progeny of aesthetics), then, Brodsky concludes—articulating the interlocutionary matrix of his poetics in the process—"a poem—any poem, regardless of its subject—is in itself an act of love."[50]

Further developing his thoughts on what he views as the poet's tendency to place his creative energies under the aegis of his passion for and abiding obsession with a particular beloved, Brodsky writes,

Hence the singularity of the addressee and the stability of the manner, or style. Often the career of a poet, if he lives long enough, emerges as a genre variation on a single theme. . . . [W]hat makes love lyrics abound is simply that they are a product of sentimental necessity. Triggered by a particular addressee, this necessity may stay proportionate to that addressee, or develop an autonomous dynamic and volume, prompted by the centrifugal nature of language. The consequence of the latter may be . . . a cycle of love poems addressed to the same person. . . . The choice here—if one can speak of a choice where necessity is at work. . . .[51]

In Brodsky's case, the *requirement* of the "singularity of the addressee," whom the poet-lover remains "obstina[tely] and obsessi[vely]" concerned with throughout his career, has been clearly met: M. B., the catalyst, inspiration, and dedicatee of what Brodsky considered the "chief accomplishment of [his] life"—from the *New Stanzas to Augusta*—emerges as his Muse's real-life embodiment. From their first encounter in Leningrad in the summer of 1962 until virtually the end of his life, Brodsky would—in what may well be called a "fanatically single-minded" manner and through all of his adult life's vagaries (including persecution and exile, rise to world fame, late marriage, and second-time fatherhood)—continue writing and thus maintain his creative fidelity to the dictates of his great lover-cum-Muse.[52] Moreover, in presenting the *New Stanzas to Augusta* as his attempt at producing a work of art rivaling the "chief accomplishment of [Dante's] life," that is, the *Divine Comedy*, Brodsky implicitly casts M. B. along the lines of Dante's source of inspiration, that is, as a "new Beatrice." Like Beatrice, to whom Dante would remain poetically faithful throughout *his* life—presumably as of the very moment he first laid eyes on her "at about the beginning of her ninth year [and] near the end of [his] ninth year," through marriage, fatherhood, persecution, and exile—M. B. was to be the lodestar of Brodsky's poetic creativity.[53] However, *unlike* Dante's "glorious lady" and epitome of virtue (married though her real-life model was), M. B. is cast—and here Brodsky radically departs from the ostensibly chivalresque-romantic setup of his poetics and ethics of love—as an unfaithful, promiscuous liar, and most crudely as a *slut* or *bitch*.[54] (Incidentally, I should point out that the shortened form of Beatrice—Bice—employed by Dante in the *Vita Nuova* and phonemically and syllabically parsed in *Paradiso*, prefigures Brodsky's *bitch,* which, although an English word, scintillates through the Russian *bljad'*.[55]

Brodsky's bathetic transformation of Dante's Beatrice into a harlot—which creates a stark contrast between the poet's presumably abiding fidelity to his beloved or Muse and hence to his moral rectitude, as it were, as opposed to the beloved's or Muse's infidelity and hence immorality—is biographically and poetically motivated: biographically to the extent that it is informed by and poetically metabolizes what Brodsky avowedly experienced as his "greatest personal trouble" and with which he was "mostly preoccupied" during the period of the "great public trouble" of his arrest, trial, sentencing, and exile—namely his betrayal by "a girl, etcetera, etcetera"; and poetically insofar as contrasting the infidelity of his "bitch" with his own unremitting fidelity to her (if only at the poetic level) allows him to throw into sharp relief what he suggests as "the monogamous nature of [the] poet's passion [and] attachment to [language and, hence, to his Muse, née language]," and to demonstrate the validity of his claim that "all [the poet's] capacity for fidelity gets spent on [his] Muse."[56]

The new Beatrice's novelty cannot fail to reflect back on and co-determine the new Dante's novelty, which accrues yet another valence in light of it—in addition, that is, to its functional dependence on Brodsky's assumption and continuation of Dante's ethical legacy. Insofar as the new Dante constitutes himself in dialogue with the new Beatrice, his novelty reveals itself emphatically as consisting in being caught up in an ethical-erotic dynamic that is radically distinct from the dynamic obtaining between Dante and *his* Beatrice, predicated as it is on the latter's exemplary rectitude and virtuousness. In other words, the new Dante is *a fortiori* new in the sense that he is faced with a "hitherto unutterable" ethical-poetic challenge, unknown to his Florentine predecessor—namely, his beloved's or Muse's infidelity. For all their differences—the beloved's mortality as opposed to the Muse's immortality being, in Brodsky's view, the "ultimate distinction"—both beloved and Muse share a weakened sense of ethical-erotic commitment. Just like M. B., who found herself another lover when "he [was] gone," the Muse too, Brodsky notes, "finds herself another mouthpiece"—mark the crudely sexual innuendo of this line—once the "[poet]'s gone." Like a hooker or groupie, he further observes, the Muse "always hangs around a language and doesn't seem to mind being mistaken for a plain girl."[57]

Brodsky's portrayal of his beloved or Muse as promiscuous and unfaithful, and hence as ethically flawed, is significant in several respects. First and most general, it brings into particularly sharp relief Brodsky's overall affairistic approach to and conceptualization of the question of poetry, the evental component of which is predicated on the postulate of the "singular nature of historical occurrence" and the erotic component of which is predicated on the anthropological-psychological axiom that "artistic *and* erotic activities are expressions of one's creative energy, that *both* are a sublimation."[58] According to Brodsky, poetry is an "affair" that constitutively implies the interface of fidelity and betrayal as it plays out specifically in the poet's relationship with his unfaithful Muse, with language, and through language with "reality."[59] Brodsky's repeated declarations of his infatuation with the English language in particular—for example, "my love affair with the English language"; "with a foreign culture [esp. Anglo-American] . . . your love affair is a lot more intense"; "I am completely crazy about the English language"; "my long-lasting affair with the English language . . . has turned into a kind of marriage"—pointedly underscore the erotic-affairistic impetus of his poetics, which in placing "an equation mark between [writing,] reading and the erotic endeavor" and short-circuiting "pen and penis" reveals the dictate of language as an *erotic* dictate above all.[60] Although Brodsky's paronomastic coupling of "pen and penis" ostensibly bespeaks the alignment of his "equation [of] reading and the erotic endeavor" with the facile metaphorical equation of language and sex based on the paronomastic link between the grammatical *copula* and the physical act of *copulation,* his concomitant, existentially saturated avowals of his love for the English language underscore the deeply personal and utterly unmetaphorical dimension of his relation to language, which for him is essentially an erotic and intimate one—a bond of "ultimate privacy . . . a *tête à tête* between you and your language."[61] The concrete interlocutionary character of Brodsky's poetic practice comes to the fore with special clarity in his palpably sexualized depiction of one exemplary poetic tryst, namely, his nocturnal tête-à-tête with Horace, to whom "everything I've written is, technically [if not factually], addressed." "Last night," Brodsky confesses to Horace,

> there I was, lying across my unkempt bed [with] the little volume of your Collected [Works], in Russian translations. . . . The heat was on. . . . This was the most vig-

orous session of its kind I've ever taken part in, whether in real life or in imagination. . . . I was as much impressed by my stamina as by my concupiscence . . . a body
of Latin poetry became the target of my relentless affection last night. . . . And for all
the relentlessness of my pursuit, which stood—no pun intended—for a lifetime of
reading you, the dream never turned wet.[62]

Second, Brodsky's portrayal of his beloved or Muse as unfaithful and promiscuous
enjoins being interpreted as Brodsky's oblique mode of responding to and engaging with—on his own, poetic terms—the cluster of real-life affairs (political and
erotic) that avowedly inform his poetics. The dialectic of fidelity and betrayal as
it unfolds in the poet's relationship with his Muse can be viewed, Brodsky suggests, as running "parallel to history,"[63] as an oblique replication and displaced
response to, as well as a *truthful* translation of, the *untruth* of the multiple betray-
als he had to face during the time of his "greatest . . . trouble" (at the personal and
public levels) in the early to mid-1960s and beyond into the truth of his poetics.
In casting the question of the Muse's dictate—that is, the question of the origin
of poetry *tout court*—in terms of the dialectic of betrayal and fidelity, Brodsky
can be said to place his poetic project as a whole implicitly under the sign of the
"Brodsky affair"—that is, the event of his multiple betrayal by lover-Muse, fellow
poet–friend, and country—thereby articulating his creative fidelity to its painful
(un)truth.

Third and last, Brodsky's portrayal of his beloved clearly suggests that his
poetic-ethical universe is not constructed according to the same ethical laws as
Dante's. Amor, the "ethicizing power" *par excellence* in Dante's poetic cosmos, has
been dethroned in Brodsky's. If the new Dante is to find his way out of the "dense
forest" in which he is metaphorically lost "in the middle of his life,"[64] it will not
be due to the intervention of a Beatrice or other well-meaning "allies" such as
Virgil or Bernard of Clairvaux—all of whom are motivated by Amor in Dante's
Divine Comedy—but due to his own, pro-active, Odyssean resourcefulness.

Nowhere does Brodsky more poignantly and wryly express his resignation at
being let down by his Muse than in the poem "Letter in a Bottle," written in
internal exile in November 1964 and addressed—as suggested by its original title,
"Entertaintment for Mary—Bottle with a Letter"—to Marianna Basmanova,
whose first name Brodsky transforms into the English *Mary* under the influence
of his love affair with the English language and its poetry, which he was avidly
perusing and translating at the time.[65] With Mandelstam's poet-sailor and the
tradition of the elegy of the "dying poet" in mind, this *divertimento* stages the

moment of the poet's shipwreck and imminent demise.[66] Fusing poetics and autobiography, Brodsky writes:

> I was sailing truthfully, but then I hit a reef
> and it scuttled my flank.
>
> . . .
>
> I realize that I have lost the trial
> much more determinedly than any
> heathen desiring to sleep with his wife.
> The water, I can see it, is reaching up to my chest,
> and I am sailing off on my last voyage.
> And as nobody is going to see me off,
> I'd simply like to shake some hands
>
> . . .
>
> I'd like to think that I didn't sing in vain.
> (lines 49–50, 110–116, 169)

The hands that Brodsky would like, yet will not be able to shake are, specifically, the hands of a certain "Madam" (that is, M. B., or Mary):

> Madam, you will forgive the disjointedness of my thoughts, my agitation.
> After all, you know, where I was sailing
>
> . . .
>
> And in this bottle at your feet,
> a humble testimony to the fact that I drowned
> like an astronaut among the planets,
> You will find what no longer exists.
> (lines 215–216, 248–252)

The irony of Brodsky's "Entertaintment" will hardly escape the reader. What for the poet is a matter of existential significance ("I realize that I have lost the trial") and, within the poem's overall conceit of the capsized sailor-poet, literally a matter of life and death is cast as a mere pastime for his Muse, who unlike Dante's Beatrice does not lift a finger on the poet's behalf.

In the process of fashioning himself as a new Dante and Marianna Basmanova, implicitly, as a new Beatrice, Brodsky crucially displaces Dante's poetics. He inverts its ethical matrix, which is predicated on the unquestionable and unimpugned virtuousness of Beatrice (as the very embodiment of love), owing to which Dante is capable of being redeemed.[67] Beatrice's moral rectitude and fidelity to Dante constitute the ethical premise of the latter's entire poetic-existential project, which forfeits its viability without it. This means that above all and against the grain of its ostensibly positive hermeneutic thrust, Brodsky's recourse to and displacement of the ethical-poetic paradigm of Dante's relationship with Beatrice ought to be read in negative terms, as an *exercise in failure.* The model of Dante and Beatrice, Brodsky suggests, is bound to fail as an ethical-poetic paradigm in a world in which Bice is—pardon my French—a "bitch" and hence not able or willing to "succor him who bore her such love [and] whom death . . . assails. . . . "[68] In other words, what Brodsky actually seems to be saying in donning the mask of Dante is that this self-figuration, which may have worked for many an exiled writer before him, does not work for him. In a world in which the very embodiment of virtue, Beatrice, has joined the ranks of those traitors who are condemned to suffering in the *Inferno*'s ninth circle, aspiring to become a new Dante is a futile endeavor. Brodsky's admonition that "one should be very careful about metaphors when dealing with history" acquires particular significance in light of the perceived moral discrepancy between Dante's Beatrice and her latter-day Russian avatar.[69]

If Brodsky's metaphorical identification with Dante is ultimately meant to signify its own impossibility, its own failure, why, we need to ask, does Brodsky choose to engage in the autobiographical conceit of donning the Italian's mask in the first place? Why this ostensibly futile endeavor of a poetic *via negativa?*

A simple and superficial answer to this question has to do with Dante's overall significance as an inflated cultural prop—that is, with the fact that more often than not the infinitely rich and detailed worlds conjured in the *Divine Comedy* (the *Inferno* in particular) come in handy, as it were, yielding images that are all too easy to graft onto many a concrete, real-life situation prior to critical reflection. At one time or another we all most likely have found ourselves in a situation that may aptly be thought of, captured, and depicted in the language and imagery of Dante. This is precisely what Brodsky has in mind when he points to such overused images as the proverbial *selva oscura* (lifted from Dante's text) where countless authors (including Brodsky) have lost their way over the centuries, or when he observes that "an exiled writer will most likely evoke Ovid's Rome, Dante's Florence, and—after a small pause—Joyce's Dublin."[70] An excellent case in point is Brodsky's casual reference in the course of an interview to the prisoner train that took him to his place of exile in the Russian North as "a kind of hell on wheels . . . straight out of . . . Dostoevsky or Dante."[71] Here Dante is invoked not on the basis of his presumed heuristic-poetic singularity—obviously the point can be made equally with Dostoevsky (and others)—but simply because, it would seem, he happens to be, along with Dostoevsky, the first to come to Brodsky's mind during the conversation.

A more complex answer, which takes into account and does justice to the high level of philosophical sophistication and self-reflection that characterize Brodsky's poetics, has to do with the question of his poetic *pedigree.* Although it can pre-

sumably be traced, according to Brodsky, "all the way back to Adam," the more
immediate and contextually relevant links in the chain of his poetic filiation are,
as I have documented, Mandelstam and Dante.[72] In fashioning himself *per impossibile* as a new Dante, Brodsky accomplishes several contextually relevant goals: (1)
He explicitly acknowledges and pays homage to his poetic descent, thus making
good on his stipulation that a poet's "real" biography is to be sited in his "meters,
rhymes, and metaphors," that is, in his intertextual relations with others—poets
in particular. (2) He stages what his poetry would or could be like *if it were indeed
possible* for him to be a new Dante, thereby endorsing and smoothly continuing
the line of poetic succession. In other words, in *pretending* to be a new Dante,
Brodsky gives us a fiction or simulacrum of what he and his poetry decidedly are
not: the work of a new Dante. (3) Finally, in so doing, he engages in a metapoetic
exercise, an *étude* of sorts in the uses and abuses—his own included—of Dante
as master trope, saying, as it were, "This is what I, as a poet who has experienced
exile, persecution, and loss, may be expected to do in line with many an exiled
writer before me, and this is what it would actually look like if I chose to pursue
this course seriously. . . . " In this reading, Brodsky's figuration of the new Dante
reveals itself as a cautionary poetic "illustration" of his theoretical caveat as to
"the reasonable element of danger" involved in any kind of "easy" recourse to
Dante as model exile, and so on—the danger, as I have suggested, of *not* taking
the road "less traveled," of following the beaten track and becoming poetically
trivial, and most important, as I explain shortly, of finding oneself metaphorically
disfigured.[73]

Which brings me to my last, historically and biographically motivated answer
to the question of why Brodsky may have chosen Dante as an alter ego by way
of a poetological *via negativa*. This answer dovetails with what I have advanced
as the cautionary aspect of Brodsky's autobiographical conceit and pertains to
his overall Stoic objective at "all costs . . . to avoid granting [himself] the status
of the victim." Insofar as Dante can be said to have cast himself as too much of
a victim of party politics for Brodsky's taste—as "a humble Italian in unmerited
exile" who had been forced to "leave everything beloved most dearly" and who has
"come to know how salt is the taste of another's bread, and how hard the path to
descend and mount by another man's stairs"[74]—he will hardly be the appropriate role model for a poet like Brodsky, who goes out of his way to cast his own
compulsory exile as "a kind of success" brought about by his "transition from a
political and economic backwater [the Soviet Union] to an industrially advanced
society with the latest word on individual liberty on its lips, [which] for an exiled
writer [is] in many ways like going home—because he gets closer to the seat of the
[democratic] ideals which inspired him all along."[75] Implicitly relying on the Stoic

conception of exile as nothing more than a "change of place," Brodsky muses, "At the end of the day, any new country . . . is merely the continuation of space. Everything depends on the conduct of any given person in this new space."[76] Thus, were Brodsky indeed to be taken at his ostensible word as far as his self-stylization as a new Dante is concerned, he would—against the overall Stoic thrust of his ethics and hence his poetics—inevitably have to be taken for what he *de facto* was, yet did not want to be taken for, namely, grist for the mills of *Realsozialismus*— that is, one in a long line of artists who have, like Ovid, Dante, Mandelstam, and countless others, been "sacrificed," in one way or another, on the altar of politics. Thus, Brodsky's taking "care of ethical matters" can be said to consist precisely and signally in disclosing the limitations of *Dante* as an ethical-poetic paradigm, in pointing up the "danger" lurking behind the temptation of fashioning oneself as a new Dante.

Given the semantic and ethical complexities of Brodsky's convoluted engagement with Dante, as I have uncovered it; furthermore, given his conceptualization of the emergence of poetry in terms of the dialectic of betrayal and fidelity; and finally, given his implicit presentation of *New Stanzas to Augusta* in terms of his own fidelity to his love for and affair with M. B., the most productive way of reading Brodsky's "experiment in Dante," I suggest, is as an exemplary instantiation and focalization of his overall attempt to explore and articulate poetically what he experienced or understood to be the truth of the event of his love and multiple betrayal, as described earlier.

This truth, however—as far as the Muse's promiscuity and the poet's putative fidelity are concerned—is not quite as clear-cut, ethically speaking, as I have made it out to be thus far for heuristic purposes. For according to Brodsky's own testimony, he is not and does not cast himself as the dejected victim of his Muse's infidelity. Like M. B., Brodsky too begins an affair with a third party. While his Russian Muse is busy inspiring a rival poet (Bobyšev), Brodsky himself is busy being the mouthpiece of a rival Muse, about whom he is "completely crazy"—the Muse of the English language and its poetry.[77] Ever since his first encounter in 1962 with the works of Robert Frost, with whom "it all started," and especially with John Donne (the latter in the epigraph to Ernest Hemingway's novel *For Whom the Bell Tolls*, on which Brodsky's 1962 "coming of age" poem "Great Elegy to John Donne" "is entirely based"), Brodsky had avowedly been smitten with the English Muse.[78] During his exile in the Russian north, in particular, this "fairly fresh [affair]" with his English mistress, carried on unbeknownst to his "Russian wife," gained momentum—that is, Brodsky "began to translate English poetry, Donne especially" while in Norenskoe—and subsequently developed into a "long-lasting affair" that would eventually turn "into a kind of marriage."[79] It is critical at this point to take note of the tension between Brodsky's postulate of the poet's "monogamous . . . attachment" to language and the Muse *as such* and his concomitant, singularizing observation that "it could . . . be argued that all *one's* capacity for fidelity gets spent on *one's* Muse [and] *one's* language" (emphasis added), which suggests, conversely, that each poet is attached to *his or her very own* Muse, and hence language, and not to either in general.[80] Brodsky, for one, overtly spends *his* "capacity for fidelity" on (at least) two very concrete Muses— his Russian and English Muses. In other words, this "poet's passion" reveals itself as not monogamous at all.[81] To the "*ménage à troi*" involving "two guys and a girl," in which he found himself willy-nilly embroiled and with which he was "mostly preoccupied" during his trial and sentencing, Brodsky opposes his actively pursued, interlocutionary *ménage à troi*—involving 'one guy and two girls' this time—with his Russian and English Muses. Brodsky's own 'poetic philandering' in the face of multiple betrayal yet again underscores his overall affairistic notion and practice of poetry, and further separates him from his ostensible role model, Dante, whose entire poetic and existential project is presented, from the *New Life* to the *Divine Comedy*, as hinging on his poetic, if not carnal, fidelity to his *one* Muse: the "blessed Beatrice."[82]

The overall upshot of my discussion of Brodsky's multipronged dialogue with Dante can be summed up as follows: Being or, rather, attempting to be a new Dante means not being able to be(come) a new Dante even though the figure of the Italian *qua* cultural prop and hermeneutic set piece virtually obtrudes itself on the poet. The overall novelty of the new Dante would then consist emphatically in the poet's *not* being (able to be) a "Dante"; in turn, the concomitant novelty of the new Beatrice would consist in her *not* being (able to be) a "Beatrice." Attempting to be a new Dante means realizing that this attempt is bound to fail because neither the new Dante nor the new Beatrice play according to the same poetic and ethical rules—the rules of the *dolce stil nuovo*—as Dante and Beatrice.[83]

If, however, the new Dante is not a "Dante" and if the new Beatrice is not a "Beatrice," then who are they? The solution to the riddle of the new Dante and his Beatrice has been out in the open all along, contained in the very name of the titular addressee—the putative new Beatrice—of the new Dante's "chief accomplishment": the *New Stanzas to Augusta*, Brodsky's most eloquent testimony to his affair with the English Muse, whose countenance he first glimpsed in the works of Robert Frost and John Donne. Unlike M. B., the English Muse can, as I explicate shortly, indeed be said to have succored "him who bore her such love [when] death . . . assail[ed]" him and when he "call[ed] upon [her] ayde," enabling him to achieve poetically his goal to "try to avoid granting [himself] the status of the victim," thereby indeed fully taking "care of ethical matters."[84] How Brodsky achieves this goal, in the process turning himself into a latter-day Byron—the real new Dante—is the focus of the remainder of this chapter.

"Dearest Augusta"

I have a passion for the name of "Mary"
For once it was a magic sound to me. . . .

But there are forms which Time to touch forbears,
And turns aside his scythe to vulgar things:
Such as was Mary's Queen of Scots. . . .

What you have with Maria, whether it lasts just through
today and a part of tomorrow, or whether it lasts for a long
life is the most important thing that can happen to a human
being.[85]

I begin with two basic questions: Who is Augusta? And why would Brodsky write *New Stanzas* to her and consider them his "chief accomplishment"?

As with the term *new Dante,* the fact that Brodsky uses the attribute *new* to qualify his *Stanzas* means that they must be modeled on a precursor text addressed to a woman named Augusta. Determining the precursor text is an easy-enough task. On July 24, 1816, three months after leaving England for good, on April 25, 1816, George Gordon, sixth Lord Byron, then residing in Diodati near Geneva, composed a set of six stanzas addressed to his paternal half-sister and erstwhile lover, Augusta Mary Leigh, that was first published as "Stanzas to ———" in December 1816 and posthumously reprinted with the addressee's name under the title with which it would go down in literary history, namely, "Stanzas to Augusta."[86] These stanzas, along with a set of eleven quatrains written on the eve of his departure from England and published in early June 1816 under the title "To ———" and a set of sixteen stanzas written in August 1816 in Geneva and posthumously published as "To Augusta" in Thomas Moore's *Letters and Journals of Lord Byron: With Notices of His Life* (1830), constitute the bulk of Byron's explicit love poems to Augusta, in which the notoriously promiscuous poet, who "sustained [his] share of worldly shocks," praises his sister-cum-lover's unwavering fidelity to him throughout their lives and especially throughout the turmoil of his messy and scandalous separation from his wife, Annabella Milbanke:[87]

Though the day of my destiny's over,
  And the star of my faith hath declined,
Thy soft heart refused to discover
  The faults which so many could find;
Though thy soul with my grief was acquainted
  It shrunk not to share it with me,
And the love which my spirit hath painted
  It never hath found but in thee. .

There is many a pang to pursue me:
  They may crush, but they shall not contemn;
They may torture but shall not subdue me;
  'Tis of thee that I think—not of them.

Though human, thou didst not deceive me,
  Though woman, thou didst not forsake,
Though lov'd, though forborest to grieve me,
  Though slandered, thou never couldst shake. . . . [88]

Similarly, in "To ———," Byron extols Augusta's "fidelity" to him in the face of the
"world's defied rebuke":

When all around grew drear and dark,
  An reason half withheld her ray . . .
Thou wert the solitary star
  Which rose and set not to the last . . .
And stood between me and the night,
  For ever shining sweetly nigh. . . .
There's more in one soft word of thine
  Than in the world's defied rebuke.
Thou stood'st, as stands a lovely tree,
  That still unbroken, though gently bent,
Still waves with fond fidelity
  Its boughs above a monument. . . .
Then let the ties of baffled love
  Be broken—thine will never break;
The heart can feel but will not move;
  Thy soul, though soft will never shake. [89]

In "To Augusta," finally, Byron is most explicit about his attachment to his half-
sister, as well as about his own role in bringing about his "proper woe":

My sister! my sweet sister! if a name
  Dearer and purer were, it should be thine. . . .
  There yet are two things in my destiny,—

A world to roam through, and a home with thee. . . .
   The first were nothing had I still the last,
   It were the haven of my happiness;
   But other claims and other ties thou hast,
   And mine is not the wish to make them less.
   A strange doom is thy father's son's, and past
   Recalling, as it lies beyond redress. . . .
   I have sustained my share of worldly shocks,
   The fault was mine; nor do I seek to screen
   My errors with defensive paradox;
   I have been cunning in mine overthrow,
The careful pilot of my proper woe.
   Mine were the faults, and mine be their reward.[90]

Without delving too deeply into the historical circumstances and particulars of arguably "the most documented and dissected marriage [and separation] in literary history," suffice it to note that in the course of Byron's and Annabella's four-month separation proceedings, such "facts" as Lord Byron's love affair with his half-sister, his homosexual practices and his physical cruelty toward and alleged engagement in sodomy with his wife became the subjects of the latest gossip among London's high society.[91] It is critical to register at this point that—notwithstanding accounts to the contrary from Thomas Moore, Byron's friend and first biographer, to more recently, Fiona MacCarthy—Byron's departure from England following the breakup of his marriage was not compulsory, even though it was certainly motivated by his just fears of the social and, potentially, legal repercussions of the coming to light of his engagement in incest and sodomy (not to mention his enormous debts, which would have contributed to his decision to "cast off the ties of love [and] enmity . . . along with the sanctions of the responsible and respectable"). Byron left England never to return not because he had to but because he decided to do so.[92] Regardless of, and however ostensibly plausible, the reasons for his departure and subsequent absence from England for the remainder of his life may have been, Byron *did* have the option to ride out the storm generated by the breakup of his marriage in England, especially given that Annabella had agreed to disavow officially the truth of the "criminal charges of incest and sodomy" that were leveled against him during their separation.[93] Unlike Brodsky (and others) and notwithstanding the threat of social excommunication and potential prosecution, Byron was *de facto* neither forced to leave his native country nor ever barred from returning to it. In other words, Byron's legendary exile—spent mainly in Switzerland, Italy, and Greece, where he died on April 19, 1824—was self-imposed. In a letter to his friend Scrope Davies of December 7, 1818, the poet sums up his predicament in April 1816 without the slightest allusion to compulsion: "You can hardly have forgotten the circumstances under which I quitted England, nor the rumours of which I was the Subject—if *they were true* I was unfit for England, if *false* England was unfit for me."[94]

Much more important in the present context, however, than the moot historical-psychological question as to the perceived degree of necessity of Byron's leaving England is the fact that Byron himself takes full responsibility for having brought about his own "overthrow," and thus for having masterminded his own exile: "The fault was mine," he writes to Augusta from Switzerland, "nor do I seek to screen / My errors with defensive paradox; / I have been cunning in mine overthrow, / The careful pilot of my proper woe. / Mine were the faults, and mine be their reward." Clearly, in his most ruthlessly honest and introspective moments, Byron viewed himself as everything but the victim of a world presumably "bent [his] deeds to crosse," suggesting instead that the "world's . . . rebuke" as well as the "many a pang to pursue" him were not only well-deserved but cunningly and carefully crafted and devised by him! As much as he would like to indulge in self-pity, stylizing himself as the victim ("They may crush . . . / They may torture") of what one of his Soviet biographers calls, in a typically tendentious attempt at casting Lord Byron as a socialist-cum-freedom-fighter *avant la lettre*, "the witch-hunt that forced him to leave [bourgeois] England for good"—at the end of the day Byron cannot but admit that *he* "was . . . to blame [for his] own misery."[95] Like all of those exiles who, according to Brodsky, "will most likely evoke . . . Dante's [exile]" when speaking about their own, Byron too dons the mask of Dante—most pointedly in the long poem "The Prophecy of Dante" (1819), a tribute to the great poet as well as to his mistress Teresa Guiccioli, whom he expressly refers to as "my own bright Beatrice."[96] Although Byron endeavors to cast his exile in terms of an undeserved punishment in writing, in the name of Dante, "They made an Exile—not a Slave of me" (Canto 1, line 178)—a statement fully applicable to Brodsky's situation—the reader knows that he intentionally obfuscates the truth about what he himself has disclosed, most explicitly in "To Augusta," as his self-made "overthrow."

With this minimum of historical-contextual information regarding the significance of Byron's "Stanzas [to Augusta]" in mind, we need to ask, what does Brodsky achieve in calling his "own bright Beatrice" Augusta and his life's "chief accomplishment" *New Stanzas to Augusta*?

To begin with, in casting M. B. in terms of Byron's half-sister—presumably a moral bedrock and epitome of fidelity—Brodsky gives back to M. B. the ethical irreprehensibility that she has ironically been credited with *qua* new Beatrice; in other words, through Byron's particular construal of Augusta (and I should stress that here I am dealing only with Augusta's image as presented in Byron's poems and not with the historical Augusta, who obviously was as guilty of infidelity and incest as her half-brother and thus not really a candidate for the first prize in virtuousness), Brodsky *poetically* vindicates *his* Augusta's status as a new Beatrice.[97] Furthermore, in casting M. B. as Augusta, Brodsky inevitably casts himself as a latter-day Byron. This move is in turn crucial in several interlocking respects.

First and most important, evidence to the contrary notwithstanding, it allows Brodsky to translate himself into the "careful pilot of [his] proper woe"—into the agent of his multiple betrayal, including his victimization at the hands of a totalitarian regime and the infidelity of a "beloved woman." As a new Byron, Brodsky poetically achieves self-empowerment and makes good on his Stoic postulate at "all costs . . . to avoid granting [himself] the status of the victim." As a new Byron, Brodsky cannot be said to *have been betrayed and exiled*; rather, he emerges as having *actively perpetrated betrayal and gone into exile.* As a new Byron, Brodsky cannot be said to have been at the receiving end of infidelity; rather, he emerges as having *actively engaged in infidelity.* Through the conduit of Byron, Brodsky can be said to succeed poetically in turning himself into an agent in a situation in which he was denied agency. In other words, it is emphatically owing to its Byronic substratum that Brodsky's self-inscription as a new Dante addressing his new Beatrice—*a fortiori* justified in light of Byron's own impersonation of Dante—acquires full significance as an act of poetic self-empowerment, that is, as an *ethical* act. In constituting himself as a new Dante-cum-Byron, Brodsky can indeed be said to be taking "care of ethical matters," to be sounding fully the concrete "ethical consequences" of his metaphysical, historical, and poetic predicament.[98]

Second, in adopting the persona of Byron, Brodsky not only writes himself into and continues the tradition of Russian and Soviet Byronism, thus bringing into full focus the literary-historical dimension of *New Stanzas to Augusta* and his poetry in general;[99] but he also underscores the emphatically *literary-biographical* thrust of his poetic engagement with his "only life," insofar as Byron's "literary enterprise: poetry as autobiography" can be said to have generated the paradigmatic literary biography or biographical legend. "Byron created," Tomaševskij notes, "the canonical biography for a lyrical poet. . . . The . . . poet *was* his own hero. His *life* was poetry. . . . "[100] In fashioning himself as a new Dante via Byron, and *vice versa*, Brodsky doubly underscores—by simultaneously impersonating two literary figures who emphatically infuse their poetry with their "only life"—that his life too ought to be viewed as feeding into (and informed by) literary biography—the poet's "real" biography, as it constitutes and articulates itself in and through his "vowels and sibilants, . . . his meters, rhymes, and metaphors," that is, in and through his poetry. By dint of the Byronic mask in particular, Brodsky admittedly transforms himself into the prototypical "romantic hero," who is none other than "the poet himself."[101] (Moreover, in casting his treatment at the hands of the Soviet state as a variation on "a remarkable theme that runs all through Russian literature, [the theme of] 'the poet and the tsar,'" Brodsky equally articulates the literary-biographical sublation of his real-life affairs.)[102]

Third and last, in injecting the new Dante with a strong dose of Byron and the new Beatrice with a dose of Augusta, thereby mapping his literary biography onto what is arguably one of the most affair-ridden literary biographies of the modern era; and furthermore, in choosing, as his literary-biographical chief point of reference what is arguably one of the most momentous events in Byron's life—the break-up of his marriage and everything that it brought to light about Byron, followed by his departure from England—Brodsky yet again unmistakably signals the affairistic thrust of his own poetics, exemplarily staged in *New Stanzas to Augusta*. Brodsky can thereby be said to articulate poignantly his creative fidelity to the truth of his poetry's real-life matrix—a truth that could be formulated as, *If you do not want to founder as a new Dante, you have to become a new Byron.* Nowhere does the latter come to the fore as vividly as in the following lines from the collection's titular poem, "New Stanzas to Augusta," written in internal exile in September 1964. In this poem the speaker meditates on his exile through the "speech masks" of both Byron and Dante simultaneously:

> Here on the hills, amidst the empty heavens,
> amidst roads that lead only into the wood,
> life recedes from itself. . . . [103]

As in the case of Celan's interlocution with Shakespeare, and Grünbein's interlocution with Seneca, *New Stanzas to Augusta* ultimately enjoins being read as the record of Brodsky's affair with Byron himself *qua* metonymic embodiment of the English Muse—literally bespoken by Brodsky's Augusta: To the extent that the Augusta we know from Byron's stanzas can be said to be a literary creation, Brodsky's poetic log of *his* obsession and affair with *his* Augusta can be said to transpire metonymically as an oblique interlocution with the creator of the poetic Augusta himself, that is, Byron. If for Byron Augusta avowedly functioned as the (idealized) safe haven where the poet imagined himself being able to make berth in times of distress, for Brodsky it was Byron himself who can be said to have functioned as an ally during the period of Brodsky's "greatest . . . trouble" (and beyond). Byron's verse can be said to have extended "all [its] gentle grace" to Brodsky when he "call[ed] upon [his] ayde."[104]

Unlike Celan's interlocution with Shakespeare, however, Brodsky's interlocution with Byron is imbued with a strong sense of that "irony grown on the soil of reality" that he explicitly brings to bear on his own situation—fully in line, by the way, with the "brickbat" irony of Byron's poetics—and which implicitly informs his overall self-fashioning as Byron-cum-Dante. This is evidenced in the following lines from "Venetian Stanzas" in which Brodsky's Byronic hero-exile is outed as merely striking the pose of a hero-exile—as a figure or trope of a particular cultural obsession with the East that is characteristic of the nineteenth century:

> O, nineteenth century! Pining for the East! The pose
> of the exile on the cliff! . . . [105]

In a famous 1808 oil painting by George Sanders that Byron commissioned in anticipation of his expedition to Greece, Albania, and Turkey, Byron is depicted as having just disembarked from a boat and standing on a rock with his page, Robert Rushton, in the background looking up at his master and holding the skiff, both men's hair and ascots afloat in the gusty wind. This image may well have inspired Brodsky's presentation of the exile as a cultural stereotype—as the figuration of what Edward Said calls (with particular reference to the Imperial aspirations of eighteenth- and nineteenth-century Europe) *orientalism,* understood as a "collection of dreams, images, and vocabularies" articulating Europeans' fascination with and longing for "what lies east of the dividing line" between Europe and "Asia or the East." The "pure East," as Goethe calls it, is on the one hand rife with "unimaginable antiquity, inhuman beauty, boundless distance," and on the other, with the "eccentricities of Oriental life, . . . its exotic spatial configurations, its hopelessly strange languages, its seemingly perverse morality."[106] In other words, the pined-for "East" of Brodsky's Byronic posturer, as well as the latter himself, are disclosed as inventions of "colonial fantasy,"[107] fueled by, among other things, such nineteenth-century personages as Lord Byron, whose own fascination with and exploration of the "East"—most vividly articulated in such "oriental" texts as *The Giaour: A Fragment of a Turkish Tale* (1814), *The Bride of Abydos: A Turkish Tale* (1813), and *The Corsair: A Tale* (1813)—certainly contributed to the creation of the very trope of the internally conflicted Romantic hero-outcast, the "self-exiled . . . stranger in this . . . world," which he has come to embody exemplarily.[108]

In light of his emphasis on the tropical character of the modern exile-poet, Brodsky's self-fashioning as Byron-cum-Dante reveals itself as ironic in at least two respects. First, it suggests that even an exile as involuntary, "unpoetic," and viscerally real as Brodsky's compulsory relegation to the Russian North and subsequent expulsion from the Soviet Union cannot avoid being partially perceived and experienced as (and thus reduced to the status of) a cultural trope, and is thereby, to a certain extent, voided of its painful existential significance and historical weight.[109] Second, it suggests that even though Brodsky's exile consisted of moving in the opposite direction of Byron's exile, that is, westward rather than eastward, Brodsky too cannot avoid succumbing to a "colonial fantasy," albeit one that is obsessed with the West rather than the East—that is to say, the occidentalist "fantasy" of an "industrially advanced society with the latest word on individual liberty on its lips[, which] for an exiled writer [is] in many ways like going home—because he gets closer to the seat of the ideals which inspired him all along."[110] Brodsky's decision, upon arriving in Vienna in June 1972, to accept Carl Proffer's invitation to immigrate to the United States rather than proceeding to Israel—his official destination in the "East"—and thus, in a way repeating the trajectory of the eastbound exile, doubly underscores the irony of the fact that although he moved westward rather than eastward, his "West" reveals itself to be as much of a cultural-poetic fiction as the "East" of Byron (and others).[111] Isn't it precisely this irony, bespoken by the inevitable tropicality of the modern exile, that warrants Brodsky's presentation of his Byronic hero's vector as a "comedy"— most explicitly in *New Stanzas to Augusta*, Brodsky's very own *Divine Comedy*?[112]

As I mentioned earlier, unlike Mandelstam and, especially, Grünbein, Brodsky is critical and chary of relying on metaphor as a historical master trope that would presumably allow the poet to travel through time and assume the identities of whomever he chooses—if only for the duration of the poetic journey—and still be able to articulate and do justice to the truth of his own existential trajectory: "One should be very careful about metaphors when dealing with history [given] the singular nature of historical occurrence," Brodsky admonishes.[113] If, as Brodsky suggests, a person's vector is constituted through the "admixture of geography / to time," then metaphorical parallelisms across time and space, while capable of equipping the poet with "a more stereoscopic picture of what amounts to [his own] life," by definition fall short of capturing the irreducible singularity of his or her vector.[114] To the extent that Brodsky would certainly not risk obliterating this singularity in metaphorically "equating what is not the same" (in *becoming* Byron and Dante, so to speak), his self-fashioning as Byron-cum-Dante cannot possibly be interpreted as being predicated on a facile metaphorical identity swap motivated by external biographical parallels or similarities such as exile, loss, and so on.[115] If it is true, as Nietzsche argues, that metaphor, language's prime operator, abstracts from the "real" and obfuscates the "truth" of the singularity of any given referent, then Brodsky could hardly be said to be able to do justice to the singularity of his vector in metaphorically sublating himself into Byron-cum-Dante.[116] If Brodsky's becoming Byron-cum-Dante is to be convincing as an exemplary instantiation of his conception of poetry as "an act of love . . . for . . . reality," if it is to do justice to and articulate his fidelity to the truth of his "personal affairs," and if it is, most fundamentally, to be acknowledged as an exemplary manifestation of what poetry *qua* "goal of our species" is capable of at its best—that is, of facilitating "lyricism becoming truth"—then it must be motivated from within Brodsky's "real" biography, that is, from within his and his interlocutors' "vowels and sibilants . . . meters, rhymes, and metaphors."[117] In other words, if Brodsky's engagement with Byron and Dante and his concomitant accession to agency is to be convincing as his mode of becoming and remaining creatively faithful to the "Brodsky affair" and its aftermath, it must perforce be grounded in the very materiality of his and his interlocutors' poetry. Only if Brodsky's ventriloquism of Byron-cum-Dante can be shown to be motivated from within his "real"—that is, literary—biography as it articulates itself in and through the very linguistic makeup of his poetry, and only if his becoming Byron-cum-Dante addressing his Augusta-cum-Beatrice-cum-M. B. can be shown to be motivated from within the very texture of his poems and thus to be poetically "true" can his interlocution with Byron (and Dante) be said to have really succeeded—if only, as I have suggested, in the key of irony—as an act of self-empowerment, as an ethical act. How Brodsky accomplishes this crucial step toward poetically acquiring agency via Byron is the focus of this chapter's concluding reflections.

The key to understanding the "real," literary-biographical motivation and plausibility of Brodsky's adoption of the Byronic persona is to be found, I suggest, in one particular onomastic coincidence between the real and literary biographies of both poets—an onomastic continuity that materially (that is, phonically-linguistically, prosodically, and semantically) warrants Brodsky's casting of his "real" biography in Byronic terms. Above all, what can be said to motivate poetically Brodsky's impersonation of Byron is, I suggest, a contingent yet highly relevant historical-turned-literary-biographical fact involving a proper name. As in Brodsky's life and art, in Byron's life and art, too, the name Marianna as well as its nominal constituents—Mary and Anna—play a central role. Notwithstanding minor orthographical differences based on linguistic "particulars, and those merely local," in the lives and works of both poets the name Marianna as well as its nominal constituents acquire crucial poetic significance.[118]

Mary Anne, Mary, Mariamne, Marianna

In the summer of 1803, while sojourning at his ancestral home of Newstead Abbey, Byron fell "desperately and hopelessly in love" with his distant cousin Mary Anne Chaworth, whom he had first met in 1798 and who did not reciprocate his feelings, opting instead for one Jack Musters as her love interest and future husband.[119] "The young poet, who was then in his sixteenth year, while the object of his admiration was two years older," Thomas Moore writes, "seems to have drunk deepest of that fascination whose effects were to be so lasting;—six short summer weeks which he now passed in her company being sufficient to lay the foundation of a feeling for life."[120] What is especially noteworthy about Mary Anne in the present context is that Byron would write several poems to or about her, thereby unequivocally turning her into one of the literary facts of his biographical legend. Among the poems addressed to and commemorating his love for Mary Anne, "To My Dear Mary Anne," written on the occasion of his parting from her late in 1804, stands out as the only poem providing both of the addressees' given names in full (in his other poems to or about Mary Anne, she is addressed as Mary or Maria), and thus as marking the material import of the name Mary Anne within the very texture of Byron's poetry.[121]

As it happens, even prior to her translation into one of the (admittedly less well known) "Byron women"—even prior, that is, to her literary-biographical appropriation by Byron as one among the motley crew of female heroines feeding into his literary biography—Mary Anne had already been poetically coded and consequently can be said to have already presented herself to Byron *as a literary fact.* For in addition to being the proper name of the poet's real-life love interest, *Mary Anne* was also (as Thomas Moore points out, with particular attention to the significance for Byron of the very name *Mary Anne*) the title of the popular "pretty Welsh air, 'Mary Anne,'" which was, "partly, of course, on account of the name, [Byron's] especial favorite" among the tunes that "Miss Chaworth [would] play" for him in the course of the summer of 1803.[122] In other words, Byron's courtship of Mary Anne reveals itself as already framed in literary terms. His ostensible translation of real life (as embodied in his feelings for Mary Anne) into literature will to a certain extent already have transpired as a *literary act*, insofar as real life will have inevitably unfolded within the literary world of folk poetry.

After making several brief appearances, albeit in the form of its separate components, in such poems as "To Mary," "To Mary, on Receiving Her Picture," and "To Anne,"[123] Marianna returns *in toto* in "Herod's Lament for Mariamne" (1815), Byron's take on the classical story of King Herod the Great of Judea and his ill-starred wife, Marianne.[124] Aside from yet again underscoring the inherently literary dimension of the name *Marianna(e)* or *Mary Anne*, Byron's recourse to this story, told first by Flavius Josephus, is especially noteworthy in the present context because it contains one detail that, although not explicitly mentioned in "Herod's Lament," implicitly bears on both Brodsky's affair with Byron and the overall literary-biographical thrust of his poetics. It is said that one day, before departing from Judea on state business, Herod—reportedly an insanely jealous husband—"left his uncle Joseph in charge of the affairs of the realm, secretly giving him instructions that if anything (fatal) happened to him while he was [away], Joseph should at once do away with Mariamme, too. For, he said, he was very much in love with his wife and feared the outrage . . . if even after his death she were pursued by another man because of her beauty."[125] Suspecting Joseph of "sexual intimacy" with his wife upon his return, Herod gave "orders for Joseph to be executed." It is said that shortly after this episode, Herod again left on official business. This time he left his wife in the care of, among others, "his steward Joseph," whom he ordered to "keep [her] under surveillance. . . . " The next time Herod returned "to his kingdom," he again suspected his wife of infidelity, "brought an elaborately framed accusation against her" to the effect that she was planning to poison him, and had her executed. Subsequently he came bitterly to regret her death, "frequently utter[ing] unseemly laments." The story behind "Herod's Lament for Mariamne" hinges on the multiple valence of the name Joseph—Josephus, the author; Joseph, the uncle; Joseph, the steward—and clearly this fact, which is implicitly summoned in Byron's poem, cannot fail to factor into the literary-biographical import of Joseph Brodsky's affair with *his* Marianna.

Yet another contextually significant onomastic detail in Byron's biography and hence in his biographical legend—a detail that *historically* justifies Brodsky's mapping of his literary-biographical coordinates onto Byron's—consists in the fact that Byron too had a lover named Marianna, with whom he started an affair soon after taking up residence in Venice in November 1816. Giving free rein to his orientalist fantasies, he wrote to his friend Thomas Moore on November 17, 1816,

> I have fallen in love, which, next to falling into the canal . . . is the best or worst thing I could do. I have got some extremely good apartments in the house of a "Merchant of Venice" [Pietro Segati, a draper], who is a good deal occupied with business, and has a wife in her twenty-second year. Marianna (that is her name) is in her appearance altogether like an antelope. She has the large, black, oriental eyes, with that peculiar expression in them which is seen rarely among Europeans—even the Italians—and which many of the Turkish women give themselves by tinging the eyelid. . . . [126]

Similarly, in a letter to his publisher, John Murray, of November 25, 1816, Byron emphasizes Marianna's oriental allure:

> I have fallen in love. . . . I am therefore in love—fathomless love—but lest you should make some splendid mistake—& envy me the possession of some of those Princesses or Countesses with whose affections your English voyagers are apt to invest themselves—I beg leave to tell you—that my Goddess is only the wife of a "Merchant of Venice"—but then she is pretty as an Antelope—is but two & twenty years old—has large black Oriental eyes—with the Italian countenance—and dark glossy hair . . . besides a long postscript of graces . . . enough to furnish out a new Chapter of Solomon's song. . . . [127]

Although the question of Brodsky's awareness of this biographical detail—available, I should note, to the general, including the Russian, public at least since the publication of Thomas Moore's *Letters and Journals of Lord Byron* in 1830—has no effective bearing on the viability of my argument, which depends primarily on the material presence of the name Marianna in Byron's poetry, it is very likely that Brodsky *did in fact know* about it, given that in 1963 an abbreviated Russian edition of Byron's *Letters and Journals* containing the poet's depictions of his affair with Marianna Segati was issued by the Soviet Academy of Sciences.[128] In light of Byron's account of his liaison in Venice with the "oriental-eyed" Marianna Segati, Brodsky's earlier-cited invocation in "Venetian Stanzas" of the Byronic "exile on the cliff" longing for "the East" emphatically enjoins being read in light of Byron's Venetian period.[129] (Significantly, the Russian translation of Byron's depiction of Marianna's eyes as "oriental eyes" is *vostochnye glaza*, that is, Eastern eyes.)

"I Loved You So Deeply, So Hopelessly!"

To be admitted as a full-fledged fact into Brodsky's "real" biography, *Marianna* must be shown to be—similar to its poetic use by Byron—a constitutive element of the very fabric of Brodsky's "vowels and sibilants . . . his meters, rhymes, and metaphors," of the very material and rhetorical texture of his poetry. Although none of Brodsky's poems or essays (not even his most overtly Byronic text, "New Stanzas to Augusta") contains the name Marianna, two of its nominal components do appear in a number of poems, such as "To the Victories of Rumjanceva," "Letter in a Bottle" (a.k.a. "Entertainment for Mary"), "Nunc Dimittis," and most important, the 1974 cycle "Twenty Sonnets to Mary, Queen of Scots," to which I now turn.[130]

In the "Twenty Sonnets" cycle, which among other things is a poetic meditation on the passage of time, history, and the human condition as well as on the vagaries of love, fidelity, and betrayal through the prism of the Scottish queen's eventful and affair-ridden life, Brodsky's interlocution with Byron reaches its peak. "Twenty Sonnets" is not only the longest unit in *New Stanzas to Augusta*; it is also the volume's most outstanding contribution from a literary-historical and aesthetic viewpoint in that it saliently testifies to Brodsky's formal departure from the Russian literary tradition, in which the "sonnet is not a favored form," and toward the English poetic tradition, in which the sonnet has been a "favored form."[131] Considering its subject matter, as well as Brodsky's presentation of its addressee as the "dark lady of my sonnets" à la Shakespeare, the sequence as a whole enjoins being read as the record of the poet's extended tryst with the English Muse.[132] What makes Brodsky's figuration of *his* sonnet sequence in terms of Shakespeare's especially noteworthy in the present context—in addition to testifying further to Brodsky's infatuation with the English Muse—is the fact that it bears signally on how we are supposed to interpret it. Insofar as Shakespeare's sonnets are centrally concerned with the poet's erotic obsessions, and insofar as the poet-sonneteer's erotic obsessions are, according to Brodsky, "essentially the dictate of the Muse," "Twenty Sonnets" must perforce be read as a poetological text—a complex and poignant instantiation of Brodsky's poetics of interlocution ("a poem—any poem, regardless of its subject—is in itself an act of love"), developed, it will be remembered, in response to the previously outlined triple void and, more specifically, to the concrete event of the poet's multiple betrayal.[133] In adding a Shakespearean twist to his sonnets, Brodsky not only injects them (and hence *New Stanzas to Augusta* as a whole) with the tension-filled dynamic of love, fidelity, and betrayal staged in Shakespeare's sonnet sequence, thereby yet again underscoring the erotic-affairistic dimension of his poetics; but more important, Brodsky also succeeds, I suggest, in creatively articulating his fidelity to the truth of the event of his "greatest . . . trouble." Like Celan, Brodsky too can be said to have poetically "to truths translated" what were the "faults" and "errors" of history, politics, friendship, and love in real life.[134]

Why does Brodsky single out Mary, Queen of Scots, from within the overall Byronic framework of *New Stanzas to Augusta*? At the most basic structural, historical, and thematic levels, Brodsky's invocation of and extended engagement with matters Scots can plausibly be read as a general tribute to Byron and Augusta—the volume's literary-biographical patrons—given that both were of Scottish extraction on the distaff side of their families.[135] In addressing the queen, moreover, Brodsky not only acknowledges and reinscribes *in his own name* Byron's explicit admiration for the queen—

But there are forms which Time to touch forbears,
And turns aside his scythe to vulgar things:
Such as was Mary's Queen of Scots. . . .

—but he also inevitably valorizes the fact (known to Byron, of course, and thus informing his admiring reference to the queen) that through her maternal grandfather, Robert, the Fourth Earl of Holdernesse and Eighth Baron Conyers, Augusta was the queen's direct descendant and is hence metonymically referenced in the queen's very name.[136] But of course Augusta's significance as the implicit addressee of the sonnets has been on the interpretive horizon all along. After all, Mary is her middle name and consequently cannot fail to contiguously signify Augusta. In implicitly apostrophizing Augusta and, by extension, M. B., "Twenty Sonnets" replicates and thereby reinforces the entire volume's pragmatic thrust.

The literary-biographical-historical skeleton of "Twenty Sonnets" is fleshed out with the concrete pragmatic-thematic details of its putative emergence. According to Sonnet 1 and Sonnet 20 (lines 1–8 and 10–14), the sequence was occasioned by the poet's encounter with a statue of the Scottish queen in the Jardin du Luxembourg in Paris:

Mary, the Scots are pigs after all.
What generation of the tartan clan
could have foreseen that you'd step down from the screen
and, as a statue, animate the gardens—
the Luxemburg, to be precise? Hither
I rambled to digest a Paris lunch and see,
with the eyes of an old ram,
the new gates and ponds.
Where I met you. And inspired by this encounter,
and because "the past revives anew
in my worn heart," having loaded
the old gun with classical grape-shot,
I am wasting, whatever's left of Russian speech,
on your *en face* and pale shoulders.

With a simple quill—not rebellious at all—
I've sung this encounter in a certain garden
with her who had, in nineteen forty-eight,
from the screen instructed me in matters of the heart.
May you adjudicate on:
(a) whether he has been a good student,
(b) this unusual company for a Russian
(c) his weak spot for gendered endings.

. . .

The contingent, being inevitable,
is of use for many a labor.
Living the life that I live,
I am grateful for the erstwhile snow-white
sheets of paper, now rolled up into a pipe.

The poet's "encounter" with the statue brings back memories. Among other things, he recalls a movie about Mary Queen of Scots that he saw as a child in 1948, and presumably an "affair of the heart" that he remembers in the *already remembered* words of Fedor Ivanovič Tjutčev's love lyric "K. B.," addressed to Baroness Krüdener:

I encountered you—and the past
Revives anew in my worn heart;
I remember the Golden days—
And my heart is so warm . . . [137]

As we find out from Sonnet 2 (lines 3–4 and 8–13), the movie in question featured Hitler's favorite actress, Zarah Leander, as Mary. It must thus have been the 1940 German production *Das Herz einer Königin,* an adaptation of the drama *Maria Stuart* by Friedrich Schiller, who is mentioned by name in the twelfth sonnet, and directed by Karl Fröhlich. It played at the Spartacus movie theater in Leningrad for a week in 1948 under the title *Doroga na Ešafot* (Road to the scaffold):

Mary, as a boy I saw Zarah
Leander walk, clip-clop, to the scaffold.
. . .
We all emerged into the light (or this world) from the movie theater,
but something calls us back at dusk
into the "Spartacus," whose plushy womb
is cozier than Europe by night.
Images of stars are there, the main attraction a brunette,
two pictures playing. . . . [138]

Sonnet 4 tells us why the statue triggers a revival of the past in the poet's *heart* in particular. The "external features" of the "beauty whom [he] . . . / loved" and with whom he—just like Mary and her third husband, James Hepburn, Earl of Bothwell[139]—would not make "a happy pair," presumably resemble those of the queen:

The beauty whom I later
loved more deeply than you loved Bothwell
shared certain external features with you

(I whisper automatically, "my God,"
when I recall them). We, too,
didn't make a happy pair.
She went off somewhere. . . .
In order to avoid destiny's straight line
I crossed another—the horizon's,
whose blade, Mary, is sharper than a knife's.
My head outstretched above this thing,
not for the oxygen, but for the nitrogen
that threatens to burst my crop—
the larynx . . . still . . . is grateful for the deal.

The fact that Brodsky's memories are quilted from swatches taken from the fabric
of others' texts (such as those by Tjutčev, Fröhlich, and Schiller, among others),
along with his reiterated avowal (in Sonnet 4, line 14; and Sonnet 20, line 13) that
he is actually "grateful," from a professional viewpoint ("the larynx . . . still . . . is
grateful for the deal"), for the fact that he did not "make a happy pair" with the
"beauty whom [he] . . . / loved" and that he subsequently migrated across the horizon (that is, was forced into exile) doubly underscores the literary-biographical
significance of both the poet's encounter with the statue and the past the statue
evokes.[140] The sublation of autobiography into biographical legend is most conspicuously accomplished in Brodsky's overt rewriting—which Peter France calls a
"wholesale deconstruction"[141]—of Pushkin's famous poem of 1829, "Ja vas ljubil"
(I loved you):

I loved you: love may not have
Completely been extinguished in my soul;
But may it not disconcert you any longer;
I do not want to make you sad anymore.
I loved you tacitly, hopelessly,
Torn between shyness and jealousy;
I loved you so sincerely, so tenderly,
May God grant you to be loved like this by another.[142]

Brodsky's "version" (Sonnet 6) reads as follows:

I loved you. Love is still (perhaps
it's only migraine) drilling through my brain.
Everything has long shattered into pieces.
I tried to shoot myself, but it's difficult
with a gun. What's more, the temples:
which one to choose? What spoiled it was not fear, but
too much thinking. Hell! What a nightmare!

I loved you so deeply, so hopelessly—
may God grant others—no way!
Although he is an expert in many things,
he won't . . . create twice
this fire in the bloodstream . . . ,
which melts one's fillings with the desire
to touch your—"breasts," strike—lips.

Brodsky's bathetic displacement into his own "illustrious vernacular" of Push-kin's stylistically elevated love lyric (in comparison with Brodsky's text, that is) is fully in line with the conversational, flippant, and vulgar tone set in the first sonnet's quite "unpoetic" depiction of the poet's quite "unpoetic" encounter with the queen's statue in the course of a casual stroll through the Luxembourg gardens to digest a presumable heavy lunch. It is also characteristic of the entire sonnet sequence, one of the central themes of which is the queen's legendary promiscu-ity[143]—subtly articulated in Brodsky's transformation of Pushkin's final "another" into "others" in Sonnet 6 (line 9), and most explicitly (if hyperbolically) addressed in Sonnet 5 (lines 1–5 and 11–14) and Sonnet 12 (lines 3–8):

The number of your lovers, Mary,
exceeded three,
four, ten, twenty, twenty-five.
For the crown, there is no greater downfall
than a one-night stand. . . .
Your Scots didn't get the difference
between a cot and a throne.
A rare bird in your century,
to your contemporaries you were a bitch.

Take Schiller, for instance: He showed it
to history. Mary, you didn't expect
that a German, snatching the bit,
would dig up this—let's be honest—ancient affair:
what does he care
with whom you did or did not sleep?

Obviously Brodsky loved not the queen or her statue but rather their real-life met-onymic avatar. In collapsing the statue's and the beloved's identities in the Pushki-nian "I loved you," Brodsky figuratively casts the "beauty whom [he] . . . / loved" in terms of the queen's perceived profligacy.[144] Brodsky suggests that what the Scottish queen and Brodsky's erstwhile lover have in common in addition to cer-tain "external features," as stated in the fourth sonnet, is their perceived adulterous proclivities. The facts of Brodsky's literary biography clearly disclose the poet's beloved "beauty" as precisely that Mary whom we have already encountered—albeit in various spellings—in such overtly M. B.-oriented poems as "Letter in a Bottle," a.k.a. "Entertainment for Mary," and "To the Victories," and whose inconstancy and sexual infidelity presumably warranted the poet's metaphorical fusion of the two Marys in the first place.[145]

That in "Twenty Sonnets" Brodsky is indeed poeticizing about M. B.—availing himself of the Scottish queen as a "screen lady" à la Dante, as it were—comes to the fore ever so subtly yet unmistakably in his comprehensive if displaced and silent articulation of his lover's first name, which, as I have noted, does not to the best of my knowledge appear *in toto* in any of Brodsky's poetic texts.[146] As noted earlier, in Sonnet 2 (lines 3–4 and 3–11), Brodsky remembers that "as a boy" he saw Zarah Leander as Mary in *The Road to the Scaffold,* which was playing at the Spartacus movie theater:

> Mary, as a boy I saw Zarah
> Leander walk, clip-clop, to the scaffold. . . .
>
> . . .
>
> We all emerged into the light (or this world) from the movie theater,
> but something calls us back at dusk
> into the "Spartacus," whose plushy womb
> is cozier. . . .

The poet recalls the movie theater in terms of a plushy womb from which "we all" emerged and into whose cozy ambiance he longs to return. This palpably eroticized memory of the Spartacus, which welcomed and seated many, would certainly appear to be a nugatory and forced conceit in line with the sequence's overall bathetic structure—if, that is, it were not motivated by one contextually crucial historical-onomastic detail: since 1939, the Spartacus occupied the space of what used to be the Church of St. Anna![147] This means that in remembering the Spartacus, Brodsky can be said to be metonymically remembering *Anna*: both Anna Akhmatova, to whom he had already paid extended homage in the 1972 poem "Sreten'e," which like "Twenty Sonnets" also commemorates a particular encounter—namely, that between Simeon, Jesus, and the prophetess Anna in Luke 2:25–36; and more important, [Mari]Anna, insofar as nostalgically thinking of Zarah Leander's *Mary* in a building that used to be the Church of St. Anna Brodsky cannot fail to be staging, in a displaced manner (both spatially and temporally), his desire to return to *Mary-Anna's* "plushy womb," which according to Brodsky has indeed welcomed more than one. Though torn apart (Brodsky's poetic revenge?) and metonymically (dis)figured, Marianna Basmanova nominally emerges from behind the Scottish queen's mask to inhabit both materially and figurally the very texture of Brodsky's poetry. Due to her *figural* (metonymic) presence in Brodsky's text in particular, *Mary-Anna* cannot fail to bear out emphatically the poet's claim that his "real" biography is to be sited in both the material ("vowels and sibilants") and the rhetorical ("meters, rhymes, metaphors") makeup of his poetry.

"What's in a name?" we may ask with Juliet, and answer, again with Juliet, that "that which we call a rose / By any other name would smell as sweet; / So Romeo would, were he not Romeo call'd, / Retain that dear perfection which he owes / Without that title. . . . "[148] In the case of Brodsky's poetics, however, Juliet's nominalism does not hold. In a semantic universe in which the poet's "real" biography transpires in his poetry, Romeo—that is, Marianna—could not possibly retain "that dear perfection which he owes"; in other words, Romeo would not be Romeo were he called by a different name. The "title"—the name—*is* essential to the "real" being of the person. It is precisely because Marianna is neither Mary nor Augusta nor Beatrice and, concomitantly, because Brodsky is neither Dante nor Byron that his speech masks and impersonations acquire pressing ethical-political significance—albeit pivoting not so much on literary-historical *parallels* as on literary-biographically germane, yet contrastively productive, foils for his poetic project of facilitating and ensuring self-empowerment and agency. Whether or not Brodsky can be said to have succeeded fully in making good on his stipulation never to grant himself the "status of the victim" in what we commonly refer to as "real life" may be debatable and something for his biographers' to think through; *that* he has fully succeeded, particularly with the help of Byron's poetic staging of his love for his "dearest Augusta,"[149] in turning himself from victim into agent and victor *in his poetry* is, if we trust his "real" biography, beyond doubt.

Closing Remarks

Throughout this book, which was born of my concomitant, genealogically motivated interest in the lives and works of Paul Celan, Durs Grünbein, and Joseph Brodsky, I have been inquiring into the workings of poetry as an articulation of life by looking at the three poets' respective inscriptions of life into poetry. By tracing the ways in which they have gone about their craft, I have suggested, we can learn a great deal about the anatomy and physiology of the poetic text, as well as about its inseverable moorings to the extrapoetic. By approaching their poetic practices as mutually complementary, I have further suggested, we are granted an unprecedented, comprehensive view of literature-in-operation.

These general claims, which bear on a specific set of authors and on questions of poetics more generally, have necessitated the pursuit of three interlocking goals: staging inventive readings of Celan's, Grünbein's, and Brodsky's lives and works; sounding in a new key, through these readings, the relationship between literature and life; and finally, elaborating on the basis of the three poets' translations of life into poetry (and vice versa) new ways of thinking about literature as an ethical practice.

To substantiate my argument, I have chosen to focus on the poetological significance of three historical events: the Goll affair, the Livilla affair, and the Brodsky affair. More specifically, I have elaborated what I consider the singular combined importance of Celan's, Grünbein's, and Brodsky's respective poetic responses to these affairs for our comprehension of the inner life of poetry, which I have interrogated through the prism of three of poetry's fundamental, mutually imbricated building blocks: the constitution of poetic signification, poetic subjectivity, and poetic (and by extension) ethical agency. I have argued that in translating the earlier-mentioned affairs into *poetic affairs*, and with the loving support of such interlocutors as Shakespeare, Seneca, and Byron, Celan, Grünbein, and Brodsky have succeeded in revealing the affairistic underpinnings of poetic signification, poetic subjectivity, and poetic and ethical agency, respectively. In other words, in light of Celan's, Grünbein's, and Brodsky's refractions of life through poetry, poetry itself has been disclosed as affairistic at the core—as the very product of the poet's love affair with a given interlocutor.

Although I leave it up to the reader to decide whether I have indeed achieved the critical goals I set for myself, I do hope that I have succeeded in enhancing and enriching our knowledge and understanding of the works (and lives) of three outstanding poets, as well as pointing out a number of avenues for future inquiry in such areas as semiotics, translation studies, poetics, and ethics-and-literature.[1] Clearly Celan's affairistic practice of poetic translation, Grünbein's affairistic staging of the emergence of poetic subjectivity, and Brodsky's accession to ethical agency through a poetic affair cannot fail to bear on how we conceive of the functioning of poetic language as essentially caught up in translation; on how we conceive of subjectivity as always already invented; and finally, on how we conceive of ethics as always already enmeshed with the literary.[2]

To have staged the semiotic, epistemological, and ethical-poetic in affairistic terms—as the creations of interlocution—will have been one of Celan's, Grünbein's, and Brodsky's most inventive individual and combined contributions to our understanding of and engagement with poetry and literature.

Appendix: Constellations

As noted in the Introduction, above and beyond each poet's literary-historical significance, personal taste, and so on, my initial interest in Celan, Grünbein, and Brodsky was triggered by the fact that all three consider themselves heirs to the legacy of Osip Mandelstam. This Appendix, an inventory of sorts of my preliminary research for this book, shares some of the historical and genealogical findings that have contributed to this book's argument.

Historical

Although Paul Celan, Durs Grünbein, and Joseph Brodsky never met one another, a network of clues can easily be uncovered that testifies to their mutual awareness and recognition, though not in the same degree and to the same extent in the case of each of them with regard to the other two. Let me point out right away, for purposes of simplicity and clarity of exposition, that:

1. Celan did not take and in fact could not have taken notice of Grünbein for purely historical-chronological reasons; at the time of Celan's death in 1970, Grünbein was eight years old and had not yet written or published poetry.

2. Brodsky did not, to the best of my knowledge, take notice of any of Grünbein's poetry and prose published up to 1996, the year of Brodsky's death.

3. As the youngest and only living poet of the three, Grünbein has the historical advantage of being able to look back on and take cognizance of—in their
entirety, so to speak—the lives and works of Celan and Brodsky, who embody the
two languages and literary traditions to which Grünbein is particularly indebted
and who trace their poetic lineage back to and develop their poetics in dialogue
with some of Grünbein's own adopted literary ancestors and central poetic interlocutors.

In a recent interview dealing mainly with the legacy of Osip Mandelstam,
Grünbein mentions Celan and Brodsky in the same breath: "He [Mandelstam]
was an emigrant in his own country . . . as Joseph Brodsky, his most faithful
disciple, put it. . . . Whatever he would write could henceforth [that is, after his
falling out with Stalin in the early 1930s and the subsequent publication ban im-
posed on him] only be a message in a bottle. . . . For very different reasons, Paul
Celan found himself in a similar situation of radical isolation. Although he had
no difficulties getting published as a German-writing Jew in Paris . . . he felt like
a new Robinson. . . . It was his tragedy that his addressee would never come to
life again. . . . "[1] Elsewhere, Grünbein highlights Brodsky's ethical significance for
himself during and immediately after the events of 1989–1990: "his refusal to be
cast as a victim, irrespective of the circumstances, became my motto . . . the basis
for all my alleged cynicisms. . . . I simply did not want to be a victim, nobody's
victim. . . . "[2] Matters are not as simple and straightforward, historically speaking,
in the case of Celan's relation to Brodsky and vice versa, to which I now turn.

CELAN AND BRODSKY

To the best of my knowledge, Celan does not mention Brodsky in any of his
extant writings and correspondence. However, residing in Paris from 1948 until
his death in 1970, he could hardly have been unaware of Brodsky's persecution
by the Soviet authorities after the publication, in the first issue (October 1964)
of the Parisian weekly *Le Figaro Littéraire*, of a French translation of Frida Vigdorova's secret transcript of Brodsky's "dramatic and comical" trial and sentence
in March 1964 to five years of forced labor in internal exile on the trumped-up
charge of social parasitism, followed by Charles Dobzynski's accusatory "Open
Letter to a Soviet Judge" in the October 1964 issue of *Action poétique.* Vigdorova's
transcript was subsequently published, in the original Russian, in the fourth issue
(1965) of the New York–based journal *Vozdušnye Puti* (Aerial ways), which Celan

purchased—judging by the handwritten date in his copy—on February 25, 1965.[3] The only "hard" evidence for Celan's active interest in the Russian poet is the fact that he owned copies of some of Brodsky's earliest published translations into German and French—but not, however, the only original collection by Brodsky, *Stixotvorenija i poemy* (Poems; 1965), published prior to Celan's suicide.[4]

The extent to which Celan actually did engage with Brodsky's poetry is a matter of speculation, although it is fair to say that he probably did not know it well given that he did not own and does not seem to have seriously perused his poems in the original Russian.[5] As Christine Ivanović plausibly suggests, Celan's interest in Brodsky must have been more ethical and political than poetic, especially in view of Brodsky's adoption of and allegiance to Marina Cvetaeva's memorable poetic-existential credo, "Poets are kikes." He must have seen Brodsky as yet another "persecuted and exiled . . . Jewish poet."[6] Aside from its obvious unfoundedness and preposterous character, "L'affaire Brodski," as Pierre Emmanuel calls it, would have struck a particular chord with Celan in view of the fact that, similarly to Celan, Brodsky too had undergone psychiatric treatment.[7] We should thus take note—if only as a matter of historical record—that whatever Celan's assessment of and relation to Brodsky's poetry may have been, the Russian poet *does* form part, if peripherally, of Celan's poetic universe to the extent that it is oriented toward (if not exclusively focused on, of course) and populated by poets from the "East," such as Osip Mandelstam, Marina Cvetaeva, and Sergej Esenin, to name only a few.[8]

BRODSKY AND CELAN

While Celan's response to Brodsky is a matter of speculation, due to the scarcity of textual and contextual evidence, Brodsky's response to Celan is not. On at least two occasions, Brodsky explicitly commented on Celan. In an interview he gave in 1979, Brodsky had the following to say about German poets—Celan among them—when asked to "suggest some reading for younger poets in addition to Cavafy and Auden":

> As for Germans, there is Ingeborg Bachmann . . . and then Peter Huchel . . . And his friend and contemporary, Günter Eich. Huchel is in the Michael Hamburger collection. Paul Celan is also a very good poet. He committed suicide in Paris in 1971 or 1970. We shouldn't buy this thing from Europeans—I mean both we Americans and we Russians; we shouldn't buy these kinds of self-dramatizations. . . . They really had a rotten lot, all of them in this century those who had the misfortune to be born in the twenties and thirties—the war, et cetera. All the same, I think some of them were making too much of their unhappiness or catastrophes. They thrived on it in a way;

they built their identity around it, unlike Czeslaw Milosz. For a poet's identity should be built more on strophes than on catastrophes. . . . Still, Celan. Also, a man I had in mind is Georg Trakl.[9]

In a later interview, conducted in 1991 and first published in 2000, Brodsky was somewhat more explicit in his assessment of Celan, without, for that matter, changing his view. After pronouncing "Trakl . . . incomprehensible" and reiterating that he doesn't "understand what his poetry is about," Brodsky turns to Celan:

> Celan—that's a different matter, but things happened to Celan. . . . What I am saying to you—that's my point of view. I think that he is an extraordinarily gifted, marvelous poet. But, all in all, he took himself too seriously—and the tragedy that happened to him and . . . I think that, in many ways, he had maneuvered himself into an impasse. He took himself too seriously.[10]

Obviously Brodsky not only was aware of but also must have known enough of Celan's poetry to be able to declare its creator an "extraordinarily gifted, marvelous poet." He must have also known enough about Celan the man—one of "those who had a rotten lot, . . . who had the misfortune to be born in the twenties and thirties"—to call what "happened to him" a "tragedy."

Although by 1979—not to mention 1991—Brodsky could have come across Celan's works in and learned about his life from a number of available sources, he most likely encountered the poet, as he himself suggests, through Michael Hamburger's mediation. The latter's bilingual anthologies, *Modern German Poetry 1910–1960* and *German Poetry 1910–1975,* as well as his translations of nineteen poems by Celan preceded by a concise, yet fairly comprehensive biographical introduction (published in 1972 as *Nineteen Poems by Paul Celan*) would have been, on Brodsky's own testimony, the likely sources of his acquaintance with the German poet. The fact that, incidentally, all of the other German poets mentioned by Brodsky (Bachmann, Huchel, and Eich) are also represented in Hamburger's collections further corroborates the likelihood that Brodsky would have come across Celan's poems in them.[11]

In view of the lack of textual and contextual evidence to the contrary—that is, explicit references to, further critical observations on, and sustained poetic dialogue with Celan in Brodsky's poems and essays—it is plausible to assume that Brodsky's engagement with and view of Celan, which neither intensified nor changed subsequent to his initial "tragic" assessment and critique of the latter in 1979, was for the most part based on the "dark" poems—such as "Death Fugue," "Tenebrae," "Psalm," "Radix, Matrix," and "There Was Earth"—and on prefatory material emphasizing Celan's role as a "survivor and witness" in the "age of genocide" included in the previously mentioned anthologies.[12] Given this at-best perfunctory acquaintance with Celan on Brodsky's part, the former can be considered neither the latter's predecessor, in the strong sense, nor even one of his serious poetic interlocutors. Unlike "Mandelstam, Akhmatova, Cvetaeva, Auden and Frost," among others, who avowedly "gave [Brodsky] life as a poet," Celan occupies a fairly inconspicuous place somewhere on the outskirts of Brodsky's poetic universe.[13]

Yet something about Brodsky's off-handed treatment, if not outright dismissal, of Celan and all "those who had the misfortune to be born in the twenties and thirties," who made "too much of their unhappiness and catastrophes" and "thrived on it in a way," along with his injunction that "we shouldn't buy this kind of thing" suggests that this cannot be the whole story. Are we supposed to take these statements at face value and admit that Brodsky is an unempathetic, morally callous brute? If so, how does the person capable of taking such a perversely "sober" stance vis-à-vis the crematoria and gulags match that other Brodsky who took his own fate seriously enough to spend the better part of his poetic career coming to grips with, among other things, his love for and betrayal by "M. B.," the "dark lady of [his] sonnets," which on all counts can be considered much less "serious" than "the tragedy that happened" to Celan and millions of others during the Holocaust?[14] How does the person capable of such dismissal—culminating in the macabre if ingenious strophes and catastrophes pun ("a poet's identity should be built more on strophes than on catastrophes")—square with that other Brodsky who had firsthand experience of racial and political persecution and did not hedge or take his own experience lightly at all when asked to name the "gravest and most difficult moment" during his life in the Soviet Union: "The psychiatric prison hospital in Leningrad. I was given terrible tranquilizer injections. I would be awakened in the middle of the night and thrown into a bath tub filled with ice-cold water. I would then be wrapped in a wet sheet and placed next to the radiators. In the heat, the sheet would dry and cut into my body."[15]

It is far more plausible to read Brodsky's remarks about Celan and all "those in this century" along the lines of that "irony grown on the soil of reality" that he sang in 1964 during his stint in internal exile in the far north of the Soviet Union and that is frequently, as Brodsky explains on another occasion, precisely in its ostensible lightness, "the mark of the most profound despair."[15] In other words, Brodsky's cavalier treatment of Celan's biography and the atrocities of the twentieth century should be taken as the ironic mask of one who is in fact profoundly attuned to others' tragedies; as the mask of one who has learned to nurture his "hope in the key of irony" and has adopted an ironic stance vis-à-vis life's vaga-ries.[17]

Brodsky is equally aware, however, of the escapist dimension of irony, of the fact that irony as a way of life is "a deceptive thing": "When you speak of the situation you are in with a smirk or with irony you pretend not to be bound by it. But this is not so. Irony does not help us solve the problem or raise ourselves above it. On the contrary, it keeps us tied to its parameters and conditions."[18] Could it be then that Brodsky's insistence on Celan's taking "himself too seriously" bespeaks (*ex negativo* and against the grain of the phrase's literal meaning) precisely his own uneasiness about the *de facto* seriousness of Celan's and, by extension, his own, in some ways similar, fate? Shouldn't we read Brodsky's dismissal as a tacit injunction directed at himself, to the effect that he should not take himself "too seriously" in spite of the "tragedy that happened" to him? And does not this attempt at ref-erential displacement (that is, obliquely admonishing Celan rather than himself) and semantic reversal bespeak, on Brodsky's own analysis of irony's ruses, precisely his own persistence within the parameters and conditions of persecution, separa-tion, loss, and exile, which are "serious" matters indeed? In other words, does not Brodsky divulge, in and through his ostensible denunciation of Celan and others, the very seriousness with which he views and experiences his own forced separa-tion from his son, parents, and friends—all of whom he had to leave behind the "ironic curtain" when he was expelled from the Soviet Union for good in June 1972?[19] Brodsky's avowal that he "didn't want to leave Russia" and that he even "wrote Leonid Brežnev" imploring him to "let [him] participate in the literary process in [his] own country, if only as a translator" rather than forcing him into exile certainly supports such a reading.[20]

What I am suggesting, then, is the following: Although Celan cannot, strictly speaking, be considered one of Brodsky's chosen *poetic* interlocutors, he can be said to be made to perform the function of an important contrastive foil to Brod-sky's self-fashioning as an *American* poet. Historically, what is at stake here is the tension between Celan's persecuted victim, survivor, and exile and Brodsky's self-fashioned and supersuccessful American poet laureate and winner of the Nobel Prize for literature who rewrites the trauma of his forced expatriation in terms of the "transition from a political and economic backwater to an industrially ad-vanced society with the latest word on individual liberty on its lips[, which is,] for an exiled writer, in many ways like going home—because he gets closer to the seat of the ideals which inspired him all along."[21] The ideals that Brodsky has in mind are, as he himself points out, those of democracy—for the poet "is a democrat by definition."[22]

Genealogical

At the risk of stating the obvious, let me stress that although an author's placement within the historical continuum certainly determines his relations with others to some extent—for instance, an author cannot escape the fact that he could not possibly have been influenced by the works of another who is not a predecessor or contemporary—it obviously does not bespeak or guarantee a line of poetic succession on purely chronological grounds. The fact that author X precedes, overlaps with, or is contemporaneous with author Y does not mean that Y will automatically elect X as an interlocutor. Much more important for the actual makeup of an author's oeuvre and for our understanding and adequate engagement with it than history *per se* is the particular literary filiation or genealogy he creates and the aesthetic and intellectual lineage he constructs, configures, and claims for himself.[23] Thus, without disregarding or being remiss in giving due credit to history, I wish my juxtaposition and orchestration of Celan's, Grünbein's, and Brodsky's works to be viewed in light of their genealogical kinship. Their cohabitation within the covers of the same book is due in large measure to the fact that all three view themselves, as I illustrate, as heirs to and members of what can be thought of as one literary configuration or constellation, that all three have chosen "to be adopted," to quote Seneca, into the same literary family, to which I wish to assign the family name *Mandelstam.*[24]

In the present context, *Mandelstam* ought to be understood not only as a proper name but also as a configurational shorthand—a cultural-historical chiffre.[25] In other words, in addition to being rigidly designated the Russian-Jewish man and poet who was born in 1891 in Warsaw, grew up in Pavlovsk and St. Petersburg, started writing poetry at the age of fifteen, published the groundbreaking volume *Kamen'* (Stone) in 1913, co-founded in the same year the Acmeist movement in Russian poetry, was romantically involved with the poet Marina Cvetaeva, married Nadežda Xazin, had an ambivalent attitude toward the Russian revolution, was accused of plagiarism and persecuted by the Stalinist regime on account of his poetry, and died, one of the millions of Stalin's victims, in internal exile in Siberia in 1938, *Mandelstam* ought also to be understood as a chiffre signifying the modern avatar of the persecuted, abused, and exiled poet *tout court*—the "sacrificial victim of empire"—whose art and existence present a threat to tyranny and who does not shy away from putting his life on the line for the sake of poetry, as well as a particular site and moment of focalization, refraction, and transmission in Western—especially Russian and early Soviet—literature (modernism and Acmeism), history (modernity), and politics (the age of totalitarianism).[26]

Among the literary and extraliterary interlocutors who have had a significant impact on and who are, in Brodsky's words, "close in spirit to" the poetics of Brodsky, Celan, and Grünbein, Mandelstam—retroactively co-created, invented, constructed, and reinscribed by the three poets within their own respective contexts—emerges as the key figure to whom all three poets have consistently turned for literary and existential patronage.[27] This is not to say that each of the three poets does not also have other perhaps equally important interlocutors—such as W. H. Auden and Marina Cvetaeva for Brodsky, Nelly Sachs and Rainer Maria Rilke for Celan, and Seneca and René Descartes for Grünbein; it is simply to underscore that Mandelstam is the *only* point of historical, poetic, and existential reference shared by *all three* to the same degree and with the same poetic zeal. Nothing evidences Mandelstam's genealogical significance for Celan, Grünbein, and Brodsky as eloquently as the fact that Celan considered him a brother in poetry and fate, calling him "Bruder Ossip"; that Brodsky was dubbed "the second Osja" by Mandelstam's widow, Nadežda; and that Grünbein concludes his manifesto essay, "Galilei Measures Dante's Hell and Gets Hung Up on the Measurements," with a long quote from Mandelstam dealing with the life-bestowing power of poetry.[28] Thus, I wish Mandelstam to be considered *the* fulcrum for my attempt at levering Celan, Grünbein, and Brodsky into a dialogic space in which critical justice is done to each poet's individual oeuvre in light of its debt to the Acmeist. Moreover, we ought to take note that for all three poets, Mandelstam is a central, if certainly not an exclusive, cultural-historical filter through which they engage with, appropriate, displace, and respond to their literary and cultural heritage, as well as their more or less immediate situations and realities. What makes Mandelstam so attractive and important for Celan, Grünbein, and Brodsky? Two key aspects of Mandelstam's poetic project, I suggest, can plausibly be singled out as determining Celan's, Grünbein's, and Brodsky's genealogical choice. I have dubbed these key aspects *polyphonic organicism* and *ethical realism,* respectively.

POLYPHONIC ORGANICISM

"The [poetic] word is psyche," Mandelstam writes. "The living word does not designate objects; it freely chooses, for its abode, as it were, this or that material significance, thingness, beloved body. And around the thing, the word roams freely, like the soul around the abandoned yet not forgotten body."[29] What makes this animating word come to life in the first place, Mandelstam specifies, is its own animation "by the breathing of all ages"; its constitution as a "sheaf" or "bundle" (*puchok*) out of which "senses [and voices] stick out . . . in different directions" such that in saying "'sun' we undertake . . . a gigantic journey" along the path of the word's infinite uses by infinite speakers.[30] Celan's belief that whatever is poetically addressed comes to life precisely in and through this very address, Grünbein's view of the poetic word as "psyche," and Brodsky's postulate that the "poet's role . . . is to animate . . . the people no less than the furniture" are all animated by Mandelstam's "living word" or word soul, which equally informs the three successor poets' own profoundly polyphonic and transhistorical poetic practices.[31]

Mandelstam's notion of the "living word" ties in with the overall Acmeist endeavor to create "an organicist poetics . . . of a biological nature"—a poetics predicated on biology and physiology, on the "infinite complexity of our inscrutable organism," and on the basic notion that a "poem is a living organism."[32] Rather than positing the metaphorical identity of text and organism, poem and body, Mandelstam suggests that the actual continuity between the two is based on the most fundamental physiological activity, the most basic involuntary human reflex: breathing. The breathing, moving human body is the ultimate ground of poetry. The "poetic foot," Mandelstam notes, is nothing but "breathing in and breathing out."[33] The poem is literally animated into existence by "the breathing of all ages" to the extent that it is the articulation of the breathing, moving bodies of the countless poets of "all ages." The genealogical significance for his three successors of the physiological, somatic aspect of Mandelstam's poetics is evidenced in Celan's conception of poetry in terms of breathing and physical contact with the other; in Brodsky's emphasis on poetry as a function of the poet's "nerves," "breath and heartbeat," and "brain functions"; and finally in Grünbein's terse definition of poetry as a "picture puzzle of physiological origin."[34]

ETHICAL REALISM

Mandelstam's poetics is informed by and gives onto a clearly delineated social, ethical-political dimension. "Acmeism is not only a literary phenomenon," Mandelstam notes in 1922. "It is also a social phenomenon in Russian history. A new ethical force was reborn with the emergence of Acmeism."[35] This new ethical force, Mandelstam specifies, consists first and foremost, in the reversal of the Symbolist denigration of the real, phenomenal world of the here and now, the "realia," in favor of a "noumenal . . . higher reality," the "realiora," whereby the poetic word is reduced to the status of a "magical," "suggestive" symbol of that "higher reality."[36] In contrast to the Symbolist claim that the "poet's business is absolutely incommensurable with the order of this world,"[37] Mandelstam emphasizes the world's very reality and materiality as the Acmeists' paradigm and horizon: "The Symbolists . . . felt ill at ease in the cage of their own organism and in the world cage that Kant had constructed by way of his categories. . . . Love for our organism . . . love for the existence and materiality of the thing more than for the thing itself, love for our very being . . . this is the highest commandment of Acmeism."[38]

A love for the here and now, for "all manifestations of life . . . in time and not only in eternity"—a love for this world and this reality, for one's "own organism," for one's singularity, cannot fail to bear on sociopolitics.[39] What kind of sociopolitical setup will foster and secure the possibility of this kind of Acmeist existence? In words that are as much an Aesopian critique of the Russian Revolution and its more or less immediate aftermath as an eerily prescient statement on the "twilight of freedom" in the age Stalinism,[40] Mandelstam lays out his sociopolitical vision:

> There are epochs that maintain that they are not concerned with singular human beings, that human beings must be put to use, like bricks, like mortar. . . . Assyrian prisoners swarm like chicks under the feet of a gigantic Tsar; warriors personifying the power of the state inimical to the human being kill shackled pigmies with long spears, and the Egyptians . . . are dealing with the human mass as if it were building material in abundant supply. . . . But there is another form of social architecture whose scale and measure is . . . man. . . . It doesn't use human beings as building material but builds for them, it doesn't build . . . on the insignificance of the human person. . . . Mere mechanical grandeur and mere numbers are inimical to humankind. We are tempted not by a new social pyramid, but . . . by the free play of weights and forces, by a human society . . . in which everything is . . . individual, and each member is unique and echoes the whole.[41]

Mandelstam's emphasis on the here and now, on the necessity of loving this world and this life—and this means loving and attending to each thing, human being, and so forth in its uniqueness—is inextricably linked to the political postulate of a social structure that will guarantee the freedom of each of its members and in which the voice of every member will be equally weighted.[42] Each successful, truly Acmeist poem can thus be said to be a miniblueprint for such a human and humane society. Mandelstam's intervention in the late 1920s on behalf of several individuals about to be executed is a case in point. In the hope of preventing what he considered a political atrocity, according to Nadežda Mandelstam and in line with his belief that poetry "is born from the desire to forestall catastrophe," he sent a copy of his *Poems* (1928) to Nikolay Bukharin, a high-ranking member of the politburo, with the following inscription: "Every line in this book speaks against what you are about to do."[3]

The ethical rigor and realism of Mandelstam's project provides an indispensable (if not exclusive) backdrop for (1) Celan's conception of poetry as counterword "in search of reality" and in the name of the "existence of the singular human being," who "remains given to it"; (2) Brodsky's view (predicated on his belief that you cannot "separate people and writing" and that consequently poetry "offers its writer an extension of himself") of the poet as "a democrat by definition" and of poetry as "an act of love" testifying to the "ethical possibilities of man," whereby *love* is to be understood as "an attitude toward reality"; and finally (3) Grünbein's practice of poetry as "anthropological realism" with an explicitly ethical bent.[44]

Mandelstam sums up the gist of the ethics of his poetics—its emphatic concern with this world and its inhabitants—in what has undoubtedly become his signature statement: "There is no lyric poetry without dialogue"; poetry is by definition concerned with and addressed to "someone, some listener."[45] Specifying what he means by poetry's "addressivity," Mandelstam draws on the classical trope of poetry as navigation, and the poet as navigator, and establishes his famous (and much-quoted) analogy between a poem and a message in a bottle:

> In the critical moment a seafarer throws a sealed bottle with his name and the description of his fate into the ocean waves. Years later, roaming about the dunes, I find it in the sand, read the letter, learn about the date of the event and the last will of the deceased. . . . The letter sealed in the bottle is addressed to the one who finds it. I found it. Consequently, I am the . . . addressee. . . . Reading [a] poem, I experience the same feeling that I would experience if such a bottle had found its way into my hands . . . both have an addressee: the letter—the one who happens to notice the bottle in the sand, the poem—the "reader in posterity". . . . Even if singular poems (in the form of missives and dedications) may be addressed to concrete persons, poetry as a whole is always directed toward a more or less distant, unknown interlocutor, whose existence the poet cannot doubt without doubting his own.[46]

Poetry's dialogic character does not simply signify that every poem is addressed to, spoken to, somebody present, ready to respond, as in live conversation; rather, it means emphatically that every poem is historical, that it inexorably reaches *through time* on its voyage toward an interlocutor whose "embrace" its author "desire[s]."[47]

Without at this point delving any deeper into the complexities and intricacies of Mandelstam's conception of poetic dialogue, suffice it to note that Celan, Grünbein, and Brodsky explicitly appropriate his nautical-postal analogy for their own poetics (and ethics).[48] This is evidenced most saliently in (1) Celan's observation that "the poem," being "essentially dialogic" and under way "through time," "can be a message in a bottle [*Flaschenpost*], entrusted to the waves in the hope . . . that someday and somewhere it may be washed upon land"; (2) Brodsky's recourse to Mandelstam's analogy in an attempt to work through poetically and make sense of his own fate (I am thinking in particular of his profoundly autobiographical manifesto poem "Letter in a Bottle," which develops some of the central themes of his ethics and poetics); and finally (3) Grünbein's dystopian invocation—by way of a jab at what he views as contemporary society's wrong-headed, misguided, and preposterous questioning of poets' and poetry's very right to exist—of a world constructed according to the blueprint of Plato's political fiction, in which the poets' "testimony to their own demise as a species . . . would have drifted, a message in a bottle, across the seas" until "many decades later, on one of the coasts, . . . some athlete or arithmetician picked it up and destroyed it after briefly perusing it with disgust."[49]

Excursus: "A Tumultuous Affair"

To bring into focus the full genealogical import of Mandelstam's polyphonic organicism and ethical realism for Celan, Grünbein, and Brodsky, yet another aspect of his poetics needs to be taken into consideration—an aspect that distally informs my affairistic approach to the three poets: Mandelstam's metaphorical identification with and ventriloquism of Dante. What do I mean by this? Two things: first, Mandelstam's poetics is inconceivable without Dante, both as a predecessor to be reckoned with and as a screen for his own poetics; and second, insofar as Celan, Grünbein, and Brodsky turn to Dante as the model of the modern poet-exile "to reflect on poetic tradition and their place in it," they do so emphatically (if not exclusively, of course) via Mandelstam's version of Dante.[50]

In my discussion of Mandelstam's reception of Dante I address only its contextually most relevant aspects. As a matter of historical record, we should keep in mind that Mandelstam's engagement with Dante spanned his entire career, reaching a peak in the 1930s when he was working on what would turn out to be his poetical *summa*, "Conversation About Dante," and that it was part of the sweeping phenomenon of Dante's impact and appropriation in the context of the tangle of literary currents and movements that have conveniently been subsumed under the general heading of *modernism*.[51] Such well-worn modernist analogies as that between "the medieval inferno and modern life," and concomitantly between Dante's exile and the modern poet sojourning in the "sordidly realistic and . . . phantasmagoric" hell of the "modern metropolis" also inform Mandelstam's vision of Dante.[52]

However, in contrast to his illustrious contemporaries, such as Aleksandr Blok,
Ezra Pound, and T. S. Eliot (to name only a few) who propagated a romanticized,
removed, mystified, and aristocratic Dante—a Dante as "monument"—Mandelstam casts the Italian as someone to whom he (and we) can immediately relate,
someone alive and breathing, someone close to us historically, poetically, and politically.[53] Unlike Pound's "austere, patrician," and "aristocra[tic]" Dante; unlike
Eliot's "seer and repository of tradition," who stands "for the thoroughly hierarchical world of scholastic thought . . . against which the relativity and agnosticism
of the present can be judged"; and finally, unlike Blok's (and other Symbolists')
sculptural, ghostly, prophetic, and "mysterious Dante . . . consisting of a hood,
aquiline nose, and busying himself among the mountain crags," Mandelstam's
Dante is rebellious, deeply human, and personalized: a "poor man," an "upstart
intellectual," commoner, and "disserter" (*raznočinec*) who does not quite "know
how to behave . . . what to say, [or] when to bow" and who "finds it insufferable
to be part of the social hierarchy" in "that most dangerous . . . and criminal age."[54]
We cannot help recognizing in these characterizations the image of Mandelstam
himself—the penurious misfit and outsider, the "angry literator-raznochinec" who
could and did not find his place in the social hierarchy of a totalitarian state and
who eventually fell prey to his own "most dangerous and criminal age."[55] "Nel
mezzo del cammin di nostra vita," Mandelstam writes, impersonating Dante, and
thus implicitly naming him as his *alter ego*; "in the middle of my life's journey, I
was accosted, in the sleepy and dense Soviet forest, by bandits who called themselves my judges. . . . "[56]

Although this impersonation in itself may not be surprising or particularly
noteworthy—after all, "when poets turn to the great masters of the past," they
often turn, as Seamus Heaney reminds us, "to an image of their own creation,
one which is likely to be a reflection of their own imaginative needs, their own
artistic inclinations and procedures"—it does drive home the point that in attending to Mandelstam's genealogical significance for Celan, Grünbein, and Brodsky,
we must not be oblivious to the fact that we are also always already dealing with a
very particular take on and version of Dante.[57] And it is the particular version of
Dante created by Mandelstam that is at stake in our three poet's recourse to and
dialogue with Mandelstam and, as we now realize, with Dante as well.

What kind of Dante does Mandelstam author? What does it mean to resort to
Dante via Mandelstam? First and foremost, it means *going beyond* (without leaving behind, for that matter) the sufficiently common, topical—mostly "tragic"

and "bleak"—functionalization of Dante's *Inferno* as a prism through which to deal with sociopolitical and historical trauma—be it the "hell" of the modern and postmodern metropolis, the "hell" of World War I and II, or the "hell" of totalitarianism in its National Socialist or Stalinist versions.[58] Christine Ivanović's caveat that Celan's "relation to Dante by far transcends the *Inferno*'s topical significance for Holocaust literature" equally applies, *mutatis mutandis*, to Brodsky's and Grünbein's approaches to Dante.[59] Although all three poets do indeed engage Dante in the topical manner just described—Celan in a sustained attempt to grapple with his firsthand experience of the Holocaust and its aftermath, Brodsky in an attempt to deal with his falling out with and subsequent expulsion from the Soviet state, and Grünbein in a general sweep against what he seems to be reading as the twentieth century's overall miserable ethical-political track record—more is negotiated in their respective dialogues with the Italian poet than the question of political violence, personal loss, and geographical displacement.[60] Two aspects in particular in Mandelstam's portrayal of Dante stand out, in my view, as crucial in the present context: Dante as a man and poet of profound passion and erotic desire, and Dante as an irreducibly corporeal, physiological figure.

Passion, Mandelstam notes, is the central ingredient, the pith of Dante's life and art.[61] I refer not merely to the cosmic "divine love" that, according to the *Divine Comedy*, moves "the sun and other stars," or to the sublimated spiritual love that prompts Beatrice to aid Dante in finding his way out of the proverbial "dark wood," but more important, and against the grain of Dante's indictment of "animal appetite" (*appetito di fera*), precisely to his "animal appetite" (*zverskij appetit*), his experience of real erotic love and carnal "passion" (*strastie*).[62] Mandelstam's observations that "Dante does not add even a single word of his own" to what he composes, that he is "moved by anything but invention and inventiveness," that "he writes to dictation, being a copyist, a translator . . . timidly cribbing from the illuminated original," pertain not only to Dante's erudition and to the profoundly intertextual and encyclopedic character of his oeuvre, referred to elsewhere as a "veritable orgy of citations," but also, and in fact more importantly, to his indefatigable pursuit of the passion that the eight-year-old Beatrice had inspired in him in 1274 when he saw her in Florence for the very first time and that would animate him and his poetry for the remainder of his earthly existence.[63] For the dictation to which Dante writes, as Mandelstam very well knows, is none other than the dictation of *Amor*. "I am the one," Dante says to Bonagiunta da Lucca, "who, when Love inspires me, takes note, and goes setting it forth after the fashion which he dictates within me." Bonagiunta responds, "Clearly I see how your pens follow close after him who dictates."[64]

In contrast to the common view of Dante as a bard of a pure and salvific kind of love—a love, as Teodolinda Barolini writes, that is "weaned from desiring even as noncarnal an earthly reward as Beatrice's greeting" and "governed by virtue and reason"—Mandelstam's is a Dante of intense sensuality and erotic desire, "a handsome young man" attracted to a "vivacious . . . young girl," "a scholar brimming with physical health making love to a city woman in full bloom."[65] Isn't Mandelstam foregrounding precisely the scandalizing, "philandering" Dante of the *Vita Nuova* (New life)—the Dante who forfeits Beatrice's greeting and attention as a result of what he claims to be "exaggerated rumors which made me out to be a vicious person" concerning his allegedly "scandalous or distasteful . . . behaviour" involving another woman—when he writes (contra Bakhtin, by the way) that the "concept of scandal in literature is much older than Dostoevsky [and that] in the thirteenth century, in Dante's work in particular, it was much more eminent"?[66]

In casting the Italian in a sensual-erotic light, Mandelstam does not take undue interpretive liberties with him; he merely emphasizes, like Lord Byron before him, those descriptive aspects of Dante's text—especially in the *New Life*—that foreground corporeality, physicality and sexuality.[67] Does not Dante openly tell us that his love for Beatrice gives him great discomfort "in that part [of his body] where our food is digested"?[68] Isn't he completely enthralled by the details of Beatrice's physique—the color of her skin ("the pallor of a pearl"), the shape of her body ("by her mold all beauty tests herself"), her "gracious eyes," the "actions of her mouth," her "sweet manner of speaking," and her "miraculous smile"?[69] Isn't he up-front about his erotic craving for at least two other women (the famous screen ladies of the *New Life*) during the period of his poetic "courtship" of the unattainable Beatrice? Does he not avow, in so many words, that he sought erotic consolation from yet another "gracious lady, young and exceedingly beautiful," not too long after Beatrice's death? Does he not admit to the "wantonness of [his] eyes" and to "amorous desires"? Does he not confess to experiencing "evil desire and foolish temptation," notwithstanding his presumably abiding love for Beatrice and despite his resolution not to "be ruled by Love without faithful counsel of reason"?[70]

Nowhere does Mandelstam's sensual-erotic portrayal of Dante come to the fore with such subtlety and force as in his eroticized, virtually anatomical depiction of poetic articulation (immediately succeeding the earlier-quoted "animal appetite")—"a smile moves the poem, . . . gaily the lips redden, the tongue . . . presses against the palate"—as well as in his ingenious fusion of the process of artistic creation with the practice of multiple sexual intercourse in calling Dante's text a "veritable orgy of citations."[71] Of course the "orgy" that

Mandelstam witnesses and in which, as Dante's reader, he necessarily becomes a participant is not an event of the past. Mandelstam's own citation-filled and thus, orgiastic "Conversation About Dante," from which most of the preceeding quotes are taken and which Seamus Heaney has perceptively called "a tumultuous affair," testifies to the ongoing turmoil of reddening lips, moving tongues, and excited, breathing bodies "of all ages."[72] Reading Mandelstam's take on Dante in emphatically sensual-erotic terms is all the more plausible given his linking of the erotics of (inter)textuality—citation as copulation—to the discourses of anatomy and physiology. To do due justice to what he considers to be Dante's conception of the "beginning of poetry" as "the footstep linked to breathing" and of prosody as "breathing in and breathing out," and to respond adequately to Dante's "anatomical lust" for the details of the human body and its physiology (manifested throughout the *New Life* and the *Comedy*), a "reflexology of speech" is required, according to Mandelstam—"an entire science, not yet established, geared toward the word's spontaneous psycho-physiological impact on interlocutors . . . and on the speaker himself."[73]

As mentioned earlier, in creating his version of Dante as *alter ego*, Mandelstam gives us, *a fortiori*, a version of himself. From a purely poetological perspective, this means that in interpreting and commenting on Dante, Mandelstam is implicitly interpreting and commenting on himself and on his sustained engagement with the Italian poet throughout his poetic career. Moreover, given the comprehensive, summational character of "Conversation About Dante," the version of himself that he offers in this late text ought to be taken as the "authoritative" version—the one by which he will want the "reader in posterity" to remember him.[74]

What is immediately obvious if we juxtapose this "authoritative" version of the 1930s with Mandelstam's poetics as articulated in his essays and poems (always, I should stress, in conversation with Dante, his "greatest teacher") up to this late text is the extent to which the later text re-endorses and validates, while elaborating on, specifying, honing, and fine-tuning, Mandelstam's long-held poetic tenets.[75] Thus, to give only one salient example, the earlier-quoted call for the creation of "an organicist poetics . . . of a biological nature" grounded in the physiology of "our inscrutable organism" and in the notion that a "poem is a living organism" animated by "the breathing of all ages," continues to resound in virtually unadulterated fashion in the Dante essay's somatic-physiological theme: poetry as a bodily affair predicated on human anatomy and physiology, and emerging as the result of bodily movement, breathing, and intercourse.[76] Concomitantly, Mandelstam's sensual-erotic take on Dante retroactively casts in an erotic light his own earlier discussions of love as a poetic force. Such postulates as the poet's and poem's "love for the organism [and] for existence," the word-soul's search for and selection of a "beloved body" to dwell in, or the poet's and poem's "desire [for the] interlocutor's embrace [and for] loving with his love" acquire against the backdrop of the Dante essay a decidedly erotic, sexual ring.[77]

What I wish to highlight in the present context as especially significant about Celan's, Grünbein's, and Brodsky's turning to Mandelstam as a reader of Dante is the fact that in placing their poetic projects under Mandelstam's aegis, they cannot fail, *ipso facto*, to endorse the fundamentally erotic thrust of his poetics and hence to subscribe implicitly to an erotic notion of poetry.

Notes

ABBREVIATIONS

The following abbreviations are used throughout the endnotes:

BK   Joseph Brodsky, *Bol'šaja Kniga Interv'ju*
BLJ   Lord Byron, *Byron's Letters and Journals*
CCL   Paul Celan—Celan-Lestrange, *Correspondance*
CPW   Lord Byron, *The Complete Poetical Works*
GA   Barbara Wiedemann, *Paul Celan—Die Goll-Affäre*
GR   Joseph Brodsky, *On Grief and Reason*
GW   Paul Celan, *Gesammelte Werke*
LTO   Joseph Brodsky, *Less Than One*
MSS   Osip Mandelstam, *Sobranie Sočinenij* (Mandelstam Society edition)
NSA   Joseph Brodsky, *Novye Stansy k Avguste: Stixi k M. B., 1962–1982*

INTRODUCTION

1. GR, 87; Lermontov, *A Hero of Our Time*, cited in Lermontov, vol. 4, 7.

2. Eminent French scholar Claude David has called Celan "[le] plus grand poète français de langue allemande" (239). Celan, who was never a German citizen, took French citizenship in 1955.

3. See Heaney, 240. It goes without saying that Celan, Grünbein, and Brodsky are not

the only poets to have claimed Mandelstam's patronage *and* that Mandelstam in turn is not their only respective point of poetic reference. For a detailed historical and genealogical discussion of this literary constellation, as well as of Mandelstam's poetics, see the Appendix.

4. See MSS, vol. 1, 183–188. Brodsky has called Mandelstam "Russia's greatest poet in this [the twentieth] century" (LTO, 145).

5. See MSS, vol. 1, 216; vol. 2, 287. For a detailed discussion of what I call *polyphonic organicism* and *ethical realism,* see the Appendix. By *life* I mean the material (biological, physiological), biographical, and sociohistorical conditions of literature in general. As forms of utterance, literary texts are by definition tied to and thus articulate the contexts of their production and reception (see esp. Bakhtin, *Sobranie,* 177, 204). By *literature* (and its cognate forms) I mean, broadly, the "body of texts from Homer to the present that have come to be called 'literature'" (Attridge, "Singularities, Responsibilities," 111); by *poetry* I mean the literary genre we call by that name. When speaking about the workings of *poetry* I henceforth wish to be understood as speaking about poetry and literature in general. My observations concerning poetry and literature pertain, *mutatis mutandis,* to works of art in general. On the question of literature, see esp. Todorov; Eagleton; Derrida, *Acts of Literature,* 33–75. For discussions of the relationship between life and literature, see Dilthey, *Das Erlebnis* (throughout) and *Die Philosophie,* 63–68; Benjamin, *Charles Baudelaire,* 103–111; Lacoue-Labarthe, esp. 18; Polhemus and Henkle; Andringa and Schreier; Agamben, 76–86. On the enmeshment of ethics and life, see Chapter Four in this volume, esp. note 4.

6. Celan stresses that the poet "remains given" to his poems (GW, vol. 3, 198); Grünbein calls the poet a "student of experience" and defines poetry as a "picture puzzle of physiological origin" (*Galilei,* 17–18); and Brodsky argues that it is impossible to "separate people from writing," (while at the same time strictly opposing the notion that "art can be explained by life") (*Conversations,* 93; GR, 85). I henceforth use, for reasons of rhetorical economy, the somewhat cumbersome adjective *poetological* to refer to questions of poetics—that is, the theory or philosophy of literature—rather than the adjective *poetic,* which is reserved for poetry as such.

7. On the catalytic method, see Parry, 41, 49.

8. I borrow the term *stratigraphic* from anthropologist Clifford Geertz (37, 41), who uses it to designate the heuristic assumption that any given phenomenon may be perceived as multileveled. In particular, Geertz discusses the "'stratigraphic' conception of the relations between biological, psychological, social, and cultural factors in human life" (37), according to which "man is a composite of 'levels,' each superimposed upon those beneath it and underpinning those above it" (ibid.). Geertz takes exception to what he views as the implicit corollary of the stratigraphic method, namely, that these "separate scientific 'levels'" are conceived of as "complete and autonomous in themselves" (41). Clearly, however, the heuristic separation of levels by no means implies their complete autonomy. On my use of *subject, subjectivity,* and *agency,* see Chapters Three and Four. My view of the creation of poetic subjectivity on the basis of poetic signification should not be confused with Julia Kristeva's influential conception of the "engendering" (219) of subjectivity by what she calls the "geno-text" (ibid.)—an impersonal linguistic process that facilitates the replacement

of intersubjectivity by intertextuality. In contrast to Kristeva and other poststructuralists, I emphasize the squarely intersubjective dimension of literature.

9. For detailed discussions of Celan's, Grünbein's, and Brodsky's poetics, see Chapters Two through Four.

10. See GR, 85.

11. "The history of literature (art)," Jurij Tynjanov and Roman Jakobson observe, is "simultaneous with other historical series . . ." (79). "The very existence of a fact *as literary* depends," Tynjanov specifies, "on its differential quality, that is, on its interrelationship with both literary and extra-literary orders" ("Literary Evolution," 69). The formalist notion of the series has been given new currency by Michel Foucault (see esp. *L'archéologie*, 14–16).

12. See Tynjanov, "Literaturnyj Fakt," 9. Since 1924, the year in which this essay was published, it has certainly not become any easier to determine what literature "is."

13. See Tomaševskij, 41, 51–52, 54–55. "There are writers with biographies and writers without biographies . . . for a writer with a biography, the facts of the author's life must be taken into consideration. Indeed, in the works themselves the juxtaposition of the texts and the author's biography plays a structural role" (55). I am thus emphatically concerned with authors as "bio-aesthetic" phenomena (Bethea, *Joseph Brodsky and the Creation of Exile*, 41) and not as merely "implied" (Booth, 74) or "hypostatized" (Fludernik, 633) instances bespeaking the reader's tendency to "attribute stylistic features to a hypothetical narrator person and/or character . . . led by the illusionism of the narrative to impose a communicational framework on the text" (Fludernik, 622–623). I am admittedly guilty of what Andrew Gibson calls (with such theorists as Gérard Genette and Monika Fludernik in mind) the "persistence of humanism even in the most advanced, contemporary, narratological work" (Gibson, 641).

14. See LaCapra (esp. 30–52) on Flaubert's trial; Lawrence (39–122), Baldick (esp. 261–263), and Coetzee (*Giving Offense*, 48–60) on the publication, trial, and reception history of *Lady Chatterly's Lover*; Boyd (esp. 288–317) on the *Lolita* affair. Tomaševskij adduces the lives and works of Pushkin, Lermontov, and Byron as examples of the translation of life into literature.

15. For detailed accounts of the three affairs, see Chapter One.

16. "There is," Nietzsche observes, "only perspectival seeing, perspectival 'cognition'" ("Zur Genealogie," 365).

17. I further explain my use of *affair* and *affairistic* in Chapter One. On the six constitutive linguistic functions (emotive, referential, poetic, phatic, metalingual, and conative), see Jakobson, 66–71.

18. On translation as the basic mode of signification, see Jakobson, 429; Gadamer, 362–366; Apel, 25; Czernin, 101–103.

19. See Herder, 43; Buber, 1–120.

20. See letter of Novalis to Fr. Schlegel, Nov. 30, 1797, cited in Apel, 99; Jakobson, 429.

CHAPTER ONE

1. Grünbein, *Galilei,* 97; Byron, *Don Juan,* Canto 1, stanza 103, line 2; Hamburger, *The Truth of Poetry,* 36; Coetzee, *Elizabeth Costello,* 224.

2. Celan arrived in France on July 13, 1948. For a detailed account of his itinerary from his native Czernowitz (Bukovina) through Bucharest and Vienna to Paris, see CCL, vol. 2, 459–603.

3. See GA, 7. Due to an inordinate number of misprints, Celan had the entire print run of *Der Sand aus den Urnen* withdrawn from circulation immediately after publication.

4. See GA, 17 (Goll's diary, Nov. 6, 1949), 18 (Celan in a letter to Erica Lilleg, Nov. 12, 1949).

5. See GA, 226.

6. "I've read [your translations] and I find them much too different from the original" (Franz Vetter of Pflug Verlag, St. Gallen, in his rejection letter to Celan of Dec. 25, 1951; cited in GA, 178). For the complete text of Celan's translations, see GA, 28–141.

7. For the complete text of Goll's letter, see GA, 187–189. Celan did not learn about Goll's charges until early 1954 (see GA, 190).

8. See GA, 198; C. Goll, "Unbekanntes über Paul Celan" (originally published in *Baubudenpoet* 5 [1960]; reprinted in GA, 251–53).

9. See GA, 281. Kaschnitz's, Bachmann's, and Demus' open letter appeared in *Die Neue Rundschau,* 3 (1960): 547–549; reprinted in GA, 280–283. See also Hans Magnus Enzensberger's (GA, 301–302) and Peter Szondi's (Celan and Szondi, 83–103; GA, 272) interventions on behalf of Celan in the context of the Goll affair. On Klaus Demus' presence during one of Celan's visits to Yvan Goll at the American Hospital in Neuilly, see GA, 226.

10. See GA, 281–282.

11. For the bulk of articles dealing with Celan's poetry in light of Goll's charges, see GA, 257–402. Goll's supporters included, among many others, such critics as Curt Hohoff and Hans Egon Holthusen, a former member of the Waffen SS, Hitler's elite combat troops, and after the war, a respected and influential member of the Berlin Academy of the Arts.

12. In a letter to Alfred Margul-Sperber, Feb. 2, 1962; cited in Celan, "Briefe," 56.

13. "Il s'agit là d'une vraie affaire Dreyfus—sui generis bien entendu. . . . C'est un vrai miroir de l'Allemagne, les voies—'nouvelles'—que sait prendre le nazisme . . . " (draft letter to Jean-Paul Sartre, Jan. 1962; cited in GA, 544). See also Celan, *Mikrolithen,* 153–176.

14. "His sad legend, which he knew how to present in such tragic terms, had shaken us: parents killed by the Nazis, homeless, a great, unrecognized poet . . . " (Goll, "Unbekanntes," cited in GA, 252). On the Bundestag's decision, see Wiedemann, "'Es ist,'" 830–831; CCL, vol. 2, 520.

15. Cited in GA, 234. "No other event," Barbara Wiedemann stresses, "has left such an imprint on Celan's life and work during his Paris years as the [Goll] affair. Its impact [on Celan] cannot be overestimated. It accompanied him for twenty years" ("'Es ist,'" 839). The Goll affair's traumatic impact on Celan is evidenced most poignantly in the fact

that in the fall of 1961—that is, in immediate connection with the plagiarism charges—he began showing first signs of mental illness, which would intensify throughout the 1960s, necessitating repeated hospitalizations (Dec. 1962–Jan. 1963, May 1965, Feb.–Oct. 1967) and psychiatric treatments for clinical depression and persecution mania (see GA, 445).

16. I discuss Celan's poetics in detail in the next chapter.

17. See GW, vol. 3, 198; Celan's letter to Anneliese Obry of Jan. 1, 1961, cited in Wiedemann, "'Es ist,'" 847. Elsewhere Celan notes, "The poem, you know it, does not exist without the poet, without this person—without *the* person" (letter to René Char, Mar. 22, 1962; cited in GA, 575).

18. See Celan's letter to Andersch of July 27, 1956; cited in GA, 233. On Celan's notion of poetry as counter-word, see Chapter Two. As Barbara Wiedemann points out, Celan was "not willing to stoop down to the level" of publicly responding to and thus honoring Claire Goll's charges ("'Es ist,'" 840). No explicit, public statements by Celan regarding the Goll affair exist. For traces of the Goll affair in Celan's poetry, see GA, 751–787.

19. See Damerau, 293.

20. My summary of these events is based on Seneca, "Ad Polybium"; Suetonius, 168–193 (esp. 187); Tacitus, *Annals*, Book 12, 8, Book 13, 42–43; Dio Cassius, Book 60, 8, Book 61, 32. See also Fuhrmann, 87–107; Giebel, 30–43; Veyne, 6–7. Although the exact date of Seneca's birth cannot be established, the philosopher is believed to have been born sometime between 4 B.C.E. and 1 C.E. (see Fuhrmann, 9; Giebel, 7–12). Tiberius Claudius Nero reigned from 41–54 C.E.

21. See Dio Cassius, Book 60, 8, 5; on Julia Livilla's execution, see also Suetonius, 187. Since the passing, under Augustus, of the "lex Julia de adulteriis" in 18 B.C.E., adultery—extramarital sexual relations with a "respectable married woman or with a widow or unmarried free woman who was not registered as a prostitute" (Baumar, 32)—was punishable by relegation, that is, exile without confiscation of property. Both culprits, the man and the woman, were subject to the sanction. On the role of exile in Roman law, see Fuhrmann, 90–91; Giebel, 31–32; McGinn, 140–143, 168; Foucault, *Care of the Self*, 73–171. Julia Livilla was married to Marcus Vinicius in 33 C.E. and had already been banished once (in 39 C.E., under Caligula) on the charge of adultery with her brother-in-law Aemilius Lepidus (see Hazel, 153; Fuhrmann, 87). Seneca was married twice. How and when his first marriage ended, as well as the name of his first wife, whom he married sometime before 41 C.E. and by whom he had a son who died shortly before Seneca's departure for Corsica, is unknown (see Seneca, *Ad Lucilium*, Book 1, 330–331; Giebel, 40; Fuhrmann, 68). According to Dio Cassius, Seneca married Pompeia Paulina, his second wife, sometime after returning to Rome from Corsica (Book 61, 10; see also Giebel, 40).

22. "Agrippina procured a remission of banishment for Annaeus Seneca, along with a praetorship" (Tacitus, *Annals*, Book 12, 8).

23. Sullius is cited in Tacitus, *Annals*, Book 12, 42. For Seneca's avowal of his innocence ("innocentem me . . . esse"), see "Ad Polybium," 394. According to a later source, Seneca had been "more or less privy to Julia's promiscuity" (cited in Giebel, 31). It will never be known whether Seneca actually committed adultery with Julia Livilla.

24. In 34 C.E., Seneca, a Corduba native and *homo novus,* became a quaestor and thus a member of the Roman senate (see Fuhrmann, 67; Giebel, 20).

25. "Deine Ruhe stört/ ein Nachfahr jener Rüpel, die euch manche Scherereien/Bereitet haben an den Grenzen eures Reiches./ . . . /Zweitausend Jahre später . . . " (Grünbein, "An Seneca," lines 1–6).

26. See "Okololiteraturnyj Truten'," co-written by A. Ionin, Ja. Lerner, and M. Medvedev; cited in Etkind, 16–22.

27. Ibid., 16, 22.

28. See Etkind, 47. On Feb. 2, 1961, social parasitism (*tunejadstvo*) was outlawed by the Soviet Supreme Court. Under the new law, any adult who did not work, study, or serve in the military was considered a social parasite and subject to severe punishment, such as internal exile and forced labor. On the harsh reality of the implementation of the Soviet Criminal Code, see esp. Feofanov and Barry; Litvinov; and Sinjavskij and Daniel.

29. Thus the concluding statement of Judge Savel'eva's verdict, cited in Vigdorova, "Process Iosifa Brodskogo," 303.

30. See Emmanuel, 12; Samuil Maršak, cited in Etkind, 108. For comprehensive documentation of the "Brodsky case," see Etkind. Frida Vigdorova's secret transcript of Brodsky's trial was quickly smuggled out of the Soviet Union and published, in 1964, in such journals as the Polish *Kultura,* the American *New Leader,* the German *Die Zeit,* and the French *Le Figaro Littéraire.*

31. In an undated letter to the editor of *Večernij Leningrad* written sometime between November 29 and December 13, 1963, Brodsky offers a point-by-point refutation of the accusations leveled against him by the authors of "A Quasi-Literary Drone." The letter is located in the Brodsky archive, box 2, at the Beinecke Rare Book and Manuscript Library, Yale University.

32. During this period Brodsky worked as a milling machine operator at the Arsenal plant in Leningrad, as the coroner's assistant at the district hospital's morgue, as a member of the Fifth Geological Administration, and as of 1962, as a professional translator and poet, a fact clearly evidenced by his publication record (even if still meager at the time of his trial), as well as by several valid publication agreements (see Vigdorova, "Process Iosifa Brodskogo," 283, 286, 299; Volkov, 23–26).

33. These include, for example, the trial of Andrej Sinjavskij and Julij Daniel' in 1966, and the trial of Jurij Galanskov, Aleksandr Ginzburg, Aleksej Dobrovolskij, and Vera Laškova in 1967–1968; on these trials, see Sinjavskij and Daniel; Litvinov.

34. See Volkov, 32.

35. See Vigdorova, "Process Iosifa Brodskogo," 280. The *Figaro Littéraire* depicted the trial as "dramatique et comique" (Vigdorova, "Le Procès," 1).

36. See Volkov, 66, for Brodsky's reminiscence; also Vigdorova, "Process," 283. For a synoptic printing of Horace's "Exegi monumentum . . . " (*Odes and Epodes,* 3, 30), Lomonosov's "Posylka" (1747), Deržavin's "Pamjatnik" (1796), and Puškin's "Ja pamjatnik" (1836), see Lachmann, 339–343.

37. See Volkov, 76–77, 105; Etkind, 93–98. The Brodsky archive, box 2, at the Beinecke Rare Book and Manuscript Library, Yale University, contains an undated letter requesting

Brodsky's early release addressed to M. P. Maljarov, then attorney general of the USSR, and signed by Kornej Čukovskij, Frida Vigdorova, Anna Akhmatova, Efim Etkind, and Samuil Maršak, among others.

38. See BK, 212; Brodsky, *Conversations,* 81–82.

39. See Bobyšev, 346. "Officially [Basmanova's given] name is Marianna," Dmitry Bobyšev explains, "but she liked Marina better" (e-mail to the author, October 15, 2004). On Basmanova's first name—"Marina-Maria, and also Marianra"—see also Bobyšev, 384). My subsequent discussion of Brodsky's "greatest personal trouble" is based on his own account of the events in question (esp. BK, 212; Brodsky, *Conversations* 82), on Bobyšev's testimony (*Ja zdes',* 361–364, 379–383), and on the memoirs of Efim Etkind (esp. 89–91); Anatolij Najman (esp. 126, 137, 233–241); and Ludmila Shtern (esp. 114–131).

40. See Etkind, 90. "He never loved anyone," Ludmila Shtern, a close friend of Brodsky's, remembers, "the way he loved Marina Basmanova. For many years, inescapable longing for her tormented him. She became his obsession and the source of his inspiration. Once he confessed that Marina was his curse" (123).

41. "They picked me up on the street," Brodsky reminisces, "and took me to a police station, where they held me for about a week . . . after which they sent me to an asylum . . . for so-called forensic psychiatric assessment. They held me a few weeks. That was the bleakest time in my life . . . " (Volkov, 66). At his trial Brodsky dated his first psychiatric confinement "from the end of December 1963 to January 5, 1964 at Kaščenko psychiatric hospital in Moscow" (Vigdorova, "Process Iosifa Brodskogo," 281). All in all, Brodsky had to undergo psychiatric evaluations twice: "The first time in December 1963. The second . . . [in] February and March of 1964" (Volkov, 67). See also Brodsky, *Conversations,* 102.

42. Alik and Galja Šejnin in a letter to Ludmila Shtern (cited in Shtern, 118).

43. Bobyšev's testimony is partially confirmed by eyewitnesses present at the scene (see Shtern, 118).

44. Bobyšev's description of Norenskoe bears out the veracity of Brodsky's references to Norenskoe in his poems (see, for example, NSA, 24, 31, 45).

45. Andrej, Brodsky's son by Marianna Basmanova, was born on October 9, 1967 (see Brodsky, *Conversations,* xix).

46. See GR, 85; Volkov, 138. Pertinently, David Bethea notes that "much of [Brodsky's] work is unabashedly *occasional,* tethered to a specific time, place, relationship, or event that needs to be contextualized before it can be meaningful" (*Joseph Brodsky,* 89). Elsewhere Bethea notes that Brodsky's "words always make us think, and that is good, but it is even better if we have enough information [about Brodsky] so that our thinking is at least on the right track" ("Joseph Brodsky's 'To My Daughter,'" 242). It is unclear how Bethea can, in view of his emphasis on Brodsky's "occasionalism," dismiss critics' attention (including his own) to the details of Brodsky's biography—such as "persecution, penury, trials, imprisonment, and exile" (7)—as "imponderables" (ibid.) feeding into the nugatory creation of an "aureole of biographical legend" (ibid.).

47. See GR, 85, 223.

48. See Volkov, 292.

49. See GR, 97; LTO, 165. Brodsky's theoretical position on the interface between life and art is far from uniform or coherent. The claim that "biographical material [is] irrelevant . . . to the analysis of a work of art in general" (GR, 223) is blatantly contradicted by such claims as that it is "a man's only life [that] goes into writing a book" (97) and that "[l]iterature . . . always lags behind . . . experience, for it comes about as its result" (LTO, 264), both of which imply that biographical material *is* relevant, to an unspecified degree, to the "analysis of a work of art" (GR, 223). What Brodsky seems to suggest is that whatever the relationship between art and life may be, it should not be conceived of in terms of causality or facile mutual explicability. In his own practice as a reader, teacher, and critic, Brodsky avails himself of anything and everything—including biographical material—that will help him get his point across. Thus, to adduce only one example, his essay "Footnote to a Poem" (LTO, 195–267)—an extended, in-depth analysis of Marina Cvetaeva's elegy on the death of Rainer Maria Rilke, "Novogodnee" (New Year's Greetings)—teems with biographical material: "On February 27, 1927, in Bellevue, outside Paris, Marina Tsvetaeva finished 'Novogodnee.'. . . Tsvetaeva's 'Novogodnee' has much less in common with [Romanticism] than does the virtual hero of her poem, Rainer Maria Rilke. As possibly the only thread connecting Tsvetaeva with Romanticism in this poem one ought to consider the fact that for Tsvetaeva 'German is more native than Russian', i. e., that German was, on a par with Russian, the language of her childhood, which coincided with the end of the last century and the beginning of the present one, with all the consequences that nineteenth-century German literature entailed for a child. . . . For a start, let us note that it was precisely her knowledge of German that Tsvetaeva had to thank for her relation to Rilke, whose death, thus, delivered an indirect blow—across the whole of her life—to her childhood. For no other reason than that a child's attachment to a language (which is not native but *more native*) culminates in adulthood as reverence for poetry (that language's highest degree of maturity), an element of self-portraiture in 'Novogodnee' seems inevitable. 'Novogodnee,' however, is more than a self-portrait, just as Rilke to Tsvetaeva is more than a poet. . . . Even irrespective of Tsvetaeva's personal feelings toward Rilke—extremely powerful ones that underwent an evolution from Platonic love . . . even irrespective of these feelings, the death of the great German poet created a situation in which Tsvetaeva could not confine herself to an attempt at a self-portrait. . . . 'Novogodnee' is above all a confession. . . . The only thing in this correspondence [between the dead Rilke and Tsvetaeva] that might be thought to have a direct bearing on the poetics of 'Novogodnee' was Rilke's 'Elegy' dedicated to Tsvetaeva, which he sent to her on June 8, 1926 . . . " (LTO, 195, 197–198, 242, 247). For further instances of Brodsky's treatment of the question of life and art, see LTO, 28, 41, 60, 133, 164, 220, 304; GR, 48, 85, 245, 353, 358, 387; BK, 119, 122, 537–538.

50. As mentioned in the Introduction, in contrast to Emmanuel, Maršak, and Etkind (see note 30) I use *Brodsky affair* in a broad, comprehensive sense, as referring to both the public *and* the private dimensions of Brodsky's life at the time.

51. See GW, vol. 3, 198; Grünbein and Böttiger, 78. Elsewhere Celan writes, "Something occurs [*ereignet sich*] in a poem, something happens [*passiert*]. . . . In the poem everything enters into an event [*Geschehen*] . . . " (*Meridian*, 115, 125).

52. See Windelband, vol. 2, 19; Heidegger, *Beiträge*, 31, and "Zeit und Sein"; on von Ranke see Bambach, 106–108; and Koselleck, 55; see also Badiou, *Ethics*, 44, and *Manifeste*, 36; Koselleck, 145; and Attridge, *Singularity of Literature*, esp. 58–64. Recourse to Badiou in the present context is warranted in particular, in view of his philosophical debt to Celan's poetics; see esp. *Manifeste*, 66–67, *Conditions*, 100, and *Petit*, 55–58. I use the term *evental* following Hallward, 17.

53. See Badiou, *Ethics*, 27.

54. See James, 572.

55. On truth as adaequatio rei et intellectus (Thomas Aquinas, *De veritate*, Q. 1, *Summa Theologiae*, Q. 16), correspondence between mind and world, see, for example, Frege, 25–35; on the verificationist view of truth, see, for example, Murdoch, *Existentialists*, 60. For a concise summary of "conceptions of truth . . . in terms of coherence, correspondence, or confirmation," see Hallward, 153. For in-depth discussions of the history and varieties of the concept of truth, see Williams; Davidson; Sklar; Blackburn.

56. Augustine's "Non intratur in veritatem, nisi per caritatem" is cited in Pascal, *Pensées et opuscules*, 1928, 185; Celan explicitly refers to Pascal in GW, vol. 3, 195. In a letter to Gleb Struve of Jan. 29, 1959, Celan depicts his encounter with Mandelstam's poetry in May 1957 as follows: "Mandelstamm: rarement j'a eu, comme avec sa poésie, le sentiment de cheminer . . . aux côtés de l'Irrefutable et du Vrai, et *grâce à lui*" [Mandelstamm: rarely have I had, as with his poetry, the sense of waking . . . alongside the Irrefutable and the True] (cited in Terras and Weimar, 363). Interestingly, this phrase borrows heavily, in wording and tone, from the following passage in a letter of Jan. 23, 1958, to Celan from his wife, written during a particularly difficult period in their marriage due to Celan's ongoing affair with Ingeborg Bachmann: "Je suis si sure d'être dans le vrai en chemin avec toi, chemin difficile mais vrai" [I am certain of being in truth on the road with you—a road that is difficult but true] (CCL, vol. 1, 99).

57. See GW, vol. 2, 89. "A Booming" literally translates the gerund *Ein Dröhnen* in the original. Celan uses the same verb to render the Russian *gudit* in his translation of Mandelstam's poem "The Horse Shoe Finder" (GW, vol. 5, 130–137), which contains the following, contextually pertinent lines: "The air is trembling [*drožit*] with similes. / No word is better than the other, / The earth is booming [*gudit*] with metaphor" (MSS, vol. 2, 42–45, lines 31–33). Celan's *Dröhnen* obviously echoes Mandelstam's *drožit*.

58. See GR, 90–91; LTO, 355; Murdoch, *Sovereignty*, 64, 68; Hemingway, *Moveable Feast*, 12. Pertinently, Derek Attridge depicts *truth* as "a value, a feeling, a way of doing things, or some complex combination of these . . . " (*Singularity*, 39).

59. See Badiou, *Ethics*, 27, and *Saint Paul*, 48; Marcel, *Creative Fidelity*, 164.

60. See Badiou, *Ethics*, 42; Marcel, *Creative Fidelity*, 162.

61. See Marcel, *Philosophy of Existentialism*, 34–43; *Creative Fidelity*, 10, 49, 53, 147–174; *Mystery of Being*, vol. 2, 89, 139.

62. See Gallagher, 72.

63. Sleigh, *Islands*, 1; Coetzee, *Slow Man*, 161.

64. See GR, 91; Grünbein, *Antike*, 50.

65. I have found the following studies dealing with the manifold character and com-

plex history of love to be particularly helpful: Arendt; Vlastos; Soble; Tillich, 18–34, 82–88; Neumann; Bergmann; Singer, vols. 1–3.

66. My decision to engage *love* in a broad, amatory-erotic sense is based on the fact that already the meanings of the paradigmatic Greek terms (not to mention their equivalents in other languages) traditionally employed to capture the multifarious experience of *love* cannot strictly be differentiated. Not only do they blend into one another in Greek, as Gregory Vlastos has demonstrated with particular attention to the semantic points of intersection between *eros, philia,* and *agape* (112–113, 116; see also Soble, xxiii), but they also overlap in translation. *Agape* and *epithymia,* for instance, have both been translated as *dilectio;* the former has also been rendered as *caritas* and *amor,* the latter as *concupiscentia* and *libido* (see, for example, Deut. 12:15, 1 Peter 1:22).

67. See Plato, *Symposium,* 203 D (*Collected Dialogues*); 1 *Cor.* 13:11–13; Augustine, *Confessions,* vol. 1, 7, 10; Tillich, 34; Marcel, *Philosophy of Existentialism,* 20; Murdoch, *Sovereignty of Good,* 27, 65; Badiou, *Manifeste,* 64. Love, according to Brodsky, manifests itself in the "intensity of attention paid to this or that detail of the universe" (GR, 90). This kind of loving attention is paradigmatically thematized in Canto 13 of Dante's *Inferno,* in which Virgil tells his charge, "Look well [*riguarda ben*], therefore, and you shall see [*vederai*] things that would make my words incredible" (lines 21–22). On the conjunction of love and knowledge, see also Nussbaum, *Love's Knowledge;* Brümmer, 47–50.

68. See GR, 90.

69. I use *intentional* in Husserl's sense (*Die phänomenologische Methode,* 23, 46–47), that is, as constitutively directed at and oriented toward an other (person, object, concept, and so on).

70. See Benjamin, "Die Aufgabe," 59: "so muß . . . die Übersetzung liebend . . . dessen [i.e., des Originals] Art des Meinens in der eigenen Sprache sich anbilden . . . " (emphasis added in translation); GR, 91.

71. See Celan's poem "Aschenglorie . . . ," lines 24–26 (GW, vol. 2, 72). "Dans le cas de la Présence du Pour-soi à l'être en-soi," Sartre writes, "il ne saurait y avoir de troisième terme. Nul témoin . . . ne peut *l'établir,* cette présence . . . originellement le Pour-soi est présence à l'être en tant qu'il est à soi-même son propre témoin . . . " [In the case of the presence of the For-itself to being in-itself there cannot be a third term. No witness . . . can establish this presence. . . . Originally, the For-itself is present to being insofar as it is its own witness]" (161). On the question of testimony, see esp. Felman and Laub. Indication is a hermeneutic method by which that which is not immediately accessible to the interpreter (such as *Being, Truth, God*) must perforce be approached by way of that which is accessible; the latter can then be said to *indicate* the former (see Husserl, *Logische Untersuchungen,* 31; Heidegger, *Sein und Zeit,* 29, 315; Levinas, 49–56).

CHAPTER TWO

1. Shakespeare, Sonnet 21, line 9; Wiesel, *Time of the Uprooted,* 94.

2. See Adorno, 26.

3. See Damerau, "'Ich stand in dir,'" 293. For criticism representative of this most

prevalent approach to Celan, see, for example, Broda; Mayer; Lacoue-Labarthe; Buck; Felstiner; Fioretos; Levinas; Felman and Laub; Baer; Pajević; Ivanović; Del Caro.

4. See Damerau, 293.

5. Ibid.

6. "Was geschah . . . " (GW, vol. 3, 186) is Celan's shorthand for the Holocaust.

7. As I have pointed out elsewhere (*Ethics and Dialogue*, 145–146), Celan never developed a clear-cut, not to mention *systematic*, poetics. The latter can only be the product of the critic's attempt to extrapolate from and synthesize into a coherent whole a series of thematically related observations and propositions presented mainly in the Bremen and Büchner Prize speeches (both cited in GW, vol. 3, 185–188 and 187–202, respectively), as well as in a small number of scattered, short prose pieces and letters (see esp. GW, vol. 3, 167–203). I focus mainly on "Der Meridian."

8. "Gestaltgewordene Sprache eines Einzelnen" (GW, vol. 3, 197–198). *Dantons Tod* is cited in Büchner, 67–133. The real Camille Desmoulins was executed, together with Georges Jacques Danton, on Apr. 5, 1794.

9. See GW, vol. 3, 188–190.

10. See GW, vol. 3, 186. The real Lucile Desmoulins was executed on Apr. 13, 1794 (see Kropotkin, 546). For recent criticism on Celan's engagement with Büchner, see esp. Müller-Sievers; Derrida, "The Majesty of the Present," 20–22. Celan, who lost both of his parents to the Nazis and their accomplices, spent twenty months (July 1942–Feb. 1944) in various concentration–forced labor camps in Romania (see CCL, vol 2: 471).

11. On (with)standing in Celan's poetry, see Pajević, *Zur Poetik*, 208–212. On the ethical-political impetus of Lucile's "Es lebe der König!" see Thunecke. On Celan's conception of poetry as counter-word, see Brierley 59–70; Ivanović, *Das Gedicht*, 319–361; Vitiello; Eskin, *Ethics and Dialogue*, 156–157.

12. See Kropotkin; Landauer, *Briefe* and *Die Revolution*. Landauer, who called Kropotkin a "revolutionary . . . socialist [and] anarchist" (*Zwang*, 144), translated the latter's *The Great French Revolution* (1909) into German. According to Celan's biographer Israel Chalfen, throughout his high school days in Czernowitz Celan would "read anything and everything by Landauer . . . that would come his way" (from a letter to Jörg Thunecke, Apr. 22, 1981; cited in Thunecke, 30). As late as 1968, Celan referred to Landauer as "spiritually constitutive" for his existence (from a letter to Gideon Kraft, Apr. 23, 1968; cited in Thunecke, 30). It goes without saying that Büchner's denunciation of state power (see esp. "The Hessian Messenger" in *Werke und Briefe*, 39–65) constitutes the overall horizon of Celan's recourse to Kropotkin and Landauer in "Der Meridian."

13. See "Eine Ansprache an die Dichter" (1918; cited in Landauer, *Zwang*, 269). *Widerrede* (literally, counter-speech) is structurally and semantically equivalent to *Gegenwort*. See also the following contextually relevant entry in Lucile Desmoulins' diary on Aug. 10, 1792: "We want to be free. O God! At any cost"; cited in Landauer, *Briefe*, vol. 1, 175).

14. See Landauer, *Shakespeare*, 5, 11.

15. Ibid., 10. Landauer locates the "radical novelty" of his reflections on Shakespeare in their overall focus on the "principle of *freedom*" (*Shakespeare*, 5). As early as 1898, in his spirited commentary on the Dreyfus affair, "Der Dichter als Ankläger," in which he presents

himself as an "antipolitician," Landauer gives voice to his lifelong concern with the singular human being by appealing to an ethical realm "where all principles come to an end and where only the human being and the cry for human justice are heard" (*Zeit und Geist,* 58).

16. See Büchner, 132.

17. Augustine's definition of love as a person's wish that the other exist comes to mind at this point: "Amo means volo, ut sis, as Augustine puts its somewhere: I love you—I want you to be." (Martin Heidegger in a letter to Hannah Arendt, May 13, 1925; cited in Arendt and Heidegger, 31; see also Arendt, 71). Pertinently, Christine Ivanović suggests reading Lucile's exclamation as an attempt at countervailing and escaping "the curse of history" (*Das Gedicht,* 360).

18. That the spouses were deeply in love and completely crushed by their fate is attested to by Camille's letters to Lucile, written from the Luxembourg prison shortly before his death: "My Lucile, . . . my angel! . . . My dearest Lucile! My most beloved Lucile! . . . My Lucile, my dear Loulou. . . . I shall see you again one day, oh Lucile! . . . is death, which delivers me from the spectacle of so many crimes, such a great misfortune? Farewell my life, my soul, my godhead on earth. . . . I see the banks of life receding. . . . I still see, Lucile! . . . my most dearly beloved! My Lucile! My shackled hands embrace you, and even after my head has been severed from my body my eyes will be resting on you." From letters of Mar. 31 and Apr. 1, 1794; cited in Landauer, *Briefe,* vol. 1, 183, 190–191. See also Schama, 819–820.

19. See GW, iii, 198. Gegenüber literally means "counter-over."

20. John Felstiner appropriately, if awkwardly, translates *Gegenüber* as "Over-against" (Celan, *Selected Poems,* 409).

21. On Celan's poetics of dialogue and encounter, see Ivanović, *Das Gedicht,* 1–16, 212–260, 319–361; Eskin, *Ethics and Dialogue,* 144–160.

22. See, for instance, Eskin, *Ethics and Dialogue,* 155–156; Eshel, "Paul Celan's Other," 61; Müller-Sievers, "On the Way"; Vitiello, "Gegenwort"; Felstiner, *Paul Celan,* 140, 163–166.

23. From a letter to Hans Bender, May 18, 1960, written when Celan was already at work on "Der Meridian"; cited in GW, vol. 3, 177. "Poetry as a mode of existence," Celan notes elsewhere, "ultimately entails not seeing any essential difference between a poem and a handshake" (*Meridian,* 134). For a chronology of the genesis of "Der Meridian," see Celan, *Meridian,* x–xiv.

24. See Büchner, 173 (emphasis added).

25. See Buber, 182, 18, 21. Celan explicitly refers to Buber in his Bremen Prize speech (GW, vol. 3, 185). On the importance of Buber for Celan, see Felstiner, *Paul Celan,* 160–161; and Fassbind.

26. See Celan, "Notiz," 67; MSS, vol. 1, 187.

27. See GW, vol. 1, 280.

28. On the language of love and eroticism in Celan's poetry—the references are too numerous to be listed—from his earliest extant texts (see esp. *Frühwerk*) to the posthumously published collections *Lichtzwang* (Light Compulsion) (1970), *Schneepart* (Snow Part) (1971), and *Zeitgehöft* (Homestead of Time) (1976), see Voswinckel, 125–143; Wörge-

bauer; Bevilacqua; Damerau; Böschenstein. Celan learned about the award from his wife on May 14, 1960 (CCL, vol. 2, 523); he worked on "Der Meridian" between May and Oct. 1960. Although some of the themes in "Der Meridian"—such as the dialogic conception of poetry and the invocation of Büchner's narrative *Lenz*—had already been explored in such texts as the Bremen Prize speech and "Gespräch im Gebirg" (Conversation in the Mountains) (GW, vol. 3, 169–173; written in Aug. 1959), the notion of poetry as counter-word was first elaborated in the Büchner Prize speech.

29. For Celan's obliteration of an essential distinction between poetic creation and translation, see Terras and Weimar, 365.

30. On Celan's profuse activity as a translator during this period, see CCL, vol. 2, 516–544. "With five book-length translations [and] over thirty short pieces published in German-language newspapers and periodicals," the translator Celan was, between 1960 and 1963, "more visible than the poet" (Wiedemann, "'Es ist,'" 849).

31. See Felstiner, *Paul Celan*, 205.

32. As remembered by philosopher Otto Pöggeler, cited in Lengeler, *Shakespeares Sonette in deutscher Übersetzung*, 31.

33. Between September 1959 and July 1964, Celan translated the following sonnets by Shakespeare into German (for the dates of the translations, provided in parentheses, see Gellhaus, 426): Sonnets 90 (Sept. 21–25, 1959) and 137 (Feb. 14, 1960), were both published in *Die Neue Rundschau*, 71, no. 1, (1960), 98–99. Sonnets 1–5 and 70–71 (Feb. 5–12, 1961); 43, 60 (Dec. 10, 1963); 50, 65, 79, 81, 115–116, and 119 (Oct. 31, 1963); 57 (Nov. 21, 1963); and 105–106 (Nov. 1, 1963) were published in *Die Neue Rundschau*, 75, no. 2 (1964), 204–213.). In 1967 all of the sonnets were published together in book form along with an additional translation (Sonnet 107, Nov. 29 and- Dec. 21, 1966) under the title *Einundzwanzig Sonette* (Frankfurt am Main: Insel; reprinted in GW, vol. 5, 316–357). While still in Romania, Celan had already tackled sonnets 34, 50, 57, 106, 109, 116, 117, 130, and 132 (all published in Allemann and Bücher. For Celan's recourse to Shakespeare in his poetry "proper," see, for instance, "Give the Word" (a quote from *King Lear*) in GW, vol. 2, 93. Certainly Celan's particular choice of sonnets may have been motivated, questions of taste and translatability aside, by the degree of their perceived thematic germaneness to his life situation at the time.

34. Byron, *Don Juan*, Canto 2, stanza 209, line 1; Wiesel, *Time of the Uprooted*, 136.

35. I should point out that although Celan was asked in the fall of 1963 by representatives of Norddeutscher Rundfunk whether he would be interested in translating some of Shakespeare's sonnets on the occasion of the upcoming quatercentenary of Shakespeare's birth (see Gellhaus, 427), Celan's intensive engagement with Shakespeare during this period was not in any way triggered by this request, which it predated and which, in a way, happened to coincide and dovetail productively with Celan's own ongoing poetic agenda. This does not mean, however, that Celan was not grateful, as he explicitly avers, for the opportunity to contribute to such a festive and honorable event (see esp. Gellhaus, 428–429).

36. "For me," Celan avers, "there is nothing more great and more beautiful than Shakespeare," in a letter to his wife of Aug. 8, 1965; cited in CCL, vol. 1, 288.

37. See GW, vol. 5, 341. Shakespeare's sonnets are cited according to the 1609 quarto

edition (reprinted, for instance, in *Shakespeare's Sonnets*, ed. Stephen Booth). Celan's translations of Shakespeare's sonnets are cited in GW, vol. 5, 316–357. I henceforth dispense with page references to the individual translations.

38. For a synopsis of the sonnet sequence's plot and themes, see Fineman, 320: "In brief, according to [accepted literary] tradition, sonnets 1–126 are addressed to a young man, and they develop the poet's increasingly complicated relationship to this young man whom the poet defines as his beloved ideal. Sonnets 127–54 are addressed primarily to a lady, also an object of the poet's desire, though this is a desire definitely lacking an ideal complexion. Two different narrative crises occur in the course of these two different relationships: (1) the affections of the young man for the poet are challenged by the appearance of a rival poet or poets (sonnets 78–86); (2) the poet's relation to the lady is disrupted by her affair with the ideal young man (133, 134, 144; other sonnets on the lady's duplicity supplement this story); this cuckoldry duplicates . . . an earlier infidelity on the part of the young man—35, 40, 41, 42—which may itself be a happier, anticipatory account of the later infidelity with the dark lady."

39. On the history of Shakespeare's reception in Germany since his first appearance in German print, in Daniel Georg Morhof's *Unterricht von der Teutschen Sprache und Poesie, deren Uhrsprung, Fortgang und Lehrsätzen* (1682), see Eskin, "The 'German' Shakespeare"; Blinn.

40. "Nature! Nature! Nothing as natural as Shakespeare's characters," Goethe wrote in 1771 ("Zum Schäkespears Tag," cited in Blinn, vol. 1, 100). In a letter to A. W. Schlegel of Nov. 30, 1797, Novalis observes that in "German [Shakespeare] is . . . better than [in] English" (cited in Apel, 99). In his 1796 essay on Goethe's Wilhelm Meister and his appropriation of Shakespeare, A. W. Schlegel notes that "next to the English [Shakespeare] does not belong to any other people as intimately as to the Germans, because by no other people is he . . . so warmly loved" ("Etwas über William Shakespeare bei Gelegenheit Wilhelm Meisters," cited in Schlegel, 99). In 1844, Ferdinand Freiligrath famously proclaimed, "Deutschland ist Hamlet!" (cited in Muschg, 21). On September 20, 1939, and July 16, 1940, the Nazi Ministry of Propaganda issued decrees to the effect that "Shakespeare . . . be treated as a German author" (cited in Habicht, 155). See also Jaspers; Schmitt; Grünbein, *Antike Dispositionen,* 134. On Jaspers' and Schmitt's discussions of Shakespeare, see Schabert, 286–287; on the vast topic of "Shakespeare and Germany," see Blinn; Habicht; Muschg; Suerbaum; Macey.

41. See Suerbaum, 61; Czernin, 100; Grünbein, *Antike,* 138. For a comprehensive bibliography of all translations of Shakespeare's sonnets into German through 1994 (140 total), see Leithner-Brauns. Since 1994 at least two more translations have appeared, both published in 1999: Christa Schuenke translated all 154 sonnets, and Franz Josef Czernin translated 45.

42. See Holthusen, *Ja und Nein: Neue kritische Versuche* (1954), cited in GA, 206.

43. After the collapse of the Austro-Hungarian Empire in 1918, Bukovina passed to Romania. Celan, who was born in Czernowitz, Bukovina, on November 23, 1920, was thus a native Romanian. Celan took French citizenship on July 8, 1955 (CCL, vol. 2, 501). On Celan's rising prominence in Germany in the wake of his public reading at the gathering

of the Gruppe 47 in Niendorf in May 1952, see Briegleb, 53–54, 76n29; CCL, vol. 2, 489. Barbara Wiedemann appositely notes that Celan was "a complete outsider within the German literary establishment" ("'Es ist,'" 341).

44. See note 36.

45. Celan's Shakespeare translations have been widely discussed in terms of their linguistic and rhetorical idiosyncrasies and, to a limited extent, in connection with his biography (see Szondi (esp. 13–45); Gellhaus (esp. 417–459); Felstiner, "Translating Celan"; Pepper; Voss; Beese (esp. 93–194); Olschner (esp. 89–90, 108, 115–118, 295–304); Lengeler; Petuchowski; Simonis; Kaußen; Leithner-Brauns). For scholarship on Celan's practice of poetic translation more generally, see, for instance, Rexheuser Ivanović, *Das Gedicht*; Eskin, *Ethics and Dialogue*. When necessary, I juxtapose Celan's translations of Shakespeare's sonnets with those of other translators especially those translations with which Celan was familiar.

46. Given the limited framework of this chapter and the overall focus of this book, I dispense with a detailed discussion of the identity of the sonnets' protagonists. Suffice it to note that critical speculation has yielded, among others William Herbert, Earl of Pembroke, Henry Wriothesley, Earl of Southampton, William Hart, and Will Hughes as candidates for the "young man" and dedicatee; Mary Fitton (Pembroke's lover), Anne Davenant (Southampton's lover), the Italian musician Emilia Lanier, and the prostitute Lucy Negro as candidates for the "dark lady"; and finally, Edmund Spenser, Christopher Marlowe, George Chapman, and Ben Jonson as candidates for the "rival poet." For studies on the sonnets' historical context, see Booth, *Shakespeare's Sonnets* 547–549; Schiffer; Laroche; Pfister. Stephen Booth's laconic observation that "William Shakespeare was almost certainly homosexual, bisexual, or heterosexual" (Shakespeare, *Shakespeare's Sonnets,* 548) and that the "sonnets provide no [conclusive] evidence on the matter" (ibid.) still applies. For studies on love and eroticism in the sonnets, see A. Bloom; Burnham; Klein; Sharney; Smith; Traub; Stallybrass.

47. For a cursory discussion of some of Celan's most overtly autobiographical poems, see Eskin, "'To truths translated,'" 82n10.

48. On January 31, 1960, Celan sent this translation to Rudolf Hirsch, then editor-in-chief of S. Fischer, Celan's publisher (see Gellhaus, 427).

49. Translation of Celan's translation of Shakespeare's "the very worst of Fortune's might" (Sonnet 90, line 12) as "Schläge . . . die da mein Los." For the reader's convenience, throughout the remainder of this chapter, in parentheses following Shakespeare's original and Celan's version, I provide crude literal English translations of the latter.

50. See CCL, vol. 1, 133.

51. In the autobiographical poem "Eine Gauner- und Ganovenweise . . . " (first draft dated Feb. 16, 1961), Celan takes up the phrase "sich bäumt": the poem ends "aber *er bäumt sich*, der Baum. Er, / auch er / steht gegen / *die* Pest" (but *it resists*, the tree. It, / it too / stands against/ *the* plague) (GW, vol. 1, 230). He thereby retroactively reinforces the anti-defamatory intent of his translation of Sonnet 90. On Dec. 10, 1963, Celan wrote to Ernst Schnabel of the Norddeutscher Rundfunk, "As I have four German translations before me the difficulty consists, among other things, in the necessity to steer clear of all of this,

at times, even of various turns of phrase prefigured and dictated by the original itself" (cited in Gellhaus, 429). The four translations to which Celan refers in this particular letter are those by Otto Gildermeister (1871), Terese Robinson (1927)—Celan owned copies of both—and most likely by Eduard Saenger (1909), and Rolf-Dietrich Keil (1959) (Gellhaus, 428). Celan was also familiar with the translations of Gottlob Regis (1836), Friedrich Gundolf (1899), Stefan George (1909), and Karl Kraus (1933) (see Gellhaus, 419; Chalfen, 83). According to Israel Chalfen, Celan was highly critical of the versions by George, Gundolf, and Kraus (83).

52. Only Saenger, like Celan, repeats "hassen, hasse" in line 1 of Sonnet 90.

53. Completed on Feb. 5, 1961, this translation was initially intended by Celan as one of the epigraphs to his collection *Die Niemandsrose* (1963), which "most overtly testifies to the [Goll] affair," as Wiedemann rightly suggests (in view of the historical coincidence of the most heated phase of the Goll affair with the collection's completion and publication, as well as with Celan's work on Shakespeare) (GA, 807). Celan's *Argwohn und Verdacht* and *beargwöhnt* hark back to Regis's and Gildermeister's translations of Shakespeare's *suspect* in lines 3 and 13 as *Verdacht und Argwohn* and *Argwohn,* respectively.

54. See GW, vol. 3, 185–186 (emphasis added).

55. *Verfinstrung*, an elided variant of *Verfinsterung*, implies processuality through the prefix *Ver* and the ending *ung* (analogous to the English *ing*). Literally it means "darkening," "eclipsing," "gloomying." Its meaning is determined by the root *finster* (dark, gloomy, sinister). See also Wiesel, *Night.*

56. Christa Schuenke, one of Shakespeare's most recent German translators, pertinently observes that "every translation is marked by the translator's biography" (Schuenke and Jansohn, 163).

57. The intensity of Celan's dismay at and anger about the Goll affair, as it is indirectly articulated in his version of Sonnet 50, clearly emerges if we compare this version with Celan's earlier version of the same sonnet, dating from the early 1940s. Although Celan had already personalized Shakespeare's anger in the earlier version—*ich ärgerlich ihn fühlen ließ* (I angrily let him feel) (cited in Allemann and Bücher, 169)—*ärgerlich* bespeaks a much softer emotional response (annoyance rather than anger) than the later *Zorn* (anger, wrath).

58. For the sonnet sequence's plot and themes, see note 38.

59. In choosing *Arg* to render Shakespeare's *ill* in line 14 of Sonnet 57, Celan again—as in his version of Sonnet 70—follows Regis's and Gildermeister's translations (see note 50).

60. See Benjamin, "Die Aufgabe des Übersetzers," 59 ("so muß . . . die Übersetzung liebend . . . und bis ins Einzelne hinein dessen [i. e., des Originals] Art des Meinens in der eigenen Sprache sich anbilden"). The title of Benjamin's essay is commonly translated "The Task of the Translator." However, it should not be forgotten that *Aufgabe* also means "relinquishment," "letting go," "obliteration," "loss." Thus an equally legitimate translation of the title of Benjamin's essay into English would be "The Obliteration of the Translator." The importance of Benjamin for Celan is most saliently evidenced in the fact that the poet refers to the thinker by name in "Der Meridian" (GW, vol. 3, 198). On Celan's familiarity with Benjamin's writings (with "The Task of the Translator" in particular) and their relevance for poetics, see Lönker, 216–217; Ivanović, "Trauer"; Weigel.

61. I should note that I do not here pursue the question of the *reader* beyond its contextual relevance as part of my argument.

62. Mandelstam's poem (lines 7–8) and Celan's translation (each followed by an English translation) are cited in GW, vol. 5, 66–67.

63. See Eskin, "Answerable Criticism." Celan's translation of "Rakovina"—"Die Muschel"—was first published in *Die Neue Rundschau*, 69, no. 3 (1958). "Rakovina," Clarence Brown observes, is "wholly . . . about poetry"; the poet "is . . . the shell" (163). Mandelstam's injunction to the reader ("you will love") is *a fortiori* directed at his very first translator into any language, that is, Celan. "Translation," Karl S. Weimar notes, "is the visible fruit of apprehension" (90).

64. For more "faithful" versions of this line, see, for instance, Regis, "Wenn ich gestorben, traure länger nicht" (When I am dead mourn no longer); Gildermeister, "Wenn ich gestorben bin, betraure mich / Nicht" (When I am dead, do not mourn); George, "Nicht länger klage um mich wenn ich tot" (No longer mourn for me when I am dead); and Robinson, "Nicht länger klag um mich, wenn ich dahin" (No longer mourn for me when I am gone).

65. As far as I can tell, only four other sonnets marginally address the actual meaning of love: Sonnets 40 ("Take all my loves"), 115 ("Love is a babe"), 124 ("If my dear love were"), and 147 ("My love is a fever").

66. Although it would be hard to imagine an Elizabethan poet calling his own feelings "kind," the semantics of this sonnet clearly suggest that "love" in line 5 is equivalent to "love" in line 1, which, as Joel Fineman has pointed out, explicitly refers to "the poet's desire" (141) and not to the "object of his desire" (ibid.), that is, to his "beloved," who is explicitly contrasted with "love" in line 2. For further instances of Shakespeare's use of "love" not in reference to his beloved(s), see, for example, Sonnets 76 and 147. I would like to thank Derek Attridge for alerting me to the necessity of explicating this point.

67. "Mir," an ethical dative case, signifies an unspecified emotional-deictic emphasis.

68. The fact that Celan capitalizes *Einen* (One), thus turning the indefinite article "ein(e/r)"/(a) into a proper noun, strongly suggests the term's reference to Freund in line 5.

69. See Vendler, *The Art,* 447. "By identifying his beloved's qualities (*fair, kind, and true*) as those of the Platonic Triad (the Beautiful, the Good, the True)," Vendler observes, "the poet opposes to his accuser's Christian Trinity an equally powerful . . . classical, cultural totem. . . . Whereas the Good is the highest value in Christian practice . . . Shakespeare . . . produces a clear . . . opposition of the (Christian) priority of the Good to the (aesthetic) priority of the Beautiful . . . " (445–446). On the notion of idolatry and the sonnet's relation to Christian doctrine, see also Stephen Booth's commentary in *Shakespeare's Sonnets,* 336–337.

70. "All imperatives are expressed through an *Ought (Sollen)*"; Kant, *Kritik der praktischen Vernunft,* 227.

71. On the meaning of *argument* in this context, Stephen Booth notes, "*argument* [means] topic [as in Sonnet 76, line 10, and Sonnet 103, line 3] . . . however . . . although the context dictates 'is my only topic' for the focal phrase of this line, the line can be read as

(and in any case carries overtones of) 'All of my reasoning is honest, natural, and accurate'" (Shakespeare, *Shakespeare's Sonnets,* 338).

72. See Vendler, *The Art,* 445–446.

73. See GW, vol. 3, 167 ("sie versucht, wahr zu sein"), and vol. 2, 89 ("Wahrheit"); Wiedemann, "'Es ist,'" 843.

74. Celan's use of heißen here instead of *nennen* indicates elevation of style.

75. See also Petuchowski for a discussion of some of Celan's colloquialisms.

76. That these lines can be and, in fact, have been rendered more faithfully is evidenced, for instance by the translations of Regis, Gildermeister, and George: "Was ich dir vormals schrieb, falsch muß ich's nennen:/ 'Nie könnte ich wärmer lieben dich als heut'./ Denn wie die Glut je heller sollte brennen,/ Sah da mein Urteil keine Möglichkeit" (What I wrote to you before, I have to call't false:/ "Never will I love you more warmly than today"./ For how the embers ought ever to burn more brightly,/ My judgment did not see a possibility) (Regis); "Die Verse, die ich schrieb, wie logen sie,/ Daß ich dich nie herzinn'ger lieben könne!/ Da wußt ich aber nicht, warum und wie/ Die volle Flamme einst noch klarer brenne" (The verses that I wrote, how they lied,/ That I could never love you more intimately!/ I did not know then, why and how/ The full flame one day even clearer would burn) (Gildermeister); "Die reihen die ich früher schrieb sind lug—/ Auch dieses: lieben könnte ich euch nicht treuer./ Damals sah ich nicht ein nach welchem fug/ Einst heller brennen sollt mein vollstes feuer" (The rows that I used to write are lies—/ This too: I could not love you more truly./ Then I did not know at the behest of which destiny/ One day brighter would burn my fullest fire) (George). Terese Robinson anticipates Celan's eroticized translation in using the words heiß and *Trieb* (drive) to capture the sonneteer's love: "Die Zeilen, die ich einst dir schrieb:/ 'Nie werde ich dich *heißer* lieben können.'/ Ich wußte nicht, aus welchem Grund und *Trieb*/ Die hohe Flamme sollte höher brennen" (The lines that I once wrote to you: "Never will I be capable of loving you more ardently." / I did not know for what reason or as a result of which drive/ The high flame should burn higher).

77. Pertinently, Christa Schuenke translates Shakespeare's "Making lascivious comments on thy sport" (Sonnet 95, line 6, which refers to the young man's promiscuity) as "Hör, wie sie lüstern, was du *treibst*, berichten" (Listen, how salaciously, they report on what you're up to) (emphasis added).

78. See GW, vol. 1, 284. "Es ist alles anders" is dated June 5, 1962 (see Celan, *Die Niemandsrose,* 136).

79. I should stress that what I have advanced as Celan's sexual or erotic notion of poetic signification is not to be confused with the common—and facile, in my view—metaphorical equation of language or speech and sex based on the semantic-morphological proximity between the grammatical *copula* and the physical act of "copulation." For a representative articulation of this view see, for instance, the following passage from George Steiner's *After Babel:* "Eros and language mesh at every point. Intercourse and discourse, copula and copulation, are sub-classes of the dominant fact of communication. They arise from the life-need of the ego to reach out and comprehend, in the two vital senses of 'understanding' and 'containment,' another human being. Sex is a profoundly semantic act. Like language,

it is subject to the shaping force of social convention, rules of proceeding, accumulated precedent. To speak and to make love is to enact distinctive twofold universality: both forms are universals of human physiology as well as of social evolution. It is likely that human sexuality and speech developed in close-knit reciprocity. Together they generate the history of self-consciousness, the process, presumably millenary and marked by innumerable regressions, whereby we have hammered out the notion of self and otherness. . . . The interactions of the sexual and the linguistic accompany our whole lives" (38).

80. Celan's biographers note that in December 1962 Celan showed the first signs of madness (CCL, vol. 2, 540). He attacked a passer-by on the street, accusing him of being "part of the plot [of the Goll affair]" (ibid.). On another occasion he tore a yellow kerchief off his wife's neck because it reminded him of the Nazis' yellow star. On Celan's psychiatric treatments, see CCL, vol. 2, 541–596.

81. See GW, vol. 3, 190, 198.

82. See GW, vol. 3, 197.

83. The familiar formula traduttore, traditore (translator, betrayer) encapsulates translation's ethical-linguistic double bind (see, for example, Ortega y Gasset, 94). Since the study and practice of translation was first adopted as part of the rhetorical curriculum in ancient Rome, translators have had to tackle the ethical-linguistic question of the extent of their obligation to be faithful, in one way or another, to the original and its author. Thus Cicero, one of the earliest theorists of translation, noted that in order to exercise fidelity to their "virtues, that is, the thoughts, the figures of thought and the order of topics" (373) he decided to render the speeches of Demosthenes and Aeschines into Latin not as an "interpreter, but as an orator . . . in a language which conforms to our usage" (365). Notwithstanding their theoretical and conceptual differences, virtually all of Cicero's translator-successors—from St. Jerome through Dryden, Pope, Humboldt, and Schleiermacher to Benjamin, Ortega y Gasset, Jakobson, and Nabokov—agree on the centrality of the question of a translation's fidelity or infidelity vis-à-vis its source text when it comes to determining its tasks and significance. On the theory of translation in ancient Rome (esp. Cicero and Quintilian), see Schadewaldt, 250–251; Bassnett, 43–45. For significant contributions to the theory of translation from antiquity to the present more generally, see Störig; Brower; Schulte and Biguenet; Venuti. For studies on the history of translation theory, see Steiner; Apel; Venuti, esp. *The Translator's Invisibility.*

84. See lines 9–10 and 13 of Celan's translation of Sonnet 115.

85. See the poem "Kermorvan," line 7 (GW, vol. 1, 262; Celan's emphasis). For this poem's date of composition, see Celan, *Die Niemandsrose,* 96.

86. The term *belles infidèles* (unfaithful beauties) was coined by Gilles Ménage in the mid-seventeenth century, with particular reference to Perrot d'Ablancourt's Gallicized versions of classical Greek and Roman authors. On the history and contemporary applications of the phrase *belles infidèles,* see von Stackelberg.

87. See GW, vol. 3, 194, 186, 201.

88. See Eskin, *Ethics and Dialogue,* 19.

CHAPTER THREE

1. Grünbein, *Vom Schnee*, 19; Ransmayr, 253, 269; Andersch, 131.

2. See Badiou, *L'être*, 429.

3. See Benveniste, vol. 1, 259–260. On the *inventedness* of the *subject*, see also Nietzsche, "Zur Genealogie," 279.

4. See Bohrer, 13. Simon Critchley offers an elegant synopsis of the "modern philosophical use of the word *subject* as the conscious or thinking . . . self or ego, as that to which representations are attributed or predicated . . . " (51). Because even a tentative list of philosophical and critical works dealing with the question of the *subject* in its multiple avatars (for example, *creator, substance, agent, mover, reason, mind, author, self, ego, bearer of ideology, voice,* and so on) would be virtually limitless, I restrict myself to mentioning (in addition to the previously cited texts by Benveniste, Critchley, Badiou, and Bohrer) the following contextually germane discussions: Žižek (esp. 149–159); Carroll; Genette, *Fiction and Diction,* 69–79 (esp. 78); Fineman. Unlike Joel Fineman, I approach poetic subjectivity not as a "poetic posture" and a "general and conventional topo[s]" (2, 14) but rather as on a par and hence coextensive with the "real" subject.

5. See Grünbein, *Schädelbasislektion,* 35.

6. See Grünbein, *Grauzone morgens,* 26; *Schädelbasislektion,* 13, 31 (also 11, 19, 49, 102); *Falten und Fallen,* 76 (also 78), *Vom Schnee* 21 ("Who is I? Paper, paper").

7. See Grünbein, *Das erste Jahr,* 171.

8. For a general discussion of Grünbein's poetics and some of its major themes, see Eskin, "Body Language." For further scholarship on Grünbein, see esp. von Albrecht; Meyer; Geisenhanslüke; Korte; Arnold.

9. See Grünbein, *Schädelbasislektion,* 73, 133. Part 5 of *Schädelbasislektion* is entitled "Der Cartesische Hund" (89–107). The germinal idea for what would subsequently grow into *Vom Schnee* can be found in the poetic sequence "Meditation After Descartes" (Grünbein, *Falten und Fallen,* 78–79). For Descartes' "Cogito, ergo sum" / "Je pense, donc je suis," see *Discours,* 54–55; *Oeuvres,* vol. 7, 140 (also *Méditations,* 75, 79). On Grünbein's re-creation of Descartes' life and thought in *Vom Schnee,* see Eskin, "Descartes."

10. See Grünbein, Oleschinski, and Waterhouse, 33. "To every logic," Grünbein writes, "there corresponds a poetic logic, to every epistemological axiom there corresponds a poetic axiom" (ibid.).

11. "Galilei vermißt Dantes Hölle und bleibt an den Maßen hängen" (cited in Grünbein, *Galilei,* 103).

12. See MSS, vol. 3, 406. I do not deal with the philosophical intricacies of Cartesianism, such as whether Descartes' insistence on the (onto)logical primacy of the *cogito* is valid. Jean-Paul Sartre's critique of Descartes' *cogito* in the name of a prereflexive *cogito* is as apposite today as it was in 1943 (see Sartre, 16–23). For an excellent discussion of the *cogito* see Broughton, 108–143. On Grünbein's emulation of Mandelstam's reading of Dante, see Eskin, "'Stimmengewirr.'" Grünbein's practice of poetry as an integral cognitive process ought also to be read as part of his overall debt to Dante, who, against the dictates of scholasticism, which "denied any cognitional value to poetry, relegating it to making ornate lies" (Greenfield, 74), was the first modern author to consider poetry "not to be a substitute

for theology and philosophy, but to include manifestations of truths pertinent to both" (67). On the relationship between philosophy, theology, and poetry throughout the late Middle Ages and the early Renaissance, see Curtius, 219–230, 352–361; Cassirer, Kristeller, and Randall, 1–21.

13. See Aristotle, *Poetics*, 1459a4–9. Aristotle defines *metaphor* as the "application of a word that belongs to another thing: either from genus to species, species to genus, species to species, or by analogy" (1457b7–9). "The simile," Aristotle explains in *Rhetoric* (1406b4), "is also a metaphor; for there is very little difference. When the poet says of Achilles, 'he rushed on like a lion,' it is a simile; if he says 'a lion, he rushed on,' it is a metaphor. . . . Similes must be used like metaphors, which only differ in the manner stated." Aristotle's understanding of metaphor and simile as more or less identical tropes was codified in Quintilian's famous definition of metaphor as an "abbreviated simile": "metaphora brevior est similitudo" (*Institutio Oratorio,* vol. 8, 6, line 8). On *metaphor* as shorthand for poetry in general, see Franke; Genette, *Figures III,* 21–40.

14. Mandelstam implicitly juxtaposes Dante's poetic method with Descartes' philosophical method and transfers the features of the latter onto the former in applying the name *Descartes*, which metonymically signifies Descartes' method *tout court*, to Dante. On Mandelstam and Dante, see the Appendix.

15. On Descartes as the "father of modern philosophy," see Watson, 3. For an exemplary instance of the practice of treating Descartes as a cultural-historical marker, see the following passage in Jürgen Habermas's *Philosophical Discourse of Modernity*, in which Descartes is reduced to the "principle of subjectivity": "In the modern era, religious life, state and society, as well as science, ethics, and art become embodiments of the principle of subjectivity. Its structure *as such* is philosophically captured in the abstract subjectivity of Descartes' 'Cogito, ergo sum' . . . " (29). For a competing account of the rise of "modern subjectivity" beginning from "Luther's famous statement that man is the excrement that fell out of God's anus," see Žižek, 157. For an alternative view of Descartes as a "perceptual, indeed *sensuous*, philosopher," see Almog, xi. On Descartes' life and thought, see Rodis-Lewis; Watson; Specht. On the philosophical-historical significance of Descartes more specifically, see, for instance, Heidegger, *Nietzsche,* vol. 2, 148–149; Habermas, 161; Badiou, *Manifeste,* 12.

16. See Habermas, 29. For Descartes' diary entry, see *Oeuvres,* vol. 10, 175 ("X Novembris 1619, cum . . . mirabilis scientiae fundamenta reperirem . . . "). On the "specter" of Cartesianism, see Žižek, 1–5.

17. Famously, Hayden White has argued that in employing "conceptual strategies . . . to explain or represent data . . . the historian performs an essentially *poetic* act, in which he *prefigures* the historical field and constitutes it as a domain upon which to bring to bear the specific theories he will use to explain 'what was *really* happening' in it" (x). On the interface between history and poetry, see also Koselleck, 51–52, 279.

18. See Descartes, *Discours de la méthode,* 25. This is only one of a number of instances in which Descartes resorts to the device of poeticization or fictionalization in his philosophical writings. See also, for instance, *Discours de la méthode* 62–63 (on fiction of the "new world"), 65–66 (on fiction, anticipating a similar move in the *Meditations,* about

God's creation of an exact replica of the human body, albeit without a soul); *Méditations métaphysiques,* 72–77 (on fiction of the "evil genius"). For definitions of *fable,* see Littré's *Dictionnaire de la langue française,* which lists, among other meanings, "Récit imaginaire" and "Petit récit qui cache une moralité sous le voile d'une fiction" (2357). In addition to signifying a field of inquiry or a series of events and their narrativization (2997–2999), *histoire* was also used in the sense of *image* and *dessin,* throughout the sixteenth century in particular (Huguet, 481). Koselleck points out that "history meant both picture and story" (17) during the period in question. Brodsky's observation that *history* "may stand simultaneously for the past in general, the recorded past, an academic discipline, the quality of the present, or the implication of a continuum" (GR, 115) neatly sums up the term's abiding polysemy. On the "faces of history," see also Kelley. For applications of *histoire* and *fable* more or less contemporary with those of Descartes, see, for instance, Cyrano de Bergerac's *Histoire comique contenant les estat et empires de la lune. L'histoire comique des estats et empire du soleil* (1657), Alain-René Lesage's *Histoire de Gil Blas de Santillane* (1715–1735), and Jean de La Fontaine's *Fables* (1668–1694). On the history of the concept of *history,* see Koselleck, 38–66.

19. See Descartes, *Discours,* 54.

20. See Descartes, *Discours,* 25; "putting into doubt" is Descartes' basic methodological device (see esp. *Discours,* 40; *Méditations,* 66–67). On Descartes' method of doubt, see Broughton.

21. See Descartes, *Discours,* 33. Descartes stayed in southern Germany for "two or three months" (41) before embarking on a nine-year stint of "crisscrossing the world, while attempting to be more of a spectator than an actor in its manifold comedies" (50).

22. See also Grünbein's most recent engagement with the question of subjectivity in "Kein reines Ich."

23. See Grünbein, *Antike Dispositionen,* 192.

24. See Nietzsche, "Jenseits von Gut und Böse," 29. On "absolute Erkenntnis" and "unmittelbare Gewißheit," see Hegel, 22, 173; on "Ding an sich," see Kant, *Kritik der reinen Vernunft,* vol. 1, 31; on "ich will," see Schopenhauer, *Die Welt als Wille und Vorstellung.*

25. See Nietzsche, "Zur Genealogie der Moral," 279 (emphasis added). Nietzsche's much-quoted early observation that "truth" is nothing but an "agile army of metaphors . . . " ("Über Wahrheit," 880, dating from the early 1870s) anticipates some of the claims of "Jenseits von Gut und Böse" (1886) and "Zur Genealogie der Moral" (1887).

26. See also Broughton, 59–61. Of course Nietzsche's assessment of the four thinkers mentioned (Descartes, Kant, Hegel, and Schopenhauer) should be read polemically. Thus Schopenhauer, Hegel, and Kant are all very much aware of and acknowledge the constructive role of the imagination in their philosophies. Consider Schopenhauer's emphasis on representation, Kant's reliance on *Einbildungskraft* and aesthetic judgment, and Hegel's modeling of the *phenomenology of spirit* on the genre of the *Bildungsroman.* On the poetic character of Kant's and Hegel's philosophies in particular, see Goetschel; Stengel; Abrams, 225–237; and Butler, *Subjects of Desire,* 17–24.

27. See Descartes, *Méditations,* 79–81.

28. See Descartes, *Discours,* 39–40.

29. The full title of the *Discourse on Method* is *Discourse on the Method of Rightly Conducting One's Reason and of Seeking Truth in the Sciences*. I do not at this point broach the vexed question of the viability of distinguishing between the discourse of poetry and literature and that of philosophy and science; I acknowledge the common practice of making such a distinction and, more important, heed the fact that Grünbein, following Descartes, relies on it. For a full discussion of this question, see Eskin, "On Literature and Ethics."

30. Greenblatt, 1; Byron, *Don Juan*, Canto 10, stanza 11 lines 6–8; Ransmayr, 241; James, 564.

31. See Grünbein, *Erklärte Nacht*, 45, lines 15–24.

32. See the final verse of Hölderlin's hymn "Andenken" (Remembrance): "What remains, however, the poets found" (173). Grünbein here also ironically alludes to Christa Wolf's much-discussed novella *What Remains* (*Was bleibt*) and retracts his own earlier poetic declaration that "poets . . . / . . . do not found anything any longer" (*Nach den Satiren*, 86).

33. See Grünbein, *Schädelbasislektion*, 35.

34. See Grünbein and Jocks, 45. For poetic endeavors akin to Grünbein's "simultaneous experience of the distinctly separate past and present through the process of memory" (Nalbantian, 103), see, for instance, Apollinaire, 7–14 ("Zone"); Sebald; Ransmayr.

35. See Grünbein, *Vom Schnee*, 41, 13.

36. See MSS, vol. 1, 216; Grünbein, *Schädelbasislektion*, 35.

37. See Grünbein, *Antike Dispositionen*, 328; Grünbein and von Törne, "Mir kann," 44. See also Mandelstam's memoir "Šum Vremeni" (The noise of time) in MSS, vol. 2, 347–392.)

38. Beginning with Aristotle's definition of it as a figure of substitution, *metaphor* has been conceived of and used in semantic-referential terms, more or less unanimously and irrespective of any given critic's varying terminology. For insightful discussions of the history and theory of metaphor, see Cooper; Sacks; Richards, 89–98; Weinrich; Franke; Derrida, "La mythologie blanche" (esp. 275). Grünbein's view and practice of metaphor as a figure of temporality is close to Paul de Man's and Walter Benjamin's notions of allegory; see de Man, 187–228; Benjamin, *Ursprung*, 138–167. For the Greek meanings of metaphora, see Liddell and Scott, 1118.

39. See Grünbein and Jocks, 45; Grünbein, "Tausendfacher Tod im Hirn," 224; *Antike Dispositionen*, 394. For further treatment of Grünbein's dialogue with antiquity, see Eskin, "Bridge to Antiquity."

40. See Sebald, 185.

41. See Grünbein, *Erklärte Nacht*, 93–94. Lucian's dialogue (396–347) begins with Charon's laughter and ends with his exclamation: "How silly are the ways of unhappy mankind, with their kings, golden ingots, funeral rites and battles—but never a thought of Charon!" (447). Halfway through the dialogue, Charon explains to Hermes, "Let me tell you, Hermes, what I think men and the whole life of man resemble. You have noticed bubbles in water, caused by a streamlet plashing down—I mean those that mass to make foam? Some of them, being small, burst and are gone in an instant, while some last longer and as others join them, become swollen and grow to exceeding great compass; but

afterwards they all burst without fail in time, for it cannot be otherwise. Such is the life of men; they are all swollen with wind, some to greater size, others to less; and with some the swelling is short-lived and swift-fated, while with others it is over as soon as it comes into being; but in any case they all must burst" (435).

42. See Kaplan, 29. For an in-depth discussion of contemporary calls—literary and political—for a return to the Greek and Roman classics in an attempt to shape the present and future, see Eskin, "Bridge to Antiquity."

43. See Machiavelli, 39; Korte, 92.

44. See Grünbein, *Antike Dispositionen,* 340, 349, 361. Insomnia caused by city noise, Grünbein observes, "became the leitmotif of Juvenal's sixteen satires" (349).

45. Aristotle already approached metaphor, as poetry's main ingredient, from an anthropological perspective, viewing it as one of the manifestations of the "instinct of human beings, from childhood, to engage in mimesis (indeed, this distinguishes them from animals: man is the most mimetic of all, and it is through mimesis that he develops his earliest understanding)" (*Poetics* 1448b5–9).

46. See Grünbein, *Galilei,* 21.

47. See MSS, vol. 1, 115, lines 11–12.

48. See Grünbein, *Nach den Satiren,* 117–118, line 7; Nietzsche, "Unzeitgemäße," 250, 252.

49. See Nietzsche, "Unzeitgemäße Betrachtungen," 252, 329–330.

50. See Grünbein, *Antike Dispositionen,* 363.

51. See Nietzsche, "Unzeitgemäße Betrachtungen," 251.

52. See Koselleck, 29.

53. See Grünbein, "Durs Grünbein im Gespräch mit Thomas Irmer," 111.

54. "Seneca-Studien" appears at the end of Grünbein's version of Seneca's tragedy *Thyestes* (165–176) and comprises the poems "In Ägypten" (In Egypt), "Julia Livilla," "Sand oder Kalk" (Sand or lime)—all three of which are also included in *Erklärte Nacht* (68–71)—"In eigener Sache" (On his own behalf), and "Seneca oder die zweite Geburt" (Seneca or the second birth). "In eigener Sache" is also included in Seneca, *Die Kürze des Lebens,* 55; Grünbein, *Der Misanthrop auf Capri,* 93. Grünbein has also published a poetic epistle to Seneca entitled "An Seneca: Postskriptum" (To Seneca: A postscript). Closely following Seneca's life and times as attested to by the philosopher's own and others' writings (such as Suetonius, Tacitus, and Dio Cassius), Grünbein creates poetic miniatures that intertwine Seneca's version of Stoicism (the main one with which I am concerned) with significant events in his *and,* as I explicate later, Grünbein's own life: Thus, "Sand oder Kalk" picks up on Suetonius' account of Caligula's critique of Seneca's style as "sand without lime" (163), "Seneca oder die zweite Geburt" harks back to (among others) Tacitus' description of Seneca's death (*Annals,* Book 15, 61–63), and "In Ägypten" thematizes, in the guise of Seneca's epistolary dialogue with his friend Lucilius, the philosopher's sojourn in Egypt, where he traveled in order to recover from a severe respiratory ailment (see esp. Seneca, *Ad Lucilium epistulae,* vol. 1, 323–331). On Seneca's stay in Egypt, see Giebel, 11–12; Fuhrmann, 46.

55. GR, 114; Ransmayr, 123.

56. See Grünbein, *Erklärte Nacht,* 70.

57. In his discussion of Badiou's philosophy, Žižek distinguishes between an "event and its aftermath, the span between the event and its final End (. . . between falling in love and the accomplished bliss of living together . . .)" (133). Of course the aftermath of an event is, as Koselleck suggests, part of the event itself (see Chapter One, p. 20 and note 50).

58. For a detailed discussion of the potential pool of Seneca's implied, "real historical" addressees, see Eskin, "Bridge to Antiquity," 369. "I am admitting you to my inmost thoughts," Seneca writes to Lucilius, "and am having it out with myself, merely making use of you as my pretext" (*Ad Lucilium epistulae,* vol. 1, 193).

59. See Seneca, "Ad Helviam," 430–431, 438–439; *Anthologia Latina,* 195–196 (fragment 237, a poem transmitted in Seneca's name and depicting Corsica). For a detailed discussion of Grünbein's appropriation of Seneca's voice, see Eskin, "Bridge to Antiquity."

60. See Seneca, "Ad Helviam," 428–429, 435–437 (translation modified).

61. See Diogenes Laertius, vol. 1, 142–143.

62. See Seneca, "Ad Helviam," 452–453. A similar expulsion of philosophers from Rome, Stoics in particular, would take place in 94 C.E. under Domitian. On Diogenes' exile and the charge of embezzlement brought against him, see Diogenes Laertius, vol. 2, 50–52; on Aristotle's flight from Athens in 323 B.C.E., see Seneca, "De otio," 200–201; on Cicero's banishment in 58 B.C.E., see Claassen, 27–29, 54–57; on Domitian, see Suetonius, 280–294.

63. See Diogenes Laertius, vol. 2, 51.

64. Ibid., 64–65, 75.

65. See Fuhrmann, 101; see also Diogenes Laertius, vol. 2, 206–207.

66. See Seneca, "De Otio," 198–201; "Ad Helviam," 456–457; *De beneficiis,* 458–459.

67. See Seneca, *Ad Lucilium,* vol. 1, 426–427.

68. See Seneca, "De providentia," 30–43.

69. See Seneca, "De tranquillitate animi," 253–255. On courage as a Stoic virtue, see esp. Seneca, "De constantia sapientis," 50–51.

70. See "Ad Polybium de consolatione," 360. On Seneca's frail health, see also Seneca, "Ad Helviam," 482–483; Seneca, *Ad Lucilium epistulae,* vol. 2, 180–182; Fuhrmann, 46; Giebel, 11–12. Already the geographer Pomponius Mela, Seneca's contemporary, called the climates of Sardegna and Corsica *paene pestilens*—virtually detrimental to one's health (cited in Giebel, 35).

71. See Seneca, *Ad Lucilium epistulae,* vol. 1, 360–361.

72. See Grünbein, *Galilei,* 17–18, 157; *Falten und Fallen,* 38.

73. See Grünbein, *Antike Dispositionen,* 74; *Galilei,* 26. On Grünbein's "physiological aesthetics," see esp. Eskin, "Body Language." In view of Grünbein's emphasis on the physiological rootedness of poetry it would be absolutely counterproductive not to acknowledge the essentially embodied meaning and presence of *voice*—a much-debated term in contemporary narratology (see, for example, Fludernik; Gibson; Genette, *Narrative Discourse*)—in his texts. In fact, so strong is the author's voice in his poems, according to Grünbein, that "the poem really penetrates the body and explodes in the unconscious . . . like the voice on the phone . . . " (Grünbein, *Galilei,* 62). For Grünbein, textual voice is not merely,

as Manfred Jahn notes, quoting Lakoff and Johnson, a "metaphor we live by" (Lakoff and Johnson; Jahn, 695), but also that which *really* sustains the poem and establishes the connection between author, text, and reader. See the special issue of *New Literary History* (2001) on "Voice and Human Experience," edited by Ralph Cohen, for the current critical debate regarding the literary significance of *voice*.

74. See Seneca, "Ad Helviam," 445 (translation modified); "De vita beata," 141, 115; "De tranquillitate animi," 244 (see also 212–213, 278–279).

75. None of the sources I have consulted (such as works by Dio Cassius, Suetonius, and Tacitus) mentions that Julia Livilla was either prudent or intelligent. "Living in an emotionally involved world," Avishai Margalit notes, "is living a risky life. The risks are on the whole worth taking, but they are risks nonetheless. . . . Stoicism . . . is a life of apatheia, of negating one's emotions and adopting a noninvolved posture toward life" (*Ethics of Memory*, 139, 144).

76. According to Pascal, love surpasses reason, taking the route of the heart: "The heart has its own order; the mind has its own, which relies on principles and demonstration; the heart has a different kind. You cannot demonstrate . . . [love] by dint of logical argument. . . . We know the truth not only through reason but also through the heart; it is through the latter that we know the first principles, and it is in vain that reason, which has no part in the matter, tries to combat them" (*Pensées*, 128–129). Dante's cosmic-religious "love that moves the sun and the stars" (*Inferno*, Canto 1, line 39) by definition exceeds reason.

77. See Seneca, "Ad Polybium," 394–395.

78. See Seneca, "De vita," 125.

79. Ibid., 124 (translation modified). On Seneca's condemnation of adultery, see *Ad Lucilium*, vol. 3, 29.

80. "Einmal fragte mich ein Amerikaner, als ich ihm sagte, ich käme aus Berlin: 'Free side or bad side?' Seither weiß ich, daß alles, was ich bisher getrieben habe, *Poetry from the bad* side ist" (Grünbein, "Poetry from the Bad Side," 449). *Von der üblen Seite* (From the bad side) would subsequently serve as the title of Grünbein's 1994 collection of poems written between 1985 and 1991.

81. See Grünbein, *Antike Dispositionen*, 12.

82. See Grünbein, *Galilei*, 141.

83. See Grünbein, *Schädelbasislektion*, 11.

84. Ibid., 105 ("So viele Jahre Peinlichkeit"); Grünbein, *Das erste Jahr*, 171 (emphasis added).

85. See Grünbein, *Schädelbasislektion*, 139 ("Rache des Fleischs / Durch den Kehlkopf"); *Das erste Jahr*, 171.

86. On sarcasm as an important ingredient of Grünbein's poetics, see esp. *Galilei*, 16, 50, 268; *Nach den Satiren*, 223; *Das erste Jahr*, 61–63.

87. A similar address to Seneca on Grünbein's part is staged in "An Seneca: Postskriptum."

88. See Diogenes Laertius, vol. 2, 134–135.

89. See Benveniste, vol. 1, 259–260.

90. See GR, 136.

91. Margalit distinguishes between commemoration and revivification: the former implies the creation and preservation of memory, the latter implies bringing "the dead back to life in essence but not in form" (66–69).

92. Grünbein's fusion of past and present should in no way be considered along the lines of Gadamer's hermeneutically motivated fusion of "historical horizons" (*Truth and Method*, 306), which "always involves rising to a higher universality that overcomes not only our own particularity but also that of the other" (305). Unlike Gadamer, Grünbein is concerned with the utmost singularity and concreteness (both cognitive-psychological *and* somatic) of the "[directly] addressed" (Grünbein, *Antike Dispositionen*, 394) subject of speech and understanding.

93. On the significance of Seneca's exile for his practice of Stoicism, see Lang, 16.

94. On Seneca's introduction to Stoicism as a student in Rome by his teachers Attalus and Sotion, see Giebel, 17–18.

95. See Grünbein, *Antike Dispositionen*, 50.

96. See Camartin, 32. Camartin refers specifically to the poetic sequence "Im Zweieck" (In the bi-angle) (Grünbein, *Falten und Fallen*, 62–68). The erotic triangle between the characters of *Vom Schnee* (Descartes, his manservant Gillot, and the neighbor's maid, Marie) is the most elaborate and extensive fictional staging to date of the link between the question of subjectivity and the question of love in Grünbein's oeuvre. For a discussion of this erotic triangle, see Eskin, "Descartes of Metaphor."

97. As, for instance, in the poems "Julianus an einen Freund" (Julian to a friend), "Mein lieber X" (My dear X), in *Nach den Satiren*, 30–32, line 1; and "Titus beklagt sich über sein Herrscheramt" (Titus complains about his duties as emperor), "Siehst du, mein lieber Quintus" (You see, my dear Quintus), in *Erklärte Nacht*, 86, line 1.

98. *Getrieben* is the past participle form of *treiben*. See Chapter Two on Celan's "doing it with" Shakespeare.

99. See Dehmel, 61–63. Significantly, Dehmel's male speaker also uses the verb *treiben*: "du *treibst* mit mir auf kaltem Meer" (literally, you are floating with me in the cold sea) (62, line 27).

100. See MSS, vol. 1, 215–216. For a detailed discussion of Mandelstam's conception of the "living word," see the Appendix.

101. On the life-bestowing power of the soul, see esp. Aristotle, *On the Soul*: "the soul is that which imparts motion to living things . . . respiration is the essential condition of life. . . . The soul may . . . be defined as the first actuality of a natural body possessing life. . . . That which has the capacity to live is not the body which has lost its soul, but that which possesses its soul . . . that which has soul is distinguished from that which has not by living . . . the soul is that whereby we live and perceive and think in the primary sense . . . the soul is the actuality of . . . body" (21, 69–71, 78–79).

102. See Grünbein, *Galilei*, 28, 79, 83.

103. See Bakhtin, *Raboty*, 18–19. "There is no philosophical, world political, or ethical problem," Grünbein notes, "which [the poets] would not have sounded with their sensitive probes" (Grünbein, *Antike Dispositionen*, 50).

104. "The branch of philosophy regulating this work [that is, the *Divine Comedy,*] both as a whole and in its parts," Dante writes to Cangrande della Scala in 1319, "is the business of morals or ethics, because it was undertaken . . . not for speculation but for practical purposes . . . " (Genus philosophiae sub quo hic in toto et parte proceditur est morale negotium, sive ethica; quia non ad speculandum, sed ad opus inventum est) (*Dantis Alighieri Epistolae,* 178). See also Dante's *Literature in the Vernacular* for a discussion of poetry as linked to ethics (esp. 16, 40). On Dante's elevation of love to the status of the "ethical and ethicizing power" *par excellence,* see Haller, 28–29; see also Auerbach, 105.

105. See *Discours de la méthode,* 47 ("milieu d'une forêt," "les voyageurs . . . se trouvant égarés"), 83 ("le bien de l'homme"). The so-called "morale par provision" (provisional ethics) (45), under the aegis of which Descartes places his four methodological maxims, most explicitly speaks to the ethical thrust of his philosophical project.

CHAPTER FOUR

1. Byron, *Prophecy of Dante,* Canto 1, line 178; *Don Juan,* Canto 2, stanza 16, lines 3–4; GR, 144.

2. For secondary material on Brodsky's life and work that I found particularly helpful, see esp. Bethea; Polukhina; Loseff and Polukhina; *Novoe Literaturnoe Obozrenie,* 45 (esp. 153–255); MacFadyen; Rančin.

3. *Agency* and *agent* derive from the Latin verb *agere* (to act, to do, to engage in, to transact).

4. Aristotle defines the domain of ethics, which he considers part of the "mastercraft . . . of politics" (*Nicomachean Ethics,* 1094a29; *Politics,* 1323a14–16), as "praxis" (*Nicomachean Ethics,* 1095a5–7), and designates "happiness," the "highest of all the goods" (1095a15–21), as its "telos" (1095a6). For contemporary approaches to ethics as concerned with "life and conduct" (*bion prazeôn*) (ibid.), see, for instance: Murdoch, *Sovereignty of Good,* 45–91; MacIntyre; Nussbaum, *Fragility of Goodness,* 2–3; Butler, *Giving an Account,* 3. See also Eskin, *Ethics and Dialogue,* 19–54, 69–95, for a discussion of the varieties of ethical theory (such as eudaimonistic, formal, material, and deontological).

5. From among the plethora of literary-historical examples undermining this separation, suffice it to mention Horace's linking of poetry and politics-ethics in "[The poet] serves the state . . . fashions the tender, lisping lips of childhood . . . turns the ear from unseemly words . . . moulds the heart by kind precepts, correcting roughness and envy and anger . . . " (*Satires, Epistles, Ars Poetica,* 407); Shelley's claim that "poets are the unacknowledged legislators of the world" (762); and Schiller's project of an "aesthetic education of mankind" (vol. 2, 570–655).

6. See GR, 48–49, 208.

7. See LTO, 267; BK, 530.

8. See GR, 50. Elsewhere Brodsky observes, "Poetry is not an art or a branch of art, it's something more. If what distinguishes us from other species is speech, then poetry, which is the supreme linguistic operation, is our anthropological, indeed generic, goal" (*Conversations,* 100). As I explain later, Brodsky's emphasis on the precedence of the aesthetic over the ethical must be read in part as a subversion of Soviet cultural doctrine. Brodsky's view

of the interface between aesthetics and ethics harks back in particular to Nikolaj Berdjaev's linking of the question of freedom with the question of creativity (see, for example, *Samopoznanie*, 456–472; *Sud'ba Rossii*, 29–263). On Brodsky's recourse to Berdjaev, see Volkov, 13, 46, 178; Loseff and Polukhina, *Brodsky's Poetics*, 42–43.

9. See Bakhtin, *Raboty*, 42.

10. See GR, 144. My approach is motivated by Brodsky's own emphasis on language as "the given" (GR, 84) and his concomitant view that the poet *must* do something with it. "All [ethical] imperatives," Kant notes, "are expressed by an *Ought* [*Sollen*]" (*Kritik der praktischen Vernunft*, 227). Elaborating on Kant's distinction between that which "the nature of cognition gives us as a task [*augibt*]" (*Kritik der reinen Vernunft*, vol. 1, 15) and the ways in which "objects [are] given [*gegeben*]" (ibid., 66) to us, the Neokantian Hermann Cohen assigns the question of the "given-as-task" (*Aufgabe*) to the domain of ethics (*Ethik*, 143). Similarly, Cohen's fellow Neokantian Heinrich Rickert distinguishes between the "category of givenness" (*Der Gegenstand*, 371) and the ethical "ought" (ibid.).

11. LTO, 355. "This may not be," Brodsky explains, "the species' definition as yet, but this is surely its goal" (ibid.).

12. See GR, 97; LTO, 165; Chapter One, this volume, note 46.

13. See Seneca, "De Constantia sapientis," 50–51 (translation modified). Brodsky's reverence for Seneca comes to the fore most audibly in his calling the Stoic, in medieval Aristotelian fashion, "the philosopher" (GR, 123). For references to Seneca and Stoicism throughout Brodsky's oeuvre, see esp. *Uranija*, 85; LTO, 123, 351–352, 355; GR, 97, 267–298; BK, 22, 67, 192, 200, 221, 239.

14. See LTO, 351. This definition echoes Brodsky's depiction of his first encounter with Robert Frost's poetry—"I was astonished at . . . that kind of restraint, that hidden, controlled terror . . . " (*Conversations*, 75)—and bears out the "truth" of his tongue-in-cheek claim that for "every Byron we always get a Wordsworth" (GR, 81). It will be remembered that Wordsworth and Coleridge highlight poetry's capacity to palliate and assuage painful emotions through its metrical makeup: "if . . . the images and feelings have an undue proportion of pain connected with them there is some danger that the excitement may be carried beyond its proper bounds. Now the co-presence of something regular, something to which the mind has been accustomed . . . cannot but have great efficacy in tempering and restraining the passion by an intertexture of ordinary feeling" (Preface to 1798 edition of *Lyrical Ballads*, cited in Wordsworth and Coleridge, 172); "from the tendency of metre to divest language in a certain sense of its reality . . . there can be little doubt but that more pathetic situations and sentiments, that is, those which have a greater proportion of pain connected with them, may be endured in metrical composition, especially in rhyme, [rather] than in prose . . . (Preface to 1802 *Lyrical Ballads*, cited in Wordsworth and Coleridge, 172).

15. Huxley, 220; Schleiermacher, 225.

16. See Volkov, 292; LTO, 402.

17. See Volkov, 292.

18. See MSS, vol. 1 216, vol. 3, 253. On Mandelstam's engagement with Dante, see the Appendix.

19. From the elegy "Pokhorony Bobo" (Funeral of Bobo), March 1972, in *Čast' Reči,* 6–7, lines 45–48. For an alternative English translation, by Richard Wilbur, see Brodsky, *Collected Poems in English,* 56–57. On "Funeral of Bobo," see Rigsbee 60–62; on Brodsky's self-stylization as a new Dante, see Loseff, "Brodsky in Florence," 5. I do not deal with the overall satirical-ironic setup of "Funeral of Bobo," which has been said to be addressed to the poet's cat or to a butterfly.

20. For further instances that saliently testify to the indelible presence of Dante's voice in Brodsky's works, see, for example, "ideš' . . . po vtoromy krugu" (you are walking . . . along the second circle) (Brodsky, *Konec prekrasnoj epoxi,* 61); "V seredine žizni, v gustom lesu, / čeloveku svojstvenno ogljadyvat'sja—kak beglecu / ili prestupniku . . . / No prošedšee vremja vovse ne puma i / ne borzaja" (In the middle of life, in a dense forest, / man is wont to look backward—like a runaway / or criminal . . . / But time past is not a puma and / not a greyhound) (NSA, 126) Brodsky's puma and greyhound hark back to the beasts encountered by Dante in *Inferno,* Canto 1, lines 32, 45, 49: lonza (leopard), Leona (lion), and lupa (she-wolf); "V seredine dlinnoj ili v konce korotkoj / žizni" (In the middle of a long or at the end of a short / life) (*Uranija,* 75); and "Novaja žizn'" (The new life) (*Pejzaž s navodneniem,* 8–10). David Bethea notes that "Brodsky read the entire *Commedia* in the famous Lozinsky translation in 1962–63, the same years in which he was reading the Bible for the first time as well as the English metaphysicals" (*Joseph Brodsky,* 265–266). On Brodsky's profound familiarity with Dante's oeuvre, see also BK, 248: "I also remember him [Robert Lowell] well because the discussion he and I had about *The Divine Comedy* [in 1975] was the most profound and detailed discussion on the subject I had had since talking about it with my friends in the Soviet Union." Brodsky mentions the same discussion in Volkov, 135.

21. Incidentally, Brodsky's "new Dante" can also be read as a tongue-in-cheek attempt to counter what may well be construed as his ostensible reduction to the status of his Acmeist predecessor's "second-order" replica by Osip Mandelstam's widow, Nadežda, who used to call him, by way of a compliment, the "second Osja" (*Osja* being the diminutive form of *Osip,* which is a version of *Iosif,* Brodsky's first name in Russian). On Brodsky as the second Osja, see Bethea, *Joseph Brodsky,* 17, 61, 265, 269.

22. See GR, 27.

23. See GR, 228, 82. On the "road less traveled," see the penultimate line of Robert Frost's poem, "The Road Not Taken" (103). On Brodsky's recourse to the image of the woods or forest (*les*), see, for instance, NSA, 8, 14, 45–46; *Sočinenija Iosifa Brodskogo,* vol. 1, 211, 248. Incidentally, the Brodsky archive at the Beinecke Rare Book and Manuscript Library, Yale University, box 1, contains a fragment of a poem written in internal exile and entitled "Ex Ponto / Poslednee Pis'mo Ovidija v Rim" (Ex Ponto / Ovid's Last Letter to Rome).

24. On the innovative and unprecedented character of Mandelstam's approach to Dante, see the Appendix.

25. See GR, 85.

26. See the Appendix. On Mandelstam's complex notion of poetic creativity and origi-

nality, which relies on the poet's engagement with and orchestration of previous texts, see Eskin, *Ethics and Dialogue*, 139–140.

27. See GR, 56–57.

28. See MSS, vol. 3, 226; GR, 228 27. For further references to the poet's "pedigree," see GR, 87, 116.

29. See GR, 118.

30. See Derrida, *Limited Inc.*, 119; Attridge, *Singularity of Literature*, 24.

31. See "24 Dekabrja 1971 Goda," "Pes'nja Nevinnosti, Ona že—Opyta," and "1972 God" in *Čast' Reči*, 3–4, 12–15, 20–23). On the *baroque* in Brodsky's writings, see esp. Mac-Fadyen, *Joseph Brodsky and the Baroque*, and Bethea, "Joseph Brodsky's 'To My Daughter.'" This is not by any means to reduce the baroque to a concern with *vanitas*, but it is to highlight the centrality of this concern for the period, especially as a function of and response to the Thirty-Years' War (1618–1648) and its aftermath (see Martini, 140; Martin, 15; and Calabrese).

32. "Naverno, posle smerti—pustota" ("Funeral of Bobo," in *Čast' Reči*, 7, line 35).

33. See GR, 86. "I am convinced," Brodsky remarked at his trial, "that what I have written will be of service . . . to future generations" (Vigdorova, "Process Iosifa Brodskogo," 283). On Brodsky's endorsement of Horace's "poetics of longevity," see Chapter One, this volume.

34. See GR, 114–137.

35. Ibid., 116.

36. Interestingly, Brodsky's figuration of the poet-historian anticipates Grünbein's figuration of the poet as historian and the historian as poet (see Eskin, "Risse," 119–120).

37. See Grünbein, *Galilei*, 99.

38. "The branch of philosophy to which [the *Divine Comedy*] belongs as a whole and in its parts," Dante explains to Cangrande della Scala, "is morals, or ethics, because it was created not for the sake of speculation but for practical purposes" (*Dantis Alighieri Epistolae*, 178; see also *Purgatorio*, Canto 18, lines 67–75; and *Literature in the Vernacular*, 16, 40, for reflections on ethics in connection with poetry). Insofar as Dante's ethics are avowedly a function of his poetics, the latter emerges as the implicit matrix and *avant-la-lettre* instantiation of Brodsky's own poetical axiom as to the precedence of aesthetics over ethics—as the model instance of the "closest possible interplay between ethics and aesthetics" (LTO, 99).

39. See GR, 140. Heeding Lenin's injunction that literature must serve the "social-democratic [that is, communist] workers' movement" and "strictly follow the party line" (*Lenin o Literature*, 10), the Soviet Writers' Union adopted, in 1932, Gronskij's concept of "socialist realism"—that is, the truthful, historically concrete representation of reality in its revolutionary growth in the spirit of socialism—as the official doctrine of Soviet aesthetics.

40. See MSS, vol. 3, 235; GR, 118. On Mandelstam's construal of Dante, see the Appendix. I am not at all suggesting that Mandelstam cannot be said to have to a certain extent been and, more importantly, thought of himself as engagé. After all, as an Acmeist he was emphatically concerned with the details of *this* life, *this* world, and *this* reality (see the Appendix). I am also not suggesting that Brodsky, conversely, must be considered engagé.

What I *am* suggesting is that Brodsky is far more interested in the abiding force of Dante's philosophical and ethical-political testament than in his seemingly inexhaustible amenability to *metaphorical* appropriation through the ages; in other words, in donning the mask of Dante, Brodsky does not so much want the reader to think of him metaphorically *in terms* of the Italian *qua* cultural trope as to indicate that he has accepted the baton of the ethics of Dante's aesthetics and will carry it forward in a yet-to-be specified direction.

41. See Brodsky, *Conversations,* 121; NSA, 97; GR, 128. For Brodsky's use of vector, see esp. NSA, 56, 60; GR, 284; and BK, 114, 313, 506, 512, 529. Brodsky's poetics vacillates between his admiration for Urania on the one hand and Clio, the muse of history, on the other. Urania ultimately takes the cake, though, on account of her historical seniority (GR, 117). For Brodsky's engagement with the Muses, see GR, 117–37; *Uranija* (esp. 62, and 161, "To Urania" [*K Uranii*], which takes up the theme of the void). On the significance of Urania as the "Muse of astronomy . . . the Muse of Christian poetry [as well as] a name for Aphrodite," see Scherr, "To Urania," 101–102. Brodsky parts company with Mandelstam on the crucial question of a person's vector and its significance for the practice of poetry as an essentially uncharted ethical and "existential process" (LTO, 267), giving the screw of ethical realism a decisive turn. The constitutive openness und unpredictability of Brodsky's vector—most poignantly expressed in "Letter in a Bottle," written in internal exile in November 1964: "I would like to know for sure, / since I will not be coming back home, / in which direction you will point me, my vector?" (NSA, 60)—explodes Mandelstam's projected neo-Gothic social architecture (see the Appendix), which is predicated on the "free [yet highly organized] play of weights and forces [and] in which each member is unique and echoes the whole" (MSS, vol. 2, 287) from his particular, charted "place . . . in the universe" (vol. 1, 102). (The irony of Brodsky's decision to displace Mandelstam's poetics in a poem that titularly endorses it—"Letter in a Bottle"—will certainly not go unnoticed.) In contrast to Mandelstam's abstract "place of the human being in the universe," which poetry *qua* "letter in a bottle" is presumably particularly well equipped to safeguard and commemorate, Brodsky foregrounds the irreducibility of the concrete human body in a concrete geographical location at a singular moment in time as the substratum of history and poetry: "What makes history?—Bodies. / And Art?—A beheaded body" (NSA, 110), be it the "body [of] John Donne . . . in his bedroom" (BK, 155), the body of Dante "taking a step . . . accompanied by breathing" (MSS, vol. 3, 219) in a concrete locale in northern Italy, or the "piles of corpses" (GR, 129) of millions of victims whose sole yet colossal mistake was, according to Brodsky, that they happened to be in the wrong place at the wrong time: "In order to become a victim, one ought to be present at the scene of the crime" (ibid.; see also LTO, 443). Brodsky's vector is much closer to Celan's notion of a person's unique "direction and fate" (GW, vol. 3, 188) than to Mandelstam's universal scatter plot.

42. GR, 85; see also 81–95.

43. GR, 56, 84 ("language is the given").

44. See note 4.

45. See *Purgatorio,* Canto 24, lines 52–54.

46. See Dante, *Inferno,* Canto 1, line 39; *Paradiso,* Canto 33, line 145; *Inferno,* Canto 1, lines 1–2. For an extended meditation on love, see also *Purgatorio,* Canto 17 (esp. lines

103–105) and Canto 18 (esp. lines 1–75). On "love as the motive force for *all* actions" in Dante, see Barolini, 31–32; on Beatrice as the embodiment of love, see Pogue Harrison, 38–42; on the erotic dimension of Dante's poetic treatment of love, see the Appendix.

47. See Haller, 28–90 (also Auerbach, 86, 131–133; Schnell, 79). On the interface between ethics and poetry, see Dante, *Literature in the Vernacular*, 16, 40.

48. See GR, 56. "When they say 'the poet hears the voice of the Muse,'" Brodsky observes elsewhere, "it's nonsense if the nature of the Muse is unspecified. But if you take a closer look, the voice of the Muse is the voice of the language" (*Conversations*, 72–73).

49. GR, 84.

50. Ibid., 91.

51. Ibid., 88.

52. Brodsky's first poem dedicated to M. B.—"Ni toski, ni ljubvi, ni pechali" (Neither languour, nor love, nor sadness)—dates from June 4, 1962 (*Sočinenija Iosifa Brodskogo*, vol. 1, 169; the poem has not been included in NSA). Brodsky's last published poem dedicated to M. B. dates from December 25, 1993, as its title, "25. XII. 1993" (*Pejzaž s navodneniem*, 140) indicates. Brodsky began writing poetry in the late 1950s, when he was "eighteen, nineteen, or twenty years old" (BK, 115; see also Volkov, 32–33). In 1990, Brodsky married Maria Sozzani (see Volkov, xiii), by whom he had one daughter, Anna Maria Alexandra, born June 9, 1993 (see Bethea, "Joseph Brodsky's 'To My Daughter,'" 243). Brodsky's son by Marianna Basmanova, Andrej, was born in the Soviet Union on October 9, 1967. I should point out that in attending to Brodsky's poetic fidelity to M. B. I obviously do not mean to suggest that he did not dedicate and address poems to persons other than M. B. or write poems that were not directly concerned with M. B. What I do suggest, however, is that M. B. can plausibly be said to constitute the overall horizon of Brodsky's poetics of love.

53. See Dante, *Vita Nuova*, 3. Dante had been betrothed to Gemma de' Donati since 1277; he married her around 1285; they had four children (see Mandelbaum; Mazzotta, 6; Rheinfelder).

54. See Dante, *Vita Nuova*, 3. As I explain later in great detail, in calling Mary, Queen of Scots, *bljad'* (slut or bitch) (see "Twenty Sonnets to Mary Stuart," NSA, 103–114, Sonnet 5, line 14), Brodsky obliquely addresses Marianna Basmanova's *nepostojenstvo* (inconstancy) (see "Zimnjaja Počta" [Winter mail], in NSA, 29–31, line 62, which is dedicated to M. B.). In the 1968 poem "Elegy," Brodsky asks, "What did you lie for? Why can't I / distinguish lying from truth anymore" (NSA, 72, line 12–13). In the 1993 poem "Itaka" (*Pejzaž s navodneniem*, 136), which harks back to Brodsky's 1972 farewell poem to his son Andrej, "Odysseus to Telemachus" (*Čast' Reči*, 19; NSA, 90), and to Cavafy's famous poem "Ithaca" (*Complete Poems*, 36–37), Brodsky imagines himself returning to Ithaca (that is, Russia) only to learn that his grown son has become a stranger to him and that his wife Penelope (that is, M. B.) "has given [herself] to all" (line 8).

55. "I saw lady Vanna and lady Bice [*monna Bice*]" (Dante, *Vita Nuova*, 53); "But that reverence which is wholly mistress of me, only by *Be* and by *ice* [*per Be a per ice*]" (*Paradiso*, Canto 7, lines 13–14). In connection with this note I would like to thank Teodolinda Barolini.

56. See GR, 83.

57. See GR, 95. Although Brodsky writes that "when [the poet]'s gone, [the Muse] finds herself another mouthpiece in the next generation" (ibid.), this observation applies equally, *mutatis mutandis*, in the case of the poet's disappearance and replacement by a "mouthpiece" of his own generation.

58. For Brodsky's discussion of history and art, see GR, 118 and 87, respectively. "What art and sexuality have in common," Brodsky explains elsewhere, "is that both are sublimations of one's creative energy" (LTO, 45). I do not discuss the plausibility or legitimacy of Brodsky's Freudian axiom.

59. See GR, 91–92. "A poem—any poem, regardless of its subject—is in itself," Brodsky observes, "an act of love, not so much of an author toward his subject as of language for a piece of reality" (ibid.).

60. See Brodsky, *Conversations*, 73, 76; BK, 250, 302; GR, 456, 439.

61. See Brodsky, *Conversations*, 66. On the linkage of *copula* and *copulation*, see Chapter Two, note 79.

62. See GR, 428, 430, 435, 439, 455. For further instances in which Brodsky casts the practice of poetry in erotic terms, see NSA, 15, 31; *Konec prekrasnoj epoxi*, 3, 33, 76, 100; *Ostanovka v pustyne*, 10; *Časť Reči*, 20, 34, 61; *Uranija*, 15, 21, 62, 103, 111; LTO, 150, 372; and GR, 206–208.

63. See GR, 48.

64. See NSA, 126.

65. See NSA, 56–64. In the poem's typescript, located in the Brodsky archive at the Beinecke Rare Book and Manuscript Library, Yale University, box 2, "Entertaintment for Mary" is written by hand in large letters in black ink immediately above the typed original Russian title, "Butylka s Pis'mom" (Bottle with a letter). Although Brodsky's spelling error in *Entertaintment* could be chalked up to his erstwhile lack of proficiency in English, the fact that the supernumerary *t* is underlined with a gentle swoosh suggests that Brodsky misspelled the word intentionally, to allude to his at-that-point already "tainted" relationship with the unfaithful "Mary." "Then I began," Brodsky remarks, reminiscing on the early to mid-1960s, "to translate English poetry, Donne especially. When I was sent to that internal exile in the north, a friend of mine sent me two or three anthologies of American poetry . . . Oscar Williams, with the pictures, which would fire my imagination" (*Conversations*, 76). The same friend, Lidija Čukovskaja, also sent him the 1952 Modern Library edition of John Donne's works, edited by Charles Coffin (BK, 154). In addition to translating Donne, Brodsky also perused in depth the works of W. H. Auden and T. S. Eliot while in internal exile (see Kulle, 291). For the volumes referred to by Brodsky, see the Bibliography. On Brodsky's familiarity and engagement with English and American poetry in the early 1960s, see also Bethea, *Joseph Brodsky*, 84, 268n16.

66. On Mandelstam's conception of poetry in terms of navigation, see the Appendix; and Eskin, "Of Poets and Sailors." For texts that stake out the tradition of the subgenre of the elegy of the "dying poet," well known in Russia since the age of Pushkin, see, for instance, de Lamartine, "Le poète mourant" in *Oeuvres poétiques complètes*, 144–149; Millevoye, "Le poète mourant," in *Oeuvres*, 77–78; Chenier, "Élégie XXV," in *Oeuvres complètes*,

76–77. "The end of [the eighteenth] century," Tomaševskij notes, "had produced the ste-reotype of the 'dying poet': young, unable to overcome the adversities of life, perishing in poverty, the fame he merited coming too late" ("Literature and Biography," 49).

67. The fact that Beatrice acts on Dante's behalf at the behest of the virgin Mary (*Inferno*, Canto 2, line 94), among others, does not in any way diminish her pivotal role in facilitating Dante's salvation.

68. See Dante, *Inferno*, Canto 2, lines 104–107.

69. See GR, 118.

70. Ibid., 228, 27.

71. See Volkov, 75.

72. See GR, 27.

73. See GR, 228; also note 23 of this chapter.

74. See Dante, *Paradisio*, Canto 17, lines 55–60. It is well known that Dante consid-ered his exile "unmerited" (cited in Mandelbaum, 327) and desired to return to Florence—a wish that was not to be granted. Giuseppe Mazzotta points out that Dante "knew de-spair and almost certainly he contemplated suicide" (9). Of course this is not to say that Dante did not endeavor to countervail his "despair" by becoming a "party by [him]self" (*Paradisio*, Canto 17, line 69) and banking on his "fair fame" (ibid.). On January 27, 1302, Dante, a White Guelph, was condemned in absentia by the Black Guelphs, who then ruled Florence, on several unproven charges (including barratry and fomenting discord) to "two years of exile, to perpetual exclusion from public service, and to the payment of a ruinous fine of five thousand florins within three days" (Mandelbaum, 325). Because Dante failed to respond to the sentence or appear in person before the Black Guelphs in Florence, a second sentence that overrode the first was delivered on March 10, 1302. Dante was con-demned to the "confiscation of all his goods and to death by burning should he fall into the hands of the commune" (ibid.). Until his death in 1321, Dante wandered the courts of Northern Italy dependent on the benevolence of wealthy patrons such as Cangrande della Scala. For concise accounts of Dante's life, see Mandelbaum; Rheinfelder; Mazzotta; Haller; Auerbach.

75. See GR, 24, 28.

76. BK, 192 (see also 67). "Exile," Seneca writes, is merely 'a change of place" ("Ad Helviam," 428–429). Elsewhere, Brodsky reiterates this Stoic tenet: "basically every country is just a continuation of space" (*Conversations*, 65).

77. See BK, 250.

78. See BK, 25; Brodsky, *Conversations*, 75; BK, 181. Brodsky notes, "My first acquain-tance with Robert Frost was when I was twenty-two. I got some of his translations, not a book . . . and I was absolutely astonished at the sensibility, that kind of restraint, that hidden, controlled terror. I couldn't believe what I'd read. I thought I had to look into the matter closely, ought to check whether the translator was really translating, or whether we had on our hands a kind of genius in Russian. And so I did, and it was all there. . . . And with Frost it all started" (*Conversations*, 75). Both the title of Hemingway's novel and its epigraph are taken from the seventeenth meditation in Donne's *Devotions upon Emergent Occasions* (cited in Donne, *Complete Poetry and Selected Prose*, 440–441). I here borrow

Helen Vendler's notion of a poet's "coming of age," by which she means a poet's "writing his first 'perfect poem'—the poem which wholly succeeds in embodying a coherent personal style" (*Coming of Age as a Poet*, 1). On Brodsky's "Great Elegy" as a coming-of-age poem, see Bethea, *Joseph Brodsky*, 94.

79. See Brodsky, *Conversations*, 73, 76; BK, 302.

80. See GR, 83.

81. Ibid.

82. See *Vita Nuova*, 86. Dante's own vacillation between two languages—Latin and Italian—certainly presents an interesting parallel to Brodsky's infatuation with Russian and English, and would be well worth inquiring into in another context.

83. The "yoking of philosophy—indeed theology—to Eros" (Barolini, 19)—that is, the joining of the question of salvation with the question of love—is the most basic feature of the "dolce stil nuovo" (ibid.), a style of Italian lyric verse in the early Renaissance.

84. See Dante, *Inferno*, Canto 2, lines 104–107; Shakespeare, Sonnet 79, line 1; GR, 144, 116.

85. Byron, *Don Juan*, Canto 5, stanza 4, lines 1–2, and stanza 48, lines 3–5; Hemingway, *For Whom the Bell Tolls*, 305.

86. The stanzas were first published in the 1816 edition of Byron, *The Prisoner of Chillon*, 16–17 (hereafter cited as "Stanzas to [Augusta]," in CPW, vol. 4, 34–35). On the circumstances of the composition and delivery to England of "Stanzas to ——," see Eisler, 538; Strickland, 25–26. In the 1898 edition of *The Prisoner of Chillon and Other Poems*, for instance, "Stanzas to ——" is printed as "Stanzas to Augusta" (33–34) and preceded by an explanatory note providing, among other things, information regarding its date and place of composition as well as its transmission "to England for publication" (ibid.). Augusta Mary Leigh (1783–1851) was the daughter of Captain John Byron and Lady Amilia D'Arcy, Baroness Conyers, who passed away shortly after Augusta's birth. John Byron subsequently married the Scottish heiress Catherine Gordon; their son George Gordon, sixth Lord Byron, was born on January 22, 1788. For a concise biography of Augusta Leigh, see Strickland, 13–39.

87. "To Augusta," line 20. For the original publication of "To ——," which would subsequently be reprinted as "Stanzas to ——," that is, as "Stanzas to Augusta" (for example, in Byron, *Poetical Works*, 88–89), *and* alternatively as "To [Augusta]" (for example, in CPW, vol. 3, 386–388; and Eisler, 514–515), see Byron, *Poems*, 9–12. In turn, "To Augusta," which was first published in Moore, vol. 2, 27–30, would subsequently be reprinted as "Epistle to Augusta" (for example, in Byron, *Prisoner of Chillon*, 1898, 35–39; *Poetical Works*, 90–91; and CPW, vol. 4, 36–40). "Stanzas to [Augusta]" (see previous note) was translated into Russian by D. Družinin, Valery Popov, Karolina Pavlova, Vilgelm Levik, and Boris Pasternak (1938), among others (for Pasternak's translation, see Pasternak, 178–181). "To [Augusta]" was translated into Russian by Vilgelm Levik (see Byron, *Izbrannoe*, 51–52).

Annabella left Byron on January 15, 1816. Byron signed the final deed of separation on April 21, 1816 (see Eisler, 505; MacCarthy, 278). The Byrons never obtained a divorce. Byron would later explain to one of his numerous Italian mistresses that "in England we can't divorce except for *female* infidelity" (letter to John Murray of May 18, 1819, in BLJ, vol. 6, 133). "Of the two possible ways to end a marriage [in Regency England]," Benita Eisler explains, "the only sane expedient was a private legal separation. The alternative, divorce, subjected litigants to a nightmare of overlapping jurisdictions. In Regency England, divorce involved the Ecclesiastical Court, or Doctors' Commons, and required an Act of Parliament (never obtainable by women), and if a father's automatic custody was challenged, the case was also referred to the Chancery. The time and money required for this . . . created a popular alternative among the better-off classes: 'private separation', defined as an 'agreement to part, negotiated between two spouses and embodied in a deed of separation, drawn up by a conveyancer . . . '" (493).

88. See Byron, "Stanzas to ——," lines 1–8, 21–28 (*The Prisoner of Chillon*, 1816, 16–17; reprinted as "Stanzas to [Augusta]" in CPW, vol. 4, 34–35).

89. See lines 1–2, 11–12, 15–16, 23–28, 37–40 (cited in Byron, *Poems*, 9–12; reprinted as "To [Augusta]" in CPW, vol. 3, 386–388).

90. See lines 1–2, 7–14, 20–25 (cited in Moore, vol. 2, 27–30; reprinted as "Epistle to Augusta" in CPW, vol. 4, 36–40).

91. See Eisler, 486. Among the many biographies of Byron's life, Benita Eisler's magisterial *Byron: Child of Passion, Fool of Fame* (esp. 486–506), which I found the most informative and least tendentious, is the one to which I would refer the reader; see also MacCarthy, esp. 261–280; Minta; Strickland; Marchand, *Byron*; McGann; Clinton; and Moore.

92. See Eisler, 506. Moore notes that Byron's exile "had not even the dignity of appearing voluntary, as the excommunicating voice of society left him no other resource" (cited in MacCarthy, 275). Echoing Moore, Fiona MacCarthy, one of Byron's most recent biographers, writes, "Had the scandal been only that of the breakdown of his marriage Byron might, if he had chosen to, have ridden out the storm. It was the additional element of incest, and more critically, sodomy, that made his departure unavoidable" (ibid.) According to Byron's close friend John Cam Hobhouse, conversely, there "was not the slightest necessity . . . for [Byron's] going abroad" (cited in MacCarthy, 275). Although incest would not be classified as a criminal offense under English Common Law until 1908, it was considered a crime under Canon Law and was punishable in Ecclesiastical Court (see Gray, 32). Regarding the place of sodomy in English law, Ed Cohen explains, "Prior to the passage of the Criminal Law Amendment Act [in 1885], legislation regulating sexual acts between persons of the same sex derived from Henry VIII's statute of 1533 which made 'Buggery committed with Mankind or with Beast' a capital offense. . . . Although the death penalty was set aside in 1861, the essential definition of the crime continued unchanged, proscribing 'sodomy' whether committed with (or by) a male or female. This legal injunction[, which] derived from canon law, against a particular type of 'unnatural act,' [was] not confined to a single sex or even a single species . . . " (*Talk on the Wilde Side*, 92). Sodomy, both heterosexual *and* homosexual, Eisler notes, "was judged, like pederasty and incest, both a sin and 'a Crime *Inter Christianos non nominandum*—not to be named among Christians" (500; see also Foucault, *L'histoire de la sexualité*, 50–57).

93. See Eisler, 500.

94. Cited in MacCarthy, 275.

95. See Elistratova, 95; Byron's letter to Lady Melbourne of Apr. 30, 1814 (BLJ, vol. 1,

110). In an earlier letter to Lady Melbourne (Apr. 25, 1814), Byron avows, in response to her query as to whether the risks involved in a liaison with his half-sister Augusta were worth taking, "Oh! but it is 'worth while'—I can't tell you why . . . " (BLJ, vol. 4, 104; see also Eisler, 423). Byron's Soviet editors and commentators tend to gloss over those aspects of Byron's life and oeuvre that do not fit the socialist mold (for example, incest, homosexuality, promiscuity, the poet's pride in and emphasis on his lineage), focusing instead on what they construe as the "socially condemning pathos of his poetry and libertarian thrust of his activities" (Elistratova, 6) and casting him as the embodiment of the "fight against [bourgeois] reaction in politics and literature" (Kondrat'ev, 15). It is certainly no coincidence that Soviet scholarship and commentary on Byron conveniently tends to drop *Lord* from his name (see, for instance, Elistratova; Kondtrat'ev; and Byron, *Dnevniki*).

96. See GR, 27; Byron's letter to John Murray of Mar. 23, 1820 (BLJ, vol. 7, 59). For further instances of Byron's explicit recourse to Dante, see esp. *Don Juan*, Canto 2, stanza 83; and Canto 3, stanzas 10–11.

97. It should be remembered that Augusta Leigh had been married to George Leigh since 1807 and thus engaged in both incest *and* adultery when she struck up an affair with her half-brother in 1813 (see Eisler, 396; MacCarthy, 205–206; Strickland, 16).

98. See GR, 116.

99. On Byron's immense impact on the Russian (and Soviet) imagination since the age of Pushkin and Lermontov, see Diakonova and Vacuro; Gilenson; MacFadyen, *Joseph Brodsky and the Soviet Muse,* 164–170; and Kondrat'ev. Vladimir Lenskoj, the ill-fated hero of Pushkin's *Eugene Onegin* (vol. 3, 32), for instance, is unmistakably related to Byron's equally ill-fated "fair-faced Lanskoi" (*Don Juan*, Canto 9, stanza 47, line 8); and Lermontov, for one, not only translated Byron's works but viewed his own life through the prism of Byron's: "There's one more parallel between my life and Lord Byron's. His mother was told by an old hag in Scotland that he would be *a great man* . . . the same thing was said about me by an old hag to my grandmother in the Caucasus . . . "(*Sobranie sočinenij*, vol. 4, 392–393). Lermontov knew about this episode in Byron's life from Moore's *Letters and Journals* (vol. 1, 21–27). Brodsky's acquaintance with the works of Lord Byron goes back to his early youth. In school, he reminisces, "we got the whole thing. The English poets would be Byron and Longfellow . . . " (*Conversations,* 75). "When I used to read Byron in Russian," Brodsky remembers elsewhere, "the echo of Pushkin was with me constantly. In the best sense, [Byron] was Pushkin; in the worst, Lermontov" (Volkov, 88).

100. See Tomaševskij, 49; on Byron's "literary enterprise," see Eisler, 109. Already Byron's contemporaries marveled at the literary-biographical dimension of the Byron phenomenon. Thus Goethe is reported as saying that "[Byron's] late separation from his wife [was] so poetical that if Lord Byron had invented it he would hardly have had a more fortunate subject for his genius" (as recorded by George Ticknor on October 25, 1816; cited in MacCarthy, 280). "Byron's fame as poet and his notoriety as man," Benita Eisler observes, "were one; the scandals of his life—whoring, marriage, adultery, incest, sodomy—became the text or subtext of his poems" (4), which in turn provided blueprints for action. The "truth of Byron's poetry," Eisler notes elsewhere, "was also that of his life" (741). Forgoing a detailed discussion of the close interface between life and art in Byron's texts, suffice it to

mention only a handful of examples that clearly blur the boundaries between the poetic and the extrapoetic. The 1806 poem "To Mary," published in *Fugitive Pieces* (17–19; CPW, vol. 1, 132–135), Byron's first, privately printed collection (1806) unequivocally metabolizes its author's affair with his promiscuous addressee, who has gone down in literary history as Naughty Mary (Eisler, 114). Parts of *Childe Harold's Pilgrimage* (Cantos 1 and 2, 1812; Canto 3, 1816; and Canto 4, 1818) can plausibly be read as Byron's poetic travelogue of his first expedition to the continent, including Greece, Albania, and Turkey (see McGann, 67–93, for an insightful discussion of the autobiographical dimension of *Childe Harold's Pilgrimage*). The theme of incest in *The Bride of Abydos: A Turkish Tale* (1813) indirectly thematizes the poet's affair with Augusta and can be said to testify to, as Eisler notes, "his need to tell and not to tell" (408). Conrad, the protagonist of *The Corsair: A Tale* (published Feb. 3, 1814), is torn, "in a characteristic Byronic triangle" (Eisler, 410), between two women, one of whom bears the name Medora, which will also become the middle name of Augusta Leigh's daughter (arguably by Byron), Elizabeth Medora, born two months after the publication of *The Corsair*, on April 15, 1814. Finally, in *The Deformed Transformed* (1824), Byron addresses head on his own congenital physical deformity.

101. See Volkov, 138.

102. Ibid., 32.

103. NSA, 45, lines 70–72. On Brodsky's "speech masks," see LTO, 251. The original typescript of "New Stanzas to Augusta" (located in the Brodsky archive at the Beinecke Rare Book and Manuscript Library, Yale University, box 2) is dated "Sept. 64." Bobyšev's depiction of Norenskoe as "huts in an open field . . . a nearby wood . . . a narrow path leading into the wood . . . " (379–380) bears out the veracity of Brodsky's description. If it is true, as Brodsky suggests, that since "the fourteenth century, the woods have given off a very strong smell of [that] *selva oscura*" in which Dante gets lost "midway on the road of life," then his description to Augusta of the actual site of his relegation and, by extension, the *New Stanzas to Augusta* as a whole are necessarily coded in terms of both Dante's and—given the poem's overall Byronic locutionary setup—Byron's texts, that is, in emphatically literary terms.

104. See lines 1–2 of Shakespeare's Sonnet 79.

105. See "Venecianskie Strofy I" (Venetian stanzas I) (1982), lines 13–14 (cited in *Konec prekrasnoj epoxi*, 105). For Brodsky's ironic approach to his own situation, see NSA, 39; and the Appendix. Leslie Marchand appositely comments on Byron's ironic stance: "For the most part one need not look for verbal subtleties in Byron. His irony is likely to be a brickbat, but hurled with such skill and force that when it does hit, it crushes" ("Byron in the Twentieth Century," 432).

106. See Said, 73, 31, 167, 166. Said refers specifically to Goethe's introductory poem in *West-Östlicher Divan* (1819): "North and West and South fall apart, / Thrones burst, Empires shake: / You, take flight, toward the pure East / To taste the air of patriarchs" (7). On the question of Orientalist stereotyping, see also Bhabha, 66–84. George Sanders' painting is located in Queen Elizabeth II's Royal Collection (reproduced in MacCarthy, illustration 1). J.M.W. Turner's famous 1842 oil painting of Napoleon on St. Helena, titled "War, the Exile and the Rock Limpet" (located at the Tate Gallery, London), equally comes to

mind as a potential subtext to Brodsky's poem. On the circumstances of the creation of Sanders' painting, see Eisler, 172–174. According to the commentary in Brodsky's *Collected Poems*, Brodsky "remarked that he fashioned ["Venetian Stanzas"] after paintings depicting cityscapes at different times of day and seasons . . . " (523).

107. See Bhabha, 82.

108. See Byron, *Lara* (1814), Canto 1, stanza 1, line 4; and stanza 18, line 3 (CPW, vol. 3, 214–256). For some key poetic examples of Russian orientalism modeled on Byron, see Pushkin's *Kavkazskij Plennik* (The prisoner of Caucasus) (1822), *Baxčisarajskij Fontan* (The fountain of Bakhchisaraj) (1824), and *Cygany* (The gypsies) (1824), all in Pushkin, *Sočinenija*, vol. 2); and Lermontov's *Izmail-Bej: A Tale of the East* (1832), *Mcyri* (1839), and *The Demon: A Tale of the East* (1839), all in Lermontov, vol. 2.

109. "Whenever you get in trouble," Brodsky observes, "you're automatically forced to regard yourself . . . as a kind of archetypal character. So who else could I think of being but Ovid?" (*Conversations*, 83).

110. See GR, 24.

111. On Brodsky's decision to go the United States rather than Israel, where he officially "had to go to" (*Conversations*, 83), see Volkov, 114–115, 130.

112. "À la fois dramatique et comique" [*both dramatic and comical*]," as the caption of the French version of Frieda Vigdorova's transcript of the poet's trial in *Le Figaro* appositely reads. On Brodsky's trial, see Chapter One, note 36.

113. See GR, 118.

114. See NSA, 97; GR, 128.

115. See Nietzsche, "Über Wahrheit," 880.

116. Ibid.

117. See GR, 91; Volkov, 138; GR, 50; LTO, 355, 164.

118. See CPW, vol. 2, 4.

119. See BLJ, vol. 1, 43, note 1. Mary Anne and Jack were married in August 1805 (see Eisler, 86).

120. See Moore, vol. 1, 53. On Byron and Mary Anne Chaworth, see also BLJ, vol. 1, 45; Marchand, *Byron: A Portrait*, 18, 26–38; Eisler, 35, 66–71.

121. "To My Dear Mary Anne" (CPW, vol. 1, 3) was first published in 1831 and would subsequently be included in all editions of Byron's *Collected Works*, such as E. H. Coleridge's 1856 six-volume set as well as its widely circulating 1905 reissue in one volume (see CPW, vol. 1, xxviii–xxxiv). For Byron's other poems addressed to or about Mary Anne Chaworth, see "To Maria ——," "Well! Thou art happy . . . ," "The Farewell to a Lady [On Being Asked My Reason for Quitting England in the Spring]," and "Epistle to a Friend, in Answer to Some Lines Exhorting the Author to be Cheerful, and to 'Banish Care'" (all in CPW, vol. 1, 129–130, 221–223, 225, 344–346). The first poem, originally published in *Fugitive Pieces* (1806, 10–11), was written, as was "To My Dear Mary Anne," on the occasion of the poet's parting from Mary Anne in 1804. The next two poems were written after the poet's visit to Mary Anne Chaworth-Musters (then a wife and mother) in November 1808 (BLJ, vol. 1, 173) and first published in *Imitations and Translations from the Ancient and Modern Classics* (edited by Byron's friend John Cam Hobhouse, 1809); in the first of these,

"Well! Thou art happy . . . ," Byron addresses Mary Anne as Mary ("Mary, adieu!" line 17). The last of these poems was written for Francis Hodgson in October 1811 and first published in Moore, vol. 1, 301–302. See also "The Dream," written in July 1816 (CPW, vol. 4, 92–97), which Moore discloses as a poem about, among other things, Byron's attachment to Mary Anne (vol. 1, 55; see also Eisler 70–71).

122. See Moore, vol. 1, 54.

123. "To Mary" and "To Mary, on Receiving Her Picture" were first published in 1806 in *Fugitive Pieces* (17–19, 28–29; CPW, vol. 1, 132–135, 50–51) and are addressed to the so-called "naughty Mary," Byron's promiscuous London mistress [see CPW, vol. 1, 367, 378; Eisler, 113–116). The addressee of "To Anne" (*Poetical Works*, 49) is unknown. The name Mary also appears, for instance, in *Don Juan*, Canto 5, stanza 4,. line 1; stanza 98, line 5; and Canto 9, stanza 71, line 5. Incidentally, 'Anne Isabella' was also the full given name of Byron's wife, Annabella Milbanke.

124. See CPW, vol. 3, 306–307. The spelling of the name Marianne varies. In the original source of the story, Josephus' *Jewish Antiquities* (written in Greek),the name is spelled μαριαμμε (Mariamme) (32–45, 86–89, 97–115); Joseph Addison, on whom Byron most likely relies, spells it *Mariamne* (*The Spectator*, issue 171, Sept. 15, 1711; vol. 2, 245–247). Others such as Christian Friedrich Hebbel and, more recently, Pär Lagerkvist, for instance, have spelled it *Marianne* (see Hebbel's 1849 tragedy *Herodes und Marianne* and Lagerkvist's 1967 novella *Herod and Marianne*).

125. See Josephus, 33. My subsequent summary of Josephus's account of Herod and Mariamne is based on Josephus, 32–45, 86–115.

126. See BLJ, vol. 5, 129–130. On Byron's liaison with Marianna Segati, which lasted from Nov. 1816 until Feb. or Mar. 1818, see Eisler, 548–589; MacCarthy, 319–335.

127. See BLJ, vol. 5, 133–134. Teresa Guiccioli, Byron's last mistress, confirms Byron's description of Marianna Segati: "She was . . . a young lady of twenty-two, with Oriental eyes, a pretty face in the Italian manner, dark hair . . . " (*Lord Byron's Life in Italy*, 90). See also Byron's letter to Thomas Moore of Dec. 24, 1816: "My flame (my 'Donna' whom I spoke of in my former epistle, my Marianna) is still my Marianna, and I her—what she pleases. She is by far the prettiest woman I have ever seen here, and the most loveable I have met with any where—as well as one of the most singular. I believe I told you the rise and progress of our *liaison* in my former letter. Lest that should not have reached you, I will merely repeat, that she is a Venetian, two-and-twenty years old, married to a merchant well to do in the world, and that she has great black oriental eyes, and all the qualities which her eyes promise" (BLJ, vol. 5, 148).

128. See Byron, *Dnevniki i pis'ma*, 134–139. As early as 1830, Lermontov refers to Moore's *Letters and Journals* (see this chapter's note 99).

129. See Byron, *Dnevniki i pis'ma*, 134.

130. See "Rumjancevoj Pobedam" (To the victories of Rumjanceva) (NSA, 40), "Pis'mo v Butylke" (Letter in a bottle) (NSA, 56–64), "Sreten'e" (Nunc dimittis, or literally, *encounter*) (NSA, 87–89; *Collected Poems*, 61–63), and "Dvadcat' sonetov k Marii Stjuart" (Twenty sonnets to Mary, Queen of Scots) (NSA, 103–114). In my subsequent discussion of "Twenty Sonnets," I dispense with page references to the individual sonnets. Brodsky sometimes

uses the spelling Мэри (*Mary*) (such as in "Rumjancevoj") and sometimes Мари (*Mari* or *Marie*) (as throughout "Twenty Sonnets," with the exception of the title). These orthographic variations are due mostly to prosodic considerations. If the name's second syllable is stressed, Brodsky uses the Francophone *Mari* or *Marie*; if the first syllable is stressed, he uses the Anglophone *Mary*. That the spelling is semantically unmarked is borne out by the fact that throughout the poeticized English version of "Twenty Sonnets to Mary Queen of Scots" (translated by Peter France and Brodsky himself and in whose Russian title, by the way, the name is spelled *Maria*, in the dative case), the original's Francophone Мари (*Mari* or *Marie*) is rendered as *Mary* (see *Collected Poems*, 226–234). In my own literal translations of the sonnets (which follow shortly), I follow the English version and use *Mary* throughout. On two occasions—in Sonnets 1, line 6 ("to digest a Paris lunch"), and 4, line 14 ("grateful for the deal")—I borrow France's and Brodsky's wording. "Sreten'e" is based on Luke 2:25–36 (Simeon's encounter with Jesus and the prophet Anna in the temple) and is, among other things, an homage to Anna Akhmatova; "Rumjancevoj Pobedam" commemorates, according to Dmitrij Bobyšev (*Ja zdes'*, 374), the role of Tanja Rumjanceva, one of Marianna Basmanova's friends from school, as mediator between Brodsky and his lover in 1964–1965. "Twenty Sonnets to Mary Stuart" was originally published in *Čast Reči*, 43–54.

131. See France, 106. France also mentions the Italian and French traditions (Petrarch, Ronsard, and Du Bellay) as distally informing Brodsky's sonnets.

132. See BK, 523.

133. See GR, 84, 91. On Brodsky's reverence of and intimate familiarity with Shakespeare, see *Conversations*, 127–128.

134. See Shakespeare, Sonnet 96, lines 8, 4, 7.

135. Byron's mother, Chatherine Gordon, and Augusta's mother, Amelia, Baroness Conyers, were of Scottish descent.

136. See Byron, *Don Juan*, Canto 5, stanza 98, lines 3–5. On Augusta's lineage, see Bakewell and Bakewell; Strickland, 13–39.

137. See Tjutčev, 247, stanza 1. Mark the parallel between the title of Tjutčev's poem—"K. B."—and Brodsky's dedication of *New Stanzas to Augusta* to M. B.

138. In the original text, line 8 of Sonnet 2 reads, "My vyšli vse na svet . . . ," which literally means "we all went out into the light . . . ," or "we all went out into the/this world. . . . " On the screening of *Doroga na Ešafot* at the Spartacus, see Brodsky, *Sočinenija Iosifa Brodskogo*, vol. 6, 17, 410; *Collected Poems*, 519; GR, 11. The irony of the fact that Brodsky—a Jew and staunch antitotalitarian—would cherish tender memories of a profoundly National Socialist artifact rather than repudiating it will certainly not escape the reader. From the viewpoint of history, it is equally ironic, as Peter France (111) points out, that Fröhlich's anti-British film made at Göbbels' behest was still being screened in the Soviet Union three years after Nazi Germany's defeat.

139. Mary, Queen of Scots (1542–1587), was first married to Francis II of France. After his death in 1560, she married Henry Stuart, Lord Darnley. It is reported that while she was married to Darnley she had an affair with David Riccio, her French secretary. After the murder of Darnley, she married Bothwell, the supposed slayer of Darnley (see Cowan; Guy).

140. For some of the additional intertexts of "Twenty Sonnets" (esp. Dante, Pushkin, Mozart, Baudelaire, Blok, and Akhmatova), which further underscore the sequence's overall literary-biographical thrust, see France, 102–103. Brodsky's attention to the physiological groundedness of poetry ("the larynx") dovetails with his earlier staging of poetic speech in terms of "coughing" (NSA, 46) and presents a remarkable parallel to Grünbein's virtually identical conception of poetry as "Revenge of the flesh / Through the larynx" (*Schädelbasislektion,* 139).

141. France, 102.

142. Pushkin, vol. 1, 271.

143. "Therefore, pay careful attention reader," Dante cautions, to "consider the illustrious vernacular, which poets . . . ought to use . . . " (*Literature in the Vernacular,* 47). On Pushkin's poem "I loved you" as an example of unadorned and straightforward poetic speech devoid of figures and images, see esp. Jakobson, 129.

144. On Mary's extramarital liaisons, see Cowan, 6, 13, 20. The "Edinburgh mob," Cowan notes, famously "decried her as a whore" (21).

145. See this chapter's note 130.

146. On Dante's "screen ladies," see the Appendix.

147. See Brodsky, *Collected Poems,* 519.

148. See Shakespeare, *Romeo and Juliet,* Act 2, Scene 2, lines 45–49, in *Shakespeare's Works,* vol. 3, 208.

149. One of Byron's formulae of address to his half sister, such as in his letters to her of Nov. 2, 6, and 11, 1816 (BLJ, vol. 5, 122–128).

CLOSING REMARKS

1. On ethics-and-literature as a discrete field of inquiry, see Eskin, "Introduction."

2. See Eskin, "On Literature and Ethics."

APPENDIX

1. See Grünbein and Böttiger, 75–76.

2. See Grünbein and von Törne, "Mir kann die ganze Ostnostalgie," 45–46.

3. For the *Figaro Littéraire* version, the caption of which depicts the trial as "À la fois dramatique et comique" (*both dramatic and comical*), see Vigdorova, "Le Procès de Yosip Brodski"; Dobzynski is cited in Etkind, 82–89. The trial transcript was also published, in German, in the weekly *Die Zeit,* numbers 26–27 (1964), under the title "Ein Dichter—ein arbeitsscheues Element." On the date of purchase by Celan of the fourth issue of *Vozdušnye Puti,* see Ivanović, "Kyrillisches, Freunde, auch das . . . ," 126.

4. For the German and French translations owned by Celan, see Brodsky, *Gedichte von Jossif Brodskij* and *Collines et autres poèmes,* both located at the Deutsches Literaturarchiv, Marbach, Germany. Some of Brodsky's poems had already appeared in German in *Akzente* 12.5 (1965; see Brodsky, "Drei Gedichte") and in *Lyrische Hefte* 8.1 (1966; see Brodsky, "Zwei Gedichte"). Brodsky's second collection, *Ostanovka v pustyne* (A halt in the desert), was not published until 1970, that is, too late for Celan, who committed suicide in April 1970, to productively take notice of it.

5. It is well known that Celan used to read and annotate in the original the works of poets whose languages he knew and who were important to him, especially Russian poets.

6. See Ivanović, "*Kyrillisches*," 39. In the epigraph to his poem "Und mit dem Buch aus Tarussa" (And with the book from Tarussa) (from the 1963 collection *Die Niemandsrose*; see GW, vol. 1, 287), Celan cites and changes Cvetaeva's lines, "V sem xristiannejšem iz mirov / Poety—židy!" (In this most Christian of worlds / Poets are kikes!); from the 1926 poem "Poema Konca" (Poem of the end; Cvetaeva, 403) to "Vse poety židy" (All poets are kikes). On Celan's relation to Cvetaeva, see Ivanović, *Das Gedicht*, 288–305.

7. See Emmanuel, 12. From December 1962 until the end of his life, Celan would intermittently undergo psychiatric treatment (see CCL, vol. 2, 541). On Brodsky's involuntary subjection to psychiatric treatment, explicitly referred to in his trial transcript, on the front page of the *Figaro Littéraire* version in fact, see discussion later in chapter.

8. "My hope is in the East—*it is there*," Celan wrote to his friend Petre Solomon in Romania on March 22, 1962 (see Solomon, 66). On Celan's imagined and mythicized "East," see Pajević, "Erfahrungen." On Celan's engagement with Russian poets, see Ivanović, *Gedicht*; Eskin, *Ethics and Dialogue*, 112–267.

9. See Brodsky, *Conversations*, 67–68.

10. See BK, 587–588.

11. In addition to being virtually identified as such by Brodsky, it is their bilingual character in particular that bolsters Hamburger's anthlogies' candidacy for being the probable sources of Brodsky's acquaintance with Celan. Insofar as, according to Brodsky, "a poem is a form of the closest possible interplay between ethics and aesthetics" (LTO, 99); and furthermore, insofar as the strength and quality of a poem are the result of this interplay; and finally, insofar as this "interplay, lamentably, is precisely what tends to vanish in translation" (ibid.), the declaration of a poet as "extraordinarily gifted" and his poems as "marvelous" implies at least some familiarity on Brodsky's part with the poet's work in the original. Now Brodsky, who avowedly "did not know a damn thing about German" (Volkov, 130) when he left the Soviet Union and would not in any case have known enough German by 1979 to read Celan's difficult poetry solely in the original, yet must have been sufficiently familiar with it, would obviously have benefited greatly from and most likely relied on a bilingual edition of it as the basis for an informed judgment about Celan. The fact that Brodsky translated only a single text from German—the popular 1930s song "Lili Marlen" (*Sočinenija Iosifa Brodskogo*, vol. 4, 301)—in contrast to his numerous translations from Polish, Czech, and Italian equally bespeaks his lack of mastery of German. Other than in Hamburger's and Middleton's translations, Brodsky could have read Celan in, for instance, the English versions by Donald White (1966; cited in Barnstone, 164–165) and Joachim Neugroschel (1971; see Celan, *Speech-Grille*). Such early criticism on Celan as Vladimir Markov's 1959 review in *Grani* of Celan's Mandelstam translations and Karl S. Weimar's 1974 translation and interpretation of "Death Fugue" in *PMLA* would also have been of interest to Brodsky. It goes without saying that Brodsky had access to Celan's individual collections, for example, *Mohn und Gedächtnis* (1952), *Von Schwelle zu Schwelle*

(1955), *Sprachgitter* (1959), *Die Niemandsrose* (1963), and *Atemwende* (1967), and all other published materials on Celan.

12. See Celan, *Nineteen Poems*, 12 ("survivor . . ."); Hamburger and Middleton, xlii ("age . . ."). For the poems listed, see Hamburger and Middleton, 318–321; Hamburger, *German Poetry*, 262–268; Celan, *Nineteen Poems*, 35–36. Hamburger's much more comprehensive, bilingual follow-up anthology, *Paul Celan: Poems* (1980), further reinforces the poet's image as a tragic poet grappling with the "impossibility of writing poems after Auschwitz, let alone about Auschwitz" (*Paul Celan: Poems*, 24).

13. See BK, 304.

14. For Brodsky's Shakespeare reference, see BK, 523.

15. See BK, 279. See also Chapter One, note 40.

16. See "Tvoj lokon" (Your lock), line 33, written in exile in 1964 (NSA, 39); and LTO, 305.

17. See NSA, 39, line 34.

18. See BK, 22.

19. See GR, 140.

20. See Volkov, 184.

21. See GR, 24. Elsewhere Brodsky observes, "the feeling of strangeness here [in the West] isn't as painful as the feeling of strangeness in your own homeland. Don't forget this when you hear all these endless, bitter-tasting arguments about the dreadful drama of writers in exile, because this is not in fact so. I even think that the audience here, in the West, for writers . . . from Eastern Europe is a more or less adequate audience . . . and frequently even exceeds what these people had back home" (Volkov, 276).

22. See LTO, 200.

23. I use *history* and *genealogy* in the most general senses. By *history* I mean the actual unfolding of events in their temporal succession, the "historical field" or "historical process" itself prior to its narrativization into an historical account (White, 5, 41). By *genealogy* I mean an account of the descent or lineage of a person, group, or thing. For a helpful discussion of the distinction between genealogy and history, see Jenkins, 9–10. I should note that, following Mandelstam (see, for example, MSS, vol. 3, 217), I subscribe to a responsive notion of literature—that is, to a view of literary creativity as ineluctably predicated on an author's responses to other authors. On literature as response, see also Bakhtin, *Sobranie sočinenij*, 337; H. Bloom; Eskin, *Ethics and Dialogue*, 92–95, 130.

24. See Seneca, "De brevitate vitae," 37.

25. I borrow Alain Badiou's method of functionalizing the names of individual historical figures as the chiffres for particular historical-conceptual configurations (*Manifeste pour la philosophie*, 14–15). I henceforth use *Mandelstam* both in reference to the poet himself and as a configurational shorthand (which also comprises the poet). It should be clear from the context which of the two senses (if not both) applies in any given instance.

26. See Bethea, *Joseph Brodsky and the Creation of Exile*, 52. Acmeism—the "organicist school in Russian lyric poetry" (MSS, vol. 1, 229)—emerged as the result of the "creative

initiative of [Nikolaj] Gumilev and [Sergej] Gorodeckij early on in 1912, who were officially joined by [Anna] Akhmatova, Vladimir Narbut, Mixail Zenkevič and the author of these lines [that is, Mandelstam]" (ibid.). On Mandelstam's assessment of the Russian Revolution, see Cavanagh, 201.

27. Reminiscing in 1981 on his first encounter with Mandelstam's poems in 1959, Brodsky remarked, "These poems fascinated me. Perhaps because for the first time in my life I was reading something really close to me in spirit" (BK, 171). The "past" is, as Hayden White notes, of an "ineluctably poetic nature" (xi); it is necessarily also an *ex post facto* creation, a retroactive invention, which does not in the least imply that it did not happen! "It is patently obvious," Keith Jenkins appositely notes, "that it is historians who create history . . . " (10). With particular attention to poets' engagement with the "great masters of the past," Seamus Heaney writes, "When poets turn to the great masters of the past, they turn to an image of their own creation, one which is likely to be a reflection of their own imaginative needs, their own artistic inclinations and procedures" (240).

28. See Ivanović, *Das Gedicht*, 230, 244, on Mandelstam as Celan's "Bruder Ossip," the title of an unpublished poem by Celan from the early 1960s; also Chapter Four, note 21, on Brodsky as "the second Osja"; and Grünbein, *Galilei vermißt*, 89–104. While certainly many a poet (from Cvetaeva and Akhmatova to Lowell and Heaney, to name only a few) has written on and engaged in dialogue with Mandelstam, none of Mandelstam's successors has, to the best of my knowledge, chosen to become his "reader in posterity" (MSS, vol. 1, 184) and enfold him, whose life and art were avowedly driven by the craving for the "interlocutor's embrace" (187), as wholeheartedly and with such seriousness, fidelity, and empathy as Celan, Brodsky, and Grünbein. On Brodsky and Mandelstam, see esp. Bethea, *Joseph Brodsky*, 10, 48–73; Polukhina; and Rančin. On Celan and Mandelstam, see esp. Parry; Ivanović, *Das Gedicht*, 212–260; Eskin, *Ethics and Dialogue*, 113–267. On Grünbein and Mandelstam, see Eskin, "Stimmengewirr vieler Zeiten."

29. See MSS, vol. 1, 215.

30. See MSS, vol. 1, 216; vol. 3, 226.

31. See GW, vol. 4, 198; Grünbein, *Galilei*, 26 ("The word is psyche"); and Volkov, 44. As David Bethea appositely notes, for Mandelstam "the miracle of the . . . Eucharist, is the basis of all poetic speech" (*Joseph Brodsky*, 61). For Mandelstam's discussions of *logos*, as mediated through the Gospel of John, see MSS, vol. 1, 177–178, 212, 214. On Acmeism's relation to Christianity, see esp. Doherty, 165, 232.

32. See MSS, vol. 1, 229, 179; Gumilev, vol. 4, 186. Of course the Acmeists were not the first to think of art in organicist terms. The development of an organicist poetics, Justin Doherty notes, "suggests a derivation from European Romanticism, which Gumilev's appropriation of Coleridge would support; indeed, German Romantic thought, particularly Schelling's *Naturphilosophie,* has been suggested as the origin of certain of Mandelstam's ideas" (112). For Mandelstam's explicit recourse to the German Romantics, especially "Schelling, Hoffmann, and Novalis," see MSS, vol. 1, 230. On the Acmeists' appropriation of the discourses of biology and physiology, see Doherty, 117, 152–156; Tihanov, 169–173. For an in-depth treatment of the organicist aspects of Romantic poetics, see Abrams, 167–225.

33. See MSS, vol. 3, 220.

34. See GW, vol. 3, 177, 188, 194; LTO, 100, 134, 141; Grünbein, *Galilei,* 18. Clearly, critical reflection on corporeality long predates the recent upsurge of interest in the body on the part of literary and cultural critics as well as historians. For insightful discussions of the body's rise to critical stardom in the 1990s, see Vidal, (esp 936–937); Erb, 107–121.

35. See MSS, vol. 1, 230. For the ethical dimension of Acmeism, see also Gumilev, vol. 4, 158, 174, 177–178; Gorodeckij, 47; Doherty 52, 276–277.

36. See Ivanov, 9, 14.

37. See Blok, *Sobranie sočinenij,* vol. 6, 165.

38. See MSS, vol. 1, 179–180. Mark Mandelstam's subtle critique of Kant's concept of the "thing in itself."

39. See Gumilev (commenting on Mandelstam), vol. 4, 327.

40. See MSS, vol. 1, 135.

41. See MSS, vol. 2, 286–287.

42. I do not deal with Mandelstam's fascination with and view of the Middle Ages— Gothic architecture in particular. Suffice it to note that he conceives of the architecture of a poem as homologous to the architecture of society, and that this rapprochement between poetry and sociopolitics in the name of a "human society" is informed by his view of Gothic architecture as the paradigm of the free play of "weights and forces" (see also MSS, vol. 1, 179).

43. See MSS, vol. 2, 256; N. Mandelstam, 120.

44. GW, vol. 3, 189, 186; Celan, "Notiz," 67; GW, vol. 3, 198; Brodsky, *Conversations,* 93; GR, 90; LTO, 200; GR, 91; LTO, 267; GR, 90; Grünbein, *Galilei,* 83; and Grünbein, *Antike Dispositionen,* 50. Elsewhere Celan notes, "I haven't written a single line that would not be related to my existence" (Celan and Einhorn, 6).

45. See MSS, vol. 1, 187; Gumilev, vol. 1, 179.

46. See MSS, vol. 1, 183–188. For a historical account of the trope of poetry as navigation, see Curtius, 128–130.

47. See MSS, vol. 1, 187.

48. On Mandelstam's poetics of dialogue, see esp. Eskin, *Ethics and Dialogue,* 129–145.

49. See GW, vol. 3, 186; NSA, 56–64; Grünbein, *Antike Dispositionen,* 52. "Only a society," Grünbein notes with reference to his own situation, "which despairs of its own destiny and does not desire anything beyond . . . economic reproduction would go so far as to question . . . poetry as such" (*Antike Dispositionen,* 46).

50. See Hawkins and Jacoff, xxiv. On Celan's, Grünbein's, and Brodsky's respective recourses to Dante, see, for instance, GW vol. 1, 112, 200, 212; Grünbein, *Falten und Fallen,* 66, 95; *Nach den Satiren,* 50; *Das erste Jahr,* 111; *Galilei,* 89–104; BK, 64, 100, 247; LTO, 204, 402; GR, 26, 87, 233; NSA, 126; *Čast' Reči,* 7, 109; and *Uranija,* 75, 63. This is not to say that Celan, Brodsky, and Grünbein had not been acquainted with Dante before coming across Mandelstam's works; it is simply to point out that their respective "mature" recourse to the Florentine is certainly mediated through Mandelstam.

51. Anna Akhmatova, a firsthand witness, points out that Mandelstam "devoted many years of his life to the study of the works of Dante" (*Sočinenija,* vol. 2, 183). Mandelstam's

"Razgovor o Dante," which has rightly been called "a synthesis of his own poetics" (N. Struve, *Ossip Mandelstam,* 200), was written in the early 1930s and not published until 1966, in the second volume of the 1964–1966 Struve and Filippov edition of his works. It was first published in the Soviet Union in 1967. On Dante's significance for Modernism, see Hawkins and Jacoff, xiii–xvi; Heaney; Ivanović, "Göttliche Tragödie," 121; Bethea, *Joseph Brodsky,* 52–60. I do not deal with the different stages of Mandelstam's engagement with Dante. Suffice it to note that his rereading of Dante in the early 1930s only reinforced and consolidated the poetics he had been developing since the early 1910s.

52. See Eliot, "What Dante Means to Me," 31, 29. Christine Ivanović even goes so far as to suggest that for the Acmeists, Dante replaced Ovid as the exemplary exile ("Göttliche Tragödie," 130).

53. See Heaney, 250.

54. See Pound, 159–160; Heaney, 251 (referring in particular to Eliot's essay "Dante"); MSS, vol. 3, 229, 224–225, 235. In mentioning the "mysterious Dante," Mandelstam specifically alludes to Blok's 1909 poem "Ravenna," which ends with the words, "The shade of Dante with his aquiline profile / Sings of a New Life to me" (Blok, *Stixotvorenija,* 399). "Now I will show you," Mandelstam writes in the same passage, inveighing, in particular, against the Romantics and Symbolists, "how little Dante's initial readers were concerned with his so-called mysteriousness" (MSS, vol. 3, 230).

55. In his autobiographical piece, *The Noise of Time* (1925), Mandelstam refers to himself as a "raznočinec" and "literator-raznočinec" (MSS, vol. 2, 384, 386).

56. See MSS, vol. 3, 176.

57. See Heaney, 240.

58. Famously, Elie Wiesel (esp. 32, 38) and Primo Levi (in, for example, *If This Is a Man,* 27–28, 56, 115–21; and *The Drowned and the Saved,* 55, 82) draw a parallel between their experience of the death camps and Dante's *Inferno.* Alexander Solženicyn, for instance, resorts to the *Inferno* in his treatment of Soviet prison life (see, for example, *V Kruge Pervom*).

59. See Ivanović, 123.

60. See GW, vol. 1, 200; Volkov, 75; Grünbein, *Galilei,* 89–90; Felstiner, 25, 123; Eskin, "Stimmengewirr vieler Zeiten," 35.

61. Although Mandelstam is specifically referring to Dante's "passion for the city [Florence], love for the city, [and] hatred for the city [as the basic] materials of the *Comedy*" (MSS, vol. 3, 250), he must be taken to suggest that this passion—the "central sun of [Dante's] entire system" (vol. 2, 256), as he notes elsewhere—is the driving force behind Dante's life and art *tout court,* insofar as the *Comedy* is Dante's poetic-existential *summa.* On Dante's "love of my native place," see *Inferno,* Canto 14, line 1; on his "hatred" of Florence during his exile, see esp. *Purgatory,* Canto 6, lines 76–151, and Canto 11, lines 112–114.

62. See Dante, *Inferno,* Canto 1, line 39; *Paradiso,* Canto 33, line 145; *Vita Nuova,* 33; *Inferno,* Canto 2, lines 72, 1–2; *Rime,* 190 ("Dolgia mi reca," line 143); MSS, vol. 3, 218, 250. With specific reference to "Dolgia mi reca," Teodolinda Barolini notes that Dante

condemns passion "ungoverned by virtue and reason" (31)—what the "depraved call by the name of 'love' [but] what is really mere bestial appetite" (ibid).

63. MSS, vol. 3, 253, 220. On Dante's first encounter with Beatrice, see *Vita Nuova*, 3; Mazzotta, 4. For an excellent discussion of Dante's passion for Beatrice, see Pogue Harrison. Auerbach calls Dante's love for Beatrice the "most fundamental fact of his life" (75). Because it would lead me too far afield, I eschew discussing Dante's poetic engagement with love in the light of the history and practice of courtly poetry and the development in the second half the thirteenth century of the *dolce stil nuovo* (*Purgatorio*, Canto 24, line 57). Suffice it to note that Dante was neither the first nor the only poet to elevate love to the status of poetry's "prime mover" (see Auerbach, 76; see also Schnell, esp. 77–181; Barolini; Robertson).

64. See Dante, *Purgatorio*, Canto 24, lines 52–54, 58–59. The main difference between Dante's *passionate* Amor and the profoundly "religious character" (Auerbach, 38) of the Amor inspiring such stilnovists as Guinizzelli, Cavalcanti, or Cino is, Mandelstam suggests, that Dante's Amor presents itself, to use Auerbach's terms, as of this "earthly world." In other words, Mandelstam valorizes—against the grain of Dante's theological, salvific bent (especially in the *Divine Comedy*)—what Auerbach calls Dante's "passionate temperament" (77).

65. See Barolini, 23, 31; MSS, vol. 3, 230.

66. See Dante, *Vita Nuova*, 16; Pogue Harrison, 37; MSS, vol. 3, 223. On Mandelstam's polemic against Bakhtin, see Eskin, *Ethics and Dialogue*, 128. Amor himself explains to Dante (*Vita Nuova*, 18) that he is shunned by Beatrice because of rumors concerning his "scandalous . . . relationship with the second screen-lady" (Musa, 116). Scandal is also at the center of the *Inferno*, Canto 28 (eighth circle, ninth pouch), which deals with the "sowers of scandal and of schism" (line 35).

67. The conflict and dichotomy between what Mark Musa calls the "Greater Aspect of Love" and the "Lesser Aspect of Love" (119–120)—that is, between spiritual or pure and carnal or erotic love—is at the heart of the *New Life* (*Vita Nuova*). Obviously Mandelstam does not engage with Dante's moral condemnation of "carnal sinners" as expressed in the fifth canto of the *Inferno* (line 38). "Some persons," Byron muses, "say that Dante meant theology / By Beatrice, and not a mistress—I, / Although my opinion may require apology, / Deem this a commentator's phantasy . . . " (*Don Juan*, Canto 3, stanza 11, lines 1–4).

68. See *Vita Nuova*, 4. "Such physiological manifestations of passion," Mark Musa notes, "are familiar to us, of course, from the Troubadour love lyrics . . . " (172). Dante's recourse to physiology in an attempt to capture his psychological-emotional state is informed by the classical doctrine of the four bodily humors (black bile, yellow bile, phlegm, and blood). On the history of this doctrine, see Klibansky, Panofsky, and Saxl, 39–54. In an explicit homage to the "Poet-Syre of Italy" (Byron, *Prophecy of Dante*, "Dedication," line 3), Lord Byron also links the experience of "first passion" to "the liver . . . the lazaret of bile" (*Don Juan*, Canto 2, stanza 214, line 1).

69. See Dante, *Vita Nuova*, 33, 40.

70. See Dante, *Vita Nuova*, 74, 76, 78, 81, 4. On Dante's "dalliance with the screen-ladies," see Musa, 121. On Dante's lovers more generally, see Pogue Harrison, 37.

71. See MSS, vol. 3, 218, 220.

72. See Heaney, 251.

73. See MSS, vol. 3, 219, 249, 252. Mandelstam's vision of Dante is informed by the fact that the latter is literally on the go—mostly walking—throughout the *Divine Comedy*. Already in the *New Life*, however, we find such contextually apposite statements as "I did not dare to begin writing, and I remained for several days with the desire to write and the fear of beginning. Then it happened that while walking down a path . . . I suddenly felt a great desire to write a poem" (31–32). "The future of Dante criticism" (MSS, vol. 3, 230), which ought to "approximate the method of living medicine" (227), belongs, Mandelstam proclaims, "to the natural sciences" (230). The reader "may . . . come to wonder," Mark Musa notes, having in mind Dante's attention to the workings of the human body, "if the lover's tears, so frequently recorded in the narrative, are not often strongly influenced physiologically" (90).

74. See MSS, vol. 2, 184.

75. See Akhmatova, vol. 2, 183.

76. See the following essays (all written between 1913 and 1922, and most in MSS): "O Prirode Slova" (On the nature of the word) (1922, vol. 1, 229); "Utro Akmeizma" (The morning of Acmeism) (1913/1919, vol. 1, 179); "Anatomija Stixotvorenija" (Anatomy of the poem) (1921; Gumilev, vol. 4, 186); "Slovo i Kul'tura" (The word and culture) (1921, vol. 1, 216).

77. See MSS, vol. 1, 177–178, "Utro Akmeizma"; vol. 1, 215, "Slovo i Kul'tura"; vol. 1, 187, "O Sobesednike" (On the Interlocutor), 1913. Mandelstam's erotic conception of poetry ties in with the profoundly gendered and sexualized thrust of Acmeism, which casts the poet as "manly and hard" (Gumilev, vol. 4, 171), as a "new Adam. . . . entering an untouched and virginal world" (Gorodeckij, 49).

Bibliography

Abrams, Meyer Howard. *The Mirror and the Lamp: Romantic Theory and the Critical Tradition*. London: Oxford University Press, 1953.

Addison, Joseph. *The Spectator with Notes and Illustrations*. 6 vols. London: Stereotype Edition, 1822.

Adorno, Theodor Wiesengrund. *Prismen: Kulturkritik und Gesellschaft* [Prisms: Cultural criticism and society]. 4th ed. Frankfurt am Main, Ger.: Suhrkamp, 1992.

Agamben, Giorgio. *The End of the Poem: Studies in Poetics*. Trans. Daniel Heller-Roazen. Stanford, CA: Stanford University Press, 1999.

Akhmatova, Anna A ndreevna. *Sočinenija* [Works]. Ed. V. A. Černyx, E. G. Gerštein, and L. A. Mandrykina. 2 vols. Moscow: Xudožestvennaja Literatura, 1986.

Allemann, Beda, and Rolf Bücher. "Paul Celan: Talmarici ale sonetelor lui Shakespeare" [Paul Celan: Translations of Shakespeare's sonnets]. *Manuscriptum* 3 (1982): 183–185.

———. "Paul Celan: Talmarici ale sonetelor lui Shakespeare (II) [Paul Celan: Translations of Shakespeare's sonnets]." *Manuscriptum* 4 (1982): 169–173.

Almog, Joseph. *What Am I? Descartes and the Mind-Body Problem*. Oxford, UK: Oxford University Press, 2002.

Andersch, Alfred. *Der Vater eines Mörders* [The father of a murderer] Zurich: Diogenes, 1982.

Andringa, Els, and Margrit Schreier, eds. *Poetics Today* 25.2 (2004). Special Issue: "How Literature Enters Life." (Introduction: 161–169).

Anthologia Latina sive Poesis Latinae Supplementum [Latin anthology, or supplement to Latin poetry]. Vol. 1, Part 1. Ed. F. Buecheler and A. Riese. Leipzig, Ger.: Teubner, 1894.

Apel, Friedmar. *Sprachbewegung: Eine historisch-poetologische Untersuchung zum Problem des Übersetzens* [The movement of language: A historical-critical inquiry into the problem of translation]. Heidelberg, Ger.: Winkler, 1982.

Apollinaire, Guillaume. *Alcools.* Paris: Gallimard, 1920.

Arendt, Hannah. *Love and St. Augustine.* Ed. Joanna Vecchiarelli Scott and Judith Chelius Stark. Chicago: University of Chicago Press, 1996.

Arendt, Hannah, and Martin Heidegger. *Briefe 1925–1975 und andere Zeugnisse aus den Nachlässen* [Arendt and Heidegger: Letters and other documents from their estates]. Ed. Ursula Ludz. 2nd ed. Frankfurt am Main, Ger.: Klostermann, 1999.

Aristotle. *Art of Rhetoric.* Trans. J. H. Freese. Cambridge, MA: Harvard University Press, 1994.

———. *The Nicomachean Ethics.* Trans. H. Rackham. Cambridge, MA: Harvard University Press, 1999.

———. *On the Soul. Parva Naturalia. On Breath.* Trans. W. S. Hett. Cambridge, MA: Harvard University Press, 2000.

———. *Poetics.* Trans. Stephen Halliwell. Cambridge, MA: Harvard University Press, 1999.

———. *Politics.* Trans. H. Rackham. London: Heinemann; Cambridge, MA: Harvard University Press, 1944.

Arnold, Heinz Ludwig, ed. *Text und Kritik* 153 (2002). Special issue on Durs Grünbein.

Attridge, Derek. "Singularities, Responsibilities: Derrida, Deconstruction, and Literary Criticism." *Critical Encounters: Reference and Responsibility in Deconstructive Writing.* Ed. Cathy Caruth and Deborah Esch. New Brunswick, NJ: Rutgers University Press, 1995. 106–126.

———. *The Singularity of Literature.* London: Routledge, 2004.

Auerbach, Erich. *Dante als Dichter der irdischen Welt* [Dante as a poet of this world]. 2nd ed. Berlin: de Gruyter, 2001.

Augustine. *Confessions.* Trans. William Watts. 2 vols. Cambridge, MA: Harvard University Press, 2002.

Badiou, Alain. *Conditions.* Paris: Seuil, 1992.

———. *Ethics: An Essay on Understanding Evil.* Trans. and introd. Peter Hallward. London: Verso, 2002.

———. *L'être et l'événement* [Being and event]. Paris: Seuil, 1988.

———. *Manifeste pour la philosophie* [Manifesto for philosophy]. Paris: Seuil, 1989.

———. *Petit manuel d'inésthetique* [Small handbook of inaesthetics]. Paris: Seuil, 1998.

———. *Saint Paul: La fondation de l'universalisme* [St. Paul and the foundations of universalism]. Paris: Presses Universitaires de France, 1997.

Baer, Ulrich. "The Perfection of Poetry: Rainer Maria Rilke and Paul Celan." *New German Critique* 91 (2004): 170–189.

————. *Remnants of Song: Trauma and the Experience of Modernity in Charles Baudelaire and Paul Celan*. Stanford, CA: Stanford University Press, 2000.

Bakewell, Michael, and Melissa Bakewell. *Augusta Leigh, Byron's Half-Sister: A Biography*. London: Chatto & Windus, 2000.

Bakhtin, Mikhail M. *Raboty 1920-x godov* [Works from the 1920s]. Ed. D. A. Tatarnikov. Kiev, Ukraine: Next, 1994.

————. *Sobranie sočinenij v semi tomax, V: Raboty 1940-x—načala 1960-x godov* [Collected works in seven volumes: Works from the 1940s through the beginning of the 1960s]. Ed. S. G. Bočarov and L. A. Gogotišvili. Moscow: Russkie Slovari, 1996.

Baldick, Chris. "Post-mortem: Lawrence's Critical and Cultural Legacy." *The Cambridge Companion to D. H. Lawrence*. Ed. Anne Fernihough. Cambridge, UK: Cambridge University Press, 2001. 253–269.

Bambach, Charles. *Heidegger, Dilthey, and the Crisis of Historicism*. Ithaca, NY: Cornell University Press, 1995.

Barnstone, Willis, ed. *Modern European Poetry*. New York: Bantam, 1966.

Barolini, Teodolinda. "Dante and the Lyric Past." *The Cambridge Companion to Dante*. Ed. Rachel Jacoff. Cambridge, UK: Cambridge University Press, 1993. 14–33.

Bassnett, Susan. *Translation Studies*. Rev ed. London: Routledge, 2000.

Baumann, Richard A. *Crime and Punishment in Ancient Rome*. London: Routledge, 1996.

Beese, Henriette. *Nachdichtung als Erinnerung: Allegorische Lektüre einiger Gedichte von Paul Celan* [Imitation as memory: An allegorical reading of some poems by Paul Celan]. Darmstadt, Ger.: Agora, 1976.

Benjamin, Walter. *Charles Baudelaire: Ein Lyriker im Zeitalter des Hochkapitalismus* [Charles Baudelaire: A poet in the age of high capitalism]. Ed. Rolf Tiedemann. Frankfurt am Main, Ger.: Suhrkamp, 1974.

————. "Die Aufgabe des Übersetzers" [The task of the translator]. *Illuminationen: Ausgewählte Schriften 1* [Illuminations: Selected writings 1]. Ed. Rolf Tiedemann. Frankfurt am Main, Ger.: Suhrkamp, 1977. 50–62.

————. *Ursprung des deutschen Trauerspiels* [Origin of the German tragic drama]. Ed. Rolf Tiedemann. Frankfurt am Main, Ger.: Suhrkamp, 1978.

Benveniste, Émile. *Problèmes de linguistique générale* [Problems of general linguistics]. 2 vols. Paris: Gallimard, 1966, 1974.

Berdjaev, Nikolaj. *Samopoznanie* [Self-knowledge]. Ed. V. V. Škoda. Moscow: EKSMO Press, 2000.

————. *Sud'ba Rossii* [The fate of Russia]. Ed. V. V. Škoda. Moscow: EKSMO Press, 2000. 29–263.

Bergmann, Martin S. *The Anatomy of Loving: The Story of Man's Quest to Know What Love Is*. New York: Columbia University Press, 1987.

Bethea, David M. *Joseph Brodsky and the Creation of Exile*. Princeton, NJ: Princeton University Press, 1994.

————. "Joseph Brodsky's 'To My Daughter'." *Joseph Brodsky: The Art of the Poem*. Ed. Lev Loseff and Valentina Polukhina. Houndmills, UK: Palgrave, 1999. 240–257.

Bevilacqua, Giuseppe. "Erotische Metaphorik beim frühen Celan" [Erotic metaphorics in Paul Celan's early poetry]. *Études Germaniques* 53.2 (1998): 471–480.

Bhabha, Homi K. *The Location of Culture*. London: Routledge, 1994.

Blackburn, Simon. *Truth: A Guide*. Oxford, UK: Oxford University Press, 2005.

Blinn, Hansjürgen, ed. *Shakespeare-Rezeption: Die Diskussion um Shakespeare in Deutschland* [Shakespeare reception: The Shakespeare debate in Germany]. 2 vols. Berlin: Erich Schmidt, 1982 (vol. 1: 1741–1788), 1988 (vol. 2: 1793–1827).

Blok, Aleksandr. *Sobranie sočinenij* [Collected works]. Ed. V. N. Orlov. 8 vols. Moscow: Gosudarstvennoe Izdatel'stvo Xudožestvennoj Literatury, 1962.

———. *Stixotvorenija* [Poems]. Ed. V. Orlov. Leningrad: Sovetskij Pisatel', 1955.

Bloom, Alan. *Shakespeare on Love and Friendship*. Chicago: University of Chicago Press, 2000.

Bloom, Harold. *The Anxiety of Influence: A Theory of Poetry*. London: Oxford University Press, 1973.

Bobyšev, Dmitrij. *Ja zdes'* (*Čelovekotekst*) [I am here (a memoir)]. Moscow: Vagrius, 2003.

Bohrer, Karl Heinz. *Der romantische Brief: Die Entstehung ästhetischer Subjektivität* [The romantic letter: The birth of aesthetic subjectivity]. Frankfurt am Main, Ger.: Suhrkamp, 1989.

Booth, Stephen, ed. *Shakespeare's Sonnets*. New Haven, CT: Yale University Press, 2000.

Booth, Wayne C. *The Rhetoric of Fiction*. 2nd ed. Harmondsworth, UK: Penguin, 1987.

Böschenstein, Bernhard. "Erste Notizen zu Celans letzten Gedichten" [First notes on Celan's last poems]. *Text und Kritik* 53/54 (1984): 55–61.

———. "'Wenn Du im Bett / aus verschollenem Fahnentuch liegst'." [When you lie in bed / made from the lost drape of a flag]." *Paul Celan "Atemwende": Materialien* [Paul Celan "Breathturn": Materials]. Ed. Gerhard Buhr and Roland Reuß. Würzburg, Ger.: Königshausen und Neumann, 1991. 85–94.

Boyd, Brian. *Vladimir Nabokov: The American Years*. Princeton, NJ: Princeton University Press, 1991.

Briegleb, Klaus. "Ingeborg Bachmann, Paul Celan, Ihr (Nicht-)Ort in der Gruppe 47 (1952–1964/65): Eine Skizze" [Bachmann and Celan, their (non-)place in the Gruppe 47]." *Ingeborg Bachmann und Paul Celan—Poetische Korrespondenzen: Vierzehn Beiträge* [Bachmann and Celan: Poetic correspondences]. Ed. Bernhard Böschenstein and Sigrid Weigel. Frankfurt am Main, Ger.: Suhrkamp, 1997. 29–81.

Brierley, David. *'Der Meridian': Ein Versuch zur Poetik und Dichtung Paul Celans* [The meridian: An essay on the poetics of Paul Celan]. Frankfurt am Main, Ger.: Lang, 1984.

Broda, Martine. *Dans la main de personne: Essai sur Paul Celan* [In the hand of no one: An essay on Paul Celan]. Paris: Cerf, 1986.

Brodsky, Joseph. *Bol'šaja Kniga Interv'ju* [Great book of interviews]. Ed. Valentina Polukhina. 2nd ed. Moscow: Zaxarov, 2000.

———. *Čast' Reči: Stixotvorenija 1972–1976* [A part of speech: Poems 1972–1976]. 1977. St. Petersburg, Russ.: Puškinskij Fond, 2000.

———. *Collected Poems in English*. Ed. Ann Kjellberg. New York: Farrar, Straus and Giroux, 2002.

————. *Collines et autres poèmes* [Hills and other poems]. Trans. Jean-Jacques Marie. Paris: Seuil, 1966.

————. *Conversations.* Ed. Cynthia L. Haven. Jackson: University Press of Mississippi, 2002.

————. "Drei Gedichte" [The poems]. Trans. Karl Dedecius. *Akzente* 12.5 (1965): 386–393.

————. *Gedichte von Jossif Brodskij.* Trans. Vera Straßburger. *Lyrische Hefte* 8.2 (1966): 1–23.

————. *Konec prekrasnoj epoxi* [The end of a beautiful era]. 1977. St. Petersburg: Puškinskij Fond, 2000.

————. *Less Than One: Selected Essays.* New York: Farrar, Straus and Giroux, 1986.

————. *Novye Stansy k Avguste: Stixi k M. B. 1962–1982* [New stanzas to Augusta: Poems for M. B. 1962–1982]. 1983. St. Petersburg, Russ.: Puškinskij Fond, 2000.

————. *On Grief and Reason: Essays.* New York: Farrar, Straus and Giroux, 1995.

————. *Ostanovka v pustyne* [A halt in the desert]. 1970. St. Petersburg, Russ.: Pushkinskij Fond, 2000.

————. *Pejzaž s navodneniem* [Landscape with inundation]. New York: Ardis, 1995.

————. *Sočinenija Iosifa Brodskogo* [The works of Joseph Brodsky]. Ed. G. F. Komarov. 7 vols. St. Petersburg, Russ.: Puškinskij Fond, 1998–2000.

————. *Stixotvorenija i poemy* [Poems]. Washington, DC: Inter-Language Literary Associates, 1965.

————. *Uranija.* St. Petersburg, Russ.: Puškinskij Fond, 2000.

————. "Zwei Gedichte von Jossif Brodskij" [Two poems by Joseph Brodsky]. Trans. Vera Straßburger. *Lyrische Hefte* 8.1 (1966): 1–2.

Broughton, Janet. *Descartes' Method of Doubt.* Princeton, NJ: Princeton University Press, 2002.

Brower, Reuben A., ed. *On Translation.* Cambridge, MA: Harvard University Press, 1959.

Brown, Clarence. *Mandelstam.* Cambridge, UK: Cambridge University Press, 1973.

Brümmer, Vincent. *The Model of Love: A Study in Philosophical Theology.* Cambridge, UK: Cambridge University Press, 1993.

Buber, Martin. *Das dialogische Prinzip: Ich und Du, Zwiesprache, Die Frage an den Einzelnen, Elemente des Zwischenmenschlichen, Zur Geschichte des dialogischen Prinzips* [The dialogic principle: I and Thou; Dialogue, The question of the individual, On the history of the dialogic principle]. Heidelberg, Ger.: Lambert Schneider, 1984.

Büchner, Georg. *Werke und Briefe* [Works and letters]. Ed. Karl Körnbacher et al. 2nd ed. Munich: Deutscher Taschenbuch Verlag, 1990.

Buck, Theo. *Muttersprache, Mördersprache: Celan-Studien I* [Mother tongue, murderers' tongue: Celan studies I]. Aachen, Ger.: Rimbaud, 1993.

Burnham, Michelle. "'Dark Lady and Fair Man': The Love Triangle in Shakespeare's Sonnets and *Ulysses.*" *Studies in the Novel* 22.1 (1990): 43–56.

Butler, Judith. *Giving an Account of Oneself.* New York: Fordham University Press, 2005.

————. *Subjects of Desire: Hegelian Reflections in Twentieth-Century France.* New York: Columbia University Press, 1999.

Byron, George Gordon, Lord. "The Bride of Abydos: A Turkish Tale." *Poetical Works.* Ed.
    Frederick Page and John Jump. Oxford, UK: Oxford University Press, 1970. 264–276.
———. *Byron's Letters and Journals,* ed. Leslie A. Marchand. 13 vols. Cambridge, MA:
    Harvard University Press, 1973–1994.
———. *Childe Harold's Pilgrimage.* In *Poetical Works.* Ed. Frederick Page and John Jump.
    Oxford, UK: Oxford University Press, 1970. 179–252.
———. *The Complete Poetical Works.* Ed. Jerome J. McGann. 7 vols. Oxford, UK: Clar-
    endon Press, 1980–1993.
———. *The Corsair: A Tale.* In *Poetical Works.* Ed. Frederick Page and John Jump. Ox-
    ford, UK: Oxford University Press, 1970. 277–303.
———. *The Deformed Transformed.* In *Poetical Works.* Ed. Frederick Page and John Jump.
    Oxford, UK: Oxford University Press, 1970. 605–623.
———. *Dnevniki i pis' ma* [Journals and letters]. Ed. Z. E. Aleksandrova, A. A. Elistra-
    tova, and A. N. Nikoljukin. Moscow: Izdatel'stvo Akademii Nauk SSSR, 1963.
———. *Don Juan.* In *Poetical Works.* Ed. Frederick Page and John Jump. Oxford, UK:
    Oxford University Press, 1970. 635–858.
———. *Fugitive Pieces.* Facsimile ed. New York: Columbia University Press, 1933.
———. *Izbrannoe* [Selected writings]. Ed. Iurij Kondrat'ev. Moscow: Gosudarstvennoe
    Izdatel'stvo Deckoj Literatury, 1960.
———. *Poems.* London: John Murray, 1816.
———. *Poetical Works.* Ed. Frederick Page and John Jump. Oxford, UK: Oxford Univer-
    sity Press, 1970.
———. *The Prisoner of Chillon and Other Poems.* London: John Murray, 1816.
———. *The Prisoner of Chillon and Other Poems.* Boston: Houghton Mifflin, 1898.
———. *The Prophecy of Dante.* In *Poetical Works.* Ed. Frederick Page and John Jump.
    Oxford, UK: Oxford University Press, 1970. 370–378.
Calabrese, Omar. *Neo-Baroque: A Sign of the Times.* Princeton, NJ: Princeton University
    Press, 1992.
Camartin, Iso. "Die Anatomie und das Lebensgefühl: Laudatio auf Durs Grünbein."
    Peter- Huchel-Preis 1995: Durs Grünbein. Texte-Dokumente-Materialien. Ed. Wolfgang
    Heidenreich. Baden-Baden, Ger.: Elster, 1998. 25–32.
Carroll, David. *The Subject in Question: The Languages of Theory and the Strategies of Fic-
    tion.* Chicago: University of Chicago Press, 1982.
Cassirer, Ernst, Paul Oskar Kristeller, and John Hermann Randall Jr., eds. *The Renaissance
    Philosophy of Man.* Chicago: University of Chicago Press, 1948.
Cavafy, C. P. *The Complete Poems of Cavafy.* Trans. Rae Dalven. San Diego, CA: Harcourt
    Brace, 1976.
Cavanagh, Clare. *Osip Mandelstam and the Modernist Creation of Tradition.* Princeton, NJ:
    Princeton University Press, 1995.
Celan, Paul. "Briefe an Alfred Margul-Sperber" [Letters to A. Margul-Sperber]. *Neue Lit-
    eratur* 26.7 (1975): 50–63.
———. *Einundzwanzig Sonette: Deutsch von Paul Celan* [Twenty-one sonnets: German
    translation by Paul Celan]. Rev. ed. 1967. Frankfurt am Main, Ger.: Insel, 2001.

———. *Das Frühwerk* [Early works]. Ed. Barbara Wiedemann. Frankfurt am Main, Ger.: Suhrkamp, 1989.

———. *Gesammelte Werke* [Collected works]. Ed. Beda Allemann. 5 vols. Frankfurt am Main, Ger.: Suhrkamp, 1986.

———. *Der Meridian: Endfassung, Vorstufen, Materialien* [The meridian: Final version, drafts, materials]. Ed. Jürgen Wertheimer. Frankfurt am Main, Ger.: Suhrkamp, 1999.

———. *Mikrolithen sinds, Steinchen: Die Prosa aus dem Nachlaß* [Microliths they are, pebbles: Prose writings]. Ed. Barbara Wiedemann and Bertrand Badiou. Frankfurt am Main, Ger.: Suhrkamp, 2005.

———. *Die Niemandsrose: Vorstufen, Textgenese, Endfassung*. Ed. Jürgen Wertheimer [The no one's rose: Final version, drafts, materials]. Frankfurt am Main, Ger.: Suhrkamp, 1996.

———. *Nineteen Poems*. Trans. Michael Hamburger. Manchester, UK: Carcanet, 1972.

———. "Notiz" [Note]. *Gedichte* [Poems]. By Osip E. Mandelstam. Trans. Paul Celan. Frankfurt am Main, Ger.: Fischer, 1959. 67–68.

———. *Paul Celan: Poems*. Trans. Michael Hamburger. New York: Persea Books, 1980.

———. *Der Sand aus den Urnen* [The sand from the urns]. Vienna: Plan, 1948.

———. *Selected Poems and Prose of Paul Celan*. Trans. John Felstiner. New York: Norton, 2001.

———. *Speech-Grille and Selected Poems*. Trans. Joachim Neugroschel. New York: Dutton, 1971.

Celan, Paul, and Gisèle Celan-Lestrange *Paul Celan—Gisèle Celan-Lestrange: Correspondance (1951–1970)*. Ed. Bertrand Badiou with Eric Celan. 2 vols. Paris: Seuil, 2001.

Celan, Paul, and Erich Einhorn. *Einhorn: du weißt um die Steine . . . : Briefwechsel* [Einhorn: You know about the stones—correspondence]. Berlin: Friedenauer Presse, 2001.

Celan, Paul, and Peter Szondi. *Paul Celan / Peter Szondi: Briefwechsel* [Celan/Szondi: Correspondence]. Ed. Christoph König. Frankfurt am Main, Ger.: Suhrkamp, 2005.

Chalfen, Israel. *Paul Celan: Eine Biographie seiner Jugend* [Celan: A biography of his youth]. Frankfurt am Main, Ger.: Suhrkamp, 1983.

Chenier, André. *Oeuvres complètes* [Complete works]. Ed. Gérard Walter. Paris: Gallimard, 1958.

Cicero, Marcus Tullius. *De inventione. De optimo genere oratorum. Topica* [On invention. On the best kind of orator. Topics]. Trans. H. M. Hubbell. London: Heinemann; Cambridge, MA: Harvard University Press, 1960.

Claassen, Jo-Marie. *Displaced Persons: Literature of Exile from Cicero to Boethius*. London: Duckworth, 1999.

Clinton, George. *Memoirs of the Life and Writing of Lord Byron*. London: Robins, 1831.

Coetzee, J. M. *Elizabeth Costello*. New York: Viking, 2003.

———. *Giving Offense: Essays on Censorship*. Chicago: University of Chicago Press, 1996.

———. *Slow Man*. London: Secker & Warburg, 2005.

Cohen, Ed. *Talk on the Wilde Side: Toward a Genealogy of Discourse on Male Sexualities*. New York: Routledge, 1993.

Cohen, Hermann. *Ethik des reinen Willens* [Ethics of pure will]. 2nd ed. Berlin: Cassirer, 1907.

Cohen, Ralph, ed. *New Literary History* 32.3 (2001). Special issue: "Voice and Human Experience."

Cooper, David E. *Metaphor.* Oxford: Blackwell, 1986.

Cowan, Ian B. *Mary, Queen of Scots.* Saltire Pamphlets, New Series 9. Edinburgh, Scot.: Saltire Society, 1987.

Critchley, Simon. *Ethics-Politics-Subjectivity: Essays on Derrida, Levinas, and Contemporary French Thought.* London: Verso, 1999.

Curtius, Ernst Robert. *European Literature and the Latin Middle Ages.* Trans Willard R. Trask. New York: Pantheon Books, 1953.

Cvetaeva, Marina. *Stixotvorenija i poemy* [Poems and epic poems]. Ed. A. A. Saakianc. Leningrad: Sovetskij Pisatel', 1979.

Czernin, Franz Josef. "Zur Übersetzung" [On translation]. *Sonnets, Übersetzungen.* [Sonnets, translations]. Munich: Hanser, 1999. 99–139.

Damerau, Burghard. "'Ich stand in dir': Bemerkungen zur Erotik bei Celan" [I was standing inside her: Notes on eroticism in Celan's poetry]. *Celan-Jahrbuch* 7 (1997/1998): 93–306.

Dante Alighieri. *Dantis Alighieri Epistolae* [Dante's letters]. Ed. Paget Toynbee. Oxford, UK: Clarendon Press, 1966.

———. *The Divine Comedy.* Trans. Charles S. Singleton. 6 vols. (1–2: *Inferno and Commentary;* 3–4: *Purgatorio and Commentary;* 5–6: *Paradiso and Commentary*). Princeton, NJ: Princeton University Press, 1989–1991.

———. *Literature in the Vernacular.* Trans. Sally Purcell. Manchester, UK: Carcanet, 1981.

———. *Rime* [Poems]. Ed. Gianfranco Contini. Torino, It.: Einaudi, 1946.

———. *Vita Nuova* [The new life]. Trans. Mark Musa. Bloomington: Indiana University Press, 1973.

David, Claude. "Préambule" [Preamble]. *Études Germaniques* 25.3 (1970): 239–249.

Davidson, Donald. *Inquiries into Truth and Interpretation.* Oxford, UK: Clarendon Press, 1991.

———. *Truth and Predication.* Cambridge, MA: Harvard University Press, 2005.

Dehmel, Richard. *Weib und Welt* [Woman and world]. Berlin: Schuster und Löffler, 1896.

De Lamartine, Alphonse. *Oeuvres poétiques complètes* [Complete poetic works]. Ed. Marius-François Guyard. Paris: Gallimard, 1963.

Del Caro, Adrian. *The Early Poetry of Paul Celan: In the Beginning Was the Word.* Baton Rouge: Louisiana State University Press, 1997.

De Man, Paul. *Blindness and Insight: Essays in the Rhetoric of Contemporary Criticism.* Minneapolis: University of Minnesota Press, 1983.

Derrida, Jacques. *Acts of Literature.* Ed. Derek Attridge. New York: Routledge, 1992.

———. "La mythologie blanche: la métaphore dans le texte philosophique" [White mythology: Metaphor in the text of philosophy]. *Marges de la philosophie* [Margins of philosophy]. Paris: Minuit, 1972. 247–324.

———. *Limited Inc.* Evanston, IL: Northwestern University Press, 1988.

————. "The Majesty of the Present." *New German Critique* 51 (2004): 17–40.

Descartes, René. *Discours de la méthode suivi d'extraits de la Dioptrique, des Météores, de la Vie de Descartes par Baillet, du Monde, de l'Homme et des Lettres* [Discours on method followed by extracts of the Dioptrics, the Meteors, the Life of Descartes by Baillet, the World, Man, and letters]. Ed. Geneviève Rodis-Lewis. Paris: Garnier-Flammarion, 1992.

————. *Méditations métaphysiques, Objections et Réponses, suivie de quatre Lettres* [Metaphysical meditations, objections and responses]. Ed. Jean-Marie Beyssade and Michelle Beyssade. Paris: Garnier-Flammarion, 1979.

————. *Oeuvres* [Works]. Ed. Charles Adam and Paul Tannery. 12 vols. Paris: Cerf, 1897–1910.

Diakonova, Nina, and Vadim Vacuro. "Byron and Russia: Byron and Nineteenth-Century Russian Literature." *Byron's Political and Cultural Influence in Nineteenth-Century Europe: A Symposium.* Ed. Graham Trueblood. London: Macmillan, 1981. 143–159.

Dilthey, Wilhelm. *Die Philosophie des Lebens: Eine Auswahl aus seinen Schriften 1867–1910* [The philosophy of life: Selected writings 1867-1910]. Ed. Hans-Georg Gadamer. Frankfurt am Main, Ger.: Klostermann, 1946.

————. *Das Erlebnis und die Dichtung: Lessing, Goethe, Novalis, Hölderlin* [Experience and poetry: Lessing, Goethe, Novalis Hölderlin]. 1912. Leipzig, Ger.: Reclam, 1991.

Dio Cassius. *Roman History.* Books 56–60. Trans. Ernest Cary. Cambridge, MA: Harvard University Press, 2000.

————. *Roman History.* Books 61–70. Trans. Ernest Cary. Cambridge, MA: Harvard University Press, 2000.

Diogenes Laertius. *Lives of Philosophers.* 2 vols. Trans. R. D. Hicks. Cambridge, MA: Harvard University Press, 2000.

Doherty, Justin. *The Acmeist Movement in Russian Poetry: Culture and the Word.* Oxford, UK: Clarendon Press, 1995.

Donne, John. *The Complete Poetry and Selected Prose of John Donne.* Ed. Charles M. Coffin. New York: Random House, Modern Library, 1952.

Eagleton, Terry. *Literary Theory: An Introduction.* 2nd ed. Minneapolis: University of Minnesota Press, 1996.

Eisler, Benita. *Byron: Child of Passion, Fool of Fame.* New York: Vintage, 2000.

Eliot, Thomas Stearns. "Dante." *The Waste Land and Other Writings.* New York: Random House, Modern Library, 2002. 186–196

————. "What Dante Means to Me." *The Poet's Dante: Twentieth-Century Responses.* Ed. Peter S. Hawkins and Rachel Jacoff New York: Farrar, Straus and Giroux, 2001. 28–39.

Elistratova A. A. *Bajron* [Byron]. Moscow: Izdatel'stvo Akademii Nauk SSSR, 1956.

Emmanuel, Pierre. "Foreword: Un Poète Métaphysique en U.R.R.S." [A metaphysical poet in the U.S.S.R.]. *Collines et autres poèmes* [Hills and other poems]. By Joseph Brodsky. Trans. Jean-Jacques Marie. Paris: Seuil, 1966. 9–24.

Erb, Andreas, ed. *Baustelle Gegenwartsliteratur: Die neunziger Jahre* [Construction site contemporary literature: The nineties]. Opladen, Ger.: Westdeutscher Verlag, 1998.

Eshel, Amir. "Paul Celan's Other: History, Poetics, Ethics." *New German Critique* 91 (2004): 57–77.

Eskin, Michael. "Answerable Criticism: Reading Celan Reading Mandelstam." *arcadia* 35.1 (2000): 66–80.

———. "Body Language: Durs Grünbein's Aesthetics." *arcadia* 37.1 (2002): 42–66.

———. "'Bridge to Antiquity': Nostalgia, Exile and Stoicism in the Poetry of Durs Grünbein." *arcadia* 39.2 (2004): 356–381.

———. "Descartes of Metaphor: On Durs Grünbein's *Vom Schnee*." *German Monitor* (forthcoming).

———. *Ethics and Dialogue in the Works of Levinas, Bakhtin, Mandelstam, and Celan.* Oxford, UK: Oxford University Press, 2000.

———. "The 'German' Shakespeare." *A New History of German Literature*. Ed. David Wellbery. Cambridge, MA: Harvard University Press, 2004. 460–465.

———. "Introduction: The Double 'Turn' to Ethics and Literature." *Poetics Today* 25.4 (2004): 558–572.

———. "On Literature and Ethics." *Poetics Today* 25.4 (2004): 573–594.

———. "Of Poets and Sailors: Celan, Grünbein, Brodsky." *German Life and Letters* 60.3 (2007): 315–328.

———. "'Risse, die durch die Zeiten führen'—zu Durs Grünbein's Historien" [Tears in time—On Durs Grünbein's histories]. In *Der Misanthrop auf Capri* [The misanthrope in Capri]. Frankfurt am Main, Ger.: Suhrkamp, 2005. 107–121.

———. "'Stimmengewirr vieler Zeiten': Grünbein's Dialogue with Dante, Baudelaire, and Mandelstam." *Germanic Review* 77.1 (2002): 34–50.

———. "To Truths Translated': Celan's Affair with Shakespeare." *New German Critique* 91 (2004): 79–100.

Etkind, Efim. *The Trial of Iosif Brodsky / Process Iosifa Brodskogo.* London: Overseas Publications Interchange, 1988.

Fassbind, Bernard. *Poetik des Dialogs: Voraussetzungen dialogischer Poesie bei Paul Celan und Konzepte von Intersubjektivität bei Martin Buber, Martin Heidegger, und Emmanuel Levinas* [Poetics of dialogue: Conditions of dialogic poetry in the works of Celan and concepts of intersubjectivity in the works of Buber, Heidegger, and Levinas]. Munich: Fink, 1995.

Felman, Shoshana, and Dori Laub. *Testimony: Crisis of Witnessing in Literature, Psychoanalysis, and History.* New York: Routledge, 1992.

Felstiner, John. *Paul Celan: Poet, Survivor, Jew.* New Haven, CT: Yale University Press, 1995.

———. "Translating Celan, Translating Shakespeare." *Parnassus* 16.1 (1990): 174–194.

Feofanov, Jurij, and Donald D. Barry. *Politics and Justice in Russia: Major Trials of the Post-Stalin Era.* Armonk, NY, and London, UK: Sharpe, 1996.

Fineman, Joel. *Shakespeare's Perjured Eye: The Invention of Poetic Subjectivity in the Sonnets.* Berkeley: University of California Press, 1986.

Fioretos, Aris, ed. *Word Traces: Readings of Paul Celan.* Baltimore, MD: Johns Hopkins University Press, 1994.

Fludernik, Monica. "New Wine in Old Bottles? Voice, Focalization, and New Writing." *New Literary History* 32.3 (2001): 619–638.

Foucault, Michel. *L'archéologie du savoir* [Archaeology of knowledge]. Paris: Gallimard, 1969.

———. *The Care of the Self: The History of Sexuality, Vol. 3,* trans R. Hurley. New York: Vintage, 1988.

———. *L'histoire de la sexualité I: La volonté de savoir* [The history of sexuality, vol. 1: The will to know]. Paris: Gallimard, 1976.

France, Peter. "Notes on the Sonnets to Mary Queen of Scots." *Brodsky's Poetics and Aesthetics.* Ed. Lev Loseff and Valentina Polukhina. Houndmills, UK: Palgrave, 1999. 98–123.

Franke, William. "Metaphor and the Making of Sense: The Contemporary Metaphor Renaissance." *Philosophy and Rhetoric* 33.2 (2000): 137–153.

Frege, Gottlob. "Über Sinn und Bedeutung" [On sense and reference]. *Zeitschrift für Philosophie und philosophische Kritik,* 100 (1892): 25–50.

Frost, Robert. *Collected Poems, Prose, and Plays: Complete Poems 1949, In the Clearing, Uncollected Poems, Plays, Lectures, Essays, Stories, and Letters.* New York: Library of America, 1995.

Fuhrmann, Manfred. *Seneca und Kaiser Nero: Eine Biographie* [Seneca and emperor Nero: A biography]. Berlin: Alexander Fest, 1997.

Gadamer, Hans-Georg. *Truth and Method.* Trans. Joel Weinsheimer and Donald G. Marshall. 2nd ed. New York: Continuum Press, 2000.

Gallagher, Kenneth T. *The Philosophy of Gabriel Marcel.* New York: Fordham University Press, 1975.

Geertz, Clifford. *The Interpretation of Cultures: Selected Essays.* New York: Basic Books, 1973.

Geisenhanslüke, Achim. "'Mensch ohne Großhirn': Durs Grünbein und das Ende der Utopien" [Man without brain: Grünbein and the end of utopia]. *Die eigene und die fremde Kultur: Exotismus und Tradition bei Durs Grünbein und Raoul Schrott* [One's own and foreign culture: Exoticism and tradition in the works of Grünbein and Schrott]. Ed. Dieter Burdorf. Iserlohr, Ger.: Institut für Kirche und Gesellschaft, 2004. 63–78.

Gellhaus, Axel, ed. *"Fremde Nähe"—Celan als Übersetzer* [Strange proximity—Celan as translator]. Marbach, Ger.: Deutsche Schillergesellschaft, 1997.

Genette, Gérard. *Fiction and Diction.* Trans. Catherine Porter. Ithaca, NY: Cornell University Press, 1993.

———. *Figures III.* Paris: Seuil, 1972.

———. *Narrative Discourse: An Essay in Method.* Trans. Jane E. Levin. Ithaca, NY: Cornell University Press, 1980.

Gibson, Andrew. "'And the Wind Wheezing Through That Organ Once in a While': Voice, Narrative, Film." *New Literary History* 32.3 (2001): 639–657.

Giebel, Marion. *Seneca.* Reinbeck, Ger.: Rowohlt, 1997.

Gilenson, Boris. "Byron in Russia." *Contemporary Review* 253.1472 (1988): 155–158.

Goethe, Johann Wolfgang. *West-Östlicher Divan.* Ed. Max Rychner. Zurich, Switz.: Manesse, 1952.

Goetschel, Willi. *Constituting Critique: Kant's Writing as Critical Practice.* Durham, NC: Duke University Press, 1994.

Gorodeckij, Sergej. "Nekotoryja techenija v' sovremennoj russkoj poezii" [Some trends in contemporary Russian poetry]. *Apollon* 1 (1913): 46–50.

Gray, Charles M. *The Writ of Prohibition: Jurisdiction in Early Modern English Law.* Vol. I: *General Introduction to the Study and Procedure.* New York: Oceana, 1994.

Greenblatt, Stephen. *Shakespearean Negotiations: The Circulation of Social Energy in Renaissance England.* Berkeley: University of California Press, 1988.

Greenfield, Concetta C. *Humanist and Scholastic Poetics, 1250–1500.* London: Associated University Presses, 1981.

Grünbein, Durs. "An Seneca: Postskriptum" [To Seneca: A postscript]. *Die Kürze des Lebens* [On the brevity of life]. By Lucius Annaeus Seneca. Trans. Gerhard Fink. Frankfurt am Main, Ger.: Suhrkamp, 2003. 9–15.

———. *Antike Dispositionen: Aufsätze* [Antique dispositions]. Frankfurt am Main, Ger.: Suhrkamp, 2005.

———. *Das erste Jahr: Berliner Aufzeichnungen* [The first year: Berlin notes]. Frankfurt am Main, Ger.: Suhrkamp, 2001.

———. *Den Teuren Toten: 33 Epitaphe* [For the precious dead: 33 epitaphs]. Frankfurt am Main, Ger.: Suhrkamp, 1994.

———. *Der Misanthrop auf Capri* [The misanthrope in Capri]. Frankfurt am Main, Ger.: Suhrkamp, 2005.

———. "Durs Grünbein im Gespräch mit Thomas Irmer" [Grünbein in conversation with Thomas Irmer]. *Thyestes.* By Lucius Annaeus Seneca. Trans. Durs Grünbein. Frankfurt am Main, Ger.: Insel, 2002. 111–114.

———. *Erklärte Nacht: Gedichte* [Night explained: Poems]. Frankfurt am Main, Ger.: Suhrkamp, 2002.

———. *Falten und Fallen: Gedichte* [Folds and traps: Poems]. Frankfurt am Main, Ger.: Suhrkamp, 1994.

———. *Galilei vermißt Dantes Hölle und bleibt an den Maßen hängen: Aufsätze 1989–1995* [Galilei measures Dante's hell and gets hung up on the measurements: Essays 1989–1995]. Frankfurt am Main, Ger.: Suhrkamp, 1996.

———. *Grauzone morgens: Gedichte* [Gray zone in the morning: Poems]. Frankfurt am Main, Ger.: Suhrkamp, 1988.

———. "Kein reines Ich: Wie Descartes in einem Brief an Elisabeth von Böhmen die Physiologie mit der Dichtkunst verband" [No pure I: How Descartes linked physiology and poetry in a letter to Elizabeth of Bohemia]. *Neue Züricher Zeitung* 269 (International ed., 2006): 31.

————. *Nach den Satiren: Gedichte* [After the satires: Poems]. Frankfurt am Main, Ger.: Suhrkamp, 1999.

————. "*Poetry from the Bad Side:* Gespräch mit Thomas Neumann. Berlin/Oktober 1991" [Conversation with Thomas Neumann]. *Sprache im technischen Zeitalter* 30.124 (1992): 442–449.

————. *Schädelbasislektion: Gedichte* [Skull crash course]. Frankfurt am Main, Ger.: Suhrkamp, 1991.

————. "Tausendfacher Tod im Hirn: Büchner-Preisträger Durs Grünbein über Utopien, das Ende der DDR und die Zukunft der Lyrik" [Death a thousandfold in your brain: Büchner prize recipient Grünbein on utopias, the end of the GDR and the future of poetry]. *Der Spiegel 41* (1995): 221–230.

————. *Vom Schnee oder Descartes in Deutschland* [On snow, or Descartes in Germany]. Frankfurt am Main: Suhrkamp, 2003.

————. *Von der üblen Seite: Gedichte 1985–1991* [From the bad side: Poems 1985–1991]. Frankfurt am Main, Ger.: Suhrkamp

Grünbein, Durs, and Helmut Böttiger. "Benn schmort in der Hölle: Ein Gespräch über dialogische und monologische Lyrik" [Benn smolders in hell: A conversation on dialogical and monological poetry]. *Text und Kritik* 153 (2002): 72–84.

Grünbein, Durs, and Heinz-Nobert Jocks. *Durs Grünbein im Gespräch mit Heinz-Norbert Jocks* [Grünbein in conversation with Jocks]. Cologne, Ger.: DuMont, 2001.

Grünbein, Durs, Brigitte Oleschinski, and Peter Waterhouse. *Die Schweizer Korrektur* [The Swiss correction]. Ed. Urs Engeler. Basel, Switz.: Engeler, 1995.

Grünbein, Durs, and Dorothea von Törne. "Mir kann die ganze Ostnostalgie gestohlen bleiben" [Screw nostalgia for the East]. *Wochenpost* (April 27, 1995): 43–46.

Guiccioli, Teresa. *Lord Byron's Life in Italy* [La vie de Lord Byron en Italie]. Trans. Michael Rees. Ed. Peter Cochran. Newark: University of Delaware Press, 2005.

Gumilev, Nikolai Stepanovič. *Sobranie sočinenij* [Collected works]. Ed. Gleb Struve and Boris Filippov. 4 vols. Washington, DC: Kamkin, 1962–1968.

Guy, John. *Queen of Scots: The True Life of Mary Stuart.* Boston: Houghton Mifflin, 2004.

Habermas, Jürgen. *Der philosophische Diskurs der Moderne: Zwölf Vorlesungen* [Philosophical discourse of modernity: Twelve lectures]. Frankfurt am Main, Ger.: Suhrkamp, 1985.

Habicht, Werner. "How German Is Shakespeare in Germany? Recent Trends in Criticism and Performance in West Germany." *Shakespeare Survey* 37 (1984): 155–162.

Haller, Johannes. *Dante: Dichter und Mensch* [Dante: Poet and human being]. Basel, Switz.: Schwabe, 1954.

Hallward, Peter. *Badiou: A Subject to Truth.* Minneapolis: University of Minnesota Press, 2003.

Hamburger, Michael. *The Truth of Poetry: Tensions in Modern Poetry from Baudelaire to the 1960s.* Manchester, UK: Carcanet Press, 1968.

————, ed. and trans. *German Poetry 1910–1975: An Anthology.* Manchester, UK: Carcanet Press, 1977.

Hamburger, Michael, and Christopher Middleton, ed. and trans. *Modern German Poetry 1910–1960: An Anthology with Verse Translations.* New York: Grove Press, 1962.

Hawkins Peter S., and Rachel Jacoff, eds. *The Poet's Dante: Twentieth-Century Responses.* New York: Farrar, Straus and Giroux, 2001.

Hazel, John. *Who's Who in the Roman World.* London: Routledge, 2001.

Heaney, Seamus. "Envies and Identifications: Dante and the Modern Poet." *Irish University Review* 15.1 (1985): 5–19.

Hegel, Georg Wilhelm Friedrich. *Phänomenologie des Geistes* [Phenomenology of the spirit]. Stuttgart, Ger.: Reclam, 1987.

Heidegger, Martin. *Beiträge zur Philosophie (vom Ereignis)* [Contributions to philosophy: On the event]. Frankfurt am Main, Ger.: Klostermann, 1989.

———. *Nietzsche.* 2 vols. Pfullingen, Ger.: Neske, 1961.

———. *Sein und Zeit* [Being and time]. 16th ed. Tübingen, Ger.: Niemeyer, 1986.

———. "Zeit und Sein" [Time and being]. *Zur Sache des Denkens* [On the problem of thinking]. Tübingen, Ger.: Neske, 1988. 1–25.

Hemingway, Ernest. *A Moveable Feast.* New York: Scribner, 1992.

———. *For Whom the Bell Tolls.* New York: Scribner, 1968.

Herder, Johann Gottfried. *Abhandlung über den Ursprung der Sprache* [Treatise on the origin of language]. Ed. Hans Dietrich Irmscher. Stuttgart, Ger.: Reclam, 1993.

Hölderlin, Friedrich. *Gedichte* [Poems]. Ed. Konrad Nussbächer. Stuttgart, Ger.: Reclam, 1963.

Horace. *Odes and Epodes.* Trans. C. E. Bennett. Cambridge, MA: Harvard University Press, 1999.

———. *Satires, Epistles, Ars Poetica.* Trans. H. R. Fairclough. Cambridge, MA: Harvard University Press, 1999.

Huguet, Edmond, ed. *Dictionnaire de la langue française du seizeième siècle* [Dictionary of the French language in the sixteenth century]. Vol. 4. Paris: Didier, 1973.

Husserl, Edmund. *Logische Untersuchungen II/1: Untersuchungen zur Phänomenologie und Theorie der Erkenntnis* [Logical investigations II/1: Investigations into the phenomenology and theory of knowledge]. Ed. Ulrich Panzer. The Hague: Nijhoff, 1984.

———. *Die phänomenologische Methode: Ausgewählte Texte I* [The phenomenological method: Selected texts]. Ed. Klaus Held. Stuttgart, Ger.: Reclam, 1985.

Huxley, Aldous. *Brave New World.* New York: HarperCollins, 1998.

Ivanov, Vjacheslav. "Zavety Simvolizma" [The legacy of Symbolism]. *Apollon* 8 (1910): 5–20.

Ivanović, Christine. *Das Gedicht im Geheimnis der Begegnung: Dichtung und Poetik Celans im Kontext seiner russischen Lektüren* [The poem in the secret of the encounter: Celan's poetry and poetics in the context of his readings of Russian literature]. Tübingen, Ger.: Niemeyer, 1996.

———. "Göttliche Tragödie? Paul Celans *Die Niemandsrose* von Dante her gesehen" [Divine tragedy? Celan's *No one's rose* read through Dante]. *Lesarten: Beiträge zum Werk Celans* [Interpretations: Contributions to Celan's works]. Ed. Axel Gellhaus and Andreas Lohr. Cologne, Ger.: Böhlau, 1996.

————, ed. *"Kyrillisches, Freunde, auch das . . . ": Die russische Bibliothek Paul Celans im Deutschen Literaturarchiv Marbach* [Matters cyrillic, friends, that, too: The Russian library in the Celan archives in Marbach]. Marbach am Neckar: Deutsche Schillergesellschaft, 1996.

————. "Trauer—nicht Traurigkeit: Celan als Leser Benjamins. Beobachtungen am Nachlaß" [Mourning—not sadness: Celan as a reader of Benjamin. Observations based on materials from the estate] *Celan-Jahrbuch 6* (1995): 111–159.

Jahn, Manfred. "Commentary: The Cognitive Status of Textual Voice." *New Literary History* 32.3 (2001): 695–697.

Jakobson, Roman. *Language in Literature.* Ed. Krystyna Pomorska and Stephen Rudy. Cambridge, MA: Harvard University Press, 1987.

James, William. *Writings 1902–1910: The Varieties of Religious Experience, Pragmatism, A Pluralistic Universe, The Meaning of Truth, Some Problems of Philosophy, Essays.* New York: Library of America, 1988.

Jaspers, Karl. "Das Unbedingte und das Böse" [The inexorable and evil]. *Erneuerung der Universität: Reden und Schriften 1945/46* [Renewal of the university: Speeches and writings]. Heidelberg, Ger.: Lambert Schneider, 1986. 77–92.

Jenkins, Keith. *Refiguring History: New Thoughts on an Old Discipline.* London: Routledge, 2003.

Josephus, Flavius. *Josephus in Ten Volumes.* Vol. 8: *Jewish Antiquities, Books 15–17.* Trans. Ralph Marcus. Ed. Allen Wikgren. Cambridge, MA: Harvard University Press, 1963.

Kant, Immanuel. *Kritik der praktischen Vernunft. Grundlegung zur Metaphysik der Sitten* [Critique of practical reason. Foundations of the metaphysics of morals]. Ed. Martina Thom. Leipzig, Ger.: Reclam, 1989.

————. *Kritik der reinen Vernunft* [Critique of pure reason]. Ed. Wilhelm Weischedel. 2 vols. Frankfurt am Main, Ger.: Suhrkamp, 1974.

Kaplan, Robert D. *Warrior Politics: Why Leadership Demands a Pagan Ethos.* New York: Random House, 2002.

Kaußen, Wolfgang. "'Ich verantworte Ich widerstehe Ich verweigere' Celans Shakespeare" [I assume responsibility, I resist, I refuse]. *Einundzwanzig Sonette: Deutsch von Paul Celan* [Twenty-one sonnets: German translation by Celan]. Rev. ed. 1967. Frankfurt am Main, Ger.: Insel, 2001. 49–90.

Kelley, Donald R. *Faces of History: Historical Inquiry from Herodotus to Herder.* New Haven, CT: Yale University Press, 1998.

Klein, Jürgen. "'Love', 'Lust' and 'Shame' in William Shakespeares Dark Lady Sonetten." *Erkenntniswunsch und Diskretion: Erotik in biographischer und autobiographischer Literatur* [The desire to know and discretion: Eroticism in biographical and autobiographical literature]. Ed. Gerhard Hare. Berlin: Winkel, 1992. 265–291.

Klibansky, Raymond, Erwin Panofsky, and Fritz Saxl. *Saturn und Melancholie: Studien zur Geschichte der Naturphilosophie und Medizin, der Religion und der Kunst* [Saturn and melancholy: Studies in the history of natural philosophy and medicine, religion and art]. Trans. Christa Buschendorf. Frankfurt am Main, Ger.: Suhrkamp, 1992.

Kondrat'ev, Jurij. "Džordž Gordon Bajron" [George Gordon Byron]. *Izbrannoe* [Selected works]. By Lord George Gordon Byron. Ed. Iurij Kondrat'ev. Moscow: Gosudarstvennoe Izdatel'stvo Detskoj Literatury, 1960. 5–8.

Korte, Hermann. "Zivilisationsepisteln: Poetik und Rhetorik in Grünbeins Gedichten" [Epistles on civilization: Poetics and rhetoric in the poems of Durs Grünbein]. *Die eigene und die fremde Kultur: Exotismus und Tradition bei Durs Grünbein und Raoul Schrott* [One's own and foreign culture: Exoticism and tradition in the works of Grünbein and Schrott]. Ed. Dieter Burdorf. Iserlohn, Ger.: Institut für Kirche und Gesellschaft, 2004. 79–95.

Koselleck, Reinhart. *Vergangene Zukunft: Zur Semantik geschichtlicher Zeiten* [Past future: On the semantics of historical times]. Frankfurt am Main, Ger.: Suhrkamp, 1979.

Kristeva, Julia. "L'engendrement de la formule" [Engendering the formula]. *Semeiotike: Recherches pour une sémanalyse* [Semiotics: Toward a semanalysis]. Paris: Seuil, 1969. 217–310.

Kropotkin, Peter. *The Great French Revolution 1789–1793.* 1909. Trans. N. F. Dryhurst. New York: Schocken, 1971.

Kulle, Viktor. "Iosif Brodskij: Novaja Odisseja" [Brodsky: A new Odyssey]. *Sočinenija Iosifa Brodskogo* [The works of Joseph Brodsky]. By Joseph Brodsky. Ed. G. F. Komarov. 7 vols. St. Petersburg, Russ.: Puškinskij Fond, 1998–2000. Vol. 1: 283–297.

LaCapra, Dominik. *Madame Bovary on Trial.* Ithaca, NY; and London: Cornell University Press, 1982.

Lachmann, Renate. *Gedächtnis und Literatur: Intertextualität in der russischen Moderne* [Memory and literature: Intertextuality in Russian modernity]. Frankfurt am Main, Ger.: Suhrkamp, 1990.

Lacoue-Labarthe, Philippe. *Poetry as Experience.* Trans. Andrea Tarnowski. Stanford, CA: Stanford University Press, 1999.

Lakoff, George, and Mark Johnson. *Metaphors We Live By.* Chicago: University of Chicago Press, 1980.

Landauer, Gustav, ed. *Briefe aus der Französischen Revolution* [Letters from the French revolution]. Trans. and ed. Gustav Landauer. 2 vols. Frankfurt am Main, Ger.: Rütten & Loening, 1922.

———. *Die Revolution.* 1907. Frankfurt am Main, Ger.: Rütten & Loening, 1919.

———. *Shakespeare.* Ed. Martin Buber. Frankfurt am Main, Ger.: Rütten & Loening, 1920.

———. *Zeit und Geist: Kulturkritische Schriften 1890–1919* [Time and spirit: Writings in cultural criticism 1890–1919]. Ed. Rolf Kauffeldt and Michael Matzigkeit. Munich: Boer, 1997.

———. *Zwang und Befreiung: Eine Auswahl aus seinem Werk* [Coercion and liberation: Selected writings]. Ed. Hans-Joachim Heydorn. Cologne, Ger.: Hegner, 1968.

Lang, A. T. "Seneca: Mensch und Werk, Lehre und Leben" [Seneca: The man and his works, his teachings and life]. *Vom wahren Leben: Ausgewählte Schriften* [On the true life: Selected writings]. By Lucius Annaeus Seneca. Gütersloh, Ger.: Bertelsmann, 1958. 9–53.

Laroche, Rebecca. "The Sonnets on Trial: Reconsidering *The Portrait of Mr. W. H.*"

Shakespeare's Sonnets: Critical Essays. Ed. James Schiffer. New York: Garland, 2000. 391–409.

Lawrence, David Herbert. *Sex Literature and Censorship: Essays.* Ed. Harry T. Moore. New York: Twayne, 1953.

Leithner-Brauns, Annette. "Shakespeares Sonette in deutschen Übersetzungen 1787–1994: Eine bibliographische Übersicht" [Shakespeare's sonnets in German translation 1787–1994: A bibliographical survey]. *Archiv für das Studium der neueren Sprachen und Literaturen* 147.232 (1995): 285–316.

Lengeler, Rainer. "Shakespeares Sonette in Celans Übertragung." *Jahrbuch der deutschen Shakespeare Gesellschaft West* (1985): 132–145.

———. *Shakespeares Sonette in deutscher Übersetzung: Stefan George und Paul Celan* [Shakespeare's sonnets in German translation: Celan and George]. Opladen, Ger.: Westdeutscher Verlag, 1989.

Lenin [Vladimir Il'ič Ul'janov]. *Lenin c Literature: Stat'i i reči* [Lenin on literature: Articles and speeches]. Moscow: Gosucarstvennoe Izdetal'stvo Xudožestvennoj Literatury, 1957.

Lermontov, Mixail Yur'evič. *Sobranie sočinenij* [Collected works]. 4 vols. Ed. I. L. Andronikov. Moscow: Gosudarstvennoe Izdatel'stvo Xudožestvennoj Literatury, 1957–1958.

Levi, Primo. *If This Is a Man: The Truce.* Trans. Stuart Wolf. London: Abacus, 2003.

———. *The Drowned and the Saved.* Trans. Raymond Rosenthal. New York: Vintage, 1989.

Levinas, Emmanuel. *Noms propres* [Proper names]. Paris: Fata Morgana, 1987.

Liddell, Henry George, and Robert Scott. *A Greek-English Lexicon.* Rev. ed. Oxford, UK: Clarendon Press, 1968.

Littré, Paul-Emile. *Dictionnaire de la langue française* [Dictionary of the French language]. Vol. 3. Chicago: Donneley & Sons, 1994.

Litvinov, Pavel. *The Trial of the Four: A Collection of Materials on the Case of Glanskov, Ginzburg, Dobrovolsky, and Lashkova, 1967–1968.* Trans. Janis Sapiets. Ed. Peter Reddaway. New York: Viking, 1971.

Lomonosov, M. Vixail Vasil'evič. *Izbrannye Proizvedenija* [Selected writings]. Ed. A. A. Morozov. Moscow: Sovetskij Pisatel', 1965.

Lönker, Fred. "Überlegungen zu Paul Celans Poetik der Übersetzung" [Reflections on Celan's poetics of translation]. *Datum und Zitat bei Paul Celan: Akten des Internationalen Paul Celan-Colloquiums Haifa 1986* [Date and quotation in Celan's works: Proceedings of the international Celan colloquium, Haifa 1986]. Ed. Chaim Shoham and Bernd Witte. Bern, Switz.: Lang, 1986. 211–228.

Loseff, Lev. "Brodsky in Florence." *Revista di poesia comparata* 23 (2003): 1–8.

Loseff, Lev, and Valentina Polukhina, eds. *Brodsky's Poetics and Aesthetics.* Houndmills, UK: Macmillan, 1990.

———. *Joseph Brodsky: The Art of the Poem.* Houndmills, UK: Palgrave, 1999.

Lucian [of Samosata]. *Lucian.* Vol. 2. Trans. A. M. Harmon. Cambridge, MA: Harvard University Press, 1999.

MacCarthy, Fiona. *Byron: Life and Legend.* New York: Farrar, Straus and Giroux, 2002.

Macey, Samuel L. "The Introduction of Shakespeare into Germany in the Second Half of the Eighteenth Century." *Eighteenth Century Studies* 5.2 (1971–1972): 261–269.

MacFadyen, David. *Joseph Brodsky and the Baroque*. Montreal: McGill-Queen's University Press, 1998.

———. *Joseph Brodsky and the Soviet Muse*. Montreal: McGill-Queen's University Press, 1999.

Machiavelli, Niccolò. *Discourses on Livy*. Trans. J. Conaway Bondanella and P. Bondanella. New York: Oxford University Press, 1997.

MacIntyre, Alasdair. *After Virtue: A Study in Moral Theory*. Notre Dame, IN: University of Notre Dame Press, 1981.

Mandelbaum, Allen. "Dante and His Age." *The Divine Comedy of Dante Alighieri: Inferno*. Trans. Allen Mandelbaum. New York: Bantam Books, 1982. 319–329.

———. *Razgovor o Dante* [Converstion about Dante]. Moscow: Iskusstvo, 1967.

———. *Sobranie Sočinenij* [Collected works]. Ed. Gleb Struve and Boris Filipoff. New York: Chekhov, 1955.

———. *Sobranie sočinenij* [Collected works]. Ed. Pavel Nerler. Mandelstam Society ed. 4 vols. Moscow: Art Biznes Centr, 1993–1997.

Mandelstam, Nadežda. *Vospominanija* [Memoirs]. New York: Chekhov, 1970.

Marcel, Gabriel. *Creative Fidelity*. Trans. Robert Rosthal. New York: Farrar, Straus, 1964.

———. *The Mystery of Being*. 1950. 2 vols. (1: *Reflection and Mystery*; 2: *Faith and Reality*). Trans. G. S. Fraser. South Bend, IN: Saint Augustine's Press, 2001.

———. *The Philosophy of Existentialism*. New York: Citadel Press, 1961.

———. Marchand, Leslie A. *Byron: A Portrait*. New York: Knopf, 1970.

———. "Byron in the Twentieth Century." *Byron's Poetry: Authoritative Texts, Letters and Journals, Criticism, Images of Byron*. Ed. Frank D. McDonnell. New York: Norton, 1978. 431–442.

Margalit, Avishai. *The Ethics of Memory*. Cambridge, MA: Harvard University Press, 2002.

Markov, Vladimir. "Paul' Celan i ego perevody russkix poetov" [Paul Celan and his translations of Russian poets]. *Grani* 44 (1959): 227–230.

Martin, John Rupert. *Baroque*. London: Allan Lane, 1977.

Martini, Fritz. *Deutsche Literaturgeschichte: Von den Anfängen bis zur Gegenwart* [German literature history: From its origins through the present]. Stuttgart, Ger.: Kröner, 1952.

Mayer, Hans. "Lenz, Büchner und Celan: Anmerkungen zu Paul Celans Georg-Büchner-Preis- Rede 'Der Meridian' vom 22. Oktober 1960" [Lenz, Büchner, Celan: Commentaries on Celan's Büchner Prize speech, 'The Meridian', delivered on October 22, 1960]. *Vereinzelte Niederschläge: Kritik—Polemik* [Occasional showers: Criticism and polemics]. Pfullingen, Ger.: Neske, 1973. 160–171.

Mazzotta, Guiseppe. "Life of Dante." *The Cambridge Companion to Dante*. Ed. Rachel Jacoff. Cambridge, UK: Cambridge University Press, 1993. 1–13.

McGann, Jerome J. *Fiery Dust: Byron's Poetic Development*. Chicago: University of Chicago Press, 1968.

McGinn, Thomas A. *Prostitution, Sexuality, and the Law in Ancient Rome.* New York: Oxford University Press, 1998.

Meyer, Anne-Rose. "Physiologie und Poesie: Zu Körperdarstellungen in der Lyrik von Ulrike Draesner, Durs Grünbein und Thomas Kling" [Physiology and poetry: Portrayals of the body in the poems of Ulrike Draesner, Durs Grünbein, and Thomas Kling]. *Gegenwartsliteratur* (January 2002) 107–133.

Millevoye, Charles Hubert. *Oeuvres* [Works]. Paris: Garnier, n.d.

Minta, Stephen. *On a Voiceless Shore: Byron in Greece.* New York: Holt, 1998.

Moore, Thomas. *Letters and Journals of Lord Byron: With Notices of His Life.* 2 vols. London: John Murray, 1830.

Müller-Sievers, Helmut. "On the Way to Quotation: Paul Celan's 'Meridian' Speech." *New German Critique* 91 (2004): 13–150.

Murdoch, Iris. *Existentialists and Mystics: Writings on Philosophy and Literature.* New York: Allen Lane, 1998.

———. *The Sovereignty of Good.* London: Routledge, 2001.

Musa, Mark. "An Essay on the *Vita Nuova.*" *Vita Nuova* [New life]. By Dante Alighieri. Trans. Mark Musa. Bloomington: Indiana University Press, 1973. 87–210.

Muschg, Walter. "Deutschland ist Hamlet" [Germany Is Hamlet]. *Der deutsche Shakespeare.* Ed. Reinhold Grimm. Basel, Switz.: Basilius, 1965.

Nabokov, Vladimir. *Lolita: A Novel.* New York: Putnam, 1955.

Najman, Anatolij. *Slavnyj Konec Besslavyx Pokolenij* [A remarkable end of unremarkable generations]. Moscow: Vagrius, 200.

Nalbantian, Suzanne. *Memory in Literature: From Rousseau to Neuroscience.* Houndmills, UK: Palgrave, 2003.

Neumann, Gerhard. "Lektüren der Liebe" [Readings of love]. *Über die Liebe: Ein Symposion* [On love: A symposium]. Ed. Heinrich Meier and Gerhard Neumann. Munich: Piper, 2001. 9–79.

Nietzsche, Friedrich. "Jenseits von Gut und Böse: Vorspiel einer Philosophie der Zukunft" [Beyond good and evil: Foreplay to philosophy of the future]. *Jenseits von Gut und Böse. Zur Genealogie der Moral* [Beyond good and evil. On the genealogy of morals]. Ed. Giorgio Colli and Mazzino Montinari. Berlin and New York: de Gruyter, 1988. 9–243.

———. "Über Wahrheit und Lüge im aussermoralischen Sinne" [On truth and lying in the extramoral sense]. *Die Geburt der Tragödie. Unzeitgemäße Betrachtungen I–IV. Nachgelassene Schriften 1870–1873* [The birth of tragedy. Untimely meditations I–IV. Unpublished writings 1870–1873]. Ed. Giorgio Colli and Mazzino Montinari. Berlin and New York: de Gruyter, 1988. 873–890.

———. "Unzeitgemäße Betrachtungen. Zweites Stück: Vom Nutzen und Nachteil der Historie für das Leben" [Untimely meditations. Second piece: On the advantages and disadvantages of history for life]. *Die Geburt der Tragödie. Unzeitgemäße Betrachtungen I–IV. Nachgelassene Schriften 1870–1873* [The birth of tragedy. Untimely meditations I–IV. Unpublished writings 1870–1873.] Ed. Giorgio Colli and Mazzino Montinari. Berlin and New York: de Gruyter, 1988. 243–334.

———. "Zur Genealogie der Moral: Eine Streitschrift" [On the genealogy of morals: A polemic]. *Jenseits von Gut und Böse. Zur Genealogie der Moral* [Beyond good and evil. On the genealogy of morals]. Ed. Giorgio Colli and Mazzino Montinari. Berlin and New York: de Gruyter, 1988. 245–412.

Novoe Literaturnoe Obozrenie [New literary survey] 45 (2000): 153–255 (Special section on Joseph Brodsky).

Nussbaum, Martha. *The Fragility of Goodness: Luck and Ethics in Greek Tragedy and Philosophy.* Cambridge: Cambridge University Press, 1986.

———. *Love's Knowledge: Essays on Philosophy and Literature.* New York: Oxford University Press, 1990.

Olschner, Leonard Moore. *Der feste Buchstab: Erläuterungen zu Paul Celans Gedichtübertragungen* [The fixed letter: Explications regarding Celan's poetic translations]. Göttingen, Ger.: Vandenhoeck & Ruprecht, 1985.

Ortega y Gasset, José. "The Misery and Splendor of Translation." *Theories of Translation: An Anthology of Essays from Dryden to Pope.* Ed. Rainer Schulte and John Biguenet. Chicago: University of Chicago Press, 1992. 93–112.

Pajević, Marko. "Erfahrungen, Orte, Aufenthalte und die Sorge um das Selbst" [Experiences, places, sojourns and the care of the self]. *arcadia* 32.1 (1997): 148–161.

———. *Zur Poetik Paul Celans: Gedicht und Mensch—die Arbeit am Sinn* [On Celan's poetics: Poem and man—working on sense]. Heidelberg, Ger.: 2000.

Parry, Christoph. "Meridian und Flaschenpost: Intertextualität als Provokation des Lesers bei Paul Celan" [Meridian and message in the bottle: Intertextuality as a provocation of the reader]. *Celan-Jahrbuch* 6 (1995): 25–50.

Pascal, Blaise. *Pensées et opuscules* [Thoughts and minor works]. Ed. and introd. Léon Brunschvicg. Paris: Hachette, 1928.

———. *Pensées* [Thoughts]. Ed. Léon Brunschvicg. Paris: Garnier-Flammarion, 1976.

Pasternak, Boris. *Zarubežnaja Poezija v Perevodax Borisa Pasternaka* [Poetry from abroad in Boris Pasternak's translations]. Ed. E. B. Pasternak and E. K. Nesterova. Moscow: Raduga, 2001.

Pepper, Thomas. "Er, or, Borrowing from Peter to Pay Paul." *Word Traces: Readings of Paul Celan.* Ed. Aris Fioretos. Baltimore, MD: Johns Hopkins University Press, 1994. 353–368.

Petuchowski, Elizabeth. "A New Examination of Celan's Translation of Shakespeare's Sonnet 105." *Jahrbuch der deutschen Shakespeare Gesellschaft West* (1985): 146–152.

Pfister, Manfred. "Mein Lebenszins, er liegt in dieser Schrift" [My life's interest is in these words]. *Die Sonette.* By William Shakespeare. Trans. Christa Schuenke. Munich: Deutscher Taschenbuch Verlag, 1999. 179–194.

Plato. *The Collected Dialogues, Including the Letters.* Ed. Edith Hamilton and Huntington Cairns. Princeton, NJ: Princeton University Press, 1989.

Pogue Harrison, Robert. "Approaching the *Vita Nuova.*" *The Cambridge Companion to Dante.* Ed. Rachel Jacoff. Cambridge, UK: Cambridge University Press, 1993. 34–44.

Polhemus, Robert M., and Roger B. Henkle, eds. *Critical Reconstructions: The Relationship of Fiction and Life.* Stanford, CA: Stanford University Press, 1994.

Polukhina, Valentina. *Joseph Brodsky: A Poet for Our Time.* Cambridge, UK: Cambridge University Press, 1989.

Pound, Ezra. *The Spirit of Romance.* New York: New Directions, 1968.

Puškin, Aleksandr. Sergeevič. *Sočinenija* [Works]. Ed. D. D. Blagoj. 3 vols. Moscow: Gosudarstvennoe Izdatel'stvo Xudožestvennoj Literatury, 1955.

Quintilianus, Marcus Fabius. *Institutio oratoria* [The education of an orator]. 4 vols. Trans. H. E. Butler. Cambridge, MA: Harvard University Press, 1963.

Rančin, Andrej. *Na Piru Mnemoziny: Interteksty Iosifa Brodskogo* [At the banquet of Mnemosyne: Brodsky's intertexts]. Moscow: Novoe Literaturnoe Obozrenie, 2001.

Ransmayr, Christoph. *Die letzte Welt* [The last world]. Frankfurt am Main, Ger.: Fischer, 1992.

Rexheuser, Adelheid. "Die poetische Technik Paul Celans in seinen Übersetzungen russischer Lyrik" [The poetic technique of Celan's translations of Russian poetry]. *arcadia* 10.3 (1975): 273–295.

Rheinfelder, Hans. "Aus Dantes Leben" [From Dante's life]. *Die Göttliche Komödie* [The divine comedy]. By Dante Alighieri. Trans. Wilhelm G. Hertz. Munich: Deutscher Taschenbuch Verlag, 1978.

Richards, I. A. *The Philosophy of Rhetoric.* London: Oxford University Press, 1965.

Rickert, Heinrich. *Der Gegenstand der Erkenntnis: Einführung in die transzendentale Philosophie* [The object of knowledge: Introduction to transcendental philosophy]. Tübingen, Ger.: Mohr, 1928.

Rigsbee, David. *Styles of Ruin: Joseph Brodsky and the Postmodernist Elegy.* Westport, CT: Greenwood Press, 1999.

Robertson, D. W., Jr. *Essays in Medieval Culture.* Princeton, NJ: Princeton University Press, 1980.

Rodis-Lewis, Geneviève. *Descartes: His Life and Thought.* Trans. Jane Marie Todd. Ithaca, NY: Cornell University Press, 1998.

Sacks, Sheldon, ed. *On Metaphor.* Chicago: University of Chicago Press, 1979.

Said, Edward W. *Orientalism.* New York: Vintage, 1979.

Sartre, Jean-Paul. *L'être et le néant: Essai de phénoménologie ontologique* [Being and nothingness: An essay in phenomenological ontology]. Paris: Gallimard, 1943.

Schabert, Ina. "Political Shakespeare: West Germany, 1970–1990." *Shakespeare and Cultural Traditions: The Selected Proceedings of the International Shakespeare Association World Congress, Tokyo, 1991.* Ed. Tetsuo Kushi, Roger Pringle, and Stanley Wells. Newark: University of Delaware Press, 1994. 285–294.

Schadewaldt, Wolfgang. "Das Problem des Übersetzens" [The problem of translation]. *Das Problem des Übersetzens* [The problem of translation]. Ed. Hans Joachim Störig. Stuttgart, Ger.: Goverts, 1963. 249–267.

Schama, Simon. *Citizens: A Chronicle of the French Revolution.* New York: Knopf, 1989.

Scherr, Barry P. "'To Urania'—K Uranii." *Joseph Brodsky: The Art of the Poem.* Ed. Lev Loseff and Valentina Polukhina. Houndmills, UK: Palgrave, 1999. 92–106.

Schiffer, James. "Reading New Life into Shakespeare's Sonnets: A Survey of Criticism."

Shakespeare's Sonnets: Critical Essays. Ed. James Schiffer. New York: Garland, 2000. 3–71.

———. ed. *Shakespeare's Sonnets: Critical Essays.* New York: Garland, 2000.

Schiller, Friedrich. *Werke* [Works]. Ed. Paul Stapf. 2 vols. Berlin: Deutsche Buch-Gemeinschaft, 1955.

Schlegel, August Wilhelm. *Sprache und Poetik* [Language and poetics]. Ed. Edgar Lohner. Stuttgart, Ger.: Kohlhammer, 1962.

Schleiermacher, Friedrich. "Über die verschiedenen Methoden des Übersetzens" [On the different methods of translation]. *Philosophische und Vermischte Schriften II* [Philosophical and miscellaneous writings]. Berlin: Reimer, 1838. 207–245.

Schmitt, Carl. *Hamlet oder Hekuba: Der Einbruch der Zeit in das Spiel* [Hamlet or Hekabe: The irruption of time into the game]. 1956. Stuttgart, Ger.: Klett-Cotta, 1986.

Schnell, Rüdiger. *Causa Amoris: Liebeskonzeption und Liebesdarstellung in der mittelalterlichen Literatur* [The cause of love: Conceptions and portrayals of love in medieval literature]. Bern, Switz.: Francke, 1985.

Schopenhauer, Arthur. *Die Welt als Wille und Vorstellung* [The world as will and idea]. Munich: Deutscher Taschenbuch Verlag, 1998.

Schuenke, Christa, and Christa Jansohn. "Die neue Lust auf die Sonette" [The new excitement about the sonnets]. *Die Sonette.* By William Shakespeare. Trans. Christa Schuenke. Munich: Deutscher Taschenbuch Verlag, 1999. 163–173.

Schulte, Rainer, and John Biguenet, eds. *Theories of Translation: An Anthology of Essays from Dryden to Pope.* Chicago: University of Chicago Press, 1992.

Sebald, Winfried Georg. *Austerlitz.* Trans. Anthea Bell. New York: Random House, Modern Library, 2001.

Seneca, Lucius Annaeus. "Ad Helviam matrem de consolatione" [To his mother Helvia on consolation]. *Moral Essays.* Trans. John Basore. Cambridge, MA: Harvard University Press, 2001. Vol. 2, 416–489.

———. *Ad Lucilium epistulae* [Letters to Lucilius]. 3 vols. Trans. Richard M. Gummere. Cambridge, MA: Harvard University Press, 1996.

———. "Ad Polybium de consolatione" [To Polybius on consolation]. *Moral Essays.* Trans. John Basore. Cambridge, MA: Harvard University Press, 2001. Vol. 2, 356–415.

———. *De beneficiis* [On benefits]. Trans. John W. Basore. Cambridge, MA: Harvard University Press, 1935.

———. "De brevitate vitae" [On the brevity of life]. *Moral Essays.* Trans. John Basore. Cambridge, MA: Harvard University Press, 2001. Vol. 2: 326–355.

———. "De constantia sapientis" [On the steadfastness of the wise]. *Moral Essays.* Trans. John Basore. Cambridge, MA: Harvard University Press, 2001. Vol. 1: 48–105.

———. "De otio" [On peace]. *Moral Essays.* Trans. John Basore. Cambridge, MA: Harvard University Press, 2001. Vol. 2: 202–285.

———. "De providential" [On providence]. *Moral Essays.* Trans. John Basore. Cambridge, MA: Harvard University Press, 2001. Vol. 1: 2–47.

———. "De tranquillitate animi" [On the tranquility of soul]. *Moral Essays,* Trans. John Basore. Cambridge, MA: Harvard University Press, 2001. Vol. 2: 202–285.

———. "De vita beata" [On the happy life]. *Moral Essays.* Trans. John Basore. Cambridge, MA: Harvard University Press, 2001. Vol. 2: 98–175.

———. *Die Kürze des Lebens* [The brevity of life]. Trans. Gerhard Fink. Frankfurt am Main, Ger.: Suhrkamp, 2003.

———. *Moral Essays.* Vol. 1. Trans. John Basore. Cambridge, MA: Harvard University Press, 1998.

———. *Moral Essays.* Vol. 2. Trans. John Basore. Cambridge, MA: Harvard University Press, 2001.

———. *Thyestes.* Trans. Durs Grünbein. Frankfurt am Main, Ger.: Insel, 2002.

Shakespeare, William. *Die Sonette.* Trans. Christa Schuenke. Munich: Deutscher Taschenbuch Verlag, 1999.

———. *Die Sonette.* Trans Rolf-Dietrich Keil. Düsseldorf, Ger.: Eugen Diederichs, 1959.

———. *Shakespears Sonette.* Trans. Eduard Saenger. Leipzig, Ger.: Insel, 1909.

———. *Shakespeares Sonette.* Trans. Otto Gildermeister. Leipzig, Ger.: Brockhaus, 1876.

———. *Shakespeare's Sonnets.* Ed. Stephen Booth. New Haven, CT: Yale University Press, 2000.

———. *Shakespeare's Works / Sämtliche Werke.* Bilingual ed. Trans. August Wilhelm Schlegel, Caroline Schlegel, Dorothea Tieck, and Wolf Graf von Baudessin. Ed. L. L. Schücking. 12 vols. Wiesbaden, Ger.: Vollmer, n.d.

———. *Sonette.* Trans. Gottlob Regis. 1836. Leipzig, Ger.: Reclam, 1964.

———. *Sonette und andere Dichtungen* [Sonnets and other poems]. Trans. Terese Robinson. Munich: Georg Müller, 1927. 8–161.

———. *Sonnette.* Trans. Stefan George. Berlin: Georg Bondi, 1909.

Shakespeare, William, and Franz Josef Czernin. *Sonnets. Übersetzungen.* Munich: Hanser, 1999.

Sharney, Maurice. *Shakespeare on Love and Lust.* New York: Columbia University Press, 2000.

Shelley, Percy Bysshe. "A Defence of Poetry." *Romantic Poetry and Prose.* Ed. Harold Bloom and Lionel Trilling. New York: Oxford University Press, 1973. 746–762.

Shtern, Ludmila. *Brodsky: A Personal Memoir.* Fort Worth, TX: Baskerville, 2004.

Simonis, Annette. "Celan und Shakespeare—Zum Problem der Dialogizität in der Lyrik Paul Celans" [Celan and Shakespeare—On the problem of dialogicity in the poetry of Paul Celan]. *Orbis Litterarum* 49.3 (1994): 159–172.

Singer, Irving. *The Nature of Love.* 3 vols. Chicago: University of Chicago Press, 1984–1987.

Sinjavskij, Andrej Donat'evič, and Iulij Markovič Daniel'. *At the Trial of A. Sinyavsky and Yu Daniel.* New York: Inter-Language Literary Associates, 1966.

Sklar, Lawrence. *Theory and Truth: Philosophical Critique Within Foundational Science.* Oxford, UK: Oxford University Press, 2000.

Sleigh, Dan. *Islands.* Trans. André Brink. Orlando, FL: Harcourt, 2004.

Smith, Bruce R. "I, You, He, She, and We: On the Sexual Politics of Shakespeare's Sonnets." *Shakespeare's Sonnets: Critical Essays.* Ed. James Schiffer. New York: Garland, 2000. 411–430.

Soble, Alan. *Eros, Agape, and Philia: Readings in the Philosophy of Love.* St. Paul, MN: Paragon House, 1989.

Solomon, Petre. "Briefwechsel mit Paul Celan 1957–1962" [Correspondence with Celan]. *Neue Literatur* 32.11 (1981): 60–80.

Solženicyn, Aleksandr I. *V Kruge Pervom* [In the first circle]. 1958. Paris: YMCA-Press, 1978.

Specht, Rainer. *Descartes.* Reinbeck, Ger.: Rowohlt, 1966.

Stallybrass, Peter. "Editing as Cultural Formation: The Sexing of Shakespeare's Sonnets." *Shakespeare's Sonnets: Critical Essays.* Ed. James Schiffer. New York: Garland, 2000. 75–88.

Steiner, George. *After Babel: Aspects of Language and Translation.* London: Oxford University Press, 1975.

Stengel, Kathrin. *Die Rolle der Einbildungskraft in Kant's Kritik der reinen Vernunft* [The role of the imagination in Kant's *Critique of pure reason*]. Munich: n.p., 1993.

Störig, Hans Joachim, ed. *Das Problem des Übersetzens* [The problem of translation]. Stuttgart, Ger.: Goverts, 1963.

Strickland, Margot. *The Byron Women.* London: Peter Owen, 1974.

Struve, Nikita. *Ossip Mandelstam.* Paris: Institut d'Études Slaves, 1982.

Suerbaum, Ulrich. "Der deutsche Shakespeare: Übersetzungsgeschichte und Übersetzungstheorie" [The German Shakespeare: Translation history and translation theory]. *Festschrift für Rudolf Stamm: Zu seinem sechzigsten Geburtstag* [Festschrift for Rudolf Stamm: On his sixtieth birthday]. Ed. Eduard Kolb and Jörg Hasler. Bern, Switz.: Francke, 1969. 61–80.

Suetonius [Gaius Suetonius Tranquillus]. *Lives of the Caesars.* Trans. Catharine Edwards. Oxford, UK: Oxford University Press, 2000.

Szondi, Peter. *Celan-Studien* [Celan studies]. Frankfurt am Main, Ger.: Suhrkamp, 1972.

Tacitus, Cornelius. *The Annals,* Books IV–VI and XI–XII, trans. John Jackson. Cambridge, MA: Harvard University Press, 1998.

———. *The Annals,* Books XIII–XVI, trans. John Jackson. Cambridge, MA: Harvard University Press, 1999.

Terras, Victor, and Karl S. Weimar. "Mandelstamm and Celan: A Postscript." *Germano-Slavica* 2.5 (1978): 353–370.

Thunecke, Jörg. "Die Rezeption Georg Büchners in Paul Celans *Meridian*-Rede" [The reception of Büchner in Celan's *Meridian*]. *Georg Büchner Jahrbuch* 3 (1983): 298–307.

Tihanov, Galin. "Contextualizing Bakhtin: Two Poems by Mandel'stam." *Russian Literature L* (2001): 165–184.

Tillich, Paul. *Love, Power, and Justice.* London: Oxford University Press, 1954.

Tjutčev, Fedor Ivanović. *Polonoe Sobranie Stixotvorenij* [Complete poems]. Leningrad: Sovetskij Pisatel', 1957.

Todorov, Tzvetan. "The Notion of Literature." *New Literary History* 5 (1973): 5–16.

Tomaševskij, Boris. "Literature and Biography." *Readings in Russian Poetics: Formalist and Structuralist Views.* Ed. Ladislav Matejka and Krystyna Pomorska. Ann Arbor: Michigan Slavic Publications, 1978. 47–55.

Traub, Valerie. "Sex Without Issue: Sodomy, Reproduction, and Signification in Shakespeare's Sonnets." *Shakespeare's Sonnets: Critical Essays,* ed. James Schiffer. New York: Garland, 2000. 431–454.

Tynjanov, Jurij. "Literaturnyj Fakt" [The literary fact]. *Arxaisty i novatory* [Archaists and innovators]. Leningrad: Priboj, 1929. 5–29.

———. "On Literary Evolution." *Readings in Russian Poetics: Formalist and Structuralist Views.* Ed. Ladislav Matejka and Krystyna Pomorska. Ann Arbor: Michigan Slavic Publications, 1978. 66–78.

Tynjanov, Jurij, and Roman Jakobson. "Problems in the Study of Literature and Language." 1928. *Readings in Russian Poetics: Formalist and Structuralist Views.* Ed. Ladislav Matejka and Krystyna Pomorska. Ann Arbor: Michigan Slavic Publications, 1978. 79–81.

Vendler, Helen. *The Art of Shakespeare's Sonnets.* Cambridge, MA: Harvard University Press, 1997.

———. *Coming of Age as a Poet: Milton, Keats, Eliot, Plath.* Cambridge, MA: Harvard University Press, 2003.

Venuti, Lawrence, ed. *The Translation Studies Reader.* London: Routledge, 2000.

———. *The Translator's Invisibility: A History of Translation.* London: Routledge, 1995.

Veyne, Paul. *Seneca: The Life of a Stoic.* Trans. David Sullivan. New York: Routledge, 2003.

Vidal, Fernando. "Brains, Bodies, Selves, and Science: Anthropologies of Identity and the Resurrection of the Body." *Critical Inquiry* 28.4 (2002): 930–974.

Vigdorova, Frida. "Le Procès de Yosip Brodski: Poète jugé et condamné à Leningrad pour . . . oisivité" [The trial of Brodsky: Poet tried and sentenced in Leningrad on charges of laziness]. *Le Figaro Littéraire* (Oct. 1–7, 1964): 1, 8, 17.

———. "Process Iosifa Brodskogo" [The trial of Brodsky]. *Vozdušnye Puti* [Aerial ways] 4 (1965): 279–303.

Vitiello, Vincenzo. "Gegenwort: Paul Celan und die Sprache der Dichtung" [Counterword: Celan and the language of poetry]. *Celan-Jahrbuch* 5 (1993): 7–22.

Vlastos, Gregory. "The Individual as an Object of Love in Plato." *Platonic Studies.* 2nd. ed. Princeton, NJ: Princeton University Press. 96–135.

Volkov, Solomon. *Conversations with Joseph Brodsky: A Poet's Journey Through the Twentieth Century.* Trans. Marian Schwartz. New York: Free Press, 1998.

Voswinckel, Klaus. *Paul Celan: Verweigerte Poetisierung der Welt—Versuch einer Deutung* [Celan's refusal to poeticize the world: An interpretive attempt]. Heidelberg, Ger.: Stiehm, 1974.

Von Albrecht, Michael. "Nach den Satiren: Durs Grünbein und die Antike" [After the satires: Grünbein and antiquity]. *Mythen in nachmythischer Zeit: Die Antike in der deutschsprachigen Literatur der Gegenwart* [Myths in a postmythical age: Antiquity in contemporary German literature]. Ed. Bernd Seidensticker and Martin Vöhler. Berlin and New York: de Gruyter, 2002. 101–116.

Von Stackelberg, Jürgen. "Blüte und Niedergang der 'Belles Infidèles'" [The heyday and demise of the "belles infidèles"]. *Die literarische Übersetzung: Stand und Perspektiven ihrer Forschung* [Literary translation: The curruent state and future of translation studies]. Ed. Harald Kittel. Berlin: Erich Schmidt, 1988. 16–29.

Voss, Robert F. *Paul Celan's Translations of Shakespeare's Sonnets.* Dissertation. University of Cincinnati. 1973.

Watson, Richard. *Cogito, Ergo Sum: The Life of René Descartes.* Boston, MA: Godine, 2002.

Weigel, Sigrid. "Die Erinnerungs- und Erregungsspuren von Zitat und Lektüre. Die Intertextualität Bachmann-Celan, gelesen mit Benjamin" [Traces of memory and arousal in quotation and reading. The Bachmann—Celan intertexts, read through Benjamin]. *Ingeborg Bachmann und Paul Celan—Poetische Korrespondenzen: Vierzehn Beiträge* [Bachmann and Celan—Poetic correspondences: Fourteen essays]. Ed. Bernhard Böschenstein and Sigrid Weigel. Frankfurt am Main, Ger.: Suhrkamp, 1997. 231–249.

Weimar, Karl S. "Paul Celan's 'Todesfuge': Translation and Interpretation." *PMLA* 89.1 (1974): 85–96.

Weinrich, Harald. "Semantik der kühnen Metapher" [Semantics of the bold metaphor]. *Deutsche Vierteljahresschrift für Literaturwissenschaft und Geistesgeschichte* 37.37 (1963): 325–344.

———. "Semantik der Metapher" [Semantics of metaphor]. *Folia Linguistica: Acta Societatis Linguisticae.* Vol. 1. The Hague: Mouton, 1967. 1–17.

White, Hayden. *Metahistory: The Historical Imagination in Nineteenth-Century Europe.* Baltimore, MD: Johns Hopkins University Press, 1973.

Wiedemann, Barbara, ed. "'Es ist eine lange, unglaubliche, bitter-wahre Geschichte': Claire Golls Angriffe auf Paul Celan—Gründe und Folgen" [It is a long, incredible, bitter-true story: Claire Goll's attacks on Celan—Reasons and consequences]. *Paul Celan—Die Goll Affäre: Dokumente zu einer Infamie* [Paul Celan—The Goll affair: Documents on an infamous affair]. Frankfurt am Main, Ger.: Suhrkamp, 2000a. 820–860.

———, ed. *Paul Celan—Die Goll-Affäre: Dokumente zu einer Infamie* [Paul Celan—The Goll affair: Documents on an infamous affair]. Frankfurt am Main, Ger.: Suhrkamp, 2000b.

———. "Paul Celan und Ingeborg Bachmann: Ein Dialog? In Liebesgedichten?" [Celan and Bachmann: A dialog? In love poems?] *"Im Geheimnis der Begegnung": Ingeborg Bachmann und Paul Celan* ["In the secret of the encounter": Bachmann and Celan]. Ed. Dieter Burdorf. Iserlohn, Ger.: Institut für Kirche und Gesellschaft, 2003. 21–43.

Wiesel, Elie. *Night.* Trans. Stella Rodway. 25th ed. New York: Bantam, 1986.

———. *The Time of the Uprooted.* Trans. David Hapgood. New York: Knopf, 2005.

Williams, Bernard. *Truth and Truthfulness: An Essay in Genealogy.* Princeton, NJ: Princeton University Press, 2002.

Williams, Oscar, ed. *A Little Treasure of American Poetry: The Chief Poets from Colonial Times to the Present Day.* New York: Scribner's, 1948.

———. *A Little Treasure of Great Poetry: English and America from Chaucer to the Present.* New York: Scribner's, 1947.

Windelband, Wilhelm. *Präludien: Aufsätze und Reden zur Philosophie und ihrer Geschichte* [Preludes: Essays and speeches on philosophy and its history]. 5th ed. 2 vols. Tübingen, Ger.: Mohr, 1915.

Wolf, Christa. *Was bleibt* [What remains]. Munich: Deutscher Taschenbuch Verlag, 1999.

Wordsworth, William, and Samuel Taylor Coleridge. *Lyrical Ballads*. 1798. Ed. W. J. B. Owen. 2nd ed. Oxford: Oxford University Press, 1969.

Wörgebauer, Werner. "Zur strukturbildenden Funktion der Liebesbeziehung in der Dichtung Paul Celans" [On the structural function of love in Celan's poetry]. *Celan-Jahrbuch* 6 (1995): 161–172.

Žižek, Slavoj. *The Ticklish Subject: The Absent Centre of Political Ontology*. London: Verso, 1999.

Index

Titles of works are listed in English with foreign titles, if given, following in parentheses. In endnotes as well as text, the topic is listed only on the page it appears, even if the note covers more than one page. Endnotes are indicated by n. (for a single reference) and nn. (for more than one note per page)